Caroline New was born in 1[...] family in a Cardiff suburb. Her father worked as an engineer in the Post Office. Her mother, a teacher, stayed at home for ten years to look after Caroline and her younger brother. She studied philosophy at Cambridge and sociology at Oxford, simultaneously becoming distanced from her working-class roots and becoming a Marxist. In 1969 she married Norman Freeman and they set up their own family. Since then, she has worked part-time, teaching sociology and women's studies, setting up a play-scheme in a community centre, and writing. She has been politically active in varying degrees since she was fourteen, first in CND, then in the women's movement and left-wing politics. Through her own experience of combining child care, work and politics Caroline became critical of the nuclear family as a basis for proper child care. She involved herself in the politics of child care, in setting up co-operative arrangements for her own young children and others and in writing about child care.

Miriam David was born in 1945 in Keighley, in the West Riding of Yorkshire, the second of three daughters of Jewish parents of whom her father was from Germany. She grew up in a typical post-war family, her father a professional engineer and her mother only returning to teaching when she and her sisters were all in their teens. She studied sociology at Leeds University and then worked as a researcher at London University and briefly at Harvard University. She now teaches social policy at Bristol University. She has been active in the women's movement since the early 1970s and has taught women's studies in Britain, Canada and the USA. She married Robert Reiner in 1974 and has two children. Becoming a mother compelled her to search for both practical and theoretical answers to the question of child care. She campaigned for, helped set up and run the Bristol University Nursery. She is now involved in school-age child care. Her publications range widely over feminist scholarship, the family, education and social policy in Britain and the USA. They include *Half the Sky: An Introduction to Women's Studies* (with the Bristol Women's Studies Group, 1979, reprinted 1984) and *The State, the Family and Education* (1980).

Caroline New and Miriam David

FOR THE CHILDREN'S SAKE

PENGUIN BOOKS

1985

Penguin Books Ltd, Harmondsworth, Middlesex, England
Viking Penguin Inc., 40 West 23rd Street, New York, New York 10010, U.S.A.
Penguin Books Australia Ltd, Ringwood, Victoria, Australia
Penguin Books Canada Ltd, 2801 John Street, Markham, Ontario, Canada L3R 1B4
Penguin Books (N.Z.) Ltd, 182–190 Wairau Road, Auckland 10, New Zealand

First published 1985

Made and printed in Great Britain by
Richard Clay (The Chaucer Press) Ltd, Bungay, Suffolk
Filmset in 9/11½ Monophoto Photina by
Northumberland Press Ltd, Gateshead, Tyne and Wear

For our mothers and our children:
Esther David and her grandchildren
Toby and Charlotte Reiner
and
Cora New and her grandchildren
Sarah, Anna and Deborah Freeman

CONTENTS

FOREWORD

We first thought of this book three summers ago in the tiny sitting-room of a holiday cottage in North Wales. Since then it has gone through many phases. The original outline was sent to friends and colleagues and distributed at the first research conference of the National Child Care Campaign. We are grateful to Sheila Allen, Pam Calder, Jeanne Golding, Hermione Harris, Diana Leonard, Sue Owen, Helen Penn, Pat Petrie, Sheila Rowbotham, Joanna Ryan and Elizabeth Wilson for their initial encouragement and comments. We then approached several people as would-be contributors and eventually met together in Pam Calder's house to discuss the whole project. In the summer of 1982 we started writing in earnest, Miki holding the fort in Bristol, Caroline enjoying the library of the Australian National University in Canberra. Together again in the autumn, we held a mini-conference around the chapters that had been drafted. As well as our contributors – Pam Calder, Audrey Maynard, Jonathan Trustram, Wiebke Wüstenberg and Stephen Castles – we would like to thank Liz Bird, Liz Clarke, Jessica James, Ellen Malos, Sarah Meadows, Kate Paul and Annie Phizacklea for giving their thoughtful attention to the stubborn questions we were wrestling with.

It was not always easy working together, and we have tried a variety of methods: some chapters we wrote and rewrote separately, some together; one, after lots of wine, into a dictaphone, punctuated with 'ers' and giggles. We eventually decided – on our last chapter – that the best method was to agree an outline, then for each to write a complete draft, and then amalgamate them jointly. Sometimes we were forced to work separately. Caroline had only twelve child-free hours a week during 1983 and Miki had the usual teaching and administrative responsibilities of her university post. She was given study leave for the summer term to work on the book, and would like to thank Peter Townsend and Paddy Hillyard particularly for making this possible.

During this trying process our friendship went through many crises. We are deeply indebted to Myna Trustram for counselling us on several such occasions and remaining a loyal friend to each of us.

In the summer of 1983, Miki taught summer school at the Ontario Institute for Studies in Education in Toronto, trying out some of our ideas. She would like to thank Alison Griffith for making the trip possible, and her students and colleagues for sharing their refreshingly distinct North American perspective.

Various people have read drafts of some of the chapters; we are grateful to them for their comments. They include Sandy Acker, Madeleine Arnot, Liz Clarke, Lynne Davis, Alan Drummond, Norman Freeman, Eva Havesi, Hilary Land, Ellen Malos, Mervyn Murch, Roy Parker and Kate Paul. Conversations with many other people have been important in framing our ideas, especially those with Sandy Acker, Vida Bayley, Liz Bird, Jill Brown, Sue Colley, Jane Cox, Bob Deacon, Alan Drummond, Margrit Eichler, Zillah Eisenstein, Sheila Ernst, Rosemary Fraser, Jane Gaskell, Jeanne Golding, Alison Griffiths, Will Guy, Annette Holman, Sonia Jackson, Jessica James, Tessa Joseph, Gail Kelly, Hilary Land, Ernie Lightman, Ann Low-Beer, Ann Manicom, Roy Parker, Jean Phinney, Robert Reiner, Sue Richards, Janet Sayers, Jenny Shaw, Dorothy Smith, Vivienne Stone, Anne Sultoon, Helen Taylor, Pat Taylor, Myna Trustram, Gillian Walker, Jackie West and Fiona Williams. Martin Richards read the draft manuscript, and his trenchant comments were invaluable in revising it for publication. He has always been a staunch supporter.

Throughout the project, child care has been a major preoccupation for us both. We have many people to thank – as well as their fathers and grandmothers – for looking after our children. There were the staff of the Bristol University Nursery, of Colstons Primary School and the nursery class at St George's Primary School, Sarah Cemlyn, Tess Crib, Julie Davis, Karen Hall, Trish Hudson, Tessa Joseph, Jenny Nott and Ann Smith. Without their practical caring we would not have been at liberty to think clearly about theoretical questions of child care.

Kathleen Brookes never fails to provide the most caring and careful secretarial help. We have really tried her patience with successive drafts on strips of sellotaped scribble. Thanks also to Liz Gibson, Pat Lees and Pauline Tilley, who have also struggled with some of our chapters.

We are equal authors of this book. Caroline's name is first because, during our years of co-authorship, the book has been her job (unpaid). Miki has been able to develop her ideas in the course of her University teaching. Finally, special thanks to our children for being such fun to be with.

Caroline New and Miriam David
Bristol, August 1984

INTRODUCTION

Motherhood is often seen as women's destiny. Whether they have children or are childless, women cannot escape being treated as mothers, whatever they make of their individual lives.

Women are given caring work on the grounds that they are mothers, or may become mothers, or should have been mothers. They are even expected to *feel* like mothers while they work as teachers, social workers, nurses or help out at the play-group, and to be satisfied with no pay or low pay. In the aftermath of the Warnock report on human fertilization – with its oddly contrasting technical mastery and social naïvety – Alice Eden wrote passionately to the *Guardian* (27 July 1984, p. 12):

> May a childless spinster, now nearer to eighty than seventy, intrude into the debate on infertility? It is not so long ago when generations of women, because of the population imbalance, were denied the opportunity of marriage and parenthood. This fact is almost forgotten today and their kind are, year by year, now dying out.
>
> Many of these women filled their lives with the care of other people's children, whether as nurses, teachers or social working (there were few alternatives open to them). It was upon the shoulders of these 'surplus women' that our expanding education and welfare services were largely supported. So far from receiving either sympathy for their plight or commendation for their work, they were at best disregarded and under-paid, at worst despised and mocked. 'How,' it was said 'can a childless spinster be expected to understand children?' ... why when the human condition itself imposes all manner of frustration and suffering, is this one above all others regarded by some today as so appalling that it must not and shall not be tolerated? ...

Involuntary childlessness in women is still seen as a tragedy, and voluntary childlessness as something of an oddity. So much else is involved in the decision to become a mother that it hardly makes sense to speak of women freely choosing to have children or not to have them. On the one hand, having a child is *the* way to full womanhood. But deciding to be a mother inevitably closes off other options. Motherhood can be uniquely rewarding, but the lack of support and restricted working conditions are unenviable. Women who go on working for money lose opportunities for paid employment which may remain open to childless women and men, even open to the fathers of their children, or else find themselves preoccupied with the acrobatic feat of juggling a baby and a job. If they abandon themselves to full-time motherhood, women accept economic dependence and share the restricted life of their own children. They become excluded from such 'adult' places as bars and pubs while they have their children with them, they cannot go into libraries without being hushed, and their relationship to the serious 'world of work' becomes that of consumers of services. Doing the proper thing as an adult woman – becoming a 'proper' mother at home – is confusingly infantilizing. The children who are their mother's beloved companions and playmates are at the same time the source of her belittlement. No wonder many women express enormous ambivalence about their charges. But women's dependence is different from that of children:

> ... for women, the experience of dependency is ... contradictory. Their dependent status – as housewives, mothers, dutiful daughters – is not absolute, but is conditional upon their being simultaneously depended upon by others. Thus for many women, being a dependant is synonymous not with receiving care but with giving it ... (Graham, 1983, pp. 24–5).

Graham goes on to say that, for children and men, economic dependence is the price that has to be paid in return for being cared for – when men are ill or disabled, for example. For women, paradoxically, economic dependence is the price they pay for *doing* the caring.

When they become fathers, men do not have to make a choice between fatherhood and a place in the wider world of work equivalent to the one that women face. Some writers see this difference as an aspect of 'patriarchy'. We shall argue that modern society is not 'patriarchal' in the sense of the 'rule of fathers'. Men's greater power in the public world does not stem from their dominance in family life, or even depend upon it. It does have a lot to do with their non-motherhood, and their relative freedom from the essential unpaid work of child care, which gives them a different place in the labour market from that of women. The structure of economic life has changed drastically, but there has been little change in the sharing of work *inside* families. Women still have to 'choose' how to fit paid work in with rearing their families. Men's choice is about how hard they will work to provide for their families. The choices men and women make are still rigidly circumscribed. We shall be looking at the reasons for this lack of change, at how it comes about that we inherit and pass on the outdated albatross of separate spheres of work.

Our theme is straightforward. It is in everybody's interests that the current way in which the care of children is organized should be completely changed. Women need their independence to be effective as carers. Children need carers who are not second-class citizens. Men need to care for children too, for their own sakes. And child care has to become an area of *public* concern all the time, not just in the last resort.

Except in a superficial way, few feminists have recognized motherhood and child care as central pillars of the oppression of women. There are plenty of *stories* of motherhood written by feminists, but few evaluations. The notable exceptions have themselves been relatively ignored or forgotten. For example, Charlotte Perkins Gilman and other 'material feminists' were expounding one powerful idea for six decades from 1850: 'That women must create feminist homes with socialised housework and childcare before they could become truly equal members of society.' But now

> The utopian and pragmatic sources of material feminism, its broad popular appeal, and the practical experiments it provoked are not well known. Since the 1930s, very few scholars or activists have even suspected that there might be such an intellectual, political and architectural tradition in the United States. In the early 1960s, Charlotte Perkins Gilman's *Women and Economics* ... had been out of print for decades ... her books reappeared without any rediscovery of the historical context of material feminist thought or political practice that had inspired them (Hayden, 1981, pp. 3–4).

Hayden calls these women 'material feminists' because of the stress they put on economic and spatial issues. They identified 'the economic exploitation of women's domestic labour by men as the most basic cause of women's inequality'. This included the care of children. Gilman understood how the identification of mother and home presented women with a romantic, appealing image of themselves which disguised the actual narrowness of such lives. This romantic appeal is embodied, in the language of her times in her poem 'Two Callings' (Gilman, 1972):

'Home!' says the deep voice, 'Home' and softly singing
Brings me a sense of safety unsurpassed;
So old! So old! The piles above the wave –
The shelter of the stone-blocked, shadowy cave –
Security of sun-kissed treetops swinging –
Safety and Home at last!

And then – ah, then! The deep voice murmurs, 'Mother!'
And all life answers from the primal sea;
A mingling of all lullabies; a peace
That asks no understanding; the release
Of nature's holiest power – who seeks another?
Home? Home is Mother – Mother, Home – to me.

Like most feminists of her time, Gilman still saw women as essentially motherly, but against the narrow conception of the private, family-orientated mother she set the bolder idea of commitment to *all* children:

The World! The World is crying! Hear its needs!
Home is a part of life – I am the whole!
Home is the cradle – shall a whole life stay
Cradled in comfort through the working day?
I too am Home – the Home of all high deeds –
The only Home to hold the human soul!

So when the great word 'Mother!' rang once more,
I saw at last its meaning and its place;
Not the blind passion of the brooding past,
But Mother – the World's Mother – come at last,
To love as she had never loved before –
To feed and guard and teach the human race.

More recently, other American feminists have seen motherhood as a central issue. Nancy Chodorow has written a striking psychoanalytic account of how the capacity and the need to mother is passed on from one generation of women to the next. But her account remains centred in family dynamics. We want to examine how different and even contrasting outside influences come together to ensure that the system of private, mainly maternal child care keeps going. Adrienne Rich, in poetry and prose, has described motherhood as an experience and an institution. But her politics don't allow her to see the extension of motherhood, and of parenthood, to fathers and others as an answer. Jessie Bernard is another challenging writer on motherhood who stops short of recommending concrete change: 'It is far easier to point to past forms that are disintegrating than it is to discern ... the new forms in the process of emerging. Or to delineate the new forms to aim for. Or to be sure how to create them. Or just how much we can actually control them ...' (Bernard, 1983, pp. 117–18). She even retreats into socio-biology, arguing that there may be 'natural mammalian patterns' that 'neither attitudes nor law can change' (ibid.).

Why is it that feminists have had so little to say about the *future* of motherhood and child care? For some it may be that it is too threatening even to think about the possibility of 'a grand domestic revolution' including shared child care and co-operative housekeeping. Nor do women's lives make it easy to think broadly about the politics of our intimate relationships. Before women become mothers, their understanding of motherhood is usually limited to observation of their own mothers, or perhaps sisters and friends. As observers, young women are not usually detached. They often feel obscurely resentful about their own mother's 'sacrifices', and sometimes find it threatening to see close friends or relatives becoming submerged in the details of looking after children. As feminists, they are more likely to be concerned about issues which affect them immediately, such as male violence or equal pay. Women who do become mothers usually have little time, and little or no money to buy themselves the space, to think through such questions. Because it is not clear what can be done to improve the conditions of motherhood, inside or outside marriage, it is quite tempting for women to spend the little child-free time they have thinking about that other self, the person who existed before the children were born and who is still somewhere about, waiting for the right conditions before she will emerge.

Of course, some mothers do have time and space to think about their condition. But even for them, it is hard to gather the needed detachment while their children are young. Some books about the experience of motherhood, interesting as they are, never get beyond the authors' intense emotions.

Certainly we became painfully aware of these dilemmas in the process of writing the book. We were both mothers when we came together to write it, inspired both by common circumstances and by divergent 'choices'. Caroline had not established a career to be sacrificed and had uneasily accepted the traditional place in the family, working part-time in a series of temporary jobs. Miki had a well-established career, and worried about sacrificing career or baby or both. Although both our partners were committed to fatherhood – both of them coming from loving Jewish family backgrounds – it was we who made whatever choices were to be made about the kinds and combinations of work and care we would create. They wanted to be very involved in parenting – but, as we shall see, fathers' involvement is not a solution by itself to the problem women face. More often it happens that such fathers take on some of the restrictions that accompany motherhood than that their partners gain the freedom of traditional fatherhood.

It was the differences between us as much as our common interests which propelled us into writing this book. Each saw the other enjoying opportunities she had had to give up. Of course it was easier for us to identify with each other because we were both highly educated and with middle-class lifestyles. Women's special oppression stands out more starkly when there is no material disadvantage coming from class position to contend with. This does not mean that what we have written is only relevant to middle-class women. Women's responsibility for child care crosses class boundaries as the central feature of their oppression today. It is no accident that it was we, the women, who came together to write this book, rather than the men we live with.

We found that writing about child care and being involved in the care of young children at the same time was a painful experience. We criticized the view that mothers are totally responsible for everything that happens to their children, but in our private lives we often believed it. We had seriously to evaluate views and feelings about the proper care of young children which went against both what we were doing with our children and our own theories. Caroline remembers an uncomfortable morning reading *A Two-Year-Old Goes to Nursery School* in the library after a sad parting with her own two-year-old, not yet settled with her new carer (Janis, 1964). She knew that the psychoanalytic view expressed in the book, that such young children cannot retain an internal image of their mothers for any length of time, must be wrong. All her experience and observation contradicted it. But it was not pleasant reading. It would have been more comfortable for us to have written a simpler book that ignored the contradictions in theory and the practical dilemmas that we have chosen to discuss.

Our own experience of motherhood and writing about it has also helped us understand why so few feminists have tackled these questions. Once past the intense years of child bearing and child rearing, many women want to put it behind them. Even when they miss the incomparable pleasures, they want to forget the worry and the exhaustion. Adrienne Rich describes her meeting with a young mother with a newborn baby in a sling: 'I am amazed to feel in myself a passionate longing to have, once again, such a small, new being clasped against my body ... The young mother ... speaks of how quickly one forgets the pure pleasure of having this new creature, immaculate, perfect.' Then she remembers:

> In the building where I live, women are still raising children alone, living day in and day out within their individual family units, doing the laundry, herding the tricycles to the park, waiting for the husbands to come home. There is a baby-sitting pool and a children's playroom, young fathers push prams on weekends, but childcare is still the individual responsibility of the individual woman. I envy the sensuality of having an infant of two weeks curled against one's breast; I do not envy the turmoil of the elevator full of small children, babies howling in the laundromat, the apartment in winter where pent-up seven- and eight-year-olds have one adult to look to for their frustrations, reassurances, the grounding of their lives (Rich, 1977, p. 33).

Isn't mothering enough, without writing about it? There must surely be more personally satisfying, more distant and safer issues to grapple with, than this obstinate, complex, contradictory one.

Besides, it is not only the practice of motherhood which has low status, it is also the study of it. Just as the care of children is 'women's work', so the sociological study of children and their carers is marginal, has little prestige, and is more likely to be carried out by women. Many feminist academics studiously avoid the whole area. Even in psychology, where the study of 'child development' has somewhat higher status, few feminists have written about its implications.

Recently a number of books and articles by feminists have been published which discuss women's caring work in *general*, deliberately including motherhood in that wider category, without emphasizing it especially. We find this puzzling because we think motherhood is central to the understanding of caring. For instance, Janet Finch and Dulcie Groves (1983) do not include a single article on conventional motherhood in their interesting book *A Labour of Love*. One contributor (Oliver) even claims that there are more women caring for elderly and handicapped dependants at any one time than for 'normal' children. Nelson, commenting on this observation, says that this 'fact ... has been overlooked in the extensive debate on mothering and child care among feminists' (Nelson, 1984, p. 7). What extensive debate? Of course it *is* important to stress that women's caring is not restricted to young ones, and that by the year 2000 there will be more elderly dependent people than dependent children. But the point of view that this is *women's* work is justified in terms of women's supposedly *motherly* natures. Because they can bear children, women are considered more able than men to give tender, loving care to whomever needs it.

Choosing to stress the other types of caring that women do leads some writers into peculiar positions. Janet Finch (1984b) argues against community care for elderly and handicapped people, on the grounds that this work falls to women. She puts a socialist case for more residential care for elderly and handicapped people, in the interests of women. The same arguments could be applied to child care, but she would probably not be prepared to argue the case for residential care for children. We need to look for solutions which do not make caring women's private, unpaid work, but which recognize that caring *about* somebody makes it much easier to care *for* them. We have chosen to concentrate on child care, but many of the issues, and the solutions, are the same for other people, not just young ones.

The women who look after elderly and handicapped people often also care for children, or did so at an earlier stage in their lives. Their situation is much like that of mothers and so is their low status as carers. But children are very different from adults, whether handicapped, old or frail. Children have to be nurtured and raised, taught the skills of the society in which they will play a part. Parents' emotional commitment to children is necessarily different from that of adult sons and daughters to their ageing relatives. Public agencies are also much more concerned with how children are brought up than with what is thought of as the 'routine' care of handicapped and elderly people.

Most feminist work is about the relationships between men and women. One simple reason for this is that women's subordination and male dominance are the two sides of the same coin. So much is written about the ways in which this relationship operates: through marriage and sexual relations; through violence, as well as the gentle side of heterosexual relationships; through law and economic and social policies. All this feminist scholarship is very important. We have used much of it in writing this book. But all these questions are simpler in a way than the ones we have chosen to tackle. They do not force the writer and the reader to ask 'How can women, men and children co-operate and live together?'. As soon as you think about children and their care, this question becomes urgent and obvious. Denunciations are not enough and quickly become frustrating. Children are not yet the men and women who dominate and are dominated. There must be a way of shaping our society that stops children ever becoming the rigid men and women we so often see.

We most definitely do not see the oppression of women as springing from male malice. Quite unapologetically we do see men, as well as women, as more or less willingly, more or less consciously, participating in a system they did not create. Most men either accept the way things are or feel helpless to change it. Yet men were not *born* sexist. It is quite true that in a sense they benefit from women's subordination. But that is nothing like an adequate explanation of male domination. For in other senses, as we shall see, men lose so much by holding on to their traditional power. How did they *come to be* people who valued money and power and status *more* than intimacy and closeness to children? Few women would like to be men, despite everything, so the superiority of male values cannot be so obvious. As they grow up, men learn to attach more importance to the benefits they get from the status quo than to the losses. If men had not been mistreated as little boys, humiliated and punished as preparation for adult masculinity, they would never accept the way things are. We are brought back to the significance of motherhood and child care for anyone who hopes for radical change.

The more we look into this, the easier it is to see that the future of child care is an uncomfortable subject, not because it is to do with liberating mothers, but because it is also to do with empowering children. As things are, mothers play the most decisive part of all in changing children who hardly know their gender into little men and little women. Child rearing is not done in the abstract. It means teaching children the language of a particular culture: what it values, what it forbids, what it expects, what it despises. And in order to become adults who feel fully at home in their own culture, children have to come to terms with its bad side: its inequalities, discriminations and injustices.

In a story about the friendship between a white boy and a coloured boy in Rhodesia, Doris Lessing (1969) shows how each of them suffers on discovering the full facts of the system of racial injustice. These particular children never stop communicating and loving each other, but each spasmodically tries to retreat into his own group, to express anger and contempt for the other, to take any path that seems to offer a simple reason for an unacceptable and nonsensical difference. We all make some such unpleasant discoveries, but most of us are disillusioned early and give in. A lot of child rearing consists of calming children down, controlling and managing them, getting them to submit and to accept the unacceptable. These processes are not at all neutral. Inevitably they are carried out by mothers who have enormous power over their children, even though they are otherwise not very powerful. As we shall see, to get social approval mothers have to get their children to 'behave', and children's feelings and future happiness are subordinated to their being 'good'. It is usually other women – health visitors, social workers, teachers, relatives – who approve or disapprove of the way mothers manage their children. In this way divisions form between mothers and women who look after children in different ways.

Mothers usually have a good idea of what it is like for their children. They may dimly recognize that the children are right to cry if they are in pain, to undress in the park if they feel too warm, to spit out a mouthful if it is too hot. But mothers have to teach the children better manners. There are more constraints on mothers' behaviour than on children's. A mother may feel the child is stronger than *she* is, a mini-tyrant who will either disgrace her publicly or, if she is lucky, let her off a public battle. Mothers are caught in the middle, between their love and understanding of the children they have to control and their own controls.

The notion of motherhood we discuss is historically linked with an exaggerated idea of children's dependence. Towards the end of the nineteenth century, when public opinion began to turn against child labour, laws were passed which kept children at home, and which limited women's working hours as well. Children have always been dependent to an extent, because of their real physical immaturity, their developmental needs, and their ignorance. But as it became illegal for them to work for money, ideas about their capacities followed suit. Today children, like their mothers, are made far more dependent than need be, and made to feel far more powerless and helpless than they really are. The 'domino' effect of overturning current forms of motherhood could be enormous.

OUTLINE OF THE BOOK

We aim to treat the complexities of child care in as comprehensive a way as possible. We show how all-pervasive is the idea that women should be motherly. We argue that the present interlocking system of parenthood, work and child care imposes unnecessary restrictions on all our lives. We look at some current solutions, at small-scale projects which raise further questions but also identify practical possibilities and help us clarify our vision. And then we turn to our ideas for the future, for changes in the organization of parenthood, work and children's care, and to the immediate steps we can take to bring it about.

Part One goes back to beginnings and looks at the present system of child care and how it came about. In Chapter 1, 'Women and Child Care', we argue that caring for children need not always condemn the carer to be a second-class citizen. Yet this is what has happened: we look at the history of the split between motherhood and power, and at the answers socialists and feminists have offered to 'the Mother problem'. In Chapter 2, 'Child Care – Public or Private?', we describe how public control underlies the conventional idea of the 'privacy of the family'. We show that social policy to date has always assumed that women will go on doing the unpaid, undervalued job of caring, and how New Right policy is designed to make sure women have no other choice. Chapter 3, 'Children's Days with Mother', shows that the ideal notion of the young child at home with mother actually covers a vast range of experiences. Chapter 4, 'Children's Days away from Mother', reviews the available forms of non-maternal care and the role of other people in children's lives.

Part Two of the book is concerned with parenthood. In Chapter 5, 'Parents and Others', we explore the specialness of the parent–child relationship and the way in which it is used to keep other adults at arm's length from children. But in practice what is expected of parents is different for mothers and for fathers. In Chapters 6 and 7 we focus on motherhood: 'Is Mother Special?' reviews the psychological literature on biological and social motherhood and the needs and capacities of infants; 'Being Mother' shows how the present isolation of motherhood often leads to completely unnecessary depression among mothers. The other side of mothers' specialness is fathers' distance. Chapter 8, 'The Changing Rule of Fathers', discusses men's control over women and children. Chapter 9, 'Fathers Today', describes what fathers actually do. We find that the foundations have been laid for great changes, but so far little has changed. We argue that the roles of mother and father are just aspects of parenthood which have been split apart and need to be brought together again in both men and women carers.

Part Three describes some things which are actually happening in the teeth of conventional practices. Chapter 10 (with Pam Calder) looks at children in day care. Our approach here is to turn the conventional argument, that children need their mothers, upside down, and to see what happens when we take children's need for *each other* as our starting point. This chapter reviews the psychological literature on day care, and shows conclusively that it is time to abandon the prejudice that the most we can expect from day care is that it shall do no damage. In subsequent chapters three contributors look at experiments in child care that have specific ambitious aims. In Chapter 11, Audrey Maynard writes about the community nursery movement in Britain and looks at two contrasting nurseries in some detail. In different ways, each of these nurseries challenges common ideas about the division of responsibility between parents and workers. In Chapter 12, Jonathan Trustram writes about his experiences working in a small co-operative crèche for babies and very young children, one of them his own child. In Chapter 13, Wiebke Wüstenberg and Stephen Castles describe a pioneering after-school venture in Bristol, where children were given the chance to make things with 'adult' tools in ways they decided for themselves. These small-scale projects, with very limited resources, are all trying to do things which could not possibly be done within the family.

We build on the insights from these exciting projects in our concluding chapter. We imagine a very different sort of society, in which work, parenthood and child care are organized quite differently and work does not take automatic precedence. Women and men will be equal partners in the care of children. How do we get there? All sorts of things are actually happening which amount to steps towards our vision, places where we can add our weight to bring about a future in which child care is more than women's business – for all our sakes.

PART ONE
NATURE AND NURTURE

CHAPTER ONE

WOMEN AND CHILD CARE

WOMEN AS CHILDREN'S CARERS

Child care is usually women's responsibility. There are some societies where women share it with men, especially the care of weaned babies and children. Boys and old men may be involved, fathers may do something – occasionally may really share the care of weaned young ones. But overwhelmingly it is women – mother, grandmother, aunt, sister, friend – who feed, carry, watch and educate babies and children. We shall be arguing that this pattern must be changed, so we certainly need to know whether it is 'natural'. For if it is, we may as well settle for a few reforms and abandon the ambitious project of reducing the sexual division of labour to its bare minimum.

A 'sexual division of labour' – a way of dividing work between women and men, and settling which sort of work is allocated to each – occurs to some extent in all known societies. Women's responsibility for the special task of child care is a part of something much bigger. A hundred years ago anthropologists often assumed that the work considered suitable for women really did fit their biological nature better – it was easier, lighter, nearer home. No one can go on maintaining this, now that comparative studies have shown that what one society will consider 'women's work', like carrying heavy weights (because they 'have stronger heads'), is what another will believe fits men's nature rather than women's. It is true that women more often cook, work closer to home, less often hunt, but every single rule you could formulate is contradicted somewhere – which would be impossible if these rules were made inevitable by women's biological nature.

These days anthropologists are more likely to try to explain women's *other* work in terms of their responsibility for children, as though that, at least, needed no explanation. But once babies are weaned, women's continued caring does need some explanation. Why shouldn't men take over or share care of weaned children? The link between women and children cannot be explained in terms of maternal instinct.

In some societies, a woman's relationship with her biological child is not recognized as unique. She is just one of a group of 'mothers', all addressed by that title. Maternal instinct, triggered by the hormones produced during pregnancy, birth and breast feeding, could only explain *biological* mothers' care of infants. Actually we have a situation where biological mothers usually continue mothering for years and years, but are often supplemented or replaced by other women. To explain women's special role as natural, we would need evidence that women are more nurturant than men by virtue of their sex alone. Many people believe this, but there is no good evidence for it. Nancy Chodorow is one of the few feminists who have asked 'Why do women mother?', meaning by 'mothering' not only the early nursing relationship but also the continued commitment and responsibility for older children, which could in theory be undertaken equally by men. She looks at the idea that the male hormones, the androgens, insure people against behaving in a 'motherly' way. But those few female embryos who accidentally receive androgens in the womb 'become nurturant mothers just as do other females, and men also can be nurturant ... Arguments from nature ... are unconvincing as explanations for women's mothering as a feature of a social structure ...' (Chodorow, 1978, pp. 29–30). It is not women's capacity to give birth and lactate that has made women continue as the main carers also for older children, in almost all the societies we know of. It is rather '... a social and cultural translation of their childbearing and lactation capacities' (ibid., p. 30). It is not women's and men's real natures, but what are *believed* to be their natures, that has determined their relative places in society.

Similarly, the wider work women do is not chosen because it 'fits' with child care in any absolute sense. Some sort of 'fit' is developed but, while the arrangement seems obvious to people of that society, it may often seem absurd and impractical to outsiders. The simple 'explanation', in terms of hunting and gathering societies, used to be that since women had a child at the breast or on the back it was easier for them to dig for roots or grubs with this burden than to chase a kangaroo. This simple explanation has recently come under fire from feminist anthropologists.

One suggestion for the origin of the division is that the relative immobility of early hominid mothers with severe infant transport problems may have encouraged a specialisation in range between the sexes. Unburdened males could travel further and when hunting was established it was males who travelled long distances after large game. This fits with popular views about the place of men and women ... but it overlooks the widespread practice of collective hunting [which] ... involves both men and women and sometimes children and is unrelated to differences in physical size or geographic range (Dahlberg, 1981, p. 11).

The Mbuti are among these collective hunters. Mbuti women 'are perfectly capable of giving birth to a child while on the hunt', and at most would take a week's leave (Turnbull, 1981, p. 212). The Agta women of the Philippines habitually hunt, as individuals as well as in groups or with men, and go for all sizes of prey. They do not hunt in late pregnancy or during the first months of nursing, but after that they leave the baby with a grandmother, older child or some other relative. Certainly they are unusual today, but such patterns may have been common in prehistory and the story of 'man the hunter, woman the gatherer' may partly be a projecting back of modern Western prejudices. It is significant that the Agta women who hunt most are those who live in the more remote areas. In the lowlands, where there is more contact with other societies, the idea of women hunting is laughed at (Griffin and Griffin, 1981). Whether it is laughable or not is a matter of social convention. Some of the Agta see it as natural for women to hunt, and possibly once all did.

  The people of any individual society may well tell you that the work women do fits in with their child care responsibilities. But the question of 'fit' is a vexed one. In our society, housework is supposed to 'fit' with child care, and factory and office work to be quite unfitting for the care of children. We shall argue that housework and child care cannot easily be combined and that, with a change of priorities, office and factory work could just as easily be made to fit in with the care of children. For most people in a particular society its arrangement will seem sensible. If the women work at or near home, this will be explained in terms of child care needs. In another society, where women work far from home, there will still seem to be a good 'fit', because people will think it obvious that the young children should stay in the village to be cared for by the old, by older children or any other available adult, away from the danger from animals and lack of shelter. In yet another society with a different view of the mother–child relationship it will seem equally clear that the children must go with their mothers to the distant fields, and the babies be laid at the edge with older children watching to make sure they do not get bitten by snakes or grow too hot. Some cross-cultural comparisons have claimed that women's work is always

> ... done near a home base, ... is monotonous and does not require rapt attention, and it is not dangerous. Women's tasks, it is argued, can therefore be readily interrupted and resumed again without difficulty ... Such a formulation of the issue does not take account of the large number of societies in which women regularly gather wild plants or cultivate crops or engage in trade in locations many miles from home base, and either walk back and forth each day or move out into distant locations for some seasons of the year taking children with them; nor does it take account of women who tend large cauldrons of boiling foods over open fires – a dangerous process – nor, on the other hand, of the frequent practice of assigning baby-tending for long periods of a day either to children no more than five or six years old or to elderly people ... (Friedl, 1975, p. 8).

Those who try to explain what work women do in terms of child care responsibilities are assuming that it is obvious, both that women must mother, and what that will involve. Certainly all societies have to reproduce themselves, so child bearing and rearing are basic in that sense. But there is reason to think that the relation between women's child caring and their other work is a two-way matter. It may be *women's customary work* that decides how they space their children and *how* they bring them up.

> It is ... more fruitful ... to look at the problem from the other end of the funnel, and to consider first how the energies of adult women are used for the acquisition of subsistence and for other economic tasks, and then, once these requirements have been established, to see how child-spacing and child-tending are accommodated to the requirements of the women's tasks (Friedl, loc. cit.).

Foragers, like Australian aboriginal women, tend to have few children widely spaced. They may use herbs to prevent conception or bring about miscarriage, as well as the inhibition of ovulation by prolonged breast feeding or taboos on sexual intercourse during nursing. In societies where women's economic contribution is crucial, and the work is not considered compatible with child care, adult women are far less likely to be in day-to-day or hour-to-hour charge of children. We cannot explain the other work women do by taking the demands of their mothering for granted, for these are very flexible: women can have fewer or more children; close together or widely spaced; they can look after them themselves or delegate a lot of their care. Explanations of why and how women care for children, why and how they do the other work that is considered theirs, need to be more subtle and more complex than the dynamics of the nuclear cave-family we see in TV cartoons.

The divergence in details makes the universal patterns that do exist even more striking. Whether mothers care for their own children, or share care, whether 'child nurses' or older people take part in caring, adult men never play a *big* part where the sexual division of labour is at all developed. We do not need to explain this in terms of men's brains or hearts or muscles.

It is easy to see that if a sexual division of labour develops at all, women are more likely than men to care for the children. Since they have to care for them as infants, the basis is laid for continuing the relationship. This also has the advantage that it frees men completely to specialize in activities such as warfare, rather than leaving each sex looking after half the children, or looking after children half the time.

BUILDING ON THE 'ORIGINAL CLUES'

If there has to be a sexual division of labour ... but *does* there have to be? The Mbuti pygmies, studied by Turnbull, place little stress on sex differences outside the sphere of actual sexual relationships. Turnbull himself became an adopted member of the tribe and went through a speeded-up transition from childhood through puberty to adulthood while he was with them. He reports that among the Mbuti the baby is very dependent on its mother until it is weaned at about three. But before that

> ... there is a significant ritual but so informal that at first it escaped me. In the middle of camp, a mother hands her child to her husband, who puts the child to his breast. The child is, of course, familiar with the father's body, since it sleeps between the two parents. It cries 'ema' (mother) as it tries to suckle at the milkless breast. The father then gives the child its first solid food and corrects the child, teaching it to say 'eba' (father). Thus all males are first perceived by their children as 'another kind of mother,' one who cannot give milk but does provide other kinds of food. The importance of this is inestimable ... The pattern of dependence that is the child's experience in the womb is continued

through the first three years by its total dependence on first one mother, then on other mothers, and then, gradually, by extension, on 'male mothers' who, however inadequate at first sight, ultimately prove to have their uses too (Turnbull, 1981, p. 212).

The Mbuti may seem to share, to take turns, but their reasons for acting as they do are doubtless very different from the desire for justice and for individual self-fulfilment which motivate women putting forward such demands here today. The road to developing complex specialized cultures has gone through the sexual division of labour, even though it is now time to reject it.

It *seems* sensible to us, looking back, to ask why the sexual division of labour should have developed, in most places, in such a rigid way. Surely the Mbuti way of life allows for great flexibility? And if greater specialization is needed, why should it be on sex lines? Why should it be 'man the hunter' – if we suspend our doubts for a moment – when some women would undoubtedly hunt better than some men? But early and subsistence societies simply cannot think of individuals and their importance and specialness, as we do, from the standpoint of developed capitalism. Margaret Mead, the anthropologist, wrote:

> The differences between the two sexes is one of the important conditions on which we have built the many varieties of human culture that give human beings dignity and stature. In every human society, mankind has elaborated the biological division of labour into forms often very remotely related to the original biological differences that provided the *original clues* [our emphasis] (Mead, 1962b, p. 30).

A sexual division of labour and all the complex rituals that reinforce it, and the beliefs that support and rationalize it, is an enormously elaborate structure, even at its simplest, to be built on such flimsy 'original clues'. Its effects have been highly oppressive since, wherever political power has developed, men have more of it. All the same, the sexual division of labour was adaptive in its day. The development of the complex categories of kinship, and the taboo on marriage within certain kinship groups, strengthened human co-operative groups and provided a way of linking them. The relationships between the sexes became subject to rules. These rules were explained in myths which are permeated with the great division of the world into masculine and feminine. The rigidities of the sexual division of labour are archaic today: they were once triumphs of human organization – early forms of specialization.

Specialization increases production, and because it makes people mutually dependent it also cements the social bonds between them. But subsistence societies cannot afford to specialize much. They cannot feed students or apprentices or intellectual workers. They cannot tolerate people discovering their multiple talents by experiment, like the Renaissance gentleman. But specialization by sex, the simple division of labour between men and women, could be very useful, both economically and to make the sexes aware of their need to co-operate. The categories 'men' and 'women' existed already. As for the content, since men *cannot* have babies, it was often adaptive for women to continue the relationship they had developed with their suckling babies, and to become 'experts' in the care of older children too. This is another case of the old argument that it is easier to go on doing what you know about than to show someone else how to do it.

Each society has done something different with the 'original clues'. Age has always been one of the great differentiating principles, and so has the division between male and female – a first principle of human thought which has flooded our thinking, rather like a river overspilling its banks and flowing where it has no business to go. Whatever the original reasons were for dividing different sorts of work between the sexes, they can no longer apply. But the sexual division of labour is still going strong. It may have started as an innocuous and adaptive form of primitive specialization; today, it looks extremely unattractive.

In modern industrialized societies, it is still women who feed and care for their children and their children's fathers. Their place in the status hierarchy, their class position, largely depends on that of their men. And the behaviour of their men can be menacing in the extreme. The governments of the most powerful societies rely on holding potentially world-destroying bombs to keep each other at bay. No wonder Frankie Armstrong sings: 'Will there be womanly times, or must we die?' No wonder the campers at Greenham Common symbolize the contrast between the male and female worlds by fastening the important trivia of everyday life to the barbed wire fence: children's clothes, nappies, drawings, photographs of smiling people playing. Motherhood and political power are hardly on speaking terms.

POWER AND MOTHERHOOD

How did motherhood and all that is thought of as 'womanly' come to be divorced from political and economic power? In those societies where women can have political power, it is very seldom women of child-bearing years who take part in collective decision-making, or hold office. There is no obvious physical incompatibility to explain this. If child care can be delegated so that mothers can work in distant fields, it can be delegated so that they can attend council meetings. Those who think the sexual division of labour a mere mirror of our natural capacities have little trouble with this. Men's political power can simply be seen as an extension of their 'protective' role as guardian of the mother–child unit. But as Adrienne Rich writes, in that case

> ... how do we account for the fact that laws, legends, and prohibitions relating to women have, from the early patriarchal myths (e.g. Eve) through the medieval witch massacres and the gynocide of female infants down to the modern rape laws, mother-in-law jokes, and sadistic pornography of our time, been hostile and defensive, rather than 'protective' (op. cit., p. 113)?

Some feminists, Rich among them, believe that patriarchal (male-dominant) rule has replaced an original matriarchy. Certainly many societies have myths to that effect. Anthropologist Jane Bamberger (1974, p. 263) describes South American Indian myths which described female misrule and chaos which preceded the rule of men. These myths have an important role as part of the initiation of boys. They make perfect psychological sense without our needing to assume a historical matriarchy for, wherever women mother, boys have at some point to move over from the women's world to the men's. This transition inevitably involves some rejection of the values and practices of women which have, up to then, been far more important and real to the growing boy than the lesser-known activities of his own sex. So wherever the sexual division of labour is strong enough to make such a move-over necessary, it is likely to be celebrated ritually so as to deal with the possible trauma and conflict. Such points of transition where the men take the boys from their mothers are easily recognizable in modern societies: ruling-class boys are sent away to boarding school at seven, to stop them 'growing into women'; Jewish boys have a Barmitzvah at thirteen when they become men; Muslim boys are circumcised at seven.

In the traditional sexual division of labour in which women mother, their control over the lives and hearts of the children in their care is certainly a potential sort of social power. Here is one anthropologist's account of this potential:

If I had knowledge only of the anatomy and cultural capacities of men and women, I would predict that women rather than men would be more likely to gain control over the technology of defence and aggression, and that if one sex were going to subordinate the other, it would be female over male. While I would be impressed with the physical dimorphism – the greater height, weight, and strength of the males – especially in relationship to hand-held weapons, I would be even more impressed by something which the females have and which the males cannot get – namely, control over the birth, care and feeding of babies. Women, in other words, control the nursery, and because they control the nursery, they can potentially modify all lifestyle that threatens them. It is within their power of selective neglect to produce a sex ratio heavily in favour of females over males. It also lies within woman's power to sabotage the development of 'masculine' males by rewarding little boys for being passive rather than aggressive. I would expect women to concentrate their efforts on rearing solidary and aggressive females rather than males. I would further expect the few male survivors per generation to be shy, obedient, hard-working, and grateful for sexual favours. I would predict that women would monopolize the headship of local groups, that they would be responsible for shamanistic relations with the supernatural, and that God would be called SHE. Finally, I would expect that the ideal and most prestigious form of marriage would be polyandry – one woman controlling the sexual and economic services of several men (Harris, 1978, p. 64).

What if women simply refused to give the children up?

... one of women's most important tasks was to teach the children ... how to procure food, that is, not only show them how to find their own food individually, but how to participate in social production. Thus women have, objectively, considerably more power (potential power) than men ... They could reproduce a labour force which could hunt and gather, and, in turn, reproduce itself. In other respects the two sexes must have been relatively equal (Kirsch, 1979, p. 328).

This writer puts forward the hypothesis that men had to be ready to use their hunting weapons to control women in order to get access to their sons. Just as conservative writers like Tiger and Fox (1974) project their own ideas of the proper way men and women should behave on to our distant ancestors, so this feminist writer seems to be projecting on to the past the modern separatist dream of a world of women and children, needing no men, where the boy children conveniently vanish when they reach an awkward age ... But her idea is no sillier than the conservative one.

There is evidence, scanty though it is, to suggest that there may be some societies with a sexual division of labour in which women mother and men do little caring of the children, yet women are 'separate but equal'. 'Every member of the group [has control] over the distribution of the resources and products that each acquires or manufactures' (Leacock, 1981, p. 158). Women among the Australian aboriginals used to distribute the food they foraged for, or the small animals they caught, among their families, while the men controlled the distribution of the game meat. Women had as much control over their own lives as men did over theirs. Other anthropologists deny that there have ever been any egalitarian societies. They assume that patriarchy has always existed, that '... the unalterable fact of long child care combined with the exigencies of primitive technology ...' has always meant that women are unequal in status and power in hunting and gathering and in horticultural societies (Gough, 1975, p. 74). We must leave the anthropologists to battle this one out. It is really a battle between the optimists and the pessimists among feminist anthropologists, for obviously if you believe patriarchy has existed since humans first evolved from apes, the attempt to abolish the oppression of women has all the uncertainty of a completely unknown venture.

We shall assume the optimists are right. Their optimism does not take us far. The most hopeful among them admit that as soon as separate political power develops, outside the household, women's status changes. If women are linked to children and, through them, to the home base, then while there is no public administration more general than the household, men and women will be equal. But as soon as the most rudimentary form of public power begins to develop, women's areas of concern will become downgraded. The household will become just one unit in the collectivity, while the male sphere will embrace the whole. So it is only in the most politically primitive societies that women are 'separate but equal'.

The distancing of motherhood and power has been a complex and long process. The important thing is that it has been just that – a historical process, not a natural incompatibility. In some societies where women and men have separate political organizations to oversee their different areas of work, women have kept some part in collective decision-making for their own sphere. Once general political institutions have developed, as they eventually do in all sorts of societies, only exceptional women have been included in political decision-making. But women have always kept some say over the sharing out of resources within the family, some voice in family decisions, and some measure of general respect due to them as contributors to the subsistence of all. In some societies women's work is considered more crucial, and in others less, and their status and autonomy are linked to their economic role. It is only industrialization that has created the 'housewife'. Ironically, in modern societies, where women can be prime ministers or millionaires, motherhood has distanced women from access to political power as never before.

It is children, rather than women, who tend to be home-based; and, where they are children's main carers, women's work tends to be based at home or nearby. Before industrialization and during much of the long process of change labelled the 'Industrial Revolution', most of the work women did, at home as well as away from home, could be termed 'social production': that is, women were working for the public good, for more than their own immediate family group. Their products which were surplus to the family's requirements would be sold or otherwise exchanged for different things made, harvested or hunted by others. What we understand as 'housework', the work of maintaining the family's environment, preparing its food and otherwise looking after family members, including children, did not then exist as a distinct activity. Women were most often in charge of cooking and child care, but the children themselves worked at whatever needed doing. So even though women's role as children's carers had long distanced them from *political* power, over the millennia women have remained powerful where they were recognized as workers for the common good. The present-day divorce of motherhood from power is a special characteristic of industrial capitalism.

DIVORCING MOTHERHOOD FROM POWER

Our present-day understanding of motherhood is intimately linked to our idea of 'work' as wage labour, and therefore *not* housework, caring and other unpaid useful activities. During the nineteenth century in Britain work left home. It did not do so overnight. Working for wages gradually became the main means of subsistence, instead of a seasonal or occasional bonus to supplement the income from the little bit of land, the few animals, and cottage industry. In Britain big landowners systematically robbed villagers of their common lands and individual fields, through the 'enclosure' movement, and created a huge number of dispossessed: impoverished landless people for whom wage labour was the only hope of survival. Wage labour was not necessarily done outside the home in the eighteenth century. The first small spinning jennies were used in cottages. Even when steam- and water-powered machinery took textile production into the factory, there were still some processes done at home. Indeed, the scale of factory production meant that demand for these temporarily rose. But by the mid-nineteenth century, 'outwork' of all kinds was declining, so that women and children, like men, had to follow work out of the home into the factories if they were to earn. Working-class women led this process. Middle-class women remained typically home-based until this century, but might be involved in family industry, supplying finance for family business and so on.

In his classic description of industrial Britain in 1844, Engels wrote: 'Manufacturers began to employ children rarely of five years, often of six, very often of seven, usually of eight or nine years . . . the working-day often lasted fourteen to sixteen hours, exclusive of meals and intervals' (1962, p. 184). The nature and intensity of the work these children were doing, and the noise and dirt and unrelieved monotony of the surroundings, made the experience quite different from participation in agricultural work or spinning or weaving at home. But for children to work was nothing new. And it seemed to many people that they *should* be in the factories, where their parents were, so that the parents could look after them.

The process of industrialization was long and complex in Britain. (It is complex everywhere, but it was a particularly lengthy transformation in Britain, the first country to industrialize.) It was marked by intense contrasts, by the very latest technology creating unemployment in one locality while, at the same time, the remaining, highly productive women factory-workers might be relatively well paid and more independent and in control of their lives than ever before. In the very next street might be sweatshops where women or children worked gruelling hours in conditions even worse than those in a factory, using labour-intensive methods for a fraction of the factory wage. In women's other occupations, like domestic service and agriculture, wages were lower than in the factories while, as the nineteenth century advanced and large-scale industry became dominant, it became more difficult for women to set up their own businesses as craftswomen because of the amount of capital needed. But overall:

Surveying the whole field of women's work activity from 1750 to 1841, it is clear that the foundations of modern women's situation were laid in the changes associated with industrialisation. The separation of the work-

place from the home was established: the tradition of family labour ...
was abolished. The increasing differentiation of child and adult roles, with
the child's growing dependence, heralded the dependence of women in
marriage and their restriction to the home. It only remained for the
conservatism of the Victorian era to formulate a doctrine of feminine
domesticity whereby women could more effectively be tied to their family
roles, and the role of housewife could emerge in its modern form (Oakley,
1974b, p. 43).

This revolution was accomplished through protective legislation.

The conditions in which working-class people lived in mid-nineteenth-
century Britain could themselves account for the massive rate of infant
mortality. Children's long hours in the factory added to the environmental
factors. Young industrial capitalism was actually destroying its future
working class, a fact which alarmed politicians when the scale of the
devastation became clear to them.

The first Factory Acts restricted children's working hours. In 1832
children under thirteen were not supposed to work longer than six and a
half hours a day – the time modern British children spend daily at school.
There were many loopholes, and the requirement that the factory owners
provide schooling for their child workers was particularly easy to get round.
But from 1832 on, there has been a steady trend to separate children from
paid work. In 1844 a new Factory Act extended the state's protection to
women:

> Women were in every respect placed on the same footing as young
> persons, their working time being restricted to 12 hours a day, nightwork
> being forbidden in their case and so on. This was the first occasion on
> which the British legislature had found it necessary to exercise direct and
> official control over the labour of adults (Marx, *Capital* vol. 1, Everyman,
> p. 288).

This move was partly an attempt to protect children. Because there was no
safe method of feeding babies artificially, when mothers of infants went out
to work their children often died of malnutrition, combined with the effects
of poisoning by the commonly used pacifier 'Godfrey's Cordial', which
contained opium. But as Oakley writes:

> ... protective legislation was both a cause and an effect of industrialisa-
> tion's most important legacy to women: the creation of the modern
> housewife role ... Victorian attempts to get women out of the factories

and mills and into the home were motivated largely by the anxiety of men whose own situation had been radically transformed by the change to factory production. The loss of traditional work roles and the new restrictions on the labour of children caused a major crisis in the life and unity of the family. The child's increasing dependence upon adults and the continuing limitations imposed by women's reproductive role came to entail a division of labour between husband and wife, whereby the husband became the main breadwinner, and the wife the main child-rearer, living off, and providing for her children out of, the earnings of the man. In this situation the woman factory worker posed the threat of competition (op. cit., p. 45).

Throughout the second half of the nineteenth century the immorality of the factories and the unnaturalness of women working became a common theme in parliament, in the newspapers, in books and in the pulpits.

Although 'protective legislation' was often welcomed by women, it placed them in the same position as children. Women and children were being protected from the harsh world of work and from economic independence by one and the same measure. Protective legislation

> usually took the shape of negative action – limitation of hours, exclusions of women from certain types of employment, or preventing them from working within a certain period before or after childbirth. And there were no reforms which gave women the means to live while not earning money. Nurseries which might have enabled them to work without damage to the health of their small infants were actually rejected as a possible solution (Bristol Women's Studies Group, 1979, p. 209).

The few day nurseries that were established in Britain were charitable institutions copying the French example. Where they were set up, their higher standards of physical care had a noticeable effect on infant mortality. But they were never popular, probably because of '... the searching enquiries into the moral virtues and financial resources usually made on application ...' (Hewitt, 1958, p. 166). In 1867 the *Lancet* proposed local-authority day nurseries, but this plea went against the dominant belief that the state should not intervene in family life, unless to force mothers of babies to stay at home. Since then, more than a hundred years has seen little lasting change. As Illich (1983, p. 46) says:

> ... women are discriminated against in employment only to be forced, when off the job, to do a new kind of economically necessary work

without any pay attached to it ... outside of and along with wage labour, which had spread during the nineteenth century, a second kind of unprecedented economic activity had come into being. To a greater extent and in a different manner from men, women were drafted into the economy. They were and are deprived of equal access to wage labour only to be bound with even greater inequality to work that did not exist before wage labour came into being.

Children were cared for before wage labour became the normal form of work, but the modern institution of motherhood did not exist.

The way we institutionalise motherhood in our society – assigning sole responsibility for child care to the mother, cutting her off from the easy help of others in an isolated household, requiring round-the-clock tender, loving care, and making such care her exclusive activity – is ... new and unique ... (Bernard, 1975, p. 9).

In Britain, as elsewhere, motherhood has become separated from paid work. Not that all mothers stop working in paid employment. The dependent housewife and mother has become an ideal, and those who could not afford it have had to find their own ways round the difficulties of combining paid work and the care of children. Child care, like housework, has become the *private* business of individual families. So far it has not paid capitalists to provide child care for profit and, in Britain, state provision for under-fives is derisory. Available child care is often for very short hours, so even those women who do combine paid work and motherhood are usually partially economically dependent. The law and the tax system enshrine the ideal of the male breadwinner and the dependent wife and mother. Employers carry that model in their heads and use it to legitimize discrimination against single and childless women, as well as mothers. The separation of motherhood from economic as well as political power affects all women's lives. The only way for a woman to acquire her full adult female status is to become a mother. A childless woman is treated as less than complete. But at the same time, a true mother, a 'good' mother, is supposed to be at least partly economically dependent on a man; and as such, *she* is not a full adult, an equal citizen, for only people who support themselves are fully adult. Women's status as citizens is highly ambiguous. Motherhood in our society really does involve surrendering economic power and, with it, full adult status. Being 'separate but equal' is not a possible strategy for women under capitalism.

STRATEGIES TO RECONCILE POWER AND MOTHERHOOD

What was called 'the Woman Question' in the nineteenth century was really the 'Motherhood Question'. Side by side with the development of wage labour, motherhood developed as a restricting and debilitating condition, occupying a different place from the male world of work.

> The changes were, by their nature, contradictory. Industrial capitalism freed women from the endless round of household productive labour, and in one and the same gesture tore away the skills which had been the source of women's unique dignity. It loosened the bonds of patriarchy, and at once imposed the chains of wage labour. It 'freed' some women for a self-supporting spinsterhood, and conscripted others into sexual peonage. And so on (Ehrenreich and English, 1979, p. 13).

Women had more choices about how they lived, but these choices were still very constricted. They were much the same as those that women face today – a choice between two worlds: to take their proper places as mothers in the women's world of the home or to struggle in the man's world with the handicap of being a woman, or uneasily to straddle both. The outlines of the solutions that were offered in the nineteenth century are still with us today (Eisenstein, 1984, pp. 144–5).

One answer to the 'Motherhood Question' is to accept the division of the world into men's and women's spheres as valid, and to romance about each as having its own sort of value and power. Into this category comes a hotchpotch of radical and conservative groups – from the romantic conservative Ruskin to the revolutionary separatist feminist philosopher, Mary Daly. They are united by the belief that men and women are essentially and naturally different.

The other most common answer to the 'Motherhood Question' is to bring women and children into the male world. Women are to be brought into the public world of the economic market, participating in full-time work, given equal rights and equal obligations with men. Those who follow this argument to its extreme have to propose abolishing private life altogether, but its proponents are usually resigned to a sort of rump 'women's sphere' of intimate relationships at home which their reforms leave untouched.

Ehrenreich and English make a similar distinction between 'romantic' and 'rationalist' answers to the 'Woman Question'. They write (op. cit., pp. 19–20):

The *rationalist* answer is, very simply, to admit women into modern society on an equal footing with men. If the problem is that women are in some sense 'out', then it can be solved by letting them 'in' ... The sexual rationalist programme is one of *assimilation*, with ancillary changes (day care, for example) as necessary to promote women's rapid integration into what has been the world of men.

In contrast

Sexual *romanticism* cherishes the mystery that is woman and proposes to *keep* her mysterious, by keeping her outside ... If she became a female version of 'economic man', an individual pursuing her own trajectory, then indeed it would be a world without love, without human warmth ... Sexual romanticism asserts that the home will be ... [the] refuge, woman will be ... [the] consolation ... The world of private life and biological existence has become suffused with a holy radiance (ibid., pp. 20–21).

What has actually happened is that the market forces of capitalism have simultaneously loosened and consolidated the sexual division of labour. Women are 'free' to work alongside men in the labour market, but not 'free' of the family commitments that have an overriding effect on their work lives. Men can push prams, women can be bank managers; but as the exceptions multiply, the rule itself is untouched. Back in the nineteenth century, the foundations were laid for the present-day version of the sexual division of labour. The movement to bring women home with their children, out of the factories, was the antecedent of today's idealized relationship of the wage-earning husband and dependent wife and children. Even such prominent radicals as Marx and Engels were unable to escape the 'two spheres' way of thinking. They were appalled by the unfeminine way in which women workers behaved, and saw their return home as allowing a return to their 'true nature'. Engels was absolutely horrified by the necessity for role-swaps in many working-class families. In 1844, he cited an unemployed worker who called on an old friend and found him mending his wife's stockings.

... as soon as he saw his old friend ... he tried to hide them. But Joe ... had seen it, and said: 'Jack, what the devil art thou doing? Where is the missus? Why, is that thy work?' And poor Jack was ashamed and said: 'No I know this is not my work but my poor missus is i' th' factory; she has to leave at half past five and works till 8 at night and then she is so

knocked up that she cannot do aught when she gets home, so I have to
do everything for her what I can, for I have no work ... and I shall never
have any more work while I live' and then he wept ... (Marx and Engels,
1962, p. 178).

Engels comments:

Can anyone imagine a more insane state of things ... ? And yet this
condition, which unsexes the man and takes from the woman all womanliness without being able to bestow on the man true womanliness, or on
the woman true manliness ... is the last result of our much praised
civilisation ... (ibid., p. 179).

In those days the great revolutionaries were firm supporters of the 'family
wage' and the consequent economic dependence of women and children on
men's labour.

Women's economic dependence can be treated romantically as part of
their glory, as evidence of their profound intelligence. Janet Caldwell, a
member of America's New Right, wrote an article called 'Women's Lib:
They're Spoiling Eve's Con Game'. She feared that if men saw through the
veneer of feminine helplessness they would

... suspect that we women conned men through the centuries. I fear they
are asking themselves – to women's terrible hurt – why they should
support an able-bodied woman who can earn a good living too, and why
should a man give his ex-wife alimony and child support cheques, when
she is just as capable ... of rolling up her sleeves and getting on the 8.30
bus of a morning for an arduous day in the factory or office (quoted in
Ehrenreich, 1983, p. 159)?

The projected loss of the 'right to be a housewife' and the obligation on men
to support their families were among the New Right's arguments against
the Equal Rights Amendment (ERA) in the USA. A more forceful attack on
equal rights feminism was that with the ratification of the ERA women
would be drafted into the US Army (David, 1983a, p. 34).

The vision of the future that 'revolutionary feminists' want could not be
further removed from the wishes of anti-feminist women of the New Right.
But both share a common logic: that the sexual division of labour is based
on natural differences. They agree that women are *naturally* 'womanly' and
'motherly'. They disagree about men. The conservative 'romantic' view
would hold that men are naturally both protective (towards the weak, such

as women and children) and aggressive in defence of their own. Being naturally more moral, men are morally responsible for the overall well-being of society as a whole, as well as of their own women and children. Revolutionary feminists see men as immoral, as naturally brutish and destructive. They point to the ecological destruction of the planet, and they argue that unless the 'male world' is rendered powerless, unless the toys are taken from the boys, there will be no future for any of us. 'Womanly' virtues are glorified as our only hope, but no hope is held out for men coming to share them. Caring for children is not an activity but a way of being. It is certainly not an area women should be seeking to share with men or to delegate to impersonal bodies. Caring is women's nature. The big difference between revolutionary feminists and the biological conservatives who agree that caring is women's essence is, of course, that the feminists absolutely abhor any dependence of women on men or the male state.

The key 'rationalist' answer to the 'Motherhood Question' is, in its extreme, virtually to abolish motherhood as a specialized activity and to bring women into the male world of work. At the same time children are brought into the public world but kept separate from work and civic affairs. While revolutionary feminists celebrate the female sphere and seek to find ways of abolishing the male one, socialist-feminists, socialists and Marxists generally agree with society's contempt for the private sphere allotted to women and seek to reduce it to its bare essentials. By 1880 Engels had reached the position associated with Marxism ever since; he saw women's paid work as the key to their liberation:

> The emancipation of women and their equality with men are impossible and must remain so for as long as women are excluded from socially productive work and restricted to housework, which is private. The emancipation of women becomes possible only when women are enabled to take part in production on a large, social scale, and when domestic duties require attention only to a minor degree. And this has become possible only as a result of modern large-scale industry, which not only permits the participation of women in production in large numbers, but actually calls for it and, moreover, strives to convert private domestic work also into a more public industry (Engels, 1968, p. 152).

The answer to the sexual division of labour was to get rid of one side of the equation. Women can become lorry drivers but men cannot become 'house husbands'. Marxists, and most socialist-feminists, have never seen a 'positive aspect' in housework.

So Lenin described how a woman wears herself out '... with trivial, monotonous work that exhausts her and consumes her time and strength, such as housework; ... her horizon sinking, her mind growing dull ... her will weak' (Zetkin, 1968, p. 42). In post-revolutionary USSR, men and women were made equal before the law. All sorts of work and training were opened to women.

> We are setting up public kitchens and dining rooms, laundries and repair shops, crèches, kindergartens, children's homes ... Our programme [is] to shift the functions of management and upbringing in the individual household to society. In this way woman is being freed from her domestic slavery and her dependence on her husband (ibid. p. 43).

Woman was free to work for the *public* good.

The revolutions in Russia and China promised to free women to work in social production on an equal basis with men. The state of affairs in the Soviet Union today is a far cry from Lenin's and Kollontai's visions and promises. Women make up half the workforce. They do have equal pay when doing the same job as men. 'However, on average, women earn between 60 per cent and 70 per cent of men's wages ... women work at lower-paid jobs ... Women work more in lower-paid industries, but where they work in higher paid ones they work in the lower-paid jobs in those industries' (Deacon, 1983, p. 151). Both parents usually work, out of necessity. There are no child benefits for the first three children, little special provision for single parents. Deacon writes (ibid. p. 197): 'It is not surprising that one of the demands to arise from the nascent women's movement in Russia was the right not to work but to concentrate on household duties. The alternative that household duties might be done by the local community or by men was clearly far from being realised.' There is a great deal of nursery provision in the USSR, although many young children are looked after by their grandmothers at home. But the USSR is a clear case of how collective child care does not automatically free women. There are still enormous waiting lists. When places are available, mothers' relationship to their children's day care is much like that of mothers to local-authority nurseries in Britain. They depend on the day care, are often forced to accept low-quality provision and defer to the views of 'experts'. It is *women* who work in child care establishments, just as in the West.

Anti-Stalinists usually blame the failure of revolutionary promises on the Stalin era and the obvious steps backward that took place then – such as the abolition of the right to abortion. But the sexual divison of labour had *never* been radically questioned. Men were *encouraged* to help with the housework. Women's other abilities had been recognized but, while housework still existed, it was seen as primarily theirs, and the 'natural' link between women and children was never challenged. In later life the feminist oppositionist Kollontai became a Soviet official. She wrote an article listing the areas in which women had made inroads into traditionally male positions. She pointed out (1977, p. 316): 'It is well known there was never a so-called women's movement, and that the Russian women ... never viewed the battle for equality as being separate from the basic task of liberating her country from the yoke of Tsarism ...' The lack of a women's movement was undoubtedly one reason for the slip backwards to the familiar 'double burden' of women, responsibility for paid and unpaid work.

In China there *were* women's movements (but not autonomous in any sense), both under the Kuomintang and under the leadership of the Communist Party. Women's oppression had been incredibly bitter in pre-revolutionary China. The revolutionary forces had offered solid, precious changes: an end to the poverty that led to female infanticide, social concern for all children, women's equality in law, including in marriage. During land reform, women had been treated as individuals who were entitled to receive land. There was no movement for free love or abolition of the family, as in the first years of the Russian Revolution. Instead, the promise was to replace the patriarchal family with

> ... new family relations based on democratic unity ... Both husband and wife are economically independent; with 'free meals provided' and collective welfare undertaken by the people's commune ... Only in such a type of family can husband and wife achieve a union of equality based on pure love ... Children are also 'independent persons' instead of the private property of their parents (Croll, 1974, pp. 57–9).

These blessings were supposed to follow from women's freedom from *economic* subordination alone. Many blessings really did come about. However, because the sexual division of labour was never radically challenged, women in China have moved into the men's world without any corresponding movement in the other direction. Almost all women work outside the home. The responsibility of fixing up child care has remained theirs, not their men's. Articles tell them to get their husbands to help, to 'handle the contradiction' between the private and public spheres well by having the right attitude (i.e. putting 'public' first). Men still rule the People's Republic of China.

The limitations of 'socialist' societies are well known to feminists. Yet the labour movement and the Labour Party in Britain have recently adopted a comparable approach to the 'Woman Question', under some pressure from feminists, to be more enlightened about the position of women in the formal labour market. Feminists have forced them to consider questions of day nurseries, equal pay and opportunities, and the like. Originally, the Labour Movement developed to defend the interests of working men. Women, not yet even voters then, had no place in the first skilled craft unions. The 'family wage' ideology has always been dominant: that is, male trade unionists have consistently fought for higher wages to cover their needs and those of their dependants – wives and children. As women entered the formal labour market and became organized, time and again they met opposition from organized men. Eleanor Rathbone, the chief proponent of family allowances to be paid by the state for the care of children, described her opponents:

An equally formidable body of opposition came, however, from the ranks of the Party whose reaction to any such proposal might have been expected to be sympathetic. Many members of the Labour Party, and particularly those sections of it which reflected Trade Union opinion, were profoundly suspicious. They visualised a measure whose practical application might complicate and possibly bedevil the traditional conception of a standard wage, the traditional machinery for collective bargaining so painfully evolved and not yet perfected by the efforts of generations of Trade Unionists ... they were reluctant to contemplate the carving of a new channel of distribution down which spendable income might be conducted to mothers whose needs had hitherto provided the great mass of male wage-earners with a telling argument for a high standard wage (quoted in Land, 1980, p. 2).

Equally the support of the Labour Movement for equal pay has always been lukewarm, except when it was clearly in men's interests to ensure that women did not undercut them by accepting lower wages for the same or similar work. There has never been an equivalent motivation for male trade unionists to oppose sex segregation in work – the only route to *real* equal pay. Until the last couple of decades, the Labour Movement's approach to the care of children was to demand enough money for men to pay for dependent wives and children. This 'family wage' idea has been modified under persistent pressure from women joining the formal labour market and trade unions. The TUC has flirted with feminism. In 1977 it set up a working party to look into the question of provision for the under-fives, which recommended a comprehensive system of care for pre-school children. Yet the working party wrote:

If women's particular role as a parent is fully recognised, and it is accepted that women will need to take fairly lengthy periods of leave to have children and may then work part time afterwards, then they cannot conform to the traditional male pattern of employment (TUC Working Party, 1977, p. 108).

The 'traditional male pattern of employment' is still seen as *the* feature of the world of work, and the 'natural' division between men and women is still the dominant view of trade unionists. The commitment on paper is just that – paper-thin – it is hardly ever reflected in action. The Labour Party's 1983 manifesto marked the high point of its *affaire* with feminism: 'Men and women should be able to share the rights and responsibilities of paid employment and domestic activities so that job segregation within and outside the home is broken down . . .' To ensure action, it has now appointed a shadow Minister for Women's Rights. This 'token' feminist is denied influence over other public policy issues and is marginalized from the real, 'male' world of politics. Job segregation in politics is not being broken down by this measure. Yet the Labour Party now sees itself as a party committed to equal rights, to getting women into the public world, the world of work, on equal terms with men.

Curiously this, too, is what most feminists are aiming at, whether declared socialists or not. They also now adopt the solution apparently tried and tested in socialist societies – of getting women into the male world of employment. In so doing they tend to pay scant attention to the care of children. Coote and Campbell state categorically (1982, p. 38) that 'child care has been a major preoccupation of the women's liberation movement'. What they really mean by this is that one of the first three or four demands of the women's movement in both the USA and Britain was 'twenty-four-hour-day nurseries'. This was acceptable to all shades of feminist opinion from traditional Marxist to more liberal or revolutionary feminism. It was quickly misunderstood everywhere outside to mean residential nurseries and women divesting themselves of their child care responsibilities, giving an impression of 'child dumping'. The idea had been that women should be able to work, work shifts and/or go out at night – just like men. Indeed, all the force behind these demands was to have women treated like men.

In a review of the arguments of the American women's movement for day care, Steinfels showed that feminists were extraordinarily conservative. They wanted to 'open ... up the present economic structures to women' rather than to challenge them. She went on (1976, p. 26):

Its thinking tends in the direction of encouraging women to adopt the ... male dominated work ethic. Its three major demands [abortion on demand, free twenty-four-hour day care, equal pay for equal work] are directly related to freeing women from their sex-role occupations and allowing them to participate equally with men in the labour market. It is interesting to note that two of the three demands are concerned with motherhood and only one with the situation at the workplace. Day care is a crucial ingredient in a view of women's liberation that focusses on 'integrating' present economic structures. It does not simply propose that women should have equal child-rearing responsibilities with men ... but ... that women should have no greater child-rearing responsibilities than do men *in our present society* [our emphasis]. Day care, in effect, would fulfil the functions women presently fill.

Yet compared to other demands of the women's movement, the demand for day care was relatively unsuccessful. Coote and Campbell note that it failed to win 'funds from government, from charitable trusts and from individual donors' (op. cit., p. 40). In contrast, appeals for money for women's refuges were often successful: 'people (usually men) who had money at their disposal were evidently unmoved at the thought of mothers and children needing nurseries'(ibid., p. 41). The demand itself was very crude. It was defended, in the USA at least, on the grounds that 'quality child care programs are good for children' and that

Young children need peer relationships, additional adult models, enriched educational programs, particularly true because half of the intellectual development of a child is achieved by age four ... A child socialized by one whose human role is limited, essentially, to motherhood may be proportionately deprived of varied learning experiences. In a circular fashion, the development of children has been intimately influenced by the development of women (cited in Steinfels, op. cit., p. 28).

But little attention was paid to the question of emotional and living relationships between men, women and children. There were a few committed groups who set up 'women's lib' play-groups and nurseries with some male workers and self-consciously anti-sexist methods. Others looked for small-scale solutions in communal households. All this had little impact on the theory, writings and major campaigns of the women's movement. Nava, speaking with all the benefit of hindsight, is very critical of those socialist-feminists who, in the early days of the contemporary women's movement, argued for 'more nurseries, launderettes and municipal restaurants rather than the entry of men into the domestic sphere' (Nava, 1983, p. 69). She saw these proposals as 'remarkably moderate and traditionally socialist'. She states crisply: 'For ... those of us with young children the issue of domestic responsibility was of overwhelming significance; the family was not only of theoretical interest, it was the sphere in which oppression was most excruciatingly experienced. Mothering was the linchpin' (loc. cit.). Like other mothers joining the women's movement in 1970, she was most influenced by a polemical essay about alternative patterns of child rearing. She goes on to say:

> The idea that men *must* take an equal part in childcare, and that this was not only *not* a trivial demand but part of the revolutionary process, seemed daring and exhilarating. It seemed a blindingly simple solution to the apparently irreconcilable needs of mothers, for time, and young children, for the kind of loving and consistent care rarely available in nurseries ... Yet ... an equal division of labour and responsibility between men and women within the domestic sphere was not always given priority or even considered in the emerging women's liberation movement. Indeed, even among those women for whom the experience of motherhood and domesticity was totally enveloping there was no consistent acceptance of the revolutionary nature of the rearrangement of domestic life. For many, it continued to appear as an individual solution, in spite of the rhetoric of the personal as political. The assertion that family change was political implied a substantive reassessment of what, for socialists, counted as politics (op. cit., pp. 70–71).

This reassessment of what is politics for socialists and for feminists still needs to be done. Those who emphasize equal rights for women usually still accept the nature of the division of work between home and paid employment. Their strategy is to minimize unpaid work at home. The old sexual division of labour would usually persist for what remains: as in socialist countries, women would still have to do most of the irreducible work of caring. Even when the demand for collective socialization of children is added, the basic question is seen as one of relationships between adults. Children's care is not seen as of equal importance with women's oppression. Children are often seen as among women's oppressors, even by socialist-feminists:

As well as being clear-eyed about what we are doing and trying to rethink our own relationships and households, we should be aware of the social impact of what we do. Each woman who is coquettish with men and each mother who indulges her child with excessive attention and toys makes it harder for other women to resist the pressures from men and children (Barrett and McIntosh, 1983, p. 143).

As we have seen, motherhood and power have long been split apart, yet there is nothing inevitable in this. Sexual divisions of labour are constructed by people, and people can change or dismantle them. To bring motherhood and power together, women have to leave home to work and men have to go home to care. More radically, the relationship between these places and these activities has to change. It is just as important to think about what sort of care could free children from these divisions. 'Economic freedom for women' is nothing like enough to bring about the breakdown of the present sexual division of labour.

CHAPTER TWO

CHILD CARE – PUBLIC OR PRIVATE?

CHILD CARE IN PRIVATE

Feminists and socialists who set their sights on 'economic freedom for women' tend to play down the value of the home as a place for nurturing children. Their solution is to bring women and children into the public world without changing it in any other respects. Home and family life, the 'private' world, would be greatly reduced in scope and importance. This approach does not win many hearts. It sidesteps the widespread, profound attachment to the ideal of the home as the centre of children's care, with the caring woman at the heart.

> In one culture men may build shelters, make fences or terrace a hill; in another these tasks are assigned to women. But only from women does bodily life come into the world ... the special space (and the time that corresponds to it) that sets the home apart from nest and garage is engendered *only* by women, because it is they who bear living bodies ... By being turned into economic producers ... women, like men, are deprived of the environmental conditions that allow them to live by dwelling in a place and, by dwelling, to make a home. To the degree that they become more productive economically both men and women become homeless (Illich, 1983, p. 122).

So runs part of Illich's diatribe against modern industrial society expressing his nostalgia for the 'gendered' past. The image of the home as the woman's body is deep-rooted. Supposedly, home is the place where men find them-selves, can be themselves and can feel intimate with others. The home and the family are thought of as men's areas of freedom from the external controls of work and government, as their refuge from the humiliations and competition of the outside world. For women, home is *the* area designated for their creativity and self-expression, including through motherhood.

In our personal myths home is the place where we are fully accepted. It is linked with the idea of a woman, mother, who gives that all-embracing approval, with the idea of the ultimate satisfaction of our needs. For most of us 'home' means our families more than our houses. Even as adults we often talk of 'going home' when we mean visiting our parents. The contrast between the 'private' family and the 'public' outside world – employment, market, government, school – reinforces these feelings about what homes should be like. Appeals to defend 'the privacy of the family' evoke powerful memories and dreams, and are thus able to strike chords in many hearts.

Real homes and real mothers are often quite different. Most people feel some disappointment, disillusion or resentment at the failure of their mothers, homes and families to live up to the standards of myth. The family is often less than it ought to be, while work is often more.

Work relationships, friendships and care for children outside the home by non-family members can all fulfil some of our needs for warmth. Nor is the family as 'private' and exclusive as it seems. Child care within the family is actually simultaneously public and private. To understand this we have to unpick the cherished notion of the 'privacy of the family', and with it the whole fabric of illusion that veils the place of the 'home' in the organization of social and economic life.

Successive governments declare their commitment to the principle of the 'privacy of the family'. This means above all that parents are responsible for their children's care and upbringing, and that it is *they* who should make the decisions about their children's lives. But governments vary in their interpretation of this principle. Roughly speaking, Labour governments in Britain and Democratic administrations in the USA believe that the state should ensure that parents have the knowledge and resources to exercise their responsibilities properly and protect children from the excesses of their adult carers. Most Tories and Republicans would argue that policy measures aimed at supporting parents can turn the state into a nanny, by pandering to infantile parents who ought to be made to take their adult responsibilities seriously. For the right wing, 'family privacy' signifies freedom from state control. Like private schools and private enterprise, parents should be able to make their own decisions about children, subject only to public law (Mount, 1983, esp. Ch. 10).

Mrs Thatcher uses 'family privacy' in this way. According to her bizarre logic, a cut in public spending is an increase in 'family privacy'. If no school meals have to be provided by local authorities (so that children have to rely on their mothers for the midday meal), mothers are 'free' to provide packed lunches, steak and chips or 'three bites of the cupboard door'. If no 'public' nursery is available, mothers are 'free' to pay for a private one (if they can find any), to employ a child minder or to stay at home. All these decisions are presented as private choices, and the freedom to make them is part of what conservative politicians mean by 'the privacy of the family'. In this political language, deciding *how* to care for one's children is a parental right as well as a parental responsibility. But in fact even under conservative regimes, parental decision-making about their children's upbringing is rigidly circumscribed. It is not really free from state control, although parents themselves may be unaware of this and feel as if their decisions are entirely their own.

Parents do have to look after their children's material welfare, under either political regime. In the left-wing version of 'family privacy', attempts are made to equalize family circumstances and to give poorer families more assets as consumers. The right-wing version sees inequality as vital to 'family privacy', and family-households as consumers are 'free' to decide what to buy and what not to buy – private education, smoked salmon or spam. The housewife personifies this notion of the family as consumer. To hear some politicians talk, you would think her 'freedom' to shop around, to boycott, to go for the quality product highly enviable. It looks less enviable for poorer housewives when you think in terms of their 'freedom' not to buy their children wool and cotton socks and leather shoes, but to buy cheaper nylon socks and synthetic or canvas shoes which are likely to damage their developing feet.

The housewife and mother is the stereotypical private person in the misleading public/private dichotomy that tends to shape modern thinking and writing about children, the family, and work. She is even more private than her children: after all, the housewife and mother doesn't have to go to school! But in fact, even as a consumer, however much her choices are limited by the amount of money at her disposal, her actions do have a direct effect on the 'public world' of production as she expresses her preference in the (super)market.

Her labour is an integral part of the whole economy, and to that extent as 'public' as the factory work making the cornflakes that she buys. But her working conditions as an individual doing an unpaid service for her loved ones really are 'private', in the sense that they do not bring her together in one place with others in the same position, nor promote the co-operation that would make it clear that mothers have interests in common. There is a real difference between domestic unpaid work and paid employment; but the phrases which represent this difference (like the 'privacy of the family') actually obscure the similarity between these types of labour and the extent to which housework and child care are vital parts of the whole economy.

Single women and men obviously have 'private lives' too. But the 'privacy of the family' has a special status in political rhetoric. At its most general, the term 'family' refers to people linked by kinship and marriage. Some of these links – such as marriage, parenthood and the 'next-of-kin' relationship – are built into the system of law (for example, inheritance law, and social security), as well as the customs of everyday life. Behind all these lurks the model of the normal family-household consisting of two parents linked by marriage, living in one home with the dependent offspring of their partnership. The man is assumed to be the main economic provider, the woman the main emotional provider and homemaker. No law forces people to live in such family-households. But like the political levy to the Labour Party, it is opting out which requires an active decision. Just as atheists in the Army are assumed to belong to the Established Church, so are heterosexual couples who cohabit assumed to be 'as man and wife'. The idea of the nuclear family is built into the houses which are our homes, as well as into the building societies and local authorities which provide the wherewithal. To be other than the 'normal nuclear family' is even more of an effort than conformity.

Present left-wing and right-wing policies for family life and parental responsibility do not differ very much. They *do* differ in their effects on families' day-to-day lives in terms of how much state provision is available and how tightly the state controls parenting. But both sorts of policy have a common basis: it is mothers who are given prime responsibility for children's day-to-day care. And under both left- and right-wing rule, in practice, mothers usually find themselves in the same economically dependent position as their children (see David, 1985a and b).

FAMILY WAGE AND SOCIAL WAGE

In all societies, some members are physically or mentally incapable of making much contribution to the economy. In addition capitalist societies depend on contributions to the economy which are disguised as purely private services. Somehow or other these non-employed members of society (the 'economically inactive') have to live. There are two ways in which resources can be distributed to these people within a capitalist economic system. One way is through the family, on the presumption that workers are paid enough to support a wife and children, ailing parents, and other dependent family members as well as themselves – a 'family wage'. (Of course, the *idea* of the 'family wage' is one thing, the actuality is quite another.)

The other way is through the *social* wage: that part of the state's public expenditure (on health, housing, education, roads and libraries) which contributes to the standard of living of the workforce, or supports groups of people (such as the very poor and disabled) who would otherwise perish. The social wage could be a bare minimum. For example, the cash element, such as family allowances, need not be provided. Roads could be toll-roads. Schools could be entirely private. 'Workers would then have to provide for their own immediate needs and those of their dependants (including their education), as well as insuring against the needs and dependencies of sickness, accidents, old age, unemployment and so on – all from their paychecks' (Adams, 1981, p. 232). Some contemporary politicians, such as Mrs Thatcher, have just such a vision. They would have to undo the work of a century, during which: '... the State has ... increasingly socialised the wage system, in the sense of taking over from the individual capitals part of the task of providing for the production and reproduction of labour power. Put differently, the worker's standard of living depends not only upon what he or she takes home in his or her paycheck but also upon the goods and services provided by the State' (ibid.).

Since the nineteenth century there have been increases in the size and scope of the social wage. In Britain, under both left- and right-wing governments, the state has provided such services as health care, maternity provision, birth control, housing, compulsory education and social work support. In the way these services are administered and financed there is a consistent assumption that women with young children will stay at home looking after them, and in general that women are responsible for the home and for family life. The state also provides cash benefits, such as old-age and retirement pensions, unemployment and sickness benefits, maternity allowances and child benefits. These too are built on assumptions about the role of women and the normality of private child care. Of course, the very existence of maternity and child provision implies *some* recognized public responsibility for children.

It took years of campaigning by radicals and reformers to get maternity services and benefits and the family allowance, now known as child bene-

fits. Campaigners such as Margaret Llewellyn Davies and Eleanor Rathbone
had to fight the idea that these sorts of provision infringed 'family privacy'.
Eleanor Rathbone described her political opponents as fearing:

> that the beauty of the tie between husband and wife, father and child will
> be impaired, and its strength weakened, if there is anything less than
> complete financial dependence . . . [and] . . . the father's motive to industry
> will be undermined if he no longer feels that he stands between his
> children and starvation (quoted by Land, 1976, p. 114).

The principle underlying the social wage that was finally given expression in public policy did recognize the public importance of children and of
their care. The Liberal MP Herbert Samuel said in 1915 that without action
to protect mothers 'The nation is weakened. Numbers are of importance.
In the competition and conflict of civilisations, it is the mass of the nation
that tells' (quoted in Davies, 1978). Seventy years ago, he gave voice to the
present-day official view of the relationship between the family and the
state.

> The conclusion is clear that it is the duty of the community, so far as it
> can, to relieve motherhood of its burdens, to spread the knowledge of
> mothercraft that is so often lacking, to make medical aid available when
> it is needed, to watch over the health of the infant. And since this is the
> duty of the community, it is also the duty of the State. *The infant cannot,*
> *indeed, be saved by the State. It can only be saved by the mother. But the mother*
> *can be helped and can be taught by the State* [our emphasis] (ibid.).

Whether in cash or in kind, maternity provision confirms the privacy of
the family – the context of child care. This is also true of family allowances.

> On balance . . . the family allowance scheme introduced in 1945 only
> incidentally recognised the needs of mothers and children and then only
> to a limited extent. By excluding the first child and failing to make the
> value of allowance equal to the subsistence cost of a child, the State was
> only taking a small share in the cost of maintaining its future citizens and
> workers (Land, 1976, p. 115).

Despite subsequent modifications, it is still true that the child benefit has
only a slight influence on the inequalities between families, and does not
in the least challenge the responsibility of families for child care.

The 'social wage' is potentially a great leveller. If benefits were linked to
the cost of living, it could offer a guarantee of a minimum standard of living

which can never be equalled by the so-called 'family wage', tossed about
on the sea of market forces and subject to the fluctuations of the balance
of bargaining power and the fortunes of industrial struggles. Yet in all its
present forms – both cash and services – the social wage rests on the
traditional family division of labour. In two -parent households the assumption is that the man's 'family wage' is still the family's main income. Where
there is no man, the mother with dependent children is presumed to remain
economically dependent herself, so that the state replaces the man. Most
recent right-wing criticisms of the welfare state want to make it harder for
women to leave their husbands by abolishing this option. 'The compas-
sionate State has cuckolded the man,' says George Gilder (1982), ideologue
of the American New Right (see David, 1985b).

The social wage is double-edged. It blunts economic hardship and allows
some children access to better lives than their parents had. In so doing, it
justifies and makes tolerable the system which cannot but produce
inequality. Schools, for example, give their pupils all sorts of information,
skills and knowledge; but at the same time they have a 'hidden curriculum'.
They try to ensure conformity to conventional standards and practices; and
the information they pass on to their students is phrased in the very
language of the social and sexual status quo. The same thing goes for social
services.

> Real benefits may be provided which constitute an enhancement of the
> recipient's standard of living, while reduced provision may constitute a
> cut in real living standards. While teachers and social workers provide
> these benefits, however, they may at the same time act as policing agents
> through the exercise of more or less open coercion or as ideological agents
> for the transmission of dominant norms and values (Adams, op. cit., p.
> 234).

One of these dominant norms and values is obviously that women are,
first and foremost, carers. It is no accident that many teachers and social
workers themselves are women (see David, 1985a).

FAMILY BACKGROUNDS AND FAMILY FATES

A declared aim of the welfare state is to create equality of opportunity for
all – without interfering in family privacy or undermining the bonds
between husbands and wives, parents and children. Both left-wing and
right-wing governments have voiced these two contradictory views. In their

policy measures, right-wing governments tend to favour family privacy for children – individual freedom, parental choice, parental rights and parental responsibility for children's behaviour. Left-wing governments are more inclined to an egalitarian-policy approach which tries to soften the impact of unequal family backgrounds – early childhood and comprehensive education, parental involvement and participation. Each type of government holds to both family privacy and equality of opportunity. Yet how can equality of opportunity be reconciled with the protection of family privacy, which in turn protects inequality between families? Children are born into families which may be well-off or struggling on the breadline. The accidents of their birth are preserved by all policies which respect the 'privacy of the family' – since this always includes its right to be rich or poor, that most basic liberty of a free-enterprise society.

The families we find ourselves in at birth can nurture us well or badly. What they have to give is very much a matter of what their members have been given. For example, infant mortality has declined in Britain since the 1930s, but this decline has been greatest in the middle classes.

> The inescapable conclusion is that occupational class differences are *real* sources of difference in the risk of infant mortality.
>
> Equally importantly, there are similar differences in the class incidence of low birth-weight which ... can have ... long-term implications for the health and development of the young child (Townsend and Davidson, 1982, p. 123).

International studies show that these patterns are similar in all countries (WHO, 1978, p. 200). A little-known factor in the causation of low birth-weight and congenital malformation 'originates in the nutritional deprivation of the mother not at the time of giving birth but *at the time of her own birth* (ibid., p. 124).

Illness and accidents are strongly linked to social circumstances, and health is in turn strongly linked to achievement. The authors of the Black Report into *Inequalities in Health* predict that

> ... any factors which increase the parental capacity to provide adequate care for an infant will, when present, increase the chance of survival, while their absence will increase the risk of premature death. The most obvious of such factors fall within the sphere of material resources: sufficient household income, a safe uncrowded and unpolluted home, warmth and hygiene, a means of rapid communication with the outside

world, for example, a telephone or car, and an adequate level of man-power – or womanpower ... (ibid.).

One-parent families are more likely to be poor, especially since eight out of every nine are headed by a woman.

Over half of lone mothers are dependent on supplementary benefit because the combination of lack of suitable childcare facilities and their low earning capacity makes taking paid work, even if they can find it, an option which leaves them financially little better off than relying on state benefits. In other words, lone mothers and their children are likely to be poor with all the disadvantages which that brings (Land, 1983, p. 23).

In Britain, at any one time about 9 per cent of all children under sixteen are living with a lone mother – that is over a million and a quarter children (CSO, 1980, p. 34). Most of these mothers are separated or divorced, and only a small proportion can rely on financial maintenance from their ex-partners. 'What evidence there is does suggest strongly that maintenance payments are uncertain and inadequate; in fact they are the main source of income for only just over 6% of all lone parents' (Popay, Rimmer and Rossiter, 1983, p. 43).

The 'feminization of poverty' is the dramatic phrase which has been used in the USA to describe the economic effects of the shift away from the 'traditional patriarchal nuclear family' (Eisenstein, 1982). In 1980, in the USA, there were over 9 million one-parent families, 8.5 million of which were female-headed households. Of these, almost 70 per cent contained a child under the age of eighteen. *Almost half* of black households and 14 per cent of white families were female-headed households. Eisenstein has written that '... female headed families with no husband present comprise only 15% of all families, but 48% of all poverty level families ... The median income in 1978 of families maintained by a woman was $8,540 or slightly less than one half (48%) of the $17,640 median income of families overall' (op. cit., p. 585).

These figures show the bare circumstances in which millions of children lead their daily lives. The figures are a snapshot and understate the extent to which children move in and out of one-parent families. It is certainly no longer an uncommon experience for children to spend at least part of their childhood in a one-parent family which is poor, including children who have previously enjoyed a middle-class lifestyle. Meanwhile all the old causes of poverty still operate: low pay, disability and ill-health, large families and, increasingly, unemployment.

The commitment to 'family privacy' implies that the responsibility for children's well-being rests only with their parents. It was their parents' choice, the argument would run, to stay together or to separate, to work hard and achieve or to fail, and so on. By the logic of a 'free enterprise' system, the sins of the parents *must* be visited on the children, since they live with them and share their good or ill fortune. Punitive treatment cannot be abolished, because the fear of it motivates people to work hard and to stay together in families. The social wage plays an ambiguous role. In 'left'-wing regimes it softens the punishment and reduces its impact on children, without actually changing the underlying logic. Under right-wing governments the social wage is reduced to a 'safety net' which is used to ensure that those who receive punitive treatment are not actually destroyed by it. At the same time the actual administration of the benefits and services tends to become more punitive – as in the recent police action in Oxford to catch social security 'scroungers'. A grim form of this paradox was spelled out by Polly Toynbee writing (1984, p. 10) about the squalid 'bed and breakfast' accommodation local authorities provide for homeless people.

The bed and breakfast hotel is the modern equivalent of the old workhouse. It serves the same purpose and is punitive in intent. It tests the genuine desperation of families awaiting rehousing. While they hang on, squeezed in with their parents, or friends, or cramped in tiny bedsits, they have no chance of getting a flat, with waiting lists growing and available housing shrinking. Making life hell for these homeless people is supposed to act as a deterrent against others throwing themselves on the mercy of the local authorities. Like the workhouses of old, these hotels keep the poor from freezing in the streets, but they keep them so miserably that only the utterly destitute would avail themselves of this form of state aid.

There are many ways in which the state acts to cushion the full force of poverty in the lives of children – family income supplement, free school meals, milk, clothing allowances, free dental treatment and medicines. Its main effort at modifying the effect of family circumstances on children's lives has been through schooling. In 1965 President Johnson introduced what must surely have been the most publicized American domestic policy – the 'war on poverty'. He claimed that 'The answer for all our national problems is a single word. That word is "education"' (quoted in Peckman, 1980, p. 208). Research throughout the 1950s had shown that, despite massive increases in the number and types of schools available and the amount of time children could spend in formal education, families remained the most powerful influence on how well children did at school. Accordingly, in the 1960s, in both Britain and the USA, policy-makers committed themselves to trying to reduce the link between educational attainment and family background. They saw low achievement as resulting from poverty. And since policy makers and their advisers blamed poor families for their own poverty, they also blamed them for their children's educational failure. Poverty was seen as a failure to cope, arising from a faulty culture which failed to value 'education, achievement, orderly family lives, sexual regularity, and to rear their children in such a way as to impel them to do likewise' (Ryan, 1976, p. 119). Ryan quotes Oscar Lewis as an example of this attitude to the poor:

> once the culture of poverty has come into existence it tends to perpetuate itself. By the time slum children are six or seven they have usually absorbed the basic attitudes and values of their subculture. Thereafter they are psychologically unready to take full advantage of changing conditions or improving opportunities that may develop in their lifetime (ibid., p. 120).

Poor children will remain poor because they have

> Fatalistic, apathetic attitudes,
> Magical, rigid thinking
> Pragmatic, concrete values
> Poor impulse control ... (ibid., p. 122)

and so on. As Ryan mockingly says:

> ... if poverty is to be understood more clearly in terms of the 'way of life' of the poor ... then money is clearly not the answer. We can stop right now worrying about ways of redistributing our resources more equitably, and begin focusing our concern where it belongs – on the poor themselves. We can start trying to figure out how to change that troublesome culture of theirs, how to apply some tautening astringent to their flabby consciences, how to deal with their poor manners and make them more socially acceptable. By this hard and wearying method of liquidating lower-class culture, we can liquidate the lower class and, thereby, bring an end to poverty (ibid., p. 123).

To 'get poverty out of the people', the American Democratic administration launched its Great Society Legislation, chiefly a series of educational strategies, such as Head Start, Follow-Through and Parent–Child Centres.

These programmes were devised to provide early childhood education in poor areas, to undo the effects of family culture, or to train poor mothers in middle-class values of child rearing. Britain followed suit with its educational priority areas (EPAs), urban aid for nurseries in inner-city areas and an abortive policy of nursery education initiated by that inimitable friend of the family, Margaret Thatcher. Neither the British nor the American government ever provided enough investment for these programmes to test the theory that early intervention in children's lives could break the 'cycle of deprivation'. Radical critics of these policies always described them as a sort of elastoplast (or bandaid). But the plaster never covered the sore. Research showed that the effects on the children of their extra education faded rapidly, and in the economic crisis of the 1970s the idea of equalizing opportunities seemed a pathetic joke (David, 1983b).

Since the mid-1970s, the New Right has come to power in both Britain and the USA. It has made short shrift of the prevailing political consensus about the aims of the welfare state. It avoids the trap that previous governments fell into, of trying to achieve 'equality of opportunity' without altering the relationship between the family and the 'public' worlds of paid work and government. 'Equality of opportunity' is not the New Right's goal.

> The New Right thinks that the welfare state is responsible for undermining the traditional patriarchal family by taking over different family functions. The health, welfare and education of individuals, it believes, should be the purview of the family. The New Right's critique of the welfare state in this way becomes closely linked to its understanding of the crisis of the family ... From the perspective of the New Right, the 'problem' of the family – defined as the married heterosexual couple with children, the husband working in the labour force, and the wife remaining at home to rear the children – stems from husbands' loss of patriarchal authority as their wives have been pulled into the labour force ... [the New Right] desires to establish the model of the traditional white patriarchal family by dismantling the welfare state and by removing wage-earning married women from the labour force and returning them to the home (Eisenstein, 1982, p. 568).

The American New Right's attitude to welfare is that 'welfare is wreaking devastation on the American poor – making the child fatherless, the wife husbandless, the husband useless' (Irving Kristol, cited in Ashford, 1981, p. 357).

The New Right's family policies are dedicated to the reversal of modern demographic trends away from the male-headed nuclear family. The Family Protection Act, 'a tidy wish list for the New Right', was debated in two long sessions of Congress in the USA. If passed, it would have reinstated paternal authority over children and male authority over woman. Parents were to be allowed to 'preview' school textbooks, to ensure that they upheld a traditional view of sex roles. Men were to be given 'tax breaks' for dependent wives and relatives. It has not been passed in full, although some titles have become law, but it gives us a clear and comprehensive view of the aims of the New Right. In Britain, too, steps have already been taken to force some women or to entice other women to remain within their marriages and homes. There have been changes in the claims that wives can make for maintenance from their ex-husbands; and women on supplementary benefits may be forced to be dependent on their children, or indirectly on the father of their children, even when the marriage is over (Land, 1984).

The New Right has another and complementary aim. To rebuild the 'privacy of the family' in all its glory, it aims to cut the system of state services for families and to give the voluntary sector paltry resources to take over the work of supporting families. Middle-class mothers of school-age or older children are being recruited, by voluntary agencies, to teach the skills of full-time, exclusive motherhood to poor and working-class mothers on a voluntary basis. These schemes have received official financial support and approval. Cutbacks in public expenditure have reduced both women's jobs and public services to families (see David 1985a).

The left-wing way of supporting families and levelling the differences between them always relied on private child care as the mother's prime responsibility. But the new right-wing view positively glorifies the role of mothers as the state's representatives in child care. It is clear that under all sorts of governments the 'private' form of child care is useful partly because it is deceptive. It makes parents seem solely responsible for their own ignorance, their own poverty and the entire inheritance they pass on to their children. It divides parents from one another, since each family is 'private' and must be judged on its own merits. These effects are most powerful on mothers.

HOUSEWIVES AND FAMILY LIVES

All family policy to date, whatever its political credo, has relied on women working and caring, without pay, in the privacy of their homes. What they have to do there, and how hard they have to work, depends partly on the size and composition of their families. It also depends on the amount of the 'family wage', if there is one, and, even more, on the amount of that money which they can actually control, and finally on the social wage – the services and cash which the state provides.

Unlike most waged work, the housewife's unpaid work in the home is elastic: it can quietly expand or contract. This applies both to household chores and to caring. If there is no public or private help with child care available, obviously mothers have to do it all themselves. If the family wage is very low and the housewife is not able to go out to work herself, or cannot find a job, then she either has to put more time into shopping around for cheap commodities, or spend most of the housekeeping on food. This flexibility means that some families of the same size have more unpaid work to do than others and also that the same family has more to do at one time than at another. Periods of recession mean cuts in the social wage so that mentally handicapped people, old people and children depend more for their care on private support. Then women's unpaid work in the home increases. But there is usually no political outcry such as would accompany any attempt to increase productivity in paid employment without consultation with the workers and without an increase in pay.

'Women's work is never done.' We all know that this refers to housework, the endless round of washing floors, dishes, clothes; of cooking and serving; of cleaning and mending, only to have the fruits of your labour spoiled or consumed within minutes. Despite the public invisibility of housework, the chores it entails are grudgingly recognized as a sort of work. Child care is not, and for a clear reason. If you care about someone, caring for them (in the sense of meeting their needs) is supposed to spring from that emotional commitment so readily and spontaneously that it cannot possibly be a form of work requiring recognition. Mothering is a way of life. Mothers themselves believe or half-believe that their work need not even be recognized, let alone rewarded, since it is 'done for love'. This belief is a central prop of the system of private child care. It can make them feel that they have no rights as mothers, not even rights to a better life for their children, for they ought to provide that all by themselves.

Women's continual responsibility for caring affects the way they behave and the way they are treated as workers. In times of economic boom it may be easier for them to get paid work and to afford to pay someone else to do some of the chores and caring if they can find anyone willing. But, in times of both recession and boom the sort of work that women take up is always determined by the basic family responsibilities which women are forced to put first, because nobody else will take them on. To meet these, large numbers of women work in the so-called 'black economy', with no legal protection, often completely unrecognized by the statistics, simply because their employer is 'understanding' about the family (Freeman, 1982, p. 135). Large numbers of women who cannot find any other way to reconcile the conflict between their need to earn money and their need to look after the children do both together. They either work at home for very low wages, or take their children with them to work, such as in offices or shops, or as cleaners. There are always far more unemployed women than the official statistics recognize. It is obviously politically useful that women's place in the family should veil the reality of their position as unemployed workers.

In the days before the modern women's liberation movement, you used to hear the view that, since the state had taken over the functions of the old-fashioned family and technology had revolutionized housework, there was almost nothing left for women at home to do. Of course this is nonsense. Women's work within the home remains a massive job, but the typical balance between chores and caring has altered.

> Time budgets show that the total time women spend on their domestic tasks has declined very little in the last half-century ... What has changed is the way in which their time is distributed between the various tasks: the proportion of time spent on childcare has increased and the time spent on cooking and cleaning has decreased. Standards change over time and broadly speaking change upwards (Land, 1981, pp. 16–17).

Schools depend upon women's unpaid work. They expect new children to be able to count and to know their letters. Those children who have not already been taught a lot by their mothers need special attention to compensate. The Health Service similarly depends on women's work within the family, most importantly for prevention.

> Health attitudes are embedded in domestic activities, and these activities – shopping, cooking, washing, watching, waiting – are moulded by the practical constraints of time, space and money ... Describing what health provision and health maintenance involves is difficult, not only because it lacks clear boundaries ... Maintaining health is most in evidence when it is not done: when clothes and faces are left unwashed, rooms and hair are untidy, and children are ill-disciplined and noisy. When the mother works successfully to maintain the standards of dress, decor and decorum her labour is at its most invisible (Graham, 1984, p. 154).

Taking the children with you on the weekly shop, to the library or getting the children to and from school, and out-of-school activities such as Cubs and Brownies, or just playing with their friends, is most certainly work, needing self-discipline and planning. It is important work, but is never recognized as such.

Marilyn French, in *The Women's Room*, aptly depicts the life of a suburban housewife:

> Ordering everyone to behave, she went into the cutrate soda place and bought a case of the cheapest canned soda. Then she drove to Elizabeth's and honked. Tom ran out and got into the car. Next she drove to Mrs Amory's where the Cub Scout meeting was being held this week. Tom helped Eric carry the case of soda. She drove to DiNapolis' and dropped Billy off, telling him to call her when he wanted to be picked up. She drove to the tailor at the other side of town, the only one Paul felt did decent work, and picked up his gray suit, ordering the children not to touch it as she hung it on a hook over the rear seat of the car. She stopped at Milkmart for a gallon of milk. By now the bottle had cooled and Mindy was peacefully sucking it. Then Adele drove home. The baby had worked herself out with screaming, and the warm milk had sent her back to sleep. She was heavy as Adele lifted her out of the car seat, her bag dangling on her arm. Linda tried to help, and picked up the milk to carry it indoors, but it was too heavy for her and she dropped it halfway up the driveway. Adele heard the crash, turned and looked. Linda's face was white and terror-stricken as she looked up at her mother. (Oh, my God, my God!) Adele turned around, walked back, put the baby back in the car seat. Linda just stopped there. Adele brought her voice into control. 'Get back in the car, Linda.' She drove to Milkmart and picked up another gallon of milk.
>
> 'Take my purse, Linda,' Adele said as they pulled again into the driveway. She lugged the now deeply sleeping baby out of the car seat again, and Linda followed her up the driveway. 'Stay away from the broken glass,' Adele ordered sharply. Linda hopped dangerously among the pieces. Adele carried the baby into the living room and laid her in the playpen. She sighed. Mindy would be awake until late tonight: three naps in one day ... (1978, p. 121).

Adele's situation is the classic one of the housewife dependent upon her husband. Not all women have a husband whose suit they have to fetch from the dry-cleaner's. Many women live with husbands who are unemployed, so that there is less fetching and carrying related to his job, but more emotional support required and less money. Most husbands who are unemployed do not take up the slack by doing more of the chores and caring. For many of them that would seem like a further emasculation. Many women do not live with a man. In some ways the lives of lone mothers are simplified, but they usually have little money and have to bear the daily responsibility entirely on their own. Women in two-parent families and lone mothers often fit paid jobs around their family responsibilities. A night cleaner, interviewed about her work, was asked when she slept:

> There's no regular time. We snatch it when we can. Sometimes I get four hours, sometimes less. Four hours is a good sleep, for me. Usually I get home by seven in the morning, get them all out of the house [she has three teenage children and a husband], do me housework and then sleep at about 11 a.m. But I'm always up at three in the afternoon, to make the dinner ... Some sleep in the evening before they go out, but I've got teenage children I want to talk to. They don't see me all day. We like to talk, I have to keep awake, or it's not fair to them (Union Place Collective, 1976, p. 12).

Women who go out to work do not slough off their unpaid work as they slam the front door. The breakfast dishes, the unmade beds, are usually waiting for them at the end of the 'working' day. They clock up an enormous number of working hours when you add together the unpaid and the paid work done. Time budget studies imply that, to get all their work done, women *must* sleep less than men.

Somehow or other, more or less well, the unpaid work which is felt necessary gets done. In the doing of it some women work much harder than others. In damp housing conditions where the bedding has to be aired before it can be slept in, in cramped rooms and flats where mothers have to take young children out whatever the weather to give them any space, in ill-equipped kitchens where cooking is dangerous so that mothers have one eye on the stove and one on the toddlers, women's unpaid work seems endless ...

Inequality between women at home in terms of the amount of work they do often reduces the inequality families *experience*. You often hear people say of their mothers, 'She worked her fingers to the bone so that we'd never go short.' On the other hand, better-off women find that the amount of work they feel they ought to do expands to fill the time available. Mothers have a duty to protect their children from poverty, and a similar duty to ensure that their children get every ounce of the benefits of affluence. There is always another thing to do for children – music lessons, giving them good holidays, decorating their rooms. Affection and attention are not distributed along class lines like these more tangible assets, yet it is these material things which are most readily seen as proofs of love.

MOTHER, BETWIXT AND BETWEEN

Herbert Samuel had expressed the offical view that only the mother can save the infant. The state's job is to help her to do it, to teach her what is expected, to encourage her to meet certain standards, and to take action to protect the child if she consistently fails to meet them. 'Private' child care takes place under 'public' supervision. The standards that mothers daily set themselves are not plucked from thin air. How white should the nappies be, how advanced the child? The power of experts as standard-setters and advice-givers has increased as the links between generations have loosened. In some more settled communities mothers still prefer to ask their own mothers or mother-in-laws ...

> One nurse'd say one thing and another nurse'd say another. It didn't worry me because the only advice I took was from my own mother. She had eleven in poor times back in Ireland and they were all lovely ... I got scared when he used to throw up his feed. And my mum said this teat is far too fast for the child ... She said the slower he takes his food, the better he digests it (mother quoted in Oakley, 1979, p. 148).

These days, women are far more likely to ask friends. The other main source of information are the 'experts' in the clinics and the ones who write in women's magazines or give their advice on the radio or television. A lot of useful and even life-saving information is available in this way. But its dissemination is haphazard, still subject to the overriding principle that the mother is in charge – until she is officially found wanting. She can listen or refuse to listen, obey the advice or ignore it.

The advice itself is variously financed. The state and industry get together to tell mothers what they need to know, often with incongruous results. In one of our hospital parentcraft classes, the man from Milton came into tell us how to sterilize the bottles, how to work the nappy bucket, and which product to use to do so. There was no discussion of whether these methods were necessary, of whether they might actually encourage nappy rash as often as they prevent it. In our local health centre, advertising posters are displayed side by side with Health Education Council posters. One tells us that to ensure that your baby doesn't get nappy rash, you should change its nappy *whenever* it is wet. They also tell you that when you do so, you should use their proprietary baby cream. The health visitors, doctors and nurses there are giving these notions publicity. In the same health centre, free samples of various baby foods are regularly provided, and the educational booklets which are given out by the health visitors are not only those produced by the Health Education Council, but also those from companies such as Robinson, Heinz or Milupa baby foods. These manufacturers invariably suggest that children should go on eating their bland and expensive food up to school age. The message is that warm water and soap are not adequate to clean babies' bottoms, minced-up or puréed ordinary foods are not as good as expensive baby foods; and child care experts co-operate with this. Many will recommend tooth-rotting fruit syrups 'for the vitamin C' as readily as they advise you to stay at home with your child until he or she reaches school age. For inexperienced mothers, it can take some time to discover that many babies with tough bottoms are happy with only three or four daily nappy changes, and that to give them water is no deprivation. Entrepreneurs can easily cash in on mother love, mother care and the need for early learning.

When a woman has a baby, she is given pamphlets from the British Medical Association, Cow & Gate, Robinsons and so on, which contain some useful information, some quite useless assurances about difficulties being only temporary, and advice not to neglect her man. She also gets a few free nappy liners or a packet of instant rice. In an odd compromise worked out between the experts of state and industry, she is told that breast feeding is the baby's birthright, and definitely best, but that proprietary milk is *just as good* and she need not feel in the slightest bit guilty if she cannot breastfeed or prefers not to. The health visitor comes to see her several times in the first month or so, and gives her an appointment for the 'six-week check-up'. After that, she is more or less on her own, although the health visitor will probably visit again from time to time. The clinic is there, the doctors are there, the magazines are there, and the goods are on sale.

And as the baby grows, new goods are on sale. Mothers with access to a video recorder can now buy video tapes to help them teach their pre-school youngsters. These can be bought at a bargain price – equivalent to the weekly living allowance of a single person dependent on state benefits.

If the woman is working full-time, and the baby is with a child minder or at a nursery and never gets taken to the clinic, the system of checks on

private child care may break down. It is organized on the assumption that
someone will be available during the hours of the working day to see the
health visitor, to take sick children to the doctor, to take babies to the clinic
and to take all children to the dentist for twice-yearly check-ups. Very
occasionally this someone is not the mother, but the expectation is that she
will do it. Laura Balbo claims (1981, p. 9) that women are expected to act
as family representatives to helpful state agencies, as part of their task of
representing the family as a consumer:

> Because many goods and services are produced outside the family, by
> other institutions (firms, schools, hospitals and so on), and because access
> to them requires time and flexibility on the part of 'clients', someone has
> to do the work of dealing with these agencies, adapting to their often
> complex, time-consuming, rigid, indeed bureaucratic procedures. It is
> women who keep in touch with teachers, school staff, who take children
> to clinics and hospitals, who visit welfare agencies to obtain what the
> family is entitled to.

The tasks that were once done entirely in families and are now paid for
out of the social wage (such as education and health care) still crucially
depend on families to back them up. Schools rely on mothers to maintain
them in their present form. Yet another advert in our local health centre
tells mothers to be at home when their children come home from school:
'Let her tell you about her day and tell her about yours.' Schools expect
mothers to be available at both ends of the school day, to fetch and carry
children to and from school. When children are unwell, they are often asked
if their mothers are at home or out shopping. Of course it is recognized that
some mothers do work outside the home; but it is always the mother's
whereabouts, not the father's, that are first inquired about and her work,
rather than his, which is interrupted (David, 1985a).

The professionals who help children and their carers – in schools, in the
health service and the social services – are working within services
administered on the presumption that there is a mother at home. Many of
them also use that model in their daily work, in the advice they give. For
example, at one clinic a heavily pregnant mother of a two-year-old asked
the health visitor if she knew of any play-group that would take two-year-
olds, because she needed a break and thought her little one would enjoy
playing with other toddlers. The expert told her that under-threes could not
yet enjoy group situations, because they could only play side by side and
not together, and that the best place for such a young child was with its

mother at home. The woman looked depressed as she collected her para-phernalia and her little one and went home.

Women deal with helpful state agencies on behalf of their families. These agencies are not only helpful; it is also part of their work to judge. For example, a friend of ours who gave birth to her second child at home was visited daily by her midwife. On the fifth day the midwife asked her why it was that she was not yet dressed, whether she had been out of the house yet. Our friend was wearing an attractive housecoat and, as far as she was concerned, she was dressed. The midwife was following a rule-of-thumb that a woman who is not geared for work and out by Day Five may have post-natal depression and need special help. Similarly, health visitors have developed a set of rules to help them judge how well mothers, especially new mothers, are coping with looking after their babies. But with the best will in the world, these rules are inadequate. They are crude, emphasizing mothers' behaviour rather than their feelings. Many cases of post-natal depression slip through this net. The health visitor represents something of a threat as well as a promise of help, so many mothers will not confide in her. To ask for help and to accept it implies a failure to cope. Mothers are *supposed* to cope, so few are going to rush to wear that label.

Health visitors and doctors are on the look-out for families which abuse or neglect their children. This work – which involves making judgements – is indispensable. Children must be protected. The problem is that child abuse and neglect spring from too heavy a reliance on private family child care. It is perfectly normal and ordinary to need more help and support in parenting than the present system can give. Unfortunately, although doctors and health visitors mean well, the only help that they can offer is conditional. Because the official rules suggest that mothers who need help are not normal, there is a threat of punishment hanging over those who have to appeal to agencies outside the family to help them cope with their children. They have no control over the sort of help that is offered. They may be forced to accept psychological advice when they know that what they need is adequate housing and more money for food and clothing. They find themselves entering relationships with official agencies that they cannot decide to end. The supposed 'privacy of the family' suddenly vanishes, and official standards of competence are applied which the client may neither know nor agree with.

A friend of ours recently took her daughter to the children's hospital three times in one week. The first time, some children had dropped a log of wood on Lucy's head from on top of a slide, and she was slightly concussed. The second time she sucked a bead up her nose, and it had to be removed in the Casualty Department. The third time she picked up a light bulb which had just fallen out of its socket. Her hand was badly burned. Such a set of coincidences make it extremely likely that the child would be put on the At Risk register, if the parents were black or poor. In most cases nothing more happens. Even so, to be listed like this has frightening connotations.

One study of child abuse showed that mothers were sometimes reluctant to let their battered children go to a day nursery, despite the difficulties in the relationship. These mothers were 'torn between the internal directive to be a good mother and to cope alone at all cost, and the desire to escape from full-time responsibility for their children' (NSPCC Battered Child Research Team, 1976, p. 23). The directive to be a 'good mother', and to *look* as if one is coping alone, is not just internal. Day nurseries are stigmatizing. Some mothers who are able to recognize their need for help have to exaggerate their difficulties to get any support at all.

In most areas pressure on local-authority day-nursery places is now so great that being on the At Risk register is a *condition* of getting a place for your child. Some social workers actually suggest to mothers that they should admit that they really cannot cope. Many routine assessments of mothers never result in any changes in family life and remain unread in some agency's files. But if things go wrong, a 'previous record' may be used against us. The 'privacy of the family' is conditional upon our good behaviour.

Those who both help and judge families are not always professionals. There have been attempts to develop a new species of social worker: the pre-school home visitor. The words suggest that the person will be a guest in the family. Pre-school home visitors are unpaid volunteers who have been briefly trained by paid social workers to help families with young children, in which the mother is feeling under enormous strain or perhaps is depressed. They help by giving emotional support, sometimes by doing practical jobs like the shopping, the housework and actually looking after the children. One trainee dropped out because she claimed the befriending scheme amounted to no more than 'glorified baby minding'. The striking thing about these unpaid workers is that while they do give real help, the sort of help they give is elementary. It is an indictment of the present way we live that so many mothers have no husband able to share this work, and no neighbour, friend or relative who automatically and spontaneously offers this help, so that the lack of it precipitates a crisis.

There is another aspect to the pre-school home visitor which is slightly more worrying. Most of these new voluntary organizations, such as 'Home-plus', 'Befriending schemes', are not independent of the state but are locked into the system of social services. Like official social workers, these volunteer helpers also act as volunteer 'policewomen'. Most of them, too, are house-wives and mothers themselves. They have to report to the social services if any of the women they have 'befriended' are not responsive to their advice. The two aspects of statutory social work – of giving support and of judging mothers – have, in these ways, simply been reproduced in the voluntary system. The system of 'home visiting' has a long history, both in social services and in the education system. In the education system, state-employed school officials used to visit homes to make sure that parents sent their children to school, from the beginning of compulsory schooling. These officials were the ancestors of the modern education welfare officer, now the education social worker. They were often retired policemen, and got nick-named 'the school bobby'. The job and the back-up organization have changed. These state employees and the voluntary helpers do more than judge the families they visit. But many mothers are inevitably sensitive to the element of judgement in the relationship.

The 'new' ways of supporting the family are being encouraged at the moment partly because it is attractively cheap to rely on the unpaid, volunteer work of housewives. Present developments are another example of the return to nineteenth-century forms of social work. Pre-school home visiting can be seen as another form of mutual or 'self-help'. Instead of being provided with play-groups and nurseries, mothers are encouraged to set them up themselves, and to staff them, unpaid. The idea is to get the mothers who can cope to support the ones who cannot. Thus when mothers are recruited for one befriending agency, the social worker in charge visits them in their homes to make sure they are clean and well organized and do not have 'too many problems themselves'. The idea is that the client will 'tidy up and put on a clean dress' to receive the visitor, so she must be up to scratch herself. The women who are recruited are those who are conform-ing to the traditional model. They are dependent wives with time on their hands because their children have left home or are at school. Men could not be recruited, we were told, because they will either be at work or registered unemployed and therefore have to keep themselves 'available for work'. In these agencies, housewives from 'good' (= coping) families are given the task of keeping up the 'moral' standards of other families, and are used both to help and to judge other mothers. One trainee told us, 'If she says it's a horrible day, we have to ask ourselves if she really means the weather or that she's depressed. If she's depressed, we report it to the social worker.'

The use of other mothers, with no official title or salary, disguises the amount of surveillance involved in pre-school home visiting. Similarly, the caring, informal aspect of the motherly volunteers of W R V S and Home Helps veils their role as state agents and preserves the appearance of family privacy.

Like housework itself, voluntary work has a useful elastic quality. Although cheap, it is not necessarily unskilled. 'We do of course acknowledge that the volunteer cannot be stereotyped as untrained, inexperienced and unreliable. On the contrary, with unemployment so high ... volunteers could be highly trained and experienced (Barclay, 1982, p. 78). It can contract or expand without causing a political uproar, for there are no workers as such to sack, no noisy victims of neglect. Services offered through voluntary organizations never come to be seen as a *right*. They may be withdrawn or cut (like meals-on-wheels) if resources become insufficient. Then women's work within the family can expand to replace some of the work the volunteers were doing.

The relatively new development of family centres, by voluntary organizations such as the Church of England Children's Society, also gets the 'adequate' to help the 'inadequate'. Family centres are really day nurseries with built-in obsolescence as their aim. They try to teach mothers how to do their work within the home, especially child care, more effectively and efficiently. 'Inadequate' mothers are 'taught' by nursery nurses, themselves partially trained 'social workers', while their children are looked after in a separate section of the family centre on the traditional day-nursery basis. The principle of the family centre is now also being used by statutory social services for their day nurseries. For example, the job specification for a nursery officer in an Avon social services day nursery includes 'To maintain and develop professionally sound interaction between families and staff and to assist parents in the development of good parenting skills ...' This underlines the whole conception of day-nursery provision as appropriate only for 'vulnerable families and children'. Ordinary coping mothers are not supposed to be vulnerable, and their children are not supposed to need care outside the family until they reach school age. In fact, increasingly, as David has argued elsewhere, motherhood is being celebrated and taught to girls at school as well as in family centres (David, 1985a, pp. 37–9).

THE CONDITIONS OF PRIVACY

The privacy of the family is both real and mythical. What we do within our private four walls is not entirely of our own choosing. As we have seen, the standards women try to meet are set for them, and they are judged unfavourably if they fail to live up to them. These standards are ill-defined and where the boundary-line is drawn depends on social class, ethnic group, family form and age. Once that boundary is crossed and women come to the notice of state agencies, which seemed, up to this point, fairly benign and supportive, then their total parental responsibility is in danger of being changed into no responsibility at all. The conditions of our privacy are rigidly circumscribed.

This privacy is none the less real. It is real enough as far as the work is concerned – the isolated conditions in which women do the chores and the caring. Mothers think of themselves as working for their own sakes and for the sake of their children. Thus the relative isolation in which they work seems like a consequence of the sort of work it is. This is ironic, since what mothers do is for the whole of society. Parasitic industries like commercial advertising have the appearance of being socially useful, but bringing up children *appears* to be purely private business. Because each mother has *her* house or flat, *her* washing and *her* children, it is difficult for her to realize that she has *working conditions* in common with Pat up the road, and that these working conditions could be changed.

The belief that child care is purely a private business has definite political effects. It makes it less likely that working people will get together and make demands on behalf of their children, the new generation, and insist on higher standards for them. It fits in with the official view that family problems and family failures can be put down to the inadequacy of particular individual parents.

As things are, inadequate people are not fully entitled to 'family privacy'. This is a right they forgo when they ask for help or are seen to have need of it. Our argument is not that parents should possess their children and the state should never interfere. On the contrary, we want a bigger role for public authority, more 'interference' of a certain kind. The help we want from the state is the sort of preventive help which reduces the *bad* side of family privacy: the isolation of parents, their near-total responsibility and the burden that it brings, and the sexism which makes the mother *the* key parent in the family but a person of low status and little power elsewhere. State intervention into the family at the moment has a clear political aim.

It aims to get families to conform as nearly as possible to the model of a male-headed two-parent family with the man as provider and the woman as emotional mainstay and child carer; in other words, to reinforce the divorce of motherhood from power, which is itself the root of much misery and mistreatment of children.

The criteria for taking children into care reflect this political aim. Children are taken away from families in order to support the *right sort* of family. But these criteria are not spelled out. Once the privacy of the family is breached, its place is taken by the private procedures of state employees.

Of course, children are only taken into care reluctantly.

> Children should be taken into care only after the most serious consideration of the other options and the possibility of rehabilitation of the family ... where intervention is necessary it should be the minimum required to enable the family to cope and should be aimed at avoiding the removal of a child from home (Association of County Councils, 1984, pp. 207–21).

This reluctance is far more readily overcome when the 'inadequate' families are poor or black or are headed by a lone mother. The supporters of the family are less than enthusiastic about such families. Their 'cure' is doubly punitive: it confirms the parents in their status as unfit, and the alternative offered the children – local-authority care, usually in a series of foster homes – confirms them too in their marginal status.

> ... present policies towards child welfare problems imply a weakening of the family life of the poor. The failure to tackle social deprivation means that some parents will be unable to provide for their children. The emphasis on facilitating removals obviously breaks up families. The reluctance to improve day-care and social-work preventive services serves to perpetuate separations. Further, the attitudes conveyed by these trends towards the parents, who are deemed unloving, irresponsible and feckless, will only intensify their sense of defeat and drive them further from their children. What, for instance, will be the reaction of parents who discover – according to the ... Children Act – that simply to have their child in care for a certain period is sufficient ground for losing their parental rights, no matter how much they love that child? What are their feelings when learning that an application is being made to adopt a child they placed for fostering (Holman, 1980, pp. 35–6)?

To have one's parents judged a failure in such a crucial way is another blow for children who have already suffered neglect or mistreatment. Even if the 'adequate' family which replaces their old 'inadequate' family gives them warmth and security, they are left with loss and damaged self-esteem. The thrust of current family policy is to sidestep the causes of 'family inadequacy' which affect *all* families to a greater or lesser extent – the isolation of mothers and the lack of public support for child care, exacerbated by poverty and racism.

Official policy assumes that 'good parenting skills' are found in intact, white, middle-class, two-parent-family households. Two parents who stay together are assumed to provide better care than one. Ideally this should be true. Yet many women who leave their husbands do so partly because of their husbands' violence to them and/or their children. In these cases the formation of one-parent families may prevent child abuse, and there is evidence that when lone mothers remarry, child abuse (by the step-father) becomes more likely than if they remain alone (private conversation with Dartington research team). Many fathers, not always willingly, see and know little of their children. And the fact that lone parent families are on average poorer than two-parent families tells us nothing about the distribution of resources *within* male-headed households. The income and other resources coming into a family are not shared out fairly between family members. The wife and mother without earnings is particularly vulnerable. She and the children may experience considerable poverty, although her husband is actually earning enough to support them (Land, 1983, p. 9). The privacy of family life means that there is no easy way of knowing how many this affects: '... the only indication we have of their numbers is from the studies of women who have left their marriages, are living on state benefits and are therefore poor but who say that they are better off than they were while still married' (ibid., p. 24). Holman argues that it is the social deprivation which lone parents suffer that handicaps them, rather than the fact that there is only one responsible adult. One example

... comes from a study conducted by the National Children's Bureau, which compares 750 children growing up with one parent with over 12,000 in two-parent families. The former children revealed many disadvantages. They scored low on reading and arithmetical tests, they moved home more frequently, their social adjustment tended to be worse. Their parents were more likely to be in poor health and clearly experienced great strains in coping with them. Most significantly, the children of one-parent families were far more likely to be taken into public care. The conclusions could be drawn that lone parents are psychologically unbalanced, that they are incapable of raising children and that therefore policies should be directed towards removing them. Yet the research also showed that if the social deprivations of the one-parent families were held constant, then the differences in attainment and adjustment did not hold. Lone parents experience child care inequality when they are subjected to conditions of poverty which make child-rearing so difficult that normal child care objectives are not reached (Holman, op. cit., pp. 19–20).

In other words, poverty is the main factor. It does not follow that a family's poverty is a valid reason for removing its children into public care. Children of upper-middle-class people can be blatantly neglected without the same response from state agencies: '. . . middle-class and upper-class parents who leave their children in the care of nursemaids or place them in private boarding schools, failing to visit them for long periods of time, would not be regarded by the community as felons' (Katz, 1971, ch. 1). In contrast '. . . the poor are visible. They are more likely than other social groups to be in contact with public officials, to live in locations which are heavily policed, on estates already classed as "problem estates"' (Holman, op. cit., pp. 34–5).

Similarly the number of black children in care is disproportionate to the number of black families in the population. Black families certainly '. . . suffer disproportionately from poverty, poor accommodation, unsupported child care and unemployment' (CRE, quoted in Equality for Children 1983, p. 3). But this is not the whole story. The effects of poverty are compounded by those of racism. As the Commission for Racial Equality put it in their evidence to the House of Commons Select Committee on Children in Care: 'Black families have imposed on them "eurocentric" assumptions of good parenting and "proper" family life which are used to justify separating parents from children' (op. cit., p. 4). And the substitute carers are far more likely to be white. A group of black women, working within the National Child Care Campaign, are convinced that 'Black children are often seen as having problems, but we believe that in fact, it is often the attitudes, assumptions and unconscious racism of white teachers and care-givers that should be seen as problematic.' They are right. It is surely problematic that, when only a minority now lives in the white, male-headed, two-parent nuclear family, with dependent housewife, it is still held up as *the* standard of good child care. Twenty years ago the poverty of black families in the USA was seen as their own fault, as a consequence of a 'faulty family structure'.

Broken homes and illegitimacy do not necessarily mean poor upbringing and emotional problems. But they mean it more often when the mother is forced to work (as the Negro mother so often is), when the father is incapable of contributing to support (as the Negro father so often is), when fathers and mothers refuse to accept responsibility for and resent their children, as Negro parents, overwhelmed by difficulties, so often do, and when the family situation, instead of being clear-cut, and with defined roles and responsibilities, is left vague and ambiguous (as it so often is in Negro families) (Glazer and Moynihan, 1963, p. 50).

Here righteous indignation surfaces at the idea of women working outside the home, and at 'ambiguous' sex roles. Such punitive attitudes have been criticized frequently on both sides of the Atlantic, but that does not mean to say that they have disappeared. On the contrary, they are resurfacing in the US in the 'anti-feminist backlash' with its concern for the break-up of the family. In Britain, too, the marriage of racism and anti-feminism is inspiring the New Right's family policies.

These supporters of the 'family' are really only supporters of the traditional nuclear family, despite the fact that most children do not live in two-parent families with a mother at home. In those households where there are two parents, the more common pattern now is for there to be two wage-earners rather than one: this is true of 57 per cent of two-parent families in the USA. In Britain, 56 per cent of mothers with dependent children are in paid employment (Martin and Roberts, 1984, p. 13). These changes in family structure have occurred without any support from the state. In fact, they fly in the face of contemporary social policy. The New Right will have its work cut out to reverse current demographic trends towards more one-parent and two-wage-earner families. Its family model will seem increasingly out of touch with reality. It will not always be effective in getting women to shoulder ever more unpaid work, both in their homes and in the community, shoring up public services. The idea of the family and of family privacy may remind us of the 1950s, but the reality is very different today. The continuing economic recession has tarnished the dreams of home-makers. For more and more women there are no ideal homes, only poor houses.

CHAPTER THREE

CHILDREN'S DAYS
WITH MOTHER

THE CONTEXT OF CHILDREN'S EXPERIENCES

How children feel about the ways that they are brought up cannot be as neatly classified as the different styles of care themselves. Yet the enormous range of experience is often dismissed with the trite phrase that we all know how children are looked after and brought up – by their mothers and, when very young, usually at home. This is clearly at best a partial picture. Even children with full-time mothers often have completely contrasting daily lives. What it is like for children depends not primarily on whether their mothers go out to work but, to a far greater extent, on a lot of other factors. What arrangements do mothers make for their daily care? Are they at home or out-of-home; at school or at play? Are the arrangements generally considered normal or unusual in the child's environment? Is the child a boy or a girl; black or white; Christian, Jewish or Muslim? Does she or he have sisters or brothers; are these older or younger; step-, half- or adopted siblings? Does she or he live with one or two parents? With whom else? Is the family well-off or poor; working or middle class? To have an idea of the quality of children's lives, we would need to know the answers to these and many other questions. In this chapter and the next we explore afresh the diversity of care given by mothers and others in a variety of contexts – at home or out-of-home – to uncover the varied quality of children's daily lives.

Our account of children's days is mainly constructed from the few observational studies that have been done. Although they are supposed to be about children, these studies are written from the adults' point of view; and adults in their interaction with the children tend to emerge as the significant figures. It needs an imaginative leap to get the flavour of children's lives from these reports. Far more is known about children's everyday experiences from the start of schooling. Schools are 'public' and available for scrutiny and, of course, children can begin to describe their experiences in words and writing. What does come through the available evidence is the inadequacy of any single research category (such as class, place in family, working status of mother) to predict children's experiences of care. To be a 'planned' third child in one family may feel very different from being an 'afterthought' in another, socially similar family. The experience of an inner-city twin in a one-parent family is worlds apart from Topsy and Tim (the eternally five-years-old middle-class, semi-rural heroine and hero of a series of popular children's books). We shall see that maternal care varies in quality just as much as non-maternal care.

All children are 'of woman born'. Even so, we do not all have the same experiences of birth or the same chance of survival. Class differences between our mothers affect our life chances even more than family size or maternal age. Our experiences of birth depend partly on how our mothers are feeling and what their social and emotional needs are at the time. They may be tired, irritable and drugged, or they may be ecstatic. A variety of factors such as pain-killers, easy or difficult deliveries, bottle- or breast-feeding, can affect the long-term relationship between mother and child so that it is not an easy or a comfortable relationship (Brimblecombe *et al.*, 1978).

Most children's first experiences of life are of maternal care, but we cannot assume that these early experiences are merely or only of love and comfort. Some babies' experience is of maternal death or loss, others experience some degree of rejection from their mothers. From the very beginning, experiences vary almost infinitely. The ideology of maternal care over-simplifies the practice. The baby or child herself or himself structures in a myriad of ways the kinds of care that she or he receives, through different behaviours such as smiling, crying, etc. And the sex of the baby is taken to be of overriding importance.

'It's a boy!' or 'It's a girl!' is usually the first comment made at birth. Gender affects children's experience from these very beginnings and early care constructs the ways in which they come to learn the supposed differences between the sexes. These are picked up by observation, almost by osmosis, as well as by mothers' gentle teaching, even through their care.

For most of us, father was not very much present in the crucial period of infantile dependency when our personalities began to form . . . For most of the week he was absent and it was mother who gave to us and to whom we turned when we wanted something ... From the little girl's point of view, Daddy is a mystery, a powerful figure who is always leaving ... He is experienced as separate and different and outside her immediate world ... (Eichenbaum and Orbach, 1984, p. 55).

Children often begin to see more clearly than adults what the power relationships are in family life. They observe the differences between their parents without pausing to question them. They come to realize that their mother is not as powerful as she at first appeared, and that it is their father who makes the most important excursions into the public world. These notions become part of them so that, when they in turn have children, it seems natural to repeat the old patterns. We are not even aware that we are learning them; we take them in as easily as we breathe the air around us.

Even when families do not follow the traditional pattern completely, the idea of the family 'as it should be' seems to be more real to children than the departures from it. One little girl of three, whose mother is a doctor, told her one day: 'Mummy, you pretend to be Daddy and then you can be the doctor and I can be the nurse.' Although this child's mother is a doctor, she only works part-time, and in her daughter's eyes and her own is obviously primarily mother – which means woman – which means nurse. It seems that children focus on experiences which confirm the dominant set of ideas. Another little girl was walking home from her nursery with her father when she spotted a little boy of about her age on his own. 'What's that little boy doing on his own? Why isn't he with his Mummy?' Yet at that moment she herself was not with her mother, and had not been all day. The lessons children learn most readily through family life are the most conventional ones – where what they experience fits what they are told ought to be.

FAMILY WORLDS

Yet what 'ought to be' is nothing like the reality for many children. Family life, described just in terms of household structure, is a great deal more complicated than the ideal of mother at home and father at work. As the *Study Commission on the Family* (1983, p. 10) put it:

the proportion of all families which might be regarded as typical, that is a married couple with dependent children, has declined from 38 per cent in 1961 to 32 per cent in 1980 ... the number of one-parent families with dependent children has increased; they formed only 2 per cent of all households in the early 1960s but made up 4 per cent by the late 1970s.

These figures even veil the variety of two-parent families, let alone the range of experiences when a marriage or relationship breaks up. In a two-parent family the mother may be in paid employment, the father may be unemployed, there may be step-brothers and -sisters, and half-brothers and -sisters, along with relatives and friends.

A report entitled *Caring for Children*, which reviewed educational and social services in member countries of the OECD, tried to summarize the variety of family types:

The family microcosm is extraordinarily differentiated and, even limiting the description to those families with children, the typology that can be constructed immediately becomes complex.

To demonstrate the great variety of possible situations ... British census recognises the following varieties of family comprising a married couple with children:
– married couple with child(ren) and no other persons
– married couple with child(ren) and with other persons
  – with one or more ancestors
  – with one or more ancestors and other relatives only
  – with one or more ancestors, other relatives and unrelated persons
  – with one or more ancestors and unrelated persons only
  – with other relatives only
  – with unrelated persons only

Now, if this typology is combined with other parameters, for example socio-economic status or number of active persons, the *immense diversity of situations experienced by children is immediately obvious. In other words, there is an enormous number of different family worlds in which they may grow up* [our emphasis]: there are not only the parents and siblings, or one of the parents, but also grandparents, uncles, aunts, cousins, grandchildren, servants, boarders, married brothers or sisters, with or without children. It must also be remembered that households undergo changes over time. Of particular interest are the changes of environment for the child whose parents have divorced and remarried. Such families are often 'corporations' including a mixture of adults and children from two families.

These observations are important, because very often the variety of 'realities' is underestimated. Through stressing the role of the parents, one ends up forgetting about all the others, as if the majority of families consisted just of one couple and their children. Certainly, this is the majority situation, in the sense that it applies to a great number of children, but a good number of other situations exist alongside it (CERI, 1982, pp. 19–20).

Forms of family life these days have a new complexity. It is no longer just a question of which sort of family you are born into but of what happens to the parents of that family who may find different partners or may find it difficult to bring the children up. The child may have to forge new relationships with step-brothers and -sisters as well as step-parents, and then often the half-brothers or -sisters born of the new partnerships. It follows that increasingly large numbers of children experience the break-up of their parents' relationship, and their own separation from at least one of their parents.

... Nearly three-fifths of the couples who get divorced have children under 16, and almost always the mother gets custody. There are now about $1\frac{1}{4}$ million dependent children – nearly 1 child in 10 – living with only one parent, in most cases the mother. Such families form a tenth of all families with dependent children ... With a third of marriages now involving the remarriage of one or both partners, the number of births to remarried women form nearly 5 per cent of all births – more than double the proportion ten years ago ... although at present 1 in 10 children are in one-parent families, many more will have experienced that situation for at least some time before they reach sixteen and will be living with a step-parent, usually step-father (Central Policy Review Staff, 1980, pp. 16–18).

Given this 'movie' rather than 'snapshot' approach to family life, it is obvious that it is not an uncommon experience for children to spend large parts of their childhood in households with other adults as well as one of their biological parents.

Yet other children will experience life in households without either of their natural parents. Some will be accepted into the care of the local authority at the request of their parents, on a temporary or permanent basis; others because of parental neglect, others because of abuse or being 'at risk' of abuse, and yet others (usually older children, especially teenagers) in 'need of care and control'. The care that these various thousands of children receive differs enormously – both between the families and homes that will care for them and over the childhood of each child. Some children move from household to household, from children's home to one foster parent then to another foster parent, and so on. Others come to have a situation of permanence relatively quickly, finding adoptive parents who are willing to provide a home and security and, above all, make the necessary decisions about the children's welfare – that is, a similarity with 'natural' parents. The quality of life for all these children is infinitely varied – some find love and security, others experience further abuse and less love than they might have had from their mothers. A big difference in the experiences of 'children in care' from those whose parents separate, divorce and remarry is that access to 'natural' parents is even more controlled by others (here, local authorities and the 'new' parents), than when parents divorce. In both sets of cases, despite official rhetoric that the interests of the children should be paramount, children find themselves with little control over their relationships with any of their various parents.

Much of the difference between 'family worlds' – structures or styles of upbringing – comes from cultural differences. As we have seen, local authorities tend to use a white Protestant middle-class lifestyle as their measuring rod in judging the adequacy of a home or a parent. Schools and health service provision are similarly geared to this 'ideal' family. Unmarried mothers are called Mrs, Asian girls are expected to go swimming in mixed baths, and in one private school in Birmingham a Sikh boy was refused admission as long as his parents insisted that he continue wearing his turban. The parents protested that this was racial discrimination, but the question went right up to the House of Lords before it was accepted as unlawful. Where there are children from various ethnic groups, schools *may* adopt a multi-cultural approach to religion and festivities. If the area is mainly white and Christian, they are unlikely to see the relevance. As one headmaster said: 'Comparative religion is not on the primary school curriculum.' Some inner-city schools have begun to develop multi-cultural teaching materials. Black faces appear in Ladybird books, and children's reading books occasionally feature one-parent families or working mothers. Despite these minor concessions, many children experience a confusing conflict between their actual family worlds and the dominant culture. Prevailing cultural norms in Britain still assume that children are or should be reared in families whose values originate in Christian morality.

We cannot describe here the multitude of family worlds which reinforce or modify the effects of the types of child care we review. The reader will have to bear in mind that the complexity we record is only a part of the story.

MATERNAL CARE AT HOME

The proper place for young children is supposed to be at home. Thus Leach says (1979b, p. 66): 'The adult returns home with relief. The baby had better stay there.' But mothers who look after their children at home are not all the same. They do so within a particular culture and family structure – a 'family world'. The 'ideal' family represents only one of many actual 'family worlds'. It is alive and well, although its importance has been exaggerated. We shall look at the extent to which life for children in the 'ideal family' measures up to what is expected of it.

In some ways life is still more sociable in the white nuclear family than you might guess from nostalgic comparisons with the past. Certainly it used to be more common than it is now for mothers and children to live in intimate neighbourhoods, in close contact with their own and their husbands' mothers and sisters, as well as with neighbours and friends. This pattern has not entirely disappeared. Dunn and Kendrick (1982) have looked at forty children between the ages of eighteen months and two years living in housing estates, private houses or rented accommodation in Cambridge, England. They say (p. 8) that

> the stability of the working-class population, and the relatively good housing, had a direct and important effect on the lives of the children we studied. The stability was reflected in the network of relatives (cousins, aunts, uncles and more distant relatives) that many of the children had in the area, a network that extended over several generations ... while the social class of the sample was, in terms of father's occupation, far from homogeneous, the *pattern of the different children's lives was in many respects remarkably similar* [our emphasis]. A predictable routine of continuous close contact with the mother, regular visits from grandparents, visits to local shops, and frequent contact with other children was common to most of the children ...

Commenting on research on a random sample of 131, mostly young, mothers in London's Tower Hamlets, Joy Melville (1983) mentioned that: 'Most of them had also been brought up in the borough where the extended family is a reality. If you ask what their social contacts are, it's their mum. And "granny" often prevents the whole system cracking up.' Bone (1977) found that grandmothers did account for a significant proportion of people caring for young children. Several other surveys, such as that by *Woman's Own* in 1979 or the Child Health and Education Survey of children born in 1970, also found that informal arrangements with relatives were a common form of child care. Where the carer is a close friend, she is often converted into a relative from the child's point of view by the title Auntie.

Many children are fortunate enough to have close relationships with adults outside the nuclear family, usually, of course, of their parents' choosing. Mothers are even more powerful in their control over their young children's playmates:

> For any preschool child, whether his friends or playmates are congenial, or indeed whether he has anyone to play with at all, is very much a matter of luck. His physical restriction to the area immediately surrounding his own house means that he is limited almost entirely to children living close at hand; he cannot go farther afield in order to widen his choice. For some children, this will mean no peer-group company at all; they are completely dependent upon being taken to other children's homes or having other children brought on visits to them (Newson and Newson, 1968, p. 63).

Children's social worlds do usually include adults besides their parents. But all relationships outside the nuclear family depend on that central figure, the mother. She is not only important because she is constantly present for many pre-school children, but also because, present or not, it is *she* who decides how her children's lives are patterned.

Dunn and Kendrick (1982, p. 9) have a graphic description of the daily life of a child aged between eighteen months and two and a half years old:

> Daily life was, for almost all the children, a life spent close to the mother – following her around the house as she cleaned and tidied, 'helping' her to hang out the wash, playing in the kitchen as she cooked, going to the local shops with her, having a drink and a biscuit with her in front of the television. Most of the children were not used to even brief separations from their mothers. [Of the sample of forty]: six had never been separated, even for an afternoon, and fourteen more experienced separations only about once a month. Only three were used to daily separations ... During these periods all the children except one had been looked after by a relative.

This thumbnail sketch shows the paucity of experiences for such toddlers. Dunn and Kendrick emphasize the lack of educational experience or cognitive development, and highlight the extent to which the mother merges her housework and child care and the child has to fit in with the mother's work.

Again this is at odds with the official ideology which stresses the importance of mother as educator. The picture of the mother at home reading to her child, sharing his or her enjoyment of mud-pies and water play, making collages, collecting leaves and so on reflects a highly educated middle-class notion of mothering. In their study of four-year-olds in Nottingham in the 1960s, the Newsons found that wives of professional and managerial men were far less fussy about neatness, quietness and cleanliness and were more likely to allow messy play and playing on the furniture. They mention two reasons for this:

> first ... education; ... second ... economic and material circumstances. Professional-class mothers ... are especially likely to have read books on child-upbringing and education, or at least to have absorbed from other sources the principles which they contain. The idea that messy play is not only natural but right is taken for granted in any discussion of nursery education and mothers of this class are typically very conscious of the educative duties entailed in motherhood (Newson and Newson, op. cit., p. 163).

In her book *Who Cares?* Penelope Leach speaks to and for these mothers of the professional and middle class (although she certainly wishes to address a wider audience, crossing class boundaries). She advocates full-time mothering for babies and toddlers mainly because she thinks the child will develop best if looked after by a single devoted carer. Realism (as she calls it – we might call it resignation) means this can only be the mother.

> When I look at the undoubted advantages which I enjoyed (and still enjoy) in my role as mother, the one which outweighs all the rest – even the decent income, the housing and so forth – is information. It was this, more than anything else, which prevented me from being bored in an all-encompassing and soul-destroying way, even when a particular afternoon or whole week contained no highspots.
>
> The more a mother knows about children's development, about the orderly processes of change, about the actions and reactions which are likely in this or that age-group, in these or those circumstances, the more interesting her own child becomes (Leach, 1979a, p. 91).

There are many points here we want to disagree with from the mothers' point of view. She may be fascinated by her children without wanting to look after them all the time. She may have lots of 'information' and still fancy doing something different, too. She may find that giving some time and space to satisfying her own needs makes her less preoccupied and more attentive and 'interested' when she is with her children. She may believe her children need other experiences. But however much truth there may be in Leach's claim that an educated mother is a good mother, in reality most mothers, whatever their educational qualifications, express their love and emotional closeness to their children by looking after them physically and by being generally companionable as they go about their daily work, rather than by giving them much concentrated direct attention.

Whether they are working or middle class, most mothers see their actual job as housekeeping rather than child care. Housekeeping here includes meeting the physical needs of all members of the family – which means managing child care so that the children are settled or at least unobtrusive when the breadwinner returns home, needing his meal in a neat and calm environment. 'If he earns his daily bread by heavy bodily exertion, a man's sleep and food requirements are likely to be given a place of special importance, and the wife feels called upon to minister to these physical needs as a matter of first priority' (Newson and Newson, 1963, p. 220).

This attention to the needs of the breadwinner is not only found among working-class wives. It springs from the nature of marriage itself, and the expectation that men are the chief breadwinners and women their economic dependants. This expectation is backed up by laws on employment, social security and taxation which define economic dependence as women's normal status. As a consequence, women think of themselves as the maintenance staff for family members and the physical and emotional environment of the home. There are major social class differences in how women interpret this role, and in what they have to do to achieve their aims, but the role itself is generally accepted.

The trouble is that housework and child care are not always compatible.

One unusual aspect of housework as a job is that it is combined with another job: child-rearer ... The child-care/housework combination ... poses certain problems. But the contradiction is not simply that children are messy creatures who untidy the tidy house, and demand to be fed and played with while a meal is being cooked or a room cleaned. The two roles are, in principle, fundamentally opposed. The servicing function is basic to housework: children are people (Oakley, 1974a, p. 166).

Oakley produces a lot of evidence to show that mothers do not concern themselves chiefly with child care but rather with housework. In *Housewife*, published in 1974, she presents four interesting interviews with different

housewives, each with a child under five. What is characteristic of them all
is their emphasis on housework at the expense of child care. Children
observe the household chores being done far more often than they participate in them. This seems to be the common experience for all children,
whether babies, toddlers, at playschool or schoolchildren proper. The
mother of just one child, an eleven-month-old baby, describes her day in
terms reminiscent of Dunn and Kendrick's description of early child care.
Her life is dominated by housework rather than baby care. This baby goes
on visits to other mothers and children and is also looked after by another
mother in a regular 'swap' arrangement. But when mother and baby are
together, much of the time is dominated by housework.

> First I make her breakfast and I usually have something myself. Then I
> wash up and sort of potter around doing things. I endeavour to get the
> place straight – not *cleaning* really, just straightening it – tidying it ...
>
> Mostly the day consists of repetitive things like sorting out the baby's
> clothes, doing the washing ... I try to do the washing every day ... I do
> a bit of shopping every day ... I don't sit down in the morning. Sara has
> her lunch about half-past twelve. I don't always cook for her – just
> occasionally I do a casserole. I feel very good about that – something super
> to eat for a change ... I don't cook for myself at lunchtime.
>
> Usually I go out in the afternoons, I suppose two or three days a week
> I see people. I've made quite a few friends round here who have babies,
> and that's rather nice. There's a girl I know who lives down on the green,
> and she's got a daughter the same age, and she brings her baby to me
> on Thursdays while she goes off for a couple of hours, and I do the same
> to her on Tuesdays. She goes off to a class – she's doing a course in Dutch
> – or she goes to a class in flower arranging. [What do you do?] Well, I
> haven't really come to terms with it all yet. I feel I should be doing
> something important ...
>
> I feed Sara about half-past five, but she doesn't go down straight away
> ... After I've put her to bed I make myself a cup of coffee and get myself
> some biscuits and I come in here and I stay, and that's it (Oakley, 1974b,
> pp. 116–18).

So far, in looking at maternal care we have concentrated on examples
of family life where there is only *one* child. This is a relatively unusual
situation; the majority of mothers care for more than one child. Life with
more children is likely to be more interesting and more hectic for both
mother and child than the rather lonely routine described above. Certainly

more children mean more work for the mother. If the children will keep each other company it may be easier to get on with the household chores; but more likely the mother will have to interrupt the meal preparation twenty times to arbitrate between them, rescue or console them. Only those who have vacuumed a house with a baby on the hip who is frightened of the noise and a toddler trailing complainingly behind, or who have first-hand experience of the fetching and carrying and general administration involved in looking after children who have to go to different places, know how much of children's lives is spent being managed: waiting for mother to finish, being 'got ready' to go out, to come home, being rushed inexplicably to meet other people's timetables.

Oakley's other three housewives all had more than one child. All of them report daily routines in which they highlight their domestic rather than their child-rearing tasks. We get no picture of the enjoyable interactions between mother and children. Of course, this could be because of the way in which Oakley posed her questions. Even so, what is, for us, most interesting is women's interpretation of being a housewife as concerning the daily chores rather than the experience of child rearing. Food and meals seem to be the dominant concerns of Oakley's housewives, when they are not detailing physical care of the children such as washing and ironing their clothes. More than one child, then, adds to the daily toll, even if one is at school. One woman describes herself as rushing to and from school, momentarily leaving the baby unattended whilst taking the daughter to school; a life punctuated by washing, cleaning, shopping, cooking and serving with the odd chance to watch TV with the schoolchild. She tells Oakley (1974b, pp. 108–9): 'That's every day, really. I do the same things in the same order every day. Stupid, isn't it?' Another of Oakley's housewives is the mother of two pre-school children and a young schoolgirl. She is relatively well-off, married to a director of a publishing firm and living in the suburban commuter belt of London, described as a 'desirable neighbourhood'. Being so quintessentially middle class, and employing a cleaning lady a couple of days a week, we might expect her to have the time and interest to concentrate her attention on child care rather than housework. Yet that is certainly not the picture we get from her description of her daily routine; again, housework seems to preoccupy her more than child care. Her three little girls lead a varied and sociable life. They spend little time alone with their mother and, some of the time, are actually in the care of others at play-group and school. Their mother sees herself as the manager of her children's lives rather than as their educator. The model of motherhood she offers her daughters is virtually that of a high-class servant, whose own needs and capacities are irrelevant.

This prosperous mother's daily life is not very different from that of Oakley's fourth housewife, who is working class, and who has a part-time job as a 'shrink-wrapper'. The similarities in their social situation – both having three children and a husband who is uninvolved in the household chores and child care – seem more significant than the differences. This mother, too, has delegated some of her child raising to the school, by getting her four-and-a-half-year-old daughter in 'early' to enable her to continue with a part-time job. The main difference between these two accounts of families with three children is that the woman with a part-time job organizes less for her children, whilst at the same time being herself much more organized with the housework. She, too, spends most of her time at home, engaged in housework, whether the children are there or not.

I would rather describe myself as a shrink-wrapper than as a housewife. I pack tins in cellophane, and the cellophane shrinks – that's what shrink wrapping is . . . My hours are nine till one Monday to Friday; in the school holidays a friend two doors away looks after the children. I normally have time off if they're ill.

You want to know what I do every day?

My husband gets up first. I get a cup of tea and toast in bed, then I get up. I get up with the aggro – the miseries, about ten to seven. I come downstairs like a mad bull and I don't stop till I leave the house at twenty-five past eight. I try to do as much as I can before I go to work. I come down, lay the table for breakfast, get dressed, and then I charge around doing what I can: the children make their own beds. I make my bed, I carpet sweep: if I'm hoovering, I leave that till I come home, I dust, draw curtains, drink tea, smoke a million fags with nerves, and then I make sure the children are all dressed and ready for school. That time goes very quick. My boys go to school on their own, the little girl goes with my friend next door. I don't take her, but I collect her . . .

I come in, prepare me dinner – get the vegetables ready – and then I do washing, ironing, have a cup of tea. I do hand washing every day for about an hour; I leave the other things for a machine wash . . .

After I've had a cup of tea, it's usually time to go and pick up my little girl. I come back about a quarter to four, change the little girl's school clothes, and then the boys come in at four. I lay the table. And then you hear my mouth, from then till they go to bed! I've got no patience. I used to, but I haven't now.

I cook an evening meal. My children have dinners at school, but they also have dinners of an evening ...

After that I wash up, put the dishes away, sweep the floor, wash the floor, and then where the children have been playing I come in here and tidy up. They go to bed at seven. I take them up, but the two boys have their light on for half an hour to read. The light goes off at half-past seven, and then I come down, make a cup of coffee, and I sit down! ... (Oakley, 1974b, pp. 142–4).

Oakley's interviews show dramatically how much of children's daily experience consists of watching their mother work, or of playing while she gets on with it. Housework has a life of its own, perhaps serving the husband's needs, but certainly not directly contributing to the growth and development of babies and children. We get only glimpses of what all of this must be like for the child: times spent with other children, with siblings, with other adults and in organized care, such as school or play-group. From these vignettes, much of maternal care appears to be housework with the children around.

Mary Georgina Boulton interviewed fifty women with pre-school children, some from a middle-class and others from a working-class background. Her emphasis, unlike Oakley's, was on the work and satisfaction of looking after children and being a mother. All the women she interviewed also tended to separate housework from child care and create 'routines' so that they could 'feel that child care was limited and contained, and therefore manageable and under control' (Boulton, 1983, p. 81). Like Oakley's interviewees, they dwelt on the daily burdens rather than the pleasures of child care. One of them, Mandy Turner, a working-class mother with a son of three and a daughter of two, is very illuminating:

I feel exhausted. I used to be cool, calm and collected before I had children. Nothing really bothered me; I wasn't a worrier. But I do find they get me down. They do seem to get on top of me. You find that with two children both in nappies and every day or every other day it's nappies, things become a bit of a drudge. People who say have children close together! When they're grown up it's probably lovely, but they tend to gloss over the fact that when they're young, it's a lot of hard work. I find I'm getting up at about 6.00 in the morning and still working at 9.00 at night; I'm still doing things. And it's too much ... you're on the go all day long ...

It's not even like going to work where you've got a lunch hour. In that hour you're completely away. You sit down for lunch with the children but you're still at the job aren't you (Boulton, op. cit., pp. 78–9).

All these women recognize a conflict 'between the responsibility of a mother and those of a housewife' (ibid., p. 84). Boulton goes on: '... virtually all the women in the study coped with this potential conflict by giving priority to children and child care ... [but] the strategy of subordinating housework to child care did not do away with the conflict between them: it simply reduced the tensions to a more manageable level' (ibid., p. 85). She quotes one:

I like my house to look reasonable: clean and tidy. But during the day I don't bother too much ... I don't think it's fair on the children if you're forever clearing up. If they're both home and have their toys around, if you keep tidying up after them, I'm sure they'd tend not to play with their toys ... And then how would they learn? They'd just sit there and be pretty little vegetables (Colleen Johnston, middle class, daughters six and three) (ibid., p. 85).

Giving priority to child care over housework need not mean doing much *with* the children. Most of these mothers simply allowed the children's toys to litter the house during the day:

They get out their toys and they have their toys all over the place and all day long this goes on, and it doesn't bother me one bit. I think, 'This is their life.' But just as soon as my husband comes in, he doesn't like to see it and he says, 'Come on, let's pick all these toys up' (ibid., p. 86).

It was only for short periods during the day that these mothers played with the children, and there were clear class differences in their attitudes to play. Working-class women would only play games they enjoyed whereas middle-class women saw play as something the children needed, and for them it was continued out of a sense of duty:

I'm in here with them after school. But I don't always play with them. Sometimes we have a rough and tumble on the floor. But I get fed up with that pretty quick. Then they have to play their own games where they don't want me to join in (Jean Elliott, working class, sons six, four and two) (ibid., p. 75).

In contrast:

I try not to do any typing (for her job which she loves) when Daniel is around. I think it is a bit unfair to him, because the afternoon *should* be his time, really (Jackie Schneider, middle class, sons four and one).

For a couple of hours or an hour and a half after lunch I always try to devote to them. But it's terribly difficult because the games that Mark can play are many and the games Emma can join in are few and she always wants to try to join in. She's too young. She can't play dominoes, picture dominoes, which I've started to play with Mark (Angela Bourne, middle class, son $3\frac{1}{2}$, daughter $1\frac{1}{2}$) (loc. cit.).

Penelope Leach sees no conflict between the two aspects of housewifery, chores and caring:

Interested mothers change mucky nappies, make beds, sweep floors, pick up toys, cook meals and then do it all again, just as uninterested ones do. But they do these external things as a means to an end: to make a comfortable environment for the internal task of relating to the child. They are able to keep their priorities straight: to put themselves and their children before the housekeeping: to keep themselves free of self-imposed domestic slavery (Leach, 1979a, p. 91).

Have we been talking only about mothers who have failed to get their priorities straight? Leach seems to think that this is entirely a matter of will. It is true that women's high standards for housework are not imposed on them by their husbands alone or by them directly. They are produced by their training, watching their own mothers and other women caring and creating order, and learning at school and through the media that this is a feminine virtue *par excellence*. Housewives

... often submit to real or imagined external moral pressure from other women because this is the only way of giving housework any rationality. Since the housewife's work is in fact so private, [as Comer says] 'if she insists on satisfying only her own requirements in a wholly utilitarian way, she risks being labelled self-indulgent and immoral' (Barrett and McIntosh, 1983, p. 63).

To label women, who feel a desperate need to maintain certain standards of order at home, as living in 'self-imposed slavery' is rather arrogant, and misses the main point: the desperation they feel is not self-imposed but is a response to their inferior social position. It is the only way open to them to feel good about themselves. After all, many housewives regard their homes as extensions of themselves. (We sometimes feel that many homes regard housewives as their extensions.) They are often confirmed in this by the 'personal' gifts they receive: a frying pan for a birthday present; a tablecloth and napkins for Christmas.

Housework and child care *can* mix, but one has to give. Some women manage to subordinate the housework to their children's needs; let them wash up, hide in the bed and so on as they work. Even they find that if they are in a hurry for some external reason (perhaps some important visitors are expected), their attitude to the children changes radically. The children become things that *will* get in the way, that *will not* leave the bathroom so that mother can mop the floor. Then she shouts at them, and so intimidates them that they stand crying as she works. To idealize the time mothers and children spend together as if this sort of incident were not common is a nonsense. Housework is isolated, individual work. It is repeated from day to day and from household to household. What children learn from it is limited to short bursts of enthusiasm.

At best, while women work in the house their children can potter securely round their own territory. All children should have the chance and time for this, but out-of-home care and group care do not rule out secure pottering round another territory that the child comes to make her own. Care which does not allow children to feel secure and in control of their environment for a large part of the time is not good enough, whether it is at home or elsewhere. Mothers' care is not necessarily good just because it is mothers', and not necessarily enough just because it is good. We turn now to look at the variety of non-maternal care currently available, knowing that we cannot prejudge its quality by the simple fact that the carers are not the children's own mothers.

CHAPTER FOUR

CHILDREN'S DAYS
AWAY FROM MOTHER

MOTHERS AT WORK

Children spend large parts of their days away from their mothers. Once they go to school this is accepted as normal, even though there is no rationale in terms of child development behind the age chosen for compulsory schooling. This is five years old in Britain, older in most other countries. But in Britain nowadays over 40 per cent of three- and four-year-olds go to nursery or primary schools. When such early childhood education is available, public opinion about when a child is old enough to be away from mother shifts to conform to what is provided.

We cannot tell what children's days are like for them simply by noting whether or not their mothers have paid work. We have seen that the simple phrase 'full-time mothering at home' actually covers a wide range of situations and relationships. 'Day care' similarly includes all sorts of experiences. Penelope Leach's book *Who Cares?* takes as a starting point that she pretends to be proving: that full-time mothering is best for under-threes, and basically for all pre-school children (although over-threes may benefit from some sessions at nursery school or play-group). She talks (1979a, p. 16) of a myth that most women now work, and says that in fact '*Most mothers with children under five do not go out to work*' (her emphasis), and goes on: 'Not only is the total percentage of [working] mothers minute, the hours worked by the minority of this minute percentage are extremely short, too ... With hours as short as this, the disruption to both mother and child is minimal' (ibid., p. 17). Let us see if she is right.

First, the facts. The most recent (1984) figures for Britain show that almost a quarter of mothers of pre-school children (20 per cent) work part-time and 7 per cent work full-time (over thirty hours a week) (Martin and Roberts, 1984, p. 13). But these figures are certainly an underestimate. As we have seen, mothers with young children are forced into the 'black economy', that statistically blurred area of casual, underpaid work that increases as the recession deepens. The attraction is that employers in this area are often tolerant of the mother's need for occasional (unpaid) time off. In return they pay little and offer no protection or security. Mothers trying to make ends meet in this way do not always recognize or admit that they are 'economically active' and would not appear in the statistics. Nor would unregistered child minders, many women with cleaning jobs, and many 'home-workers'. But even without these mothers, 30 per cent is not a 'minute percentage'.

It is quite true that most employed mothers work *short* hours outside the home, which Leach welcomes as minimizing the 'disruption'. What on earth does she mean? Is cleaning the kitchen a 'disruption' of our relationships? If a toddler plays with a friend in the friend's mother's house twice a week, is that a (fortunately minimal) 'disruption' of full-time maternal care? We have seen that many full-time mothers do make such arrangements. It is nonsense to assume that the mother's employment *in itself* disrupts the child's and the mother's lives. What *is* 'disruptive' (in the sense of being anxiety-creating) is the lack of public provision and support for child care for working mothers. In this sense, the short hours worked may be out of all proportion to the way in which they dominate the week.

Mothers who work full-time are obliged to have some sort of reliable, constant child care. Those who work part-time often cobble arrangements together, and are continually having to renegotiate or start again. Ellen has managed to find a reasonable play-group that will take Kate at two and a half. Ellen's mother will fetch her and give her lunch . . . Catherine has found a neighbour who will fetch Luke from nursery school and have the baby, but only on Tuesdays and Fridays. Her husband can do Wednesdays and his mother Thursdays and Mondays. What if one of them is ill? Perhaps Rosemary would step in . . . no good, her children have chickenpox. Arrangements like these, with relatives, husbands and friends, are by far the commonest, not only for pre-school children but also for schoolchildren out of school hours and in the holidays. Many people feel that it is somehow more 'natural', and therefore better, for the child to be cared for in another family.

Care in the home while a mother is at work may be provided by the father, grandmother, older sibling, neighbour, friend, babysitter, nanny, housekeeper, maid, live-in students, or *au pair*. This may be the most common form of 'day care', but it is the one about which we know least. It simply has not been studied – perhaps because it is so private, because it varies so much from home to home, or because it seems to be so much like care by the mother (Clarke-Stewart, 1982, pp. 46–7).

This kind of arrangement is not unique to Britain, although in this country it has to compensate for lack of formal provision. In the USA, over half of children whose mothers go out to work are cared for by relatives (Clarke-Stewart, ibid., p. 46). 'As with playgroups and nursery schools and classes, so too in full day care the private, more improvised arrangement has outstripped the official, statutory one as far as numbers are concerned. We cannot even account for where many of the children go when their mothers work' (Bruner, 1980, p. 36).

In 1979 about 16 per cent of pre-school children of mothers working full-time and almost a third of mothers working part-time did not use day care (Study Commission on the Family, 1983, p. 27). Many of these will have been mothers who leave for work in a factory twilight shift, behind a bar, as a night nurse or office-worker or cleaner, or in a shop, as soon as their husbands come in from their work and take over. Other mothers, as Leach says, '... take their children with them ...' (1979a, p. 17). These are arrangements Leach sees as satisfactory because they hardly 'disrupt' mother and child's life together. In fact, carrying shift work into the home and into child care means reorganizing the family as a factory or office, so that the partners rarely see each other and the children have virtually no time with both parents together. This is experienced as a real emotional deprivation by all concerned. It is equally disturbing to find Leach giving her support to the idea that mothers should bring work home or take their children to the workplace. Home workers who do outwork for manufacturers often have their living space cluttered up with machinery and materials, which necessitates constant control of the children who will either damage themselves or the products. In a Low Pay Unit survey,

... homeworkers criticised the inconvenience or hazards of their work. Inconvenience in the shape of the space in small flats taken up by sewing machines, desks or in several cases sacks of balls or toys to be prepared. Many also criticised the unhealthy aspects of working in the home such as the abnormally large quantities of dust or fluff in the air, the evil-smelling nature of glues used in manufacture, or the excessive noise to be borne by the family (Crine, 1979, pp. 11–13).

Women who take their young children with them when they go to clean offices or work in shops feel worried, irritated and apologetic, as they struggle to divide their attention. It is highly irresponsible to idealize these compromises forced on mothers by the lack of recognition of their right to paid work and to have good care for their children.

DAY CARE AT HOME AND ABROAD

Non-maternal care for children tends to be more systematic and organized in most European and North American countries than it is in the UK. For all these countries we have little statistical evidence about where children are throughout the day. We do know that half of all under-fives in Britain experience some form of 'day care' (defined to include individual carers at home as well as schools and nurseries). For three- to five-year-olds, play-groups now challenge nursery schools as the main form of provision. About 12 per cent of under-fives go to nursery or primary school, far more to play-groups. But available figures do not include informal swaps set up between mothers and often used to extend the short hours of much play-group and nursery-school provision. Nor do they include care by fathers, grand-mothers and other relatives. Official figures suggest that child minders are only a tiny proportion of carers of pre-school children. But researchers have found that child minders are a vast hidden pool of carers and that their numbers extend into the millions. The picture that emerges for Britain is of vast demand for non-maternal forms of care which is inadequately met by private rather than public provision (Sharpe, 1984, Ch. 4).

A similar picture emerges for Canada where:

> Overall in 1981, 47.8 percent of all preschool children (age 0 to 5) were cared for exclusively by their parents, while 52.2 percent were cared for in some shared childcare arrangement, including 22.3 percent in nursery schools or kindergartens, 5.8 percent in day care centres, 18.6 percent in their own homes by somebody other than a parent and 18.6 percent in another home (computed from Statistics Canada, 1982, p. 16 + 1). Shared arrangement figures add up to more than 52.2 percent, since children may experience more than one type of shared child-care arrangement (Eichler, 1983, p. 249).

Those parents in Britain whose children go to nurseries, nursery schools and play-groups are not only interested in day care so that they can work. Quotations from interviews with mothers carried out by the Thomas Coram

Research Unit show the range of reasons for wanting out-of-home group care.

> 'While Ben (aged $3\frac{1}{4}$ years) is at nursery, I go shopping, do housework. I think of it as a time to do all my jobs in the morning so that I can take him into the park in the afternoon ... I've benefited from having a couple of hours on my own. I'd certainly be more grumpy having to get through my housework with them around.'

> '... The children are so restricted here; we've no garden. I'm such a worrier I won't even let the big one go across the square. If I had the children on top of me all day, I don't think I would have coped ...'

> 'I find toddlers very boring and exhausting. Even if I didn't work I'd like Emma (aged $3\frac{1}{2}$ years) to have gone ...' (Hughes, *et al.*, 1980, p. 12).

> 'We get on better. Alan's less dependent. Before, everything was Mummy – now he seems to get on better with my husband, he shares us ...'

> 'We form a better relationship. When they've been away from you, you've both got more to talk about ...'

> 'John's made new friends, copes with different kids, relates to girls more, he's much more sociable. He also knows more about shapes and puzzles and his vocabulary has improved dramatically. It's a lovely little oasis in the middle of the city. He likes sand-pits and pools and to run about in the big garden ...'

> 'I felt I couldn't offer Neil enough. Living (in a second-floor flat) is very restricting. He enjoys going, talks about it happily and openly and is never reluctant to go. He's got a lot of energy and having the garden at nursery is very important – he can slosh around in puddles and mud. They can offer him far more than I can ...' (ibid., pp. 36–7).

Hughes and his co-authors sum up the potential benefits of nursery attendance:

> ... Parents ... value the opportunities for their children to mix, play, explore, and become independent. Many believe their children can benefit in these ways from a very early age, often well before the officially recommended age of 3. The great majority of children also appreciate the opportunities for play and companionship offered by nurseries: like the children described earlier they enjoy going and are often disappointed when they can't go at weekends or holidays. This is of course a crucial point: whatever else children get from attending nurseries, they should at least get pleasure and enjoyment from going (ibid., p. 40).

Several surveys have shown that the majority of mothers of pre-school children want some form of out-of-home care for their children. In Britain, not only is little such care available, but much of what is available is of such a low standard that mothers with any choice often reject it. This may not mean that they feel that their exclusive care is best for their child, only that they feel it is better than the poor quality out-of-home care offered them. A survey conducted by Bone for the OPCS found that only two-thirds of the sample of mothers of under-fives wanted 'day provision' (Bone, 1977, p. 15). She defined 'day provision' as what was currently available, so her figure is probably an underestimate of the unmet need.

Another clue to the extent of this unmet need lies in the way in which so many mothers with pre-school children make informal arrangements to share a small part of their child care responsibilities with others outside the home. These arrangements between women are very valuable ways of reducing the isolation from which mothers and children suffer, but they cannot compensate for the lack of public support and facilities. Through 'swaps' children gain new, familiar, safe second homes, new friends, the experience of another family culture. The mothers get a breathing space. But those who see these arrangements as better than more formal ones (like play-groups, nurseries and schools) probably do not understand how much work goes into setting them up and keeping them going. All the administration, negotiation and cost is borne by the mothers, instead of by public agencies. The trouble is that just when mothers and children most need the respite such 'swaps' can give, in times of illness and family crisis, they tend to fail. If a mother has a new baby or the parents split up, the mother may lose her swap, or the relationship may become one-sided because she cannot do her share. The continuity of care for the child is always more precarious than in formal arrangements. For many children, play-groups and nurseries represent another secure environment that can become a life-line in times of family crisis.

Some countries do see a potential value in group care for little ones. The authors of the international Organization for Economic Co-operation and Development's (OECD) report mentioned above write:

A new awareness of children, whether it be on the part of the society in general or within the family, is developing ... this awareness explains the attention given to children's education that is to be found at all levels of society. Nowadays, sending children to school at the age of six no longer seems enough, and there is general acceptance that learning begins long before this age. This belief combined with other factors favouring pre-school (mothers in the workforce, desire for peer relationships) have resulted in an increased nursery attendance ... today more and more levels of the population are becoming aware of the importance of the education of young children and want appropriate forms of preschool facilities to be provided for their own (1982, p. 26).

We cannot add British figures to Table 1 since no statistics are even collected about the numbers. Blatchford (CERI, 1982, p. 7) estimated that in 1978 less than 10 per cent of the under three-year-olds were in day nurseries or play-groups. We do know very few are in group care because so few nursery places are provided, and hardly any play-groups will take under-threes.

TABLE 1: *Where the Young Children Are* (1975)

COUNTRY	NUMBER OF UNDER-3S (MILLIONS)	ATTENDING CENTRES (NURSERIES) (%)	IN FAMILY DAY CARE (CHILD-MINDERS) (%)	TOTAL % OF UNDER-3's IN DAY CARE	CHILDREN AGED 3–6 IN PRE-SCHOOL (%)
Sweden	0.323	7	16	23	28
France	2.5	11	20	31	95 +
GDR	0.532	50	0	50	85
Hungary	0.519	12	–	12	78
FDR	1.8	(4)*	(5)*	3	75 +
USA	9.4	3–4	7	10–11	64

*These are the percentages of children under three with working mothers, who go to nurseries or child minders. The figures are probably underestimates.

Adapted from: Kamerman and Kahn, 1981, p. 86

In Belgium, in contrast with the UK, over a quarter of under-threes, in 1979–80, attended pre-school education and, even more significantly, 94 per cent of three- to four-year-olds and 99 per cent of four- to five-year-olds were in some kind of school. Of the OECD countries surveyed in 1976, Britain had one of the lowest rates of pre-school *educational* attendance (CERI, op. cit., p. 227). Belgium's is the highest for three- to six-year-olds (98.9 per cent), followed by the Netherlands (95 per cent) and France (93 per cent). Denmark and Sweden, with rates of attendance of 43 per cent and 22 per cent, are the only two countries surveyed that provide for less than half the age group (and this is partly because they have so much crèche provision). Even the USA claims a rate of pre-school educational attendance of 45 per cent. All these figures cover full- and part-time attendance at public or private schools, none of them compulsory. But even if Britain included in its statistics compulsory attendance at primary school for five-year-olds and part-time attendance at play-groups (classified as private school), it would remain unusual in its limited offering of pre-school facilities.

Van der Eyken describes (1982, pp. 1–5) a way of life for young children in Belgium:

> In May 1980, the city of Antwerp celebrated the centenary of the opening of its first municipal nursery school ... Jan, a three-year-old resident of one of Antwerp's suburbs, comes to his own *kleuterschool* with his father at quarter to nine in the morning ... At lunch-time, Jan's mother comes to fetch him home for his mid-day meal. In this school, three-quarters of the children attend only part-time. Some stay at the school for lunch, others do not. The school is designed for maximum flexibility on the part of the family. Children can stay all day, from seven in the morning until six at night if the parents are both working. Or they can come just for the morning session, or stay for both sessions but go home in the middle of the day. There is even, within the school itself, a quite separate ... day centre run and staffed by a different government agency, where children from the age of 18 months to three years are catered for on a sliding-scale charge to parents ... It is, of course, not only ... the 'extended hours', nor the lack of payment for education, which help working families. On Wednesday afternoons, when most *kleuterschools* are closed, there are play sessions supervised by helpers to care for the children whose parents are not at home, and during the three major school holiday periods, play schemes operate within the schools to cater for these families.

This extensive provision enables the family to adjust to new circumstances without affecting the education of its children. As one father explained it:

'My wife does not go out to work at the moment, but she brings the children to school, fetches them at lunch-time, makes them lunch, brings them back again in the afternoon and then fetches them again at four o'clock. She is very busy! It's good for her to be able to get on with her housework and shopping during the day, so that she can give the children her full attention when they come home. We live in a small apartment, and there isn't much room for the children to play, so they're very much better off here. Anyway, they love coming here – we wouldn't be able to keep them away. But perhaps my wife will decide to get a job, and she is free to make that decision if she wants, without worrying about what will happen to the children ... '

A daily life like Jan's is very unusual for pre-school children in Britain, but not in other countries. Yet, as Jan's father makes clear, life is not so different for mothers. Mothers are still primarily responsible for child care and intimately involved with organizing it. The care itself is modelled on a notion of good 'parental care', but all the workers are women. Van der Eyken's claim only a paragraph later that the aim of such provision is to free family life from 'oppressive role stereotyping' is clearly implausible. Children's daily experiences can be improved by early childhood education even when the division of labour in the family is not altered one iota.

NON-MATERNAL CARE AT HOME

Access to good non-maternal care is partly a matter of class and income. There is very little direct British evidence but, in France, social class is a very important influence on a child's experiences. For instance, the percentage of children with no pre-schooling increases as one goes down the 'socio-occupational' categories (CERI, 1982, Table 11, p. 83). In Britain play-groups, private nurseries and nursery schools tend to be in middle-class areas (and, except for play-groups, to charge far higher rates than child minders). State day nurseries are not available for most mothers. State nursery schools, which often *are* in working-class areas (as a result of previous policies), have no catchment areas, and so take middle-class children from some distance away. As for non-maternal care at home, most evidence for Britain, Canada and the USA suggests that middle-class working mothers rely on nannies, housekeepers, maids or au pairs, whereas working-class working mothers are more likely to use relatives, neighbours and child minders (Eichler, 1983; Johnson and Dineen, 1981). So that even if the care children receive *at home* is by an individual, and there-fore theoretically on the maternal model, what this is like for the children can vary enormously – what a difference between Gran and the French au pair!

The turnover of au pairs and nannies, be they English or foreign, is extremely rapid. Nowadays most nannies are young women who see the job as a stepping stone to marriage and their own families. The lack of job security and the changing demands from the employing family also make movement likely. One woman wrote:

In the nine years that I have had living-in help, I have had nine nannies, which sounds neat but actually doesn't work out at one a year. Some have stayed three years and have since become family friends and surrogate aunts; some stayed three weeks; some have been treasures; some have been trials and a couple were straight liabilities (Arnold, 1983, p. 27).

Whereas the working-class parents who send their children to child minders entrust them to other 'family worlds', middle-class parents who use nannies try to ensure that their child's day is much as it would be if the parents were caring for the child themselves. Whether or not she is a 'mother's help' and does some housework, her function is to serve the family's needs – she is more like a servant than a child minder.

On the face of it, to find a girl who will fit in with your routine, your household and, above all, yourself – your quirks, your moods – is tantamount to netting the Holy Grail ... There is no hard and fast rule about finding a good nanny. It is a matter of luck. I have had qualified nannies who will waive the official rules of *only* undertaking housework directly related to their charges (ironing your husband's shirts does not come into this category) and I have had qualified girls who let the baby play with the oven cleaner ... (ibid.).

If you employ a nanny, she will want to know how you manage the children, what standards of behaviour you expect and whether to smack the child or punish him or her in some other way. This means that the nanny, who is almost always young, often in her teens, becomes for the child both a loved person and also someone who is subordinate to the parents. The child sees the nanny as like herself, but with an important difference: the child belongs in the family and the nanny does not. This contradiction can be difficult for the little one to handle. So are the changes of personnel – last month Jenny, this month Karen. These sudden changes are likely to coincide with family events like a move or the birth of a new baby, and are crises in themselves for the little ones. Children's days with nanny are reliable in some ways. The child is on home ground and is aware of the mother's stamp on the daily routine. The nanny only has to be shared with brother and sister, just like the mother, and in some ways the relationship may be very similar. But the child has been protected from the threat of the world outside home, only to be faced, in many cases, with another threat – loss and change.

FAMILY DAY CARE

Childminders form the largest single group of all homeworkers and in March 1975, 29,469 registered childminders provided full-time and part-time care for 85,616 children. It is further variously estimated that between 100,000 and 500,000 additional children are with unregistered childminders ... it is obvious that childminding has expanded to fill the yawning gap left by inadequate provision of state day-care services (TUC Working Party, 1977, p. 37).

Child minding is done at home, but the child is not at home. As a result mothers have far less control over the way in which child minders care for their children. This often mirrors the lack of control working-class mothers have over other aspects of their lives. They feel like customers rather than employers of their child minders, and would not dream of telling her how to feed or potty train, or how to discipline their children, even when they are profoundly uneasy about it.

Proponents of informal, private day-care arrangements often describe it as care by neighbours or trusted friends. In reality, most of the in-home care arrangements are made between strangers – parents and caregivers who make contact with one another by advertisements on notice boards, in supermarkets, in laundromats, advertisements in daily newspapers, or by referrals from acquaintances ... How can parents who use classified advertisements to find sitters be certain that they are hiring qualified persons (Johnson and Dineen, op. cit., p. 35)?

There is no basis for discussion. The mother either puts up with it or takes her child away. One mother quoted in the Jacksons' book *Childminder* said:

'I thought she was OK at first. The house was quite neat. I paid her £4 per week. There were about 5 other children there so she wasn't doing too badly. It used to worry me sometimes that Sharon cried so whenever I got near her house. But I thought it was because she didn't want to leave me. Well, one day she came home with this awful mark on her face. At first you couldn't tell what had done it but next morning you could see it was a cigarette burn. I went straight round with her ...'

Mary gave up work for a short while after this incident (Jackson and Jackson, 1981, p. 106).

Other mothers do not have that option.

Phyllis describes mornings when, at 5 o'clock she's stood on a minder's doorstep with Tommy in her arms, trying to wake her.

'I've been that scared. Not wanting to ring in case she'd be cross and not take Tommy in. And there was my bus going in 5 minutes. That was always happening' (ibid., p. 104).

Another time, faced with a minder suddenly giving up, the same woman explained that she could not tell her employers the truth and take the day off because 'she'd have lost her job altogether if she'd told them she has a child under five that she couldn't cope with' (ibid., p. 105).

The mother who uses a child minder is in a weaker position both in relation to her and, usually, in her own job than the mother who can afford a nanny. Of course, this need not mean that the minder's care will be less good than a nanny's.

In many other countries this private system of day care is more organized. In Australia, child minding is known as 'family day care', and federal funding has meant a decade of rapid expansion. Yet the individual women have not received 'wages commensurate with out-of-home employment' but rather 'payment for a woman who was primarily a housewife and mother' (Davis, 1983, p. 83). In the USA, family day care is also growing rapidly.

Family day care is legally defined as the care of up to six children (including the provider's own) in a private residence during all or part of the day. There is a big difference between being a babysitter and providing family day care. Babysitters might take care of a child for a few hours while his parents are away. But a person who cares for children on a regular basis in her own home, either part- or full-time, for up to five days a week, certainly plays a large part in the development of those children, and deserves to be called something other than a babysitter ... Someone who cares for children unrelated to her in her own home is, in fact, providing a public service (Squibb, 1980, pp. 5–6).

The Australian and American systems of licensing minders also allow formal and informal support in the way of funds and materials.

In one or two local authorities in Britain similar changes are taking place. The child minder is salaried and so is not directly employed by the mother. The agency supports the child minders by offering them such facilities as toddler groups, discussion groups, toy libraries and back-up care in case of illness. It also maintains certain standards of care. But most child minders in Britain have no such support. Registration offers no guarantee of quality since it is chiefly about physical standards the home has to meet. Making someone buy a fireguard does not mean that she will use it. There is some control over the number of children a child minder can look after, although not all authorities enforce their own bylaws. But there is little incentive for child minders to register. Most of them make little or no money:

> Minders in traditional working-class areas, where charges are low, and in immigrant areas, where they can be lowest of all, are often worried lest some official discovers their earnings and then, in some undefined way, harasses, taxes or prosecutes them. This is one of the barriers to their coming forward for registration. But if we looked at minding through business eyes, it is often clear that the financial gain is tiny and that sometimes (when one allows for the heating, light, washing, TV consumption and food required) it represents a net *loss* (Jackson and Jackson, op. cit., p. 169).

The marginal profitability of child minding means that to make it financially worth doing, child minders will be tempted to take more children than they should. Even so, many child minders are loving, responsible and imaginative. If the minder is a good carer, it may be a good thing for the child that she is in charge in her own home. Friendships between mother and minder often develop

> About half (of 63% surveyed) said they saw their minders as friends:
> 'She's a personal friend. She was before Peter went to her.'
> 'She's becoming a friend. I didn't know her at all, gradually got to know her more. She's the sort of person you might invite in for a drink ...'
> (Bryant, Harris and Newton, 1980, p. 131).

In other words, the quality of care offered by child minders varies enormously. It is something of a lottery, but with a clear tendency for the prizes to go to those with a lot going for them already.

What is it like for the children? They may have a very early start. The Jacksons' research team tried to track down unregistered minders. They went into city streets at 5.30 a.m. and saw toddlers and babies being hurried along by parents on their way to work (op. cit., ch. 1). The day is often long. According to Mayall and Petrie (1977, pp. 36–7):

> The children had a long day. 33 out of 40 (82%) spent eight or more hours at the minder's and eight of these spent ten or eleven hours there

... the children seemed to eat enough food,according to the minder's account; the pattern seemed to be a snack in mid-morning, cooked dinner, a snack in mid-to-late afternoon ... Almost all the children had a sleep: minders tended to use this time to do housework, or for resting themselves ... The children typically spent the day indoors, with brief excursions in some cases. The minder's housing is an important factor in the quality of the child's day ... Altogether 26 (out of 39 children) had access to a safe, enclosed outside space. However, some minders are cautious about letting their charges play outside ... The children spent their day in a small space ... crowded with furniture ... often restricted by the minder from running, climbing and investigating; it was after all her dwelling, her carpets, wallpaper and furniture ... The vast majority of outings were to accompany the minder and other children to and from nursery schools, play-groups and primary schools ... Eight had been to a public play-ground or play-group in the last week.

Toys become important if space is limited. Yet only a third of the minders in this survey had a good range.

... minder's pay is atrocious. Out of it they feed the children and provide any treats and expeditions; they have to heat the rooms used by the children and pay for wear and tear to the property and furnishings. It is not surprising if buying and replacing toys and other equipment comes low on the list of priorities (ibid., p. 40).

Child minding continues to be popular, partly because it is cheap and partly because it is considered to be most similar to maternal care at home. But Mayall and Petrie have documented (op. cit., p. 52) clear differences in the relationships between minder and child and mother and child.

It seems, then, that the child does not treat his minder in at all the same way as he treats his mother. He does not touch her as often, nor does he speak to her as much: in fact, in these respects *she is not a substitute mother* for him ... All this suggests that the relationship between many of the minders and the children was a rather distant one. It is not sufficient for a woman to have had children herself to be able to generalize her motherly behaviour towards other people's children ... When a minder's own young children were present it was noticeable that they approached their mother much more frequently than did the minded children ... It seemed to us that, for whatever reason, most of the minders did not avail themselves of the opportunities open to them ... Whether it is desirable for them to become substitute mothers is itself open to question. Perhaps the sort of commitment which many mothers have towards their children is too difficult for a stranger to acquire, and perhaps for some children there would be conflicts arising from such attachment which would be difficult for them. In any case, the natural mother might well be jealous of another person showing such a commitment to her child.

Bryant, Harris and Newton (op. cit., p. 216) came to almost exactly the same conclusions as Mayall and Petrie:

That minding is emotionally the next best thing to being with mum we can see is quite untrue when we look at the large numbers of children who are passive and detached from their minders ... many of the minders do not seem to be particularly warmly involved with the children, and the idea that they provide some kind of compensation for a lack of love from home is just wrong. Indeed the children we knew to have poor relationships with parents very often had the least warm minders, and one might even say that for these children the minder was a substitute *bad* mother, with the pattern of poor relationships between child and parent repeated between child and minder.

Children with their mothers at home lead fairly restricted lives, as do children with child minders. Both women have to do their housework, make meals for the rest of the family and so on, and are unlikely to spend much time concentrating on the children. But we have seen that the relationship children have with their minders is usually less close and stimulating than the one with mother. In our opinion, this is not simply because the children 'belong to the mother'. It is because, like mothers, child minders are isolated, lack support, are unpaid (as well as underpaid) workers and have the extra burden of looking after more pre-school children at once than most mothers do. Yet the women who take up child minding are usually those with least room to manoeuvre. It is seldom an act of choice from a position of strength.

Nannies tend to be under less economic pressure and a different strain. There is *no* research into children's lives with modern nannies. Care by nannies and child minders has both been compared with maternal care, but we can see that this is a gross over-simplification. The individual care that mothers, nannies and minders all give is only one aspect of these complex relationships.

OUT-OF-HOME GROUP CARE

What is out-of-home group care like for babies, toddlers and pre-school children? Although few little ones in Britain have the possibility of that experience, as we have seen in Table I, group care is not unusual for young children in many other countries. Penelope Leach believes that babies should be at home with their mothers.

> A baby who does not have anybody special, but is cared for by many well-meaning strangers in turn, or one who is cared for sketchily and without concentration, sharing his caretaker with other needful small people, is like an adult who moves from country to country, knowing the language of none. Baby and adult must rely on the universal language of gross gesture and tolerate high levels of isolation and low levels of understanding. Neither can develop any subtlety of communication nor certainty as to whether or why things have been understood or have taken place (Leach, op. cit., p. 60).

A little examination shows how unthinking this is. First, babies in nurseries *do* have special people: their families *and* their carers in the nursery. As we shall see in Chapter 10, attachment to parents is not changed by the daily experience of nursery care. The nursery staff are *not* strangers because the babies get to know them through their daily contact. 'Bobs' or 'Miss Bobs' – whose real name was Forbes – became a household name for many parents of little ones at the Bristol University nursery: she was clearly significant to them despite their early inept attempts at language. Sylvia, the new deputy supervisor, is the most wanted guest nowadays in the children's homes: 'Can Sylvia come and have breakfast tomorrow because she loves porridge?' 'Can Sylvia come to tea and watch our TV?' are familiar questions. Nurseries usually organize their care so that the babies have their own special carers, either within a baby room or in 'family groups'. The ratio for nursery staff to under-two-year-olds has to be at least 1:3, which in practice is comparable with home situations, since most mothers have more than one child. Nursery staff will not wilfully care for children 'sketchily and without concentration'. Certainly this *may* happen, but it also may happen at home, just as children at home also have to learn to share their mothers or minders with other children.

Leach goes on:

> Many toddlers are already in some form of group-care, part- or full-time, and if bureaucracy ever puts institutions where its red tape is, thousands

more will be. I neither believe group-admission is right for toddlers or the groups they are admitted to, nor that this is the only solution for their mothers ...

The toddler is not ready to share his mother's attention with strange children and he hates her to get involved with strange adults. He will fight to keep her to himself and if he cannot he will want to leave ... It is in the vital area of language development that the two-way damage done by groups to toddlers, but also by toddlers to groups, is often most clearly seen. The toddler's language will not progress as fast as it could (and therefore should) if he is expected to manage without constant adult conversation (op. cit., p. 80).

It may have been Leach's personal experience that her toddlers could not bear to share her – ours is quite different. We find that 'strange' children and adults do not remain strange for long. Our toddlers have become very fond of the other children with whom they have been looked after. They do not usually mind us cuddling their friends, including friends whom we look after regularly. What they cannot bear is for us to pay more attention to another sibling. No sooner does Toby choose his bedtime story than Charlotte storms out of the room; no sooner does Anna climb on to Caroline's lap than Debbie tries to push her off. Yet Leach does not mention this everyday painful side of mother–children relationships.

In her points about language development, Leach is misreading the evidence. Little careful research has been done on the developmental differences between toddlers at home and in group care. Most of the work is American and has used children from disadvantaged homes in University-provided day care. But in one study on 'non-disadvantaged' children, Rubinstein and Howes matched a sample of home-reared and day care eighteen-month-olds, and followed them up at four years. Their findings are much more equivocal than Leach's; indeed, if anything, they found language and play development were higher in the day care children than the home-reared children.

In fact, they suggest that day care, in several ways, may be a more enriching experience for young toddlers than being constantly at home with mother. For example:

Mothers may need to exercise more control than do centre caregivers because more objects are present that are not suitable for infant play. However, mothers tend to impose more control than do centre caregivers where control is optional, for example, in suggesting how the infant should play with his or her peer. Our speculation is that in the isolated setting of the home the infant makes more social demands of the caregiver than he or she does in the centres; the infant's needs compete with the needs of the household and with the mother's needs for adult social contact. *Longer hours of exclusive responsibility for infant care* in this context *contribute to maternal irritation and restrictiveness* (our emphasis) (Rubinstein and Howes, 1979, p. 20).

Most important, they find that language development is as highly developed amongst the day care children as the home-reared children. Their follow-up study of the children at $3\frac{1}{2}$–4-years-old showed that 'day care children had significantly more complex speech and day care mothers used more complex speech to their children ...' (Rubinstein, Howes and Boyle, 1981, p. 217). Rubinstein and Howes (1979, p. 19) feel that

infant care is more pleasurable for both infants and caregivers in a social rather than isolated context. In day care adults had the company of other adults, and infants had the company of other children. Thus, the infants enjoyed the social stimulation of other toddlers who relieved the adult of the burden of being the sole sources of social contact for the infant.

The positive benefits of social care have to be weighed against the risk of staff turnover. Adults are not the only important people in children's lives. Nurseries usually have lots of play space, indoors and out, exciting big equipment that most families could not afford, let alone house. They can allow daily use of sand, water, paints, play-dough – all the materials which seem to involve far more time to prepare and clear away for one or two children at home than the five minutes or so that they are actually played with. Nurseries stretch children's imagination and develop their physical skills and musical potential.

Nurseries vary in their capacity to do this. Private nurseries differ in philosophy, while local-authority nurseries start off with a massive disadvantage. After the Second World War, state nurseries in Britain were reserved for 'children whose mothers are constrained by individual circumstances to go out to work or whose home conditions are themselves unsatisfactory from the health point of view or whose mothers are incapable for some good reason of undertaking the full care of their children' (Ministries of Health and Education joint policy statement, 1945; quoted in Garland and White, 1980, p. 4). The conditions of entry are even more narrow now and, with honourable exceptions, they are poor nurseries for poor children.

Some of the potential advantages of day nurseries are converted into their opposites. Concentrating children from 'vulnerable families' does not tend to further their development. In family centres 'inadequate' mothers, instead of being relieved of some of their responsibilities, are invited to learn how to look after and play with their children. This still leaves untouched the problem of segregation and the poverty underlying family strain.

Children in day nurseries typically have a shorter day away from home than children who go to child minders. Their day is more likely to be between six and eight hours compared with eight to ten hours at a child minder's. Of course many children go for shorter (part-time) periods in both forms of day care. Nursery schools' interpretation of full- and part-time attendance is different again because it is not linked to concepts of the working day (except in those few places which have 'extended hours' specifically to meet the needs of working mothers). Part-time nursery schooling, which is the norm for three-year-olds, is usually for only $2\frac{1}{2}$ hours, and the full day is $6\frac{1}{2}$ hours. Many children whose mothers are working will be involved in after-school or before-school informal private arrangements.

Nursery schools have a completely different history from day nurseries. Their stated aim has always been to develop children's potential, rather than to replace their mothers as carers. This has led to 'the familiar dichotomy between day nurseries as a necessary evil and nursery schools as a positive opportunity' (Clarke-Stewart, 1982, p. 42). This dichotomy is an offshoot of the artificial split between 'care' and 'education', solidified by social policy, which now worms its way into all our minds. The split has now been taken right into nurseries and nursery schools themselves, since the former employ teachers and the latter nursery nurses. The combination has caused all sorts of problems. Nursery nurses cannot be expected to work contentedly alongside nursery teachers whose actual work overlaps considerably with theirs, but whose pay and conditions reflect the superior status given to 'education' over 'care'. Garland and White conclude by criticizing nurseries for having educational goals; yet what they think inappropriate for two- to five-year-olds in a day nursery is the essence of the nursery school. The children who are in day nurseries are not likely to have different needs from those in nursery schools. It is quite often absurd that these two sorts of daily care should be kept separate and that one should be valued so much more highly.

The artificiality of the split between 'care' and 'education' can be clearly seen in a lot of what's written about how to treat children in nursery schools. Education is seen as something separate from life: as a very special skill that needs to be taught to the educators. One research team used tape-recordings of conversations between adults and children in nursery schools and play-groups. It concluded that we should talk to a child in certain ways in order to 'see him [sic] at his linguistically most active' (Wood et al., 1980, p. 81). Some workers who were tape-recorded tended to ask children a series of questions and would receive short monosyllabic replies, and often ruin the game into the bargain. Open questions, on the other hand, such as 'Where are you going for your holidays?' and contributions from the adult herself like 'I can't stand washing up', resulted in much more lively and interesting conversations. The authors conclude that 'the task of getting young children active in conversation' is best carried out by giving children more chance to control what is said. If we forgot about trying to 'teach' children and related to them as people (in the course of a 'caring' relationship), we would do this anyway.

Whatever advice books give nursery teachers, many of them *do* relate to children as 'whole people', not just as subjects to be taught. Like all carers of young children, nursery teachers model themselves on ideal mothers, this time primarily on mother-as-educator. As with nursery workers, the limits to this are inherent in the situation. The motherly role has to be fairly general and managerial with a class of twenty and only one assistant. Because they model themselves on mother-as-educator, the conflicts are not as difficult for teachers as for nursery workers.

What is it like for children in nursery school? This account is based upon our own observations of our children in a nursery class, once they had settled in.

Sally bursts into the nursery school shrugging her coat off as she comes, already calling out to a friend spotted over the partition. The day starts with 'free play', which includes, today, finger painting, or collage. Sally glances round with a practised eye, notes what jigsaws and games are out on the low tables, who is playing with what. The teacher's assistant greets her, and invites her to start off with a painting. The room is full of busy children, already moving from one activity to another. They are operating according to rules that they do not usually find oppressive, perhaps because they have been presented as conventions to make social life more enjoyable. Sally in fact refuses to wear an apron to paint, and the teachers tolerate this although they often bring the subject up in an offhand way. Sally finishes her painting, takes it to the teacher to have her name written on it, receives her due praise and hangs it on the clothes horse to dry. She joins some friends who are constructing a tower of Lego bricks. The teacher, passing by, shows them how to strengthen the tower by laying the bricks in alternate directions. An hour and a half and several games and puzzles later, Sally is drinking milk with others around a small table in the kitchen. She spills it, and several children jump out of the way of the threatening stream. The nursery nurse tut-tuts and says, 'Now don't do that again, or that's your lot,' as she refills the cup. Milk is drunk in shifts, and as each group of children finish they go outside. The lid is off the big sandpit and the bikes and cars are out. Sally wants a car, but a little boy has it. She asks if he will let her have it. He ignores her, keeping off to a safe distance. She asks the teacher, who promises she shall have it once he has had a fair turn, and goes to be a monkey with another group on the climbing frame ... They go in for the story. The children all sit cross-legged around the teacher in the book corner, while the other staff clear up and prepare the room for lunch. She reads to them, when she has enough quiet for them all to hear. Sally is told off for sprawling and kicking another child. Later, she sings 'Miss Polly had a Dolly'. The teacher tries to be responsive and considerate to individuals who chip in with their own contributions, yet has to limit the attention each can have so as to avoid losing the others. In the middle of 'news time' Sally needs to go to the toilet. She puts her hand up, and is taken by the assistant who wipes her bottom and chats to her while she washes her hands. As eleven thirty approaches the teacher asks, 'Who can sit nicely? Who is best today, boys or girls?' The girls win, and those of them who are going home are shepherded into the cloakroom and helped to dress in outdoor clothes by the assistant, who releases them to the waiting mothers before doing the same for the boys. Meanwhile the teacher is playing a game of 'Simon Says' with the full-time children. At twelve they have lunch, with an adult at each table of six. The children take turns to serve the lunches and to clear away, and are heavily encouraged to eat at least some of the food they like least. The afternoon programme is much like the morning, but, during the long play before the afternoon part-time children arrive, the teacher takes the chance to chat with each of the full-time children or takes a small group of them into another room for some special project.

Physically, nursery schools are like day nurseries. They score over private homes in terms of play space, equipment, toys and materials. Despite the formality of the aims, the programme is seldom very formal, so that the main source of difference between them and nurseries is the different training of their chief staff and the narrower age-range.

Like nursery schools, play-groups are seen as opportunities for children rather than necessities for parents.

Playgroups began in Britain as a middle-class response to the lack of nursery school places ... one woman ... wrote a letter to the *Guardian* suggesting that mothers could get together and provide their own substitutes, until ... the Government could be persuaded to increase state funding. Initially such groups flourished in suburban and similar areas, although by the mid-seventies, people associated with the playgroup movement were claiming that they had moved well beyond their middle-class origins, and the PPA now promotes the 'community' playgroup as a permanent and distinctive form of provision, not as a temporary, substitute nursery (Finch, 1984a, p. 3).

What makes PPA play-groups distinctive is their emphasis on parental involvement. Mothers are expected to work on a rota assisting the play-group leader, which of course means that working mothers find it almost impossible to use them. As Janet Finch says: '... setting up and running a voluntary organization historically is an activity strongly associated with the middle classes' (ibid.). Play-groups do exist in working-class areas, some run on the approved self-help model and some 'provided' by community associations and other agencies. These play-groups are often used as part of day care so that the children involved, like many nursery-school children, experience complex, interlocking daily arrangements.

We have been comparing professionals to mothers. PPA play-groups actually take pride in being staffed by 'ordinary mums' although, since the staff cannot actually be mothers to all the children and are actually often mothers of schoolchildren (just like nursery teachers!), it is doubtful whether this has any relevance for the children. The actual content of the play-group session varies along lines similar to nurseries and nursery schools. The play-group is likely to be smaller-scale and to feel more improvised. From the child's point of view it is likely to be more like a pleasant place to visit regularly (rarely every day) than an extra secure territory, partly of course because the room is often used for other purposes on other days, and the equipment has to be cleared away at the end of each session.

Play-groups are the most common form of pre-school provision: most children's first experience of out-of-home care and, for many, the only one they have before primary school. One play-group leader in an inner-city area told us:

> There's plenty of nursery school provision in our area but I see our play-group as doing something the nursery school can't do. We're a much smaller group and more able to cope with a wide ability range. We can allow children who aren't ready to sit still all through the storytime to get up and do their own thing – often the mother who's helping out will keep an eye on them.

Play-groups only work for families who conform to the PPA philosophy which assumes a full-time mother at home. She will take her young child(ren) to mother-and-toddler groups a couple of times a week as an antidote to feelings of isolation, until the child is 'ready' at age three for transition to play-group, perhaps twice a week, and three or four times a week at age four. The aim is to ease the transition from home to school in gentle steps. In fact, from the child's point of view these steps may be too gentle and not sufficient preparation for school bustle.

PROPER SCHOOL DAYS

During their pre-school years, children are ideally supposed to be looked after by their mothers. As we've seen, this common assumption permeates the pre-school care itself so that the workers (whether they are teachers, nurses or play-group leaders) feel obliged to model themselves on some aspect of a preconceived notion of mothering. Once children start compulsory schooling they are all in the same situation at last, and the notion of substituting for mothers gives way to the milder idea of compensating for a 'deprived' family situation or complementing a 'good' one. Schoolteachers still consciously 'mother' to some extent. It is no accident that almost all infant teachers are women, and so are heads of separate infant schools, whereas the head of a primary school (incorporating juniors and infants) is more likely to be a man.

In a perceptive study of American inner-city elementary schools, Lightfoot describes (1977) how a teacher becomes 'the other woman' in a child's early schooldays. Because schools are defined as places where children are 'educated', it is easy to forget that for at least $6\frac{1}{2}$ hours a day, five days a week, 39 weeks a year, children are 'cared for', more or less well, in schools. Even for children who are used to full-time out-of-home care, school is the biggest, most complex, noisiest place they have ever encountered. Much of the child's first year is spent learning the rules:

'You have to shut the toilet door when you are weeing, at school. I don't know why ...' said one puzzled four-year-old.

'You are not allowed to take your own play things to school. You have to put them in a box in the corner ...' said another.

'Miss Brown won't choose children who shout out to be a leader. She chooses ones who sit up straight, nicely with their fingers on their lips.'

'Paper towels are all made from trees so we're very lucky to have them so we mustn't scrumble in the middle of the floor ...'

Children who stay to dinner have to cope with an hour-long playtime in an enormous playground with perhaps a hundred other children and minimal supervision. Compared with all their previous experience they are really on their own. The rules that they have to learn are not just those of the school and adults but the ones which govern the intimate negotiations between other schoolchildren themselves. We're amazed at the speed with which four- and five-year-olds become acclimatized to the foreign country of the school. For all of them there can be a joy and liberation in discovering new territory for themselves alone, and this is certainly one reason why new schoolchildren often refuse to share their experiences with their mothers: 'It's a secret.'

The rules of the classroom and playground are only the superficial expressions of deeper principles, which the children gradually grasp, although they will already have met some of them in their pre-school years. Some of these principles are:

'Children are subordinate to adults.

'Children progress up an age hierarchy in yearly steps, becoming more capable and responsible as they go.

Boys and girls are profoundly different, and so are men and women.

'Work is different from play. It's less fun but more praiseworthy.

'In order to be good at something you have to be better than your age-mates.

'White middle-class Christian culture is normal and best.'

The modern 'child-centred' approach to primary education is actually a more efficient way of teaching these principles than an authoritarian approach. These principles are not invented by primary schools, which take them from the wider society. But it is in these years that children come to internalize them and make them their own. Despite this sinister-sounding process, children can be happy. The process continues in secondary schools with a rather different gloss. For a start, children are older and allowed more autonomy by schools, as well as by families. But their autonomy is limited and still constrained by school rules. For example, secondary schools require some school uniform, although they may relax a few of the rules for older pupils. When they break the rules, however apparently informal, they are subject to humiliating discipline. In all sorts of ways – the demeanour expected in the classroom and the corridor, homework, hours of attendance – they learn to accept a lack of self-determination as normal. By a curious contradiction, they also learn, through these processes, that individuality (rather than collectivity) is a hallowed principle.

Individuality is not the same for boys and girls. In secondary schools these differences begin to find more concrete expression. In the curriculum, some subjects are provided specifically to teach girls about family responsibility and child development, such as health education, domestic science or preparation for parenthood. Despite the education provisions of the Sex Discrimination Act 1975, schools proceed, unabashed, to present girls with this maternal fare. Boys, on the other hand, are not usually taught about responsible parenthood, except perhaps through religious education and the odd sex-education class. Other school subjects which are not deliberately segregated have acquired sex stereotypes. On the whole, science subjects, apart from biology, are seen as masculine and the arts as more feminine. In the 'hidden curriculum', too, there are processes at work which reinforce sex difference: for example, teachers' treatment of boys and girls – girls are neat, boys are curious and untidy. Through these various deliberate and unconscious processes, girls learn that one day they will, in all likelihood, become wives and mothers; boys learn that parenthood for them takes second place to the search for work (David, 1984).

This 'learning' is reinforced for those children whose mothers orchestrate such extra-curricular activities as music, swimming and sports; Brownies, Guides, Cubs and Scouts, in many cases acting as unpaid chauffeur. In this way, girls are shown what work is entailed in motherhood and boys what services women provide for them.

A few girls take these lessons to heart whilst still at school and, accidentally or not, themselves become mothers. Their subsequent experiences are not usually very happy. Although they are no longer treated as though they were contaminating and contagious, they are still segregated off from normal schooling into, perhaps, schoolgirl mother units, with day care for their babies attached, or home tuition. They, and other girls, quickly learn the lesson that children should not have children and that, in some mysterious way, they have broken one of the most sacred of school rules.

DAY CARE FOR SCHOOLCHILDREN

Children spend a very large part of their lives in schools, yet the gap between school hours and the conventional 'full-time' working day, between school holidays and work holidays, causes enormous problems for employed mothers. Many mothers 'solve' this problem by working part-time, or in a series of casual jobs given up before the long summer holiday, by leaving their children to fend for themselves at home or in the street, or in the vague care of a neighbour. The children themselves may not mind this too much: 'I been in the house on my own . . . it was nice because I could muck about and steal the chocolate biscuits. I could do anything when my mummy was out,' said one eight-year-old girl we talked to. But city streets are physically dangerous, and the ethos of privatized child care is too widespread to permit reliance on the goodwill of neighbours in most areas. No one knows how many children are regularly left on their own or in the care of eight- to ten-year-olds, without the support they might have in small-scale societies. Our society's priorities (cars over people, property over people, profit over people) make it necessary to gather children together in special places, simply to keep them safe. Out of school hours in the morning and evening and in school holidays, these special places are called play-schemes in Britain, day care or camps in North America.

In Britain, few play-schemes or camps exist. In some countries (such as France, Australia and the USA) most schoolchildren spend at least a part of the summer at camp, either a day camp or a residential one. In the Inner London Education Authority, unusually, about one in every five schools runs a holiday and after-school scheme. The children have to find their own way to the schools used for the purpose, if they go to a different school; and the ILEA is not responsible for what may happen to them on the way. These play-schemes tend to be large-scale and fairly impersonal, although they suit some children who like football, badminton, board games, or just reading after school. A number of other schemes have been set up in the voluntary sector. Some, like most of the Bristol schemes federated in the Bristol Association of Neighbourhood Daycare (BAND), began as self-help schemes. They were set up by lone working parents who coaxed them along from holiday to holiday, leaving their own labour out of the accounts. Most provincial voluntary sector schemes still live from hand to mouth. This affects the children's experience, because of the high turnover of workers (since they are employed on a casual basis and low paid), inadequate premises and not enough toys, equipment or money for trips.

Few schemes are run or even helped by local authorities. This is because play-schemes fall right in the middle of the (literally) man-made gulf between 'care' and 'education'. They cannot be 'care', because Social Services departments abdicate responsibility for the over-fives unless they are judged to be in danger of abuse or neglect. But they cannot be 'education' because they happen *outside* school hours. One play-scheme could not get a health visitor to come and look at the children's heads during an epidemic of headlice because they were neither at home nor at school. Only the voluntary sector, it seems, has the capacity of mind to overlook such an irresponsible mixed marriage.

The result is that after-school and holiday care is not standardized. There is no training for it, except courses in youth work, teaching qualifications, or training for adventure playgrounds. Of course play-schemes do overlap with adventure playgrounds, and often use them. There is a considerable movement for improving facilities for children to play in Britain; and people with this concern, as well as those involved with formal play-schemes, come together in the National Out-of-School Alliance. Some people think that only free 'drop-in' centres and adventure playgrounds can give the children a safe, exciting, out-of-school territory without robbing them of their autonomy and their right to come and go and make friends as they please. Others, less convinced that independence should be valued above physical safety, argue that registered care is essential if there is no responsible adult available at home.

Caroline was involved in setting up a play-scheme and helped with it for several years. Even that single scheme (in Barton Hill, Bristol) has changed over the years, and the differences between schemes are enormous. But the following extracts from an unpublished report written about the scheme in its fourth year give some idea of what it is like. The scheme is housed in a community centre, which has a large room with a small office partitioned off and an enclosed garden for the use of children. Some twenty-five to thirty children use the scheme at any given time in the holidays; a total of forty-five or fifty might be 'on the books', and eight or ten would be collected from their schools and looked after in the late afternoons in term time. The children are of primary-school age, mostly around seven to nine, with one or two four-year-olds from the nursery school. The scheme has been variously staffed, but usually there is one worker attached to the community centre who is still there between holidays, one part-time casual paid worker (usually women, but occasionally men) who may, perhaps, bring a child of her own along, a volunteer or two and perhaps a young trainee from a Manpower Services Commission (MSC) scheme.

We know that children come willingly to the play-scheme, but I have been deliberately considering the possibility that this is because the alternatives are worse. However, the parents reported in three separate surveys that their children enjoyed coming ... some parents actually went into detail about how their children had benefited ... One girl of nine, an only child, was said to have become more sociable and co-operative and to be much happier than she had been alone with her gran, despite the love between them. A boy of five, who had been described by the GP as hyperactive and whose home was very cramped, was also said by his mother to be happier. A boy of nine, whom workers found very difficult and rather disturbed, has a brain-damaged brother with whom he used to quarrel during the holidays. His mother said he was happier since the play-scheme separated the boys for part of the time ...

I interviewed the children myself recently and came away with an impression that they were genuine when they said they liked the play-scheme ... They always mentioned the trips as their favourite thing, but other significant points they made were:

'In the playscheme you can play and muck about and shout and that ...'

'The playleaders are kind ... I really like them, because if you go and ask them if you can get something out they'll let you.'

'Best of all is the inflatable. You fly through the air.'

'I like the trips – we went ice skating. First I couldn't skate. Then these two girls helped me round. I went round a few times and then I could skate. I can skate backwards and it's only the second time we've been.'

'At home you haven't got plasticine and dough and modelling clay and arts and crafts but you have here.'

My inquiries about 'what do you wish was different?' mostly brought comments about the heating, which was inadequate that week as the boiler was faulty.

I have criticized the scheme for being too dependent on trips out, but it's worth mentioning that these frequent trips planned for them, the parties, shows and so on, certainly make the children feel valued ...

One of the children wrote a little piece for the playscheme newsletter:

'I like the playscheme because ... I can paint and draw ... I like the teachers because when I fall down they help me and put a plaster on it to make it better, and I play with my friends ... Sometimes I go out into the garden and play on the swing and in the sand pit where I can build a castle ... I like the running around best. I like to drive the teachers up the wall' (Emma, aged seven).

A ten-year-old whose very talented puppet shows could keep other children attentive for nearly an hour wrote:

'I like the playscheme ... because of the things you can do. When I get there I play snooker or table football, other times I do painting. After orange juice we go into groups. I am in the green weightlifters.'

These children had been asked what they liked about the play-scheme. But a feeling of power to decide how to use the scheme comes through in both pieces, and in observations and conversations with the children. Extracts from the Day Book kept up by staff:

None of the kids were into organization this morning.

But another day:

I began to make animals from tissue paper and twine, encouraging the children to join in which some did gradually. This went down well till everyone was ready for swimming ... we stayed in around 1½ hours. I think one or two non-swimmers are on their way to becoming swimmers.

And a vignette from observation:

It is 11.30. At the moment two boys are in the kitchen baking cakes. One little boy who always eats his lunch early creeps into the quiet room unnoticed, takes his lunch from the shelf and starts eating outside, where about ten children are on the adventure equipment. Suddenly a girl tumbles into the quiet room fighting with two boys. There are mild protests from two trainees. The two girls who were drawing come in to get some sellotape to fix their drawings on the front of exercise books. It is lunch time.

The play-scheme was not highly structured, although various sorts of structure were experimented with at different periods, like dividing the children into 'gang-like' small groups, with their own badges and bases. But on the whole the nature of the play-scheme was determined not only by its (inadequate) resources but also by its role as the complement of school.

We have said that schools *do* care for children as they educate them. The trouble is that because they see their job as education rather than care, they are often emotionally parasitic on homes, failing to provide children with places to relax, with space over which they have control, with concern for particular children's special needs and individual rates of development. Even when the adults are kindly (which they usually are), because they are the agents of a tight bureaucracy, relationships tend to be rather formal and ritualized. Play-schemes, like homes, have to try (especially after school) to provide places where children can flop and be accepted without any need to achieve *and* (especially in school holidays) to stretch the children to enjoy their own capacities and believe in themselves. In some respects they score over homes, especially for some children. On the other hand, they do not offer emotionally intense relationships with adults, and they also cannot allow the child to be really alone. In the play-scheme described above, quiet pursuits always lost against noisy ones. If you wanted to read quietly or to glaze a pot, you were likely to be violently bumped by someone escaping from an enemy or playing fighting games with water in squeezy bottles.

CARE VARIES

We have looked at children's days at home with mothers, with relatives or nannies, in another home with a minder, in nurseries, nursery schools, play-groups, schools and play-schemes. We have drawn out some general points; but on the whole, the most important feature of forms of child care is the variety within each type (including care at home), so that our descriptions can illustrate only one set of possibilities. We have emphasized how far home care falls short of the ideal, not because we are in any sense against homes as places for children to be in, but because this ideal has been used as a stick to beat mothers with, whether they opt to work outside the home or exclusively within it. We have argued that nurseries and other forms of out-of-home care can have advantages for children. We do not pretend that these potential advantages always exist. Nor can we say that, because we support nurseries, nursery schools and play-schemes, we think it is necessarily a good idea for children to spend eight or ten hours a day in these places. Any single form of care may be very good – just what the child needs and enjoys – for some hours; but a time may come when some other form would be better. It is the form of care, and the carers, who tend to get blamed for this. Thus mothers at home are held responsible for under-stimulated children, and nurseries and their workers for children who are sick of sharing. The real blame lies with a rigid society that has defined the normal working day as eight hours long, and has decreed that all other paid work must take priority over the paid and unpaid labour of looking after children.

The lives of children are infinitely varied, whether at home or out-of-home and at school. To pose the question, whether out-of-home care for pre-school children harms them, now seems as absurd as asking whether mothers or schools harm children. It all depends. There are as many kinds of out-of-home care as there are mothers. In the last analysis what is crucial is the particular blend of experiences, not any single one. The one thing that the vast majority of children's lives have in common is that mothers are at the heart of the arrangements. It is almost invariably women's work to care for and educate children, whether at home, in school, at play-group or nursery. The single lesson that we can draw from all this variety is that by itself out-of-home care does not change the nature of the particular gendered work of parents. It merely interrupts it, if anything, to confirm the vitality of motherhood.

PART TWO
PARENTING

PARENTS AND OTHERS

COMMITMENT

Parents are everywhere. Any discussion of child care ... child rearing ... education ... the family ... inevitably includes discussion of what parents do, should do or are failing to do. Countless manuals on child care or children's education include homilies for parents. Schools tell you how to be a successful parent; headteachers demand 'parental help'. Doctors worry about what parents are doing to children. Single people are so overwhelmed with the rhetoric and ideology that they have to excuse themselves by saying that they are not a parent or don't have children. Being a parent, then, signifies a special relationship to children. That relationship endures even in circumstances when family structure has changed. We talk of single-parent families or one-parent families. As Roy Parker (1984, p. 1) puts it:

> Most children are looked after by one or both of their parents. The crucial characteristics of that relationship are threefold. They are:
> (i) the unity of care and responsibility,
> (ii) permanence, and
> (iii) partisan commitment – love.
> These are the cornerstones upon which the care of dependent children has been built. Kinship supplies the rationale. Of course, variations occur in the mixture and in the extent of the characteristics ...

But if we try to understand what we mean by the term 'parent', it quickly becomes difficult not to give it a sex. There is almost no such relationship at present in our society as the parent–child relationship. The responsibilities of being a parent are gendered. As we shall see, being a mother is, in fact, very different from being a father. Indeed, the term 'fathering' a child is only used, in ordinary speech, to refer to the act of procreation. 'Mothering', on the other hand, is about the daily physical and social tasks. These differences are obscured in the word 'parent'. 'Single-parent families' are almost invariably made up of mothers alone rearing their children. 'Parental participation' in schools was a slogan born in the 1960s and is now common to teachers and school administrators. But how often do we hear of fathers helping in the classroom? When one of our husbands volunteered to help take the reception class on a school trip to the American museum, the teacher was rather wary of him. The museum curator was even more surprised – he had assumed this man was either another teacher or the headmaster. After all, shouldn't it be a mother helping out?

Of course, the tasks of being a parent are not rigidly segregated sexually, and more and more of the divisions are slowly changing. In any event, being a parent is both more and less than being a mother or a father. It is not just producing children, or just their daily physical care, or the financial responsibility for their upbringing. To be a parent in the active sense is to accept a long-term commitment to be responsible for your child's welfare. Some such commitment is expected from all those who conceive children and allow them to be born, although just what they are expected to do or to give varies widely. Although in practice there is often a gulf between mothers' and fathers' responsibility for their children, they usually share a basic commitment. It is in this sense that upper-class people 'parent', even if they delegate almost all the child care to others.

'Well I'm very fond of Daddy, but he hasn't time to play,
And I'm very fond of Mummy, but she often goes away,
And I'm often cross with Nanny when she wants to brush
    my hair ...'

complained A. A. Milne's Christopher Robin.

Overall responsibility is more crucial to the definition of a parent than daily care. Together with parents' responsibilities for children go their rights over children. 'Although modern statutes often mention parental rights, powers or duties, the law does not provide us with a neat list of them. There is only a patchwork of legislation and decided cases on particular points' (Hoggett, 1977, p. 5).

Legal relationships between parents and children are different from those between adults. Children are too young to look after themselves, and also too young to make their parents do it. In giving parents so much responsibility and, as we've seen, in most cases little help, society has to allow parents considerable leeway about *how* they bring children up. Parents' legal rights over children's lives are a consequence of the enormous responsibility they carry for the quality of children's lives.

Parental rights have thus largely depended on the degree of practical power which parents enjoy over their children coupled with the extent to which other people or authorities will either recognise or limit that power, while parental responsibilities depend largely on the ability of other people or authorities to oblige the parents to adopt acceptable standards of child care (ibid.).

The law can be used to prevent child abuse, yet '... child abuse is inherent in the discretion that legal rules confer on parents. Child abuse is one end of a continuum starting with the legitimate exercise of parental authority' (Olmesdahl, 1978 p. 253). We have seen that the parent's class has some influence on whether or not official agencies interpret certain treatment of children as child abuse or neglect. In general, the interpretation of parental duties is affected by the class of the parent.

Sharp and Green (1975) list criteria for the good and successful parent: 'The successful parent is the one who is interested in his child's education, and is motivated for his child to succeed' (p. 198). By this criterion, most successful parents are middle class. Working-class parents are often blamed for not having the 'right' attitudes for their children's educational success – although they were not usually given the knowledge or opportunity to form the habits that help the children. Upper-class parents, on the other hand, are not enjoined to help their children succeed. Success is presumed to flow automatically from the accident of their birth. In any case the British system of schooling for upper-class children gives parents no direct role in their education. Boarding schools rely on teachers and parents to agree about what constitutes a good education; and parents delegate their responsibility for their children term by term. Middle-class and working-class parents, whose children go to day schools, have to play a much greater part in encouraging and supporting their children's success and progress through schools; for example, much is made of such parents having to help their children with their homework – constantly demonstrating and redemonstrating their commitment to their children.

Whatever is expected of parents in day-to-day terms, in order to be a good parent they are expected to put their children first. This is a modern Western expectation of parenthood, born of the recognition that our children are the future. It begs a lot of questions about what *is* best for children. And note that it is parents, not society, who are to put children first. Technologically advanced societies are not very child-centred. The conflict of interests that exists between parents and children is not even recognized. Children's needs have been listed by Kellmer Pringle (1980): love, food, security, shelter, new experiences, praise, recognition, responsibility. All of these are adults' needs too. As the Rappaports say:

> Parents who may be able to give up fulfilling their own needs in the early years of parenthood may find it difficult to sustain this year after year … the degree of sacrifice that some parents experience in the present may invest the whole experience with an element of stress that makes it difficult to give emotionally, despite being on hand all the time (Rappaport, Rappaport and Strelitz, 1977, p. 211).

Especially for mothers, but also for fathers, fulfilling children's needs in a society that gives parents overwhelming responsibility for their care and little help and support does mean putting aside the parent's own needs. How easy this is to do depends on all sorts of factors in the parent's own past. If the parent constantly feels he or she never had enough of whatever was going, it is very difficult to live with little children who call for their needs to be fulfilled as naturally as nestlings open their beaks to be filled. 'As much as adults need and cherish children, they also resent and fear them as competitors, replacements and consumers of the limited resources of affection, energy, privacy, space, food and valued materials' (Solnitt, 1978, p. 250). How easy it is to parent also depends on what resources are *really* available at the time. Whatever feelings we bring with us from our own childhoods are easier to cope with if we are not required to make too great a sacrifice in the present.

When people have babies, they rarely think about the commitment they are making. Many people do not even ask themselves if they have the material resources to cope, let alone the psychological ones. They conceive the child by accident, or half on purpose, and think about the pleasure it will be to have someone around who *has to* love them, who will understand them, who will share their pleasures and interests. These thoughts look absurd written down, but probably most parents cherish them sometimes. At most they will think of cots, prams and nappies, sleepless nights, babysitters and money. Their vision will rarely extend to the next twenty years of parenting. Most commitments work best if they are consciously taken after due consideration of available information. When we conceive children we know nothing about them, except that they will need us; we know little about our own reactions. If it is to be our first baby, we may not know what practical difference being a parent will make to our lives. There is no one to advise us . . . we take this step in the dark.

FAMILIES: THE CONTEXT OF PARENTING

Most children are brought up by one or both of their biological parents. At birth, children take their place in a kinship system which has all sorts of symbolic meanings. They are told: 'Your red hair comes from Auntie Susie', 'You've got your dad's temper'. For the parents, their children are 'heir-looms of flesh and blood' (Mount, 1983, p. 255). They are the pledge of the parents' adult status, independent of their own parents. They are also a gift for their own parents: grandchildren. Children allow their parents to re-experience childhood: 'in a sense, one regains the child one once was in one's own child, and one regains the parents that one has lost in becoming a parent oneself' (Rappaport *et al.*, op. cit., p. 29). They also represent a 'second chance' for the parent – 'it's not going to be as bad for you', 'I don't want you to make my mistakes'. If the second chance is missed, the parent feels profoundly disappointed. So children enter a world which has already assigned them a place. This can be reassuring, especially when it means a place in a ready-made extended family who all accept the child by right of kin. But it also means that all sorts of feelings which have nothing to do with the individual child are reactivated by her or his presence.

Genetically children inherit from both the family systems which have been easily or uneasily linked by the parents' sexual relationship. Usually, each family has a stake in the child. The little one's similarity to each 'side' is assessed and negotiated. If the baby is judged to look like his father's father, this somehow strengthens the sense that he belongs to that side of the family – the one from which he gets his name. The baby can become a battleground in the power struggle between the families which often wages in the parents' minds, if not in their living-rooms. Before they can think for themselves, children are bombarded with pseudo-explanations of their looks and behaviour, innocently presented in family anecdotes. It becomes difficult to see who each child really is.

It is considered normal and appropriate for children to be parented by two people, a man and a woman, who have a sexual relationship with each other. This presents more potential for confusion. The two people who depend on each other to fulfil their physical and emotional needs are now jointly responsible for a third one, physically and emotionally enormously demanding. They are likely to get jealous of each other with the child and jealous of the child's success in bidding for their partner's attention. Sexual relationships are not well understood by the participants. We do not usually think rationally about someone whom we love sexually, and now we have to share this person with our children – and share our children with this special person.

To find out who are considered ideal parents we have to look at what happens to people who break the rules, or try to break them. It is very difficult for a lesbian couple to get custody of a child. One woman wrote to a newspaper complaining about an article which had failed to make this point:

> As someone who lost custody of my daughter on the grounds of my lesbian relationship with another woman, I felt angry and hurt that this issue was so lightly passed by in her article ...
>
> Does she realise how punitive the courts are towards lesbians, and that 95% of lesbian mothers who are involved in custody disputes lose their children, often without even subsequent access? And all because we have chosen to have close emotional and physical relationships with other women, and not with men. There is no evidence of our being worse mothers because of our preferences yet the legal system devised and run by men for their benefit punishes us and, yes, breaks us down – through our children ... (*Guardian*, 11 October 1983, p. 10).

Lesbian mothers who live alone are also often denied custody of their own children on the grounds that they are not 'normal' parents; and homosexual men may find it more difficult to get access to their children.

Parents are not only supposed to be a male and female couple, they should also follow traditional sex roles. A woman wrote to the *Guardian* about the assumptions of a divorce court judge:

> I was interested to read that only $4\frac{1}{2}$ per cent of court orders following divorce are for joint custody ...
>
> In my own case, an application for joint custody was refused by the court. The judge delivered a lengthy speech, claiming that joint custody was the prerogative of people who read about their rights in trendy liberal newspapers, and that he had no intention of indulging the whims of the children's father.
>
> After all, since I, as their mother, was the one who wiped their noses and washed their socks, it made sense that I should be totally responsible for decisions concerning their upbringing (loc. cit.).

Adoption is another procedure which indicates the standards parents are supposed to follow. We know an infertile couple who have been trying to adopt a child for a number of years. After numerous social work interviews, they were turned down as unsuitable to parent a child. They are not suitable because the woman has a full-time job, as a lecturer in higher education. To be deemed a suitable parent, to this particular local authority, a woman has to commit herself to give up paid employment for five years. In every other respect this couple fit the middle-class parental model: they have a steady and regular pair of incomes, they have been together for a number of years, and are in their mid-thirties. In an illuminating article, a woman helping a society for mentally handicapped children to recruit foster or adoptive parents explained her own background and experience. The article started, 'Julia Traill first met her daughter, Kirsty, in the ward for newborn babies at the local hospital. But at that time, just over five years ago, Julia wasn't her mother. She was a nursery nurse doing her job – and an onlooker when the baby's parents tragically decided to reject her.' Julia herself then writes:

> Gordon (my husband) was doubtful at first when I went home and suggested we should adopt her. Then he came to see her, fell in love with her – and that was that. It took three months for the paperwork to go through. That was for long-term fostering with a view to adoption. I gave my notice one day and left the next. I must say the hospital was very understanding.
>
> I can't have children and Gordon was over the age for normal adoption. You don't need to be a professional person to look after a Downs child. All you want is a happy secure home (*Bristol Evening Post*, 4 October 1983, p. 25).

A happy, secure home is taken to require a full-time mother, unfettered by the requirements of paid employment.

So the ideal family is supposedly based on a heterosexual union. Children should have a parent of each sex, the argument runs, behaving appropriately to offer good models to their little boys and girls. Nancy Chodorow (1978) has studied the experiences of boys and girls in such families, and the effect on their feelings about men and women. She believes that the nuclear family within which the woman is the main child carer sets the scene for the same pattern in the next generation. She sees these 'ideal' families as essentially conservative.

As babies, both boys and girls have the experience of love and physical unity with their carers, which provides a basis for their own parenting later. But boys' and girls' experiences are also very different. Mothers of girl babies feel them as similar to themselves, are much less aware of their separateness than are mothers of boys.

> When my daughter was born, each time I looked at her I thought she *was* me; I couldn't tell at all that she was different from me. You know that feeling when you look at yourself in a mirror, well it felt something like that. When my son was born that never even crossed my mind. He was different, he was something else (motioning out there and away with her hand). It was completely clear that he was a different person (quoted in Eichenbaum and Orbach, 1982, p. 32).

There is plenty of evidence from observation that boys are encouraged to become separate, to do their own thing, to explore, far more than girls. Girls soon learn that they are like their mothers, and identify with them and with their place in the world. There is evidence that daughters of working mothers are more ambitious and achieve more at school. Boys learn equally soon that they must turn away from womanly things and become like men. This involves to some extent denying their love for their mother and undoing their original identification with her, when they followed her round with a dustpan and brush copying her actions. Chodorow attributes men's relative lack of ease with emotional and personal life to this necessity for them as boys to turn their back on their first love. Both boys and girls are mothered by women, but the effect this has is very different. Boys come to be highly aware of themselves as separate beings, while girls come to feel only fully themselves within relationships, and far less sure of the boundaries between themselves and others.

When they grow up, men can return to their love for women – in the form of a heterosexual relationship. For girls it is both easier and harder. They never have to give up their first love – a woman – in order to grow up approved of as a female. But they have to turn towards their father, and eventually towards other men, to become heterosexual. Women's emotional needs are not usually fully gratified in relationships with men, Chodorow argues, because men '... do not define themselves in relationship and have come to suppress relational capacities and repress relational needs. This prepares them to participate in the ... world of alienated work, but not to fulfil women's need for intimacy and primary relationships' (Chodorow, 1978, p. 207). So while men find reminders of the blissful unity with their mothers in the arms of other women, women find an upside-down way of returning to their mothers by having children themselves. In caring for their own children, they sometimes feel as if they are caring for themselves. Most women feel fully themselves when they are caring for someone, while most men feel more themselves dealing with impersonal things.

Chodorow is summarizing a great range of experience, and inevitably simplifying it. We have simplified her argument further; for us, the important points to stress are that all people, both men and women, are capable of parenting, of caring, of 'mothering'. Various experiences have got in the way of that capacity, most commonly for men. The ability to nurture and to enjoy doing it is most often left undistorted in women. In addition, women often suffer a *disability*: the incapacity to feel themselves as separate beings, outside of caring relationships. The effects of this *dis*-ability are superficially similar to the ability to care for people, but the difference is that *real* nurturing is adjusted to the needs of the cared-for, not the carer. Women are far more likely than men to feel incomplete unless they have children. It is easy to see that if Chodorow is right and the division of labour in the traditional nuclear family has these effects on our adult personalities, then we are likely to reproduce a similar division of labour in our own parenting. Is the ideal family so ideal?

UN-'NATURAL' PARENTS

As we've seen, a sexual relationship between parents is considered normal. The assumption is that men and women who live together have (or should have) a sexual relationship, if they are not too far apart in age, while couples of the same sex who live together should not. A further assumption is made that if a man and a woman do have a sexual relationship and live together, they are an economic unit, pooling all their resources, and the man is responsible for the welfare of the woman's children – in other words, he has become a parent. The ruling about 'living together as man and wife' in supplementary benefits can make it a very short step from a man's sponge-bag hanging up in a woman's bathroom to a new daddy for her children. Many people, especially men, find themselves step-parents for all practical purposes, although the only commitment they wanted to make was to another adult and may not have been a long-term one. Others think long and hard about becoming step-parents.

Even though I had already begun to think quite seriously about somehow living with children, the reason I live with them now is because I fell in love with Harriet, and they came with her. This may sound callous, but it is accurate; I tried, at first, to rationalise it in other ways – to believe I would have chosen to live with these children anyway. It was easy to believe this about Anyika, who was younger, more trusting and easier to love. But the fact is that I had to work hard at developing relationships with the children, since I had fallen in love with their mother, not with them. Many traditional step-parent problems arose: I was tested, struggled against; I inspired jealousy (Downick and Grundberg, 1980, p. 154).

As Rappaport, Rappaport and Strelitz point out, the step-parent is in the impossible position of appearing to replace the irreplaceable (op. cit., Ch. 3). The displaced parent may have a thriving relationship with the child, or may have lost contact – each situation brings problems, probably because there is no model except that of parent for the step-parent to follow. One young divorced woman we know had two young children and married a widower with two young boys. She stayed at home to care for all four children, and in her situation the parental model was obviously appropriate even though difficult, since her ideas about child care differed from her predecessor's. In a day-to-day sense she *had* replaced the boys' dead mother. But the step-parental duties can be less clear. Another friend of ours who has two young children remarked that she sometimes forgets that she has responsibility for four children, not two, since her partner had two children, now in their early twenties, by a previous marriage. Despite her occasional lapses of memory, she feels that her responsibility as a step-parent is '... not just financial or things like that but a commitment to be concerned about them'. The step-parents who do best seem to start by making no assumptions of parental rights, and gradually create their own distinct committed relationships with the children, whom they allow to set the pace.

When an 'incomplete' family becomes 'reconstructed' by marriage and a new nuclear-family household is set up, the family starts to look more like the ideal again. This surface conformity can cover up the lack of any real relationship between the step-parent and the children. The step-parent is catapulted into parenthood without the preparation of pregnancy, and finds an existing set of relationships. Sometimes the results are disastrous, as in those cases where step-fathers abuse the children they were unready to take on and whom they probably feel are rejecting them. Whatever the quality of the relationship, marriage legitimizes it. In contrast, the woman whom we quoted above cannot marry her lover. 'Voices in her head' keep telling her:

'You have no legitimate connection to this child; you are nothing; you
are not a legal guardian; what claim could you ever have to credibility?
What rights do you have? If you do not stay with Harriet, you will have
no relationship with the child; she will be taken away, no matter how
much you love her; you cannot claim any parental rights; two years of
parenting does not make you anything. Who are you anyway? Her father
is the one who has the rights – he is her father after all; nothing can
change that; even though he lived with her for less time than you have,
and it was a long time ago; even though he knows her less, sees her rarely;
he is legitimate; you are nothing; you have no rights; you are nothing; be
prepared; you will lose her if . . .' (Downick and Grundberg, op. cit., p. 155).

Despite all the ambiguities of their situation and the horrible stories of
wicked step-mothers and step-fathers, step-parents' right to have a relationship with children whom they did not conceive is recognized. For most non-
parents it is very difficult to get close to children.

Where did I fit in? I had never really decided not to have children: in fact,
whenever I managed to think about it without pressure or guilt, I rather
liked the idea of teaching a child about the world and watching her grow.
I knew that I did not want to raise a child alone, as a single mother; the
isolation experienced by some of my friends and their anger warned me.
I nursed fantasies of collective households that included children, but
none of the women I was living with seemed to be thinking about it
seriously . . . My solution was to volunteer as a helper in a daycare centre.
I thought that by being around children I would find out if I really liked
them and how much of my awkwardness was simply unfamiliarity.
   All the other volunteers were mothers of children who were in the
centre and they viewed me with suspicion, thinking – quite rightly – that
I knew nothing about children . . . I felt so inadequate that it took me
weeks to learn the names of the children, even after I had developed
favourites and was familiar with all of them . . . (ibid., p. 152).

Because parents are responsible for their children to the point of ownership, they tend to control the children's relationships with other adults. It
is often hard for such an adult to become friendly or involved with a child.
It is much easier for two *adults* to get together, because there is no third party
or intermediary involved, and the two adults can behave as fully autonomous beings. Parents do have reason to be cautious. For one thing, the
increase in urbanization and the business of city and town life have in-

creased the danger for children out alone. Local communities and city councils have not put a high priority on making the streets safe for children. This is one reason why children's relationships with adults are so limited: they cannot go out to meet any. Parents also fear that strange adults who are friendly towards children might have a sexual motive. One of the contributors to *Ourselves and Our Children* (Boston Women's Health Book Collective 1981, p. 130) remembered:

> We live across the street from a large park, and when Rob was seven, he made his own adult 'friend' there. Obviously, talking to that man had real meaning for the child – you could see it in the way he'd walk up, very important and grown-up, to the man's bench, and the way he'd talk about his 'park friend' to us at home.
>
> Wow! What a problem that raised for us. The guy was a merchant seaman who was sometimes drunk, sometimes with really low characters in the neighbourhood. Both Rob's father and I made it a point to talk to the man, to get to know him and – sort of – to make our presence felt, but the whole thing made us very uneasy. Could we allow Rob to go down to the park by himself any more? What were they talking about? Etc.

This letter to a newspaper gives an example of the real danger to children.

> I would like to reply to your correspondence on PIE (Paedophilia Information Exchange) and the right of free speech. Nearly 30 years ago, as an 8-year-old girl, I was the recipient of the affection of a gentleman who would probably now belong to PIE. He was my school-teacher's husband and a respected friend of my parents.
>
> It is true that he did not physically harm me but he enveigled me by subtlety and persuasion into sexual contact with him. Any attempt I made to tell him I did not like it led to gentle pleading: 'Don't you love Uncle?'
>
> The effect this had on me and my sexual development took me many years to get over.
>
> Where children have sexual experiences among their peers, they are all equally equipped to deal with whatever happens. But where an adult seeks to satisfy himself (well, let's be honest, how many members of PIE are women?) with a child, it is his own satisfaction that interests him, not the well-being of the child ...
>
> There is an imbalance of judgment, emotional maturity and plain factual knowledge. The child is far too vulnerable to be considered capable of consent (The *Observer*, 25 September 83, p. 28).

It is significant that the man, who called himself 'Uncle', was a close friend of the family. Just as far more parents than non-parents kill children, so sexual abuse is more likely within the family circle than outside it. The danger to children from more powerful adults is very real, but it stems more from 'normal' conventional attitudes than from the activities of so-called perverts. The 'normality' of child abuse was shockingly expressed by the judge who said that he had considerable sympathy with a man who had sexual intercourse with a friend's seven-year-old daughter, because 'it strikes me as being one of the kind of accidents that could almost happen to anyone' (*The Times*, 17 December 1983).

Stevi Jackson (1982) sums up some of these issues:

> Children are under the ownership and control of particular adults and to an extent they must accept whatever life their 'owners' or parents arrange for them ... The concern to keep sex hidden from children stems from and is sometimes equated with the idea that childhood itself is in need of preservation, so that it is the sexual 'innocence' of children that above all else distinguishes them from adults (pp. 25–8).

But she then goes on to argue that:

> There may, however, be a more immediate and valid reason for our concern to protect children from sex, for in a real sense it is dangerous to them. In our society sexuality has a darker side that is closely connected with violence, aggression and exploitation. The words that name sexual acts and organs are also used as terms of abuse ... This may help to explain adult fears about children and sex, but it hardly makes our behaviour look any more rational. Keeping children in ignorance of sexuality does not protect them; it is more likely to make them more vulnerable. Telling them not to talk to strangers or accept lifts or sweets is not enough to keep them from danger. When children are molested it is usually not by strangers but by neighbours, family friends and relatives, people who have the chance to gain the child's confidence and to be alone with him or her. Even when the molester is a stranger, he can often easily persuade a young child that he is not; children are taught to defer to adults and accept what they say, which renders them powerless in situations that might harm them ... (ibid., pp. 58–9).

Parents are made the guardians of their children's innocence and safety, and this is one reason why non-parents are so often kept away from children ... not the only reason. Many parents would be delighted to find other adults prepared to share in their children's care or simply their interests – but they don't know how. Parenting is so much the model of adult relationships with children that any others are seen as slightly suspect. In addition, because children are seen as recipients of care, parents feel uneasy if their children go to see childless adults whom they cannot 'pay back' for their supposed services. Many people would find it hard to imagine that friendship between adults and unrelated children could be rewarding for the *adult*. Even for parents it can be difficult to have a significant relationship with 'other people's children'. Feelings about the parents can get in the way of clear-cut communication between two separate people. Just because of these obstacles, we always find it exhilarating when we manage to make friends with another child, or our own children take control of a relationship with an adult outside the family.

But parents or step-parents are not the only adults who are allowed to be close to children. There are also the approved relationships of the extended family: uncles and aunts and grandparents, who can often be committed and yet relaxed, free from the daily responsibility. The children lucky enough to get on with these extra people, and to have them available nearby, can use them as alternative resources when the going gets rough with their parents.

Since they are based on kinship, these relationships are vulnerable if the parents split up or get divorced. If the dispute is acrimonious the children may be separated not only from one parent, but also from a set of grandparents and several aunts and uncles. As Wallerstein and Kelly (1980) found in their research:

> Although most of the families had lived several years in the community and maintained stable residence in one place, few resources outside the immediate family were of help to the children during the family crisis. Even within the families, approximately three-quarters of the children were not helped by grandparents, uncles or aunts, many of whom lived in different parts of the country. Some grandparents living close by were very helpful and provided special treats and took children into their homes occasionally. These children appeared to benefit considerably from this special concern and care (p. 43).

Some grandparents have recently begun to demand that they be involved in the divorce settlement, and occasionally grandparents rather than parents get custody of the children. More often, children acquire more than two sets of grandparents, uncles and aunts, giving them the potential benefit of a wide family network.

There is another exception to the general rule that adults other than parents cannot take on a commitment to a child. Yet another vestige of our old kinship system is that of 'godparents', who are still frequently named by Christian families, even by those that do not consider themselves religious. (Boys usually have *two* godfathers and *one* godmother, girls *two* godmothers and *one* godfather.) Being a godparent certainly involves taking a caring concern about the child, but otherwise, godparents' responsibilities are ill-defined. They may be interpreted as spiritual or as everyday or, if necessary, stepping in to become the 'real' parent or guardian in the event of the parents' death. An Australian friend of ours was worried in case her husband, who was of Irish origin but had lived in Australia for over ten years, had been a 'bad' godparent to an Irish godchild. They were en route for Ireland to visit this family and were anxious to make amends.

For those families who do not come from a tradition in which children are given godparents, there may be anxieties about who will look after the children if the parents both die, since parents are so irreplaceable. Miki's cousin started to think in these terms when she moved from South Africa to the USA with her husband and two young children. She and her husband felt they had to find guardians, in the USA, for their children, in case of sudden or unexpected death. The only people they could think of whom they felt were suitable were an old second cousin and his younger wife, who lived over a thousand miles away. He had three young adult children who could take over responsibility, if necessary. Many mothers rearing children on their own are forced to think about who could take over if they died. It can be difficult to think of an appropriate person who would be able and willing to accept the responsibility. Many parents worry about landing a friend with such a commitment and believe no one would choose it freely. They are more likely to choose someone less suitable but who is related to them. Kin are the obvious parent-substitutes in societies which have no way of imagining anyone else wanting to make a permanent 'partisan commitment' to children.

Children with no godparents or extended family have only their parents to turn to. Wallerstein and Kelly (1980) found that, when the parents are splitting up, it is even worse for the children if there are no other committed adults in their lives. Sometimes friends' mothers manage to fill that gap, but this is not common.

Tina was one of the lucky ones: 'Tina was asked four years later what had helped her at the time of the separation. She said: "Other people. My school counselors knew about it, and I adopted my girlfriend's parents. I slept over there as much as possible. My grandparents, also, were very helpful"' (p. 44). They found that the children who did have 'other people' were among those who coped best. It is in an emergency that such lacks become visible. In fact, children's lives would be enriched if they could have committed (and casual) relationships with people other than parents *all the time*.

IN LOCO PARENTIS

Parents are irreplaceable, but their place is constantly being taken by professionals. In some extreme cases children may have to be separated from their parents on a long-term basis. More usually, parents themselves delegate daily care to others such as child minders, nursery nurses, teachers, etc., as well as to babysitters. Most of these people who temporarily replace parents are expected to reproduce parental responsibilities in some way. For schoolteachers, the legal terminology is very explicit if confusing in practice – it is *in loco parentis* (in the place of the parent).

As so often when a Latin phrase is used to name a legal right or duty, the appearance of precision covers confusion of meaning (Shaw, 1981). Legally, *in loco parentis* means the parent-substitute has temporary rights over the child, the authority that parents have in law. Although the law does not spell out which parent is to be the model, the emphasis is on the old patriarchal subordination of children to adults: until recently, paternal authority. This authority can be used to justify punitive behaviour of which the parents themselves disapprove. Peter Newell described a case in which a boy was threatened with a beating for 'trying to take a prohibited shortcut across a cemetery on his way home from school'. His mother complained, Newell wrote (1983, p. 13).

> It is over 18 months since Britain was found to be in Breach of the (European) Convention (on Human Rights) by not respecting parental objections to corporal punishment ... Over this issue, the Government shows a strange (perverted?) reluctance to take the obvious course of abolition, thus bringing it in line with every other European administration ... Other forms of degrading and inhuman treatment still persist ... (there is) new evidence of young girls being forcibly injected with largactil and valium (in these cases without even the presence of a doctor) and

others placed in solitary confinement in a secure unit for up to 36 hours (three stripped cells in Lambeth were used 169 times in 1982).

Comparing children's legal position with other articles in the Convention demonstrates a less than consistent respect for young people's rights: a single magistrate can still authorize detention in a 'Place of Safety' for up to 28 days without a court hearing ...

One old argument still used to counter any attempt to increase the legal rights of children living in institutions is that 'caring authorities' and their staff are *in loco parentis* and must retain parental discretion if their relationship with young people is not to become over-formal and controlled. It is a diversionary argument, because none of the carers would actually advocate 'degrading or humiliating treatment' – but it also has the dangerous if unintended effect of forcing children's advocates to consider the biggest and most challenging issue of all – that of parental 'ownership' of children.

The general *idea* of *in loco parentis*, as opposed to the legal meaning, is that the parent-substitute should decide what is in the child's long-term interests and act on that. In practice we find a conflict in the behaviour of professionals. On the one hand, they accept the traditional idea that the best care for children is given by parents within the family, so they model themselves on ideal parents. On the other hand, their professionalism asserts itself: they feel they know *more* than parents because they are trained or have wider experience. Even so, most caring professionals see it as part of their duty to respect and protect the child's relationship with the parents, however imperfect. The conflict could be summed up very simply: professionals are to be parent-like in their behaviour, since parents are the best carers, but they must *not* be parent-like in the sense of having individual loving relationships with their charges, for that would threaten the *real* parents.

This explains some odd features of carers' training. It is the carers of very young children who are really seen as doing what parents (here, mothers) should be doing. Nursery nurses are generally trained in the physical care of young children. Their training fulfils two purposes at one and the same time: it prepares the young women for the world of paid employment in hospitals, nurseries or private homes as nannies, and it prepares them for their future work as mothers. In the early arguments for their training through the Nursery Nurses Examination Board (NNEB) these twin purposes were very explicit. Many of the courses that are taught at colleges are about 'family responsibility and child development' or 'preparation for parenthood'. Nursery nurse training focuses on the domestic skills of being a mother, rather than the educative skills. Ironically one nursery nurse described the training as 'getting rid of all the motherliness in you'. Unlike mothers, these professionals are expected to behave consistently, to keep cool and to treat all the children in much the same way.

Being parent-like or, rather, motherly or fatherly can affect the *selection* of teachers. Women are considered most suitable for nursery and infant classes, men for posts of authority. The PTA at an Oxfordshire school objected to the appointment of a headmistress merely because of her sex. They argued that the school's catchment area contained 'some pupils ... from broken homes and many fathers were temporarily absent from home on business ... The school had a clear need for a man "to act as a father figure"' (*Times Educational Supplement*, 24 June 1983, p. 1).

Despite this, being motherly or parental does not figure significantly in the training of teachers. For primary school teachers, the emphasis is on a 'child-centred' approach, with the teacher enabling or facilitating the child's learning when the child chooses. The teacher's job is to help children acquire certain skills and become independent, to wean them from their parents, to treat each child 'as an individual', and yet to be impersonally benevolent.

Children are most successfully 'weaned' from their dependence on their parents if the transition is gradual and based on their own wish for autonomy. So nursery school teachers still wipe bottoms, infant teachers tie laces and cuddle, even if these activities are not stressed at training college. When the children go home they inevitably take the opportunity to test whether they are still loved unconditionally by flying into rages, expressing the feelings that were controlled at school, bossing their baby brother or sister around and showing little of their responsible classroom selves. Teachers cannot help sometimes feeling that the child is better in their care, and sometimes letting this feeling show.

Manicom quotes (1984, pp. 80–81) some Canadian teachers talking about their pupils: '"At times, *sure* I get frustrated ... Because you see evidence in front of you, a little kid who is coming in who doesn't have any food in her stomach and has been up all hours of the night, and you are damn frustrated with the mother ..." What we seem to hear in many teachers' voices is not respect but judgement.' Professionals not only criticize parents for their inadequate parenting or mothering: they also set clear standards for what work mothers have to do to prepare their children to go outside the home and into school. Dorothy Smith provides a beautiful example:

A little pamphlet addressed to parents published by the Ontario government makes recommendations for how children's reading and writing skills can be improved . . . the list of suggestions includes many items which are like the kinds of activities children might be engaged in in kindergarten or primary grades . . . All presuppose and make invisible expenditures of time, effort, skill and materials. Paints, crayons, scissors, paper, photographs, works of art are supposed to be available. Many of the activities suggested presuppose also some if not considerable preparatory work on the part of the parent in preparing photographs and reproductions of works of art, in making puppets and certainly considerable further work in cleaning up after these events have taken place. Space is presupposed in which these messes can be made without damage to household furnishings etc. Presupposed also are skills involved in knowing how to discuss works of art with your children, how to extend their vocabulary etc. . . . It is the investment of mothers' work and thought in activities of these kinds which prepares children for school (1983, pp. 16–17).

Inevitably teachers are the people who find out how well mothers have done this work.

Sara Lawrence Lightfoot has explored the relationship between schools and families. She points out (1978, pp. 395, 402) that in the frequent conflicts between families and schools,

because all mothers and many elementary school teachers are women, the antagonisms will largely be between women . . . Ironically, mothers and teachers are caught in a struggle that reflects the devaluation of both roles in society. Their generalized low status makes them perfect targets for each other's abuse.

She adds that both mothers and teachers are obliged to raise children 'to conform to a society that belongs to men'. The resulting ambivalence about their tasks makes them more likely to undervalue each other's contributions. She argues that a professional woman facing the disapproving social attitudes directed at 'career women'

. . . must justify her choice of life-style, and the locus of this justification lies in the family rather than in her professional work. One of the obvious ways women seek to establish an integration of their domestic and professional roles is to find work in the fields traditionally conceived of as feminine. Choosing a profession like teaching provides a continuity of this sort (op. cit., pp. 405–6).

So women teachers partly choose their jobs *because* they involve being mother-like, and then have to cope with the professional ethic that insists on a clear separation between parental and teaching relationships. As one teacher, quoted by Lightfoot, said: 'I try my best to be *asexual* in the classroom in order not to be confused with mother or motherly things' (op. cit., pp. 405–6).

Such conflicts and discontinuities are not confined to schools. In fact, the relationships between parents and child minders, nursery nurses or nannies are, if anything, more fraught with tension. This is because these workers care for the younger children, who are supposed to be with their mothers. It follows that the mothers are failing by the very act of using mother-substitutes. This idea makes it difficult for mothers and carers to develop relationships of mutual respect. The work of child minders, nannies and nursery nurses is even less valued than that of teachers. They feel they *care* for the children, but the parents retain all the rights over them. It can make them feel better to criticize the parents. For example, a child minder we know used to criticize her charges' parents to the children themselves because their mothers never made gravy. She took great pride in the gravy that she made for her charges' lunches, which the children loved, and made sure they had plenty of it every day at her house. She certainly felt that she was nourishing the children in a way that the parents were not. Having no training, and no recognition of the importance of her work, she needed to reassure herself that she was not just an inferior parent-substitute.

When children go 'into care', parents are replaced in a far more radical sense than what happens in schools and day care. Roy Parker has argued that when children are accepted 'into care' 'a shift occurs from personal responsibility (1984 p. 1). Yet the agencies who take responsibility for the child try 'to provide ... family-like environments for the separated child – a laudable objective' (ibid., p. 2) which Parker argues is actually impossible. Grouping children in 'family groups' in children's homes or using foster parents gives the impression that 'corporate care' can be like parental care. 'That attractive but dubious assumption has, I believe, hampered the development of a critical analysis of just what can be done to provide good care for the separated child' (ibid., p. 3). In corporate care:

... day-to-day care is separated from responsibility for the children. Those who carry responsibility for them on behalf of corporate bodies, rarely, if ever look after the children. In any case certain rights and duties remain vested in the parents. Secondly, both the personnel who carry responsibility and those who look after the children frequently change ... The third reason why the advantages of 'ordinary parenting' are lost when a child enters care is that special commitments to each child become exceedingly difficult to maintain. In a residential home, for instance, the child to adult ratios are high in comparison with family care, and the same adults are not always on duty during the day and at night ... On the face of it the foster home appears to overcome this practical difficulty. Yet there is a good deal of evidence which points to the existence of severe conflicts of loyalty for the foster parents as between their own children and foster children. Other evidence indicates that, by comparison with a residential home, a foster home is liable to accentuate the conflicts which children face in sharing commitments between their caretakers and the 'lost' parent. Under such circumstances children may not allow the foster parents to establish a partisan commitment, or they may reject their natural parents (ibid., pp. 1–2).

When children go into care, the conflict is clear between the wish to replace their families and the belief that families *should not* be replaced. These are 'separated children', as Parker says. It is quite realistic of them to feel that a close relationship with foster parents may threaten their relationship with the 'natural' parents.

Children in school and day care are in a different situation. There is *no need* to try to make schools and day care 'like families', although many do with 'family groups' and so on. In any case, it cannot be done in daily settings any more than in the residential homes or foster homes Parker was discussing. In schools and day care, too, the people who look after children for most of the day are not those who have overall responsibility for them. As in residential settings, the personnel frequently changes – teachers, like social workers, leave for promotion or retraining; nursery nurses also leave for retraining or a change of scene. Thirdly, special commitments of teachers or nursery nurses are hard to maintain, not only because of the high child-to-staff ratios but also because the very organization of the nursery or school into developmental stages makes 'special' relationships less likely. The child minder may be in a similar position to the foster parent, with divided and sometimes conflicting loyalties and an ambiguous relationship with the child.

People who think schools and nurseries should be 'like home' and carers 'like parents' do not usually spell out what they mean. What are homes like? What are parents like? And which of their qualities do children need in out-of-home care? Precisely because the relationship between parents and children is based on identification as well as love it is not always rational or stable. Indeed, there have been occasions when out-of-home care has been taken as the basic, normal form instead of family care, and non-parental care has been used to set standards for parents. For example, in the early days of mass universal schooling (in the mid-nineteenth century) some people in authority argued not that schools should be like homes, but that homes should be like schools. In particular, middle-class mothers were encouraged to be more didactic (teacher-like), imitating the kindergartens to which their children were sent. More recently, Margaret Mead (1962a) asked whether mothers should be like nurses or nurses more like mothers. She was drawing attention to the question of who has more consistent standards, the mother or the professional. It has often been claimed that people who are not so involved and committed in a passionate way can give better care in some respects. They can allow children to feel separate and autonomous, without feeling threatened.

If family care suffers from inconsistency and makes the children vulnerable to the parents' distress, nurseries and schools tend to suffer from too much consistency – rigidity. But to avoid this, nurseries and schools do not need to ape families. They need only aim to be *good* nurseries and schools. The idea that parents are the only 'special people' for children leads other carers to try to be motherly or fatherly. At the same time, the idea that parents have the right to an exclusive relationship with their children often holds non-parents back. Professionals trying to walk this tightrope end up being *generally* motherly: an absurd contradiction in terms. Children have the right to real relationships with their carers as well as to consistent and thoughtful treatment. Nursery workers and teachers, nannies and child minders need to be able to forget about infringing parental rights. They need to know that important relationships they make with children – whether they last hours or years – will be respected by their parents. Like other non-parents, they need to be freed to have closer and more reciprocal relationships with the children they look after.

We have already hinted at the issues that divide mothers from fathers and forbid an easy solidarity between all parents. Parenthood exists, nevertheless. Mothers and fathers are on the same side of the gulf that divides parents from non-parents. Both mothers and fathers are likely to identify with their children, to love them passionately, to expect all sorts of things for them and of them. In law and in practice, parents' responsibilities are transferable and interchangeable. But in the 'normal' state of affairs, mothers are the parents who *do* most of the parenting so that 'mother' is often a euphemism for 'parent' which covers up that inequality. Many fathers can jump the abyss and join the non-parents for hours, days or even weeks at a time, in mind as well as in body. Few mothers have that choice. For that reason, we now go on to ask what it means to be a mother or a father.

CHAPTER SIX

IS MOTHER SPECIAL?

THE BOWLBY HERITAGE

Mothers are constantly being told, in the media and popular literature, what it is like to mother and how essential their love is for their children. Bowlby has been one of the most influential writers on this subject. Since his work became the official creed in the 1950s, it is now a truism that young children need their mothers above all. It is partly thanks to Bowlby and his fellow workers that when our children are in hospital we can now visit them daily, even stay with them, in contrast to the half-hour a week which was normal in the late 1940s. Bowlby also played a progressive role in exposing the appalling conditions in many children's residential homes, which has ultimately led to a dramatic drop in the number of children who live in such homes. But these valuable reforms have only been granted in the name of the nuclear family with the full-time mother at home, an ideal consolidated during the 1950s and still persisting, increasingly out of touch with reality. How did this sort of mothering come to seem natural and desirable?

The story is a long one, but a crucial chapter began with the publication by the World Health Organization in 1951 of Bowlby's monograph *Maternal Care and Mental Health*. It was to receive wide-scale publicity and popularization, and was later published in Penguin as *Child Care and the Growth of Love*. The timing was right. During the Second World War psychological theories which saw human beings as very flexible received official support because they fitted the turbulent times: war necessitates moving people around and treating them instrumentally. Psychoanalysis (Bowlby's kind of psychological theory) was not very useful to these purposes, since it studies personality formation and emotional life, and offers no quick cures. During the subsequent period of social reconstruction it became possible to face up to the emotional costs of war. The psychoanalysts Anna Freud and Dorothy

Burlingham, for example, published an account of their residential nursery in Hampstead which suggested that these costs had been very high for children deprived of family life through the events of war.

In his monograph, Bowlby brought together studies of children reared in residential homes and of children separated from their families by admission to hospital or residential nurseries. In doing so he exposed dreadful cruelties, which in the aftermath of war could be recognized and condemned. His message was that the homeless and displaced children of war needed foster mothers, and that mothers of young children should in general be at home caring for them full-time. He got an audience: women who had been working in munitions factories, obliged to send their children for nine or ten hours daily to indifferent nurseries, men who had for years been equating peace with the haven of the family, governments which saw the social and financial potential of idealizing motherhood and family life.

Bowlby's argument was to become known as the 'maternal deprivation' thesis. It had two prongs. First, drawing on clinical experiences, his own study of juvenile thieves and other published work, Bowlby argued that if babies have no opportunity to become attached to a mother-figure they become 'affectionless' adults, lacking a conscience and unable to make close relationships. Secondly, he argued that children who have already become attached to their mothers can be permanently disturbed by separation from them during infancy. If the separation lasts too long, these children too become emotionally withdrawn, even if reunited with their mothers or families.

Goldfarb, in the USA, had looked at children in foster homes. He had tested two groups of children aged ten to fourteen: one group of fifteen children had been in foster homes since babyhood, while the other group of fifteen had been in residential homes until they were fostered at the age of three. When tested, the institutional group was found to be intellectually retarded and emotionally disturbed in a specific way: the children were demanding of affection but unable to reciprocate. Goldfarb concluded (and Bowlby agreed): '... if babies are entirely denied any opportunity for close contact with a mother, they show a singular inability to achieve close, reciprocating human relationships. In other words, they cannot love another person' (Goldfarb, 1955).

Since Bowlby first presented these arguments many studies have shown that children in institutions need not become intellectually retarded. The babies in Goldfarb's study suffered almost every sort of deprivation. They were confined in cots in separate cubicles up to the age of nine months, and their only social contact was with a nurse who perfunctorily changed and fed them. Even when, as bigger babies, they were 'cared for' in a group, there was no chance to make a relationship with *any* adult (not just a mother). It now seems clear that it was early and constant stimulus deprivation, near solitary confinement and lack of social interaction, rather than the lack of a mother, which produced the intellectual backwardness of the children in the institutional group. However, Bowlby's position on the emotional ill-effects of institutionalization has stood the test of time relatively well. Tizard (1975) reports that in institutions which give children the chance to become attached to members of staff (sometimes by assigning a 'special' nurse to each child, who gives special attention and treats) the children are emotionally more hopeful, more alive, though as a consequence they may be harder to manage.

Michael Rutter has been Bowlby's best-known critic. He points out (1972, p. 49) that the work Bowlby uses as evidence for the importance of *mothers* to a child's development actually '... suggests the relevant variable is the child's attachment to the person ... it is irrelevant whether or not this person is his mother'. The Goldfarb study we have described did show the importance of early experience – the change in the institutional children's lives came too late, at three. It also backed up the view that '... the ability to have tender feelings is ... derivative of social experience' (Goldfarb, op. cit.). It is true that if the children had all been fostered at birth, then the two groups would almost certainly not have diverged in this distressing way. But it is also probably true that if they had all been brought up by their fathers or their aunts, or by anyone at all who cared for them in the full sense of the word, they would have developed normally. Bowlby and Goldfarb would quickly reply: 'Ah, but that simply means the father, aunt or whoever have taken mother's place. They are, for our purposes, mothers.' Since we are interested in just who *can* give children the care they need for healthy development, we cannot possibly accept the idea that anyone who does so must be a mother or mother-substitute. This sounds too much like 'Heads I win, tails you lose'.

Bowlby argued that for children who *had* already become attached to their mothers, separation could have disastrous consequences. Children who were hospitalized or admitted to a residential nursery at first would cry for their mothers, call for them and protest vociferously at their absence. This behaviour, which Bowlby called the phase of protest, would after some hours or days shade into (or alternate with) a phase of despair, where the child was much quieter, but sad. If the mother returned during this period she was likely to be ignored or greeted with anger, tears and reproaches, and any attempt on her part to leave again would lead to hysterical clinging, even if she just intended to go to the shops. If the separation lasted even longer, after some weeks the child would appear to come out of the phase of grief and despair and would seem either withdrawn from people or, with some children, friendly but undiscriminating. Bowlby wrote that this phase tended to be welcomed by the staff, but actually marked a most dangerous progression since the child's capacity to make attachments might have suffered long-term damage. The mother's return, or the chance for a new relationship with a mother-figure, might come too late if the child had unconsciously concluded that love brought too much pain to be risked again. Bowlby's descriptions of children's reactions to loss of their loved people are deeply moving, though not at all sensational, while some of his critics tend to write about children's behaviour much as they might of monkeys. This may be one reason why Bowlby's conclusions have been too readily accepted.

It is hardly surprising that young children who have been cared for mostly by their mothers will suffer considerably if separated not only from her but also from home, father, brothers and sisters and all familiar people, places and routines. Bowlby's own account of children's separation experiences shows that it is not only mother they are missing. Children who were admitted to residential nurseries together with a brother or sister, or who were visited by their fathers, were less distressed than those whose links with home were completely severed. Bowlby's colleague Robertson and his wife temporarily fostered two children and recorded their reactions. They had met the children once with their mother. While they looked after them they were careful to talk about the absent mother and to allow the little ones to express their sadness. These children did become attached to the Robertsons to some extent, and when reunited with their mother showed fewer signs of anger and distress than do children who have not had comparable support. Of course, Bowlby admitted that the sort of sensitive care the Robertsons gave lessened the impact of separation. But he attributed the comforting effect of such care precisely to its 'motherliness'. Similarly, if a nurse comforts a child in hospital, Bowlby sees her as a mother substitute, and if two-year-olds in an institution who are usually given routine physical care improve intellectually after a particular nurse regularly shows them tenderness, Bowlby sees that as evidence of the power of 'maternal care'. Small wonder he concludes that 'maternal deprivation' is the key factor in the causation of children's distress.

The confusion arises from the fact that in this society it is generally mothers who care for children, so in that sense anyone other than a mother who cares for a child could be called a 'mother substitute'. Of course, if all caring is called 'mothering', then the discovery that children need to love and be loved, and need the presence of their loved ones much of the time to keep up these crucial relationships, can be misrepresented as the discovery that children *have to* have mothers in order to develop well. And this is essentially what has happened. The useful aspects of Bowlby's work have become obscured by this guilt-inducing message, which gets its credibility only by redefining the terms.

One mother known to us told us of a separation with a happy outcome, in that the child is now a capable adult with a strong personality and a family of her own. Linda has been deaf since her birth in the mid-1950s. When she was two and a half, her parents were told that she would never learn to talk if she stayed at home, and were offered a place for her in a residential nursery for deaf children in Somerset, far from their home in London. The little girl's father was low paid, and the mother was pregnant again. The parents had read the media reports of Bowlby's conclusions about the danger of separation from the mother and were seriously worried, but felt they could not risk depriving their daughter of speech. One weekend her mother left Linda in the nursery, having done her best to explain to the child that she would come back. Linda's deafness made this difficult. It was impossible for the mother to visit for two whole weeks. She still remembers those weeks, and the train journey during which she steeled herself to face anger, rejection and sadness on Linda's part. She still remembers waiting at the end of a long corridor, and seeing Linda running towards her, joy on her face and her arms outstretched. They hugged each other, crying and laughing. With the help of the staff, who used photographs of the family to communicate the assurance that they were standing in for them and that they would come back, Linda had been able to cope with her distress without losing hope. Perhaps she had picked up clues from her parents' behaviour that the separation was for a good purpose. In this particular case the guilt the mother felt, and continued to feel, was probably more harmful than the separation.

Some of Bowlby's adherents, including his close colleague Ainsworth, have said that his views have been exaggerated, that he never, for instance, opposed the short-term daily separation involved in day care. In the following passage Bowlby is ostensibly talking about continuity as opposed to separations of weeks or months, but the received meaning is that separation of even hours is bad.

The mothering of a child is not something which can be arranged by roster; it is a live human relationship which alters the characters of both partners ... Such enjoyment and close identification of feeling is only possible for either party if the relationship is continuous. Just as the baby needs to feel that he belongs to his mother, the mother needs to feel that she belongs to her child, and it is only when she has the satisfaction of this feeling that it is easy for her to devote herself to him. The provision of constant attention day and night, seven days a week and 365 in the year, is possible only for a woman who derives profound satisfaction from seeing her child grow from babyhood, through the many phases of childhood, to become an independent man or woman, and knows that it is her care which has made this possible. It is for these reasons that the mother-love which a young child needs is so easily provided within the family, and is so very very difficult to provide outside it (1951, p. 67).

Certainly it is true that the care of a child does demand commitment and, if the relationship is only to be temporary, such commitment is less likely. It is also true that the best child care is enjoyable much of the time. But the overall impact of this passage is untrue and highly guilt-inducing. Bowlby has set standards which no mother can reach, condemned her to no relief, and capped it all by saying that a *good* mother would enjoy it and find it 'easy'. Bowlby is aware that women who feel they want to do something else as well as mother are in a dilemma. He writes (1979, p. 9): '... it ill becomes those of us fortunate enough not to be faced with the problem to lay down the law to the other sex how they should resolve it'. But that the care of children is *women's problem* he never doubts, and his certainty on this point comes from his belief that the biological mother is *naturally* going to be the best carer for her child, and that her responsibility for day-to-day care should be almost total. Justifying his failure to discuss fathers, he wrote that it is after all the mother who looks after the child,

... who feeds and cleans him, keeps him warm and comforts him. It is to his mother that he turns when in distress. In the young child's eye father plays second fiddle ... Nevertheless, as the illegitimate child knows, fathers have their uses even in infancy. Not only do they provide for their wives to enable them to devote themselves unrestrictedly to the care of the infant and toddler, but, by providing love and companionship, they support her emotionally and help her maintain that harmonious contented mood in the aura of which the infant thrives (1951, p. 13).

This early work of Bowlby's was only the beginning of a long tradition of research which is still going on and which has long since bypassed its cruder early formulations. For instance, it is now well known that children become attached to their fathers at an early age; and no modern psychologist would talk as Bowlby did thirty years ago. But some of Bowlby's early assumptions are still conventional wisdom, while more recent and sophisticated concepts and techniques are unheard of outside of academic circles. It is still widely believed that children are best cared for (full-time, in the early years) by their biological mothers. At the same time, whatever goes wrong with children is laid at their mother's door. There is a contradiction here, as Ann Dally, a psychiatrist, has pointed out in her book, *Inventing Motherhood*. She speaks of 'a curious inconsistency ... running through most literature on child care and child rearing during the last thirty years' (Dally, 1982, p. 189). Babies and young children are believed to need mothering, and their own mothers (because of their mothering instinct) are believed to be the best people to give it. At the same time a darker theme is playing: some mothers are not fit to be mothers. They damage – or even psychologically cripple – their children. The only clear idea that emerges from the contradictory hotch-potch we encounter in our daily exposure to the media is that mothers are inevitably responsible for their children, for better or worse, and that the nuclear family is a biological grouping, the natural context for mothering. Both these ideas are prejudices that we must put aside to ask 'Is the biological mother likely to be her children's best carer?'

THE BIOLOGICAL MOTHER

Children discover the facts of their birth long after they have come to love their carers. As babies they have no way of knowing their biological mother. For them, the question is how good are their experiences. There may be a smooth transition from the womb to the mother's breast and warm enclosing arms, with the minimum of pain and shock, or they may have to suffer unpleasant sensations, ungratified needs, in their first hours and days. This could happen if they remain with their biological mothers, if the birth was difficult or hospital procedures or illness intervene. The range of experience for babies who stay with their biological mothers is wide, but they probably have a better chance of consistent handling. Theorists differ about how much this matters in the early weeks. Those who stress learning would probably think it mattered less than would psychoanalysts and others who emphasize emotional development. Winnicott writes (1964, p. 57): 'Something must be reliable for the infant at the beginning, otherwise there is no hope that he or she may start well on the road to mental health.' However, Winnicott is here suggesting that if necessary the bottle and the feed could serve this role.

To know whether care by the biological mother is best for babies, we need to know something about their capacities in the early days, which are quite beyond the ordinary. Recent research (MacFarlane 1977, Ch. 6) shows that mothers were right to affirm that their babies could see them and recognize their voices very early on. From birth, babies find people fascinating to look at. Experiments in which babies were shown various shapes and patterns and the experimenter measured how long they looked at each sort have shown that babies prefer complex, solid, moving, three-dimensional patterned objects – and people combine all these qualities perfectly. Babies will smile at a cardboard face (as well as at real ones) within a few weeks. The smiling response is very much in the interests of babies' survival, because adults are in turn very responsive to smiles. You could say that babies are predestined to like their carers if they get half a chance, for that automatic smile is the forerunner of the true social smile. But babies' responsiveness is not too specific: '... if, for instance, it were confined to the particular woman who had given birth to him, difficulties would ensue in the comparatively large number of cases where a change in mother-figure has to take place subsequently' (Schaffer, 1971b, p. 59).

Cognitive psychologists talk of babies as 'programmed' in certain ways. At birth, babies are not blank slates, on which anything can be written. They have a repertoire of reflexes, they have innate preferences, and an amazing capacity to learn. Other 'progammes' become evident at later maturational stages, and some only show themselves if the conditions are right. Most of new babies' programming would allow various sorts of caring. They can be comforted by being held closely, by being rocked. They prefer soft surfaces to lie on, they like to be warm, they respond to music, they dislike and fear loud noises and jerky movements. From their earliest days they like the cadences of the human voice. None of these preferences suggests the biological mother, or even a single carer. Others seem to point to her, or at least to a woman. New-born babies seem to prefer high-pitched voices, so they usually prefer women's voices to men's. There is even some recent research suggesting that they remember their own mother's voice from their time in the womb and turn towards it rather than towards another woman's voice if placed on their backs on a bed, with mother on one side and another woman on the other side. At birth, babies' rooting and sucking reflexes are very strong. Within days, they learn to tell the smell of their own mother's milk from that of others, and will turn their heads towards a breast pad soaked in it. (But the corresponding experiment on babies' ability to discriminate their 'own' brand of powdered milk from others needs doing, too.)

Babies make little speech-like sounds from very early. By about six weeks, this babbling is followed by a pause, in which (if anyone is listening) the carer usually responds, chatting away as if the baby had said something intelligible. While the carer speaks, the baby gazes at her face. The carer pauses, and the baby replies.

Another typical form of interaction involves imitation. The carer gives the baby feedback on how she or he looks or sounds, by copying the baby's face and imitating her noises. As with babbling, imitation usually takes the form of taking turns, and cognitive psychologists think this timing of the inter-action is itself programmed rather than learnt for both baby and carer. In the literature on the subject it is usually assumed – quite realistically, of course – that the carer will be the biological mother or a woman who has taken her place. Unfortunately, this assumption often makes it sound as if such conversations between adult and baby need the biological mother if they are to take place at all. For example, one psychologist says: '... almost from the time of birth there seems to be a marked tendency for mothers to reflect back to their infants certain gestures which occur spontaneously within the baby's natural repertoire of activities. She appears, however, to select actions which she can endow with communicative significance' (Pawlby, 1977, p. 221). Of course this is literally true. Yet the reference to 'birth' and the use of the term 'mother' makes it harder for us to remember that any people who know the baby well (and some who do not, but who are 'naturals' with babies) are likely to behave in this way.

What are we to make of this information? Most of it has only recently become known by psychologists and paediatricians, although people who knew babies well always gave them credit for greater capacities than they were officially allowed. But the cultures into which babies are born have scant respect for their 'programmes', which are always violated at some point or another. Babies may be cared for from birth by men, in 'role swaps' in our own culture. They may be bottle fed by their biological mothers, by various people or just by their parents. They may be looked after most of the time by children. They may be breast fed by several women. They may be fed 'by the clock' instead of when they feel hungry. They may never be rocked. Despite the flouting of their innate preferences, most of these babies will grow up to be what their societies consider normal adults (which is, of course, the least exacting standard of mental health we could set). We know there are limits to babies' flexibility, and we know, from the casualties, where some of them lie, but they have not yet been investigated systematically in cross-cultural studies. Cross-cultural studies are essential to establish the range of caring behaviour that babies, *as members of the human species*, require for development into social adulthood. If you only study societies with a similar social organization and similar ideas of how a normal adult should behave (for instance achievement-orientated Western societies, organized in nuclear families with the mother as main child carer), and conclude that children have such-and-such needs (for instance, near continuous sensitive caring from their biological mothers), you risk mistaking something which has some truth *in a certain type of society* for a characteristic of the *human species*.

ATTACHMENT THEORY

One attempt to chart the boundaries of babies' tolerance makes exactly this mistake. This is ironic, since attachment theory has been developed using the concepts of ethology, the study of behaviour characteristic of human beings as a species, and one would expect the points we have made to be second nature to workers in this area. Attachment theory was developed by Bowlby and Ainsworth, among others. Over the last thirty years it has generated an enormous amount of research and made real contributions to knowledge. It takes as its starting point one of babies' 'programmes', but one which is not evident until the middle of the first year, though it is based on earlier happenings. At about six months, babies become *attached* to their carers. They begin to make it quite clear that they like them to stay close. They begin to discriminate between the people they know well and strangers and less familiar people, and gradually develop a hierarchy of preferences. 'He'll let my mother change him if I'm not around, but if he can see me or he hears my voice he won't stop creating until I do it,' a mother might report. 'If he's feeling cheery he'll go to anyone, but if his teeth are bothering him it's got to be me or his father – and he won't have his dad if I'm there.' As they become mobile, babies crawl, then walk, after their 'attachment figures'. Sometimes they seem not to need them, and scoot off happily, bottom-shuffling perhaps, exploring some grubby corner until a carer retrieves them as a mother-dog might her puppies. On other occasions they seem to need to be assured of the availability of an 'attachment figure' in order to feel free to explore and play. This attempt to get close, especially in times of stress, in unfamiliar situations, or if the child feels tired or ill, has been termed 'attachment behaviour'. This is what you are witnessing when your little girl cannot be quieted until you gather her into your arms, or when your little boy breaks off his play and wanders towards you as if to check up on you, and only goes back to his toys after a reassuring word. Attachment behaviour is said to be '... a form of instinctive behaviour that develops in humans, as in other mammals, during infancy, and has as its aim or goal proximity to a mother-figure. The function of attachment behaviour is ... protection from predators' (Bowlby, 1979 p. 87).

Just as hunger is satisfied by eating, so attachment behaviour is satisfied by getting physically close to the mother-figure. How close the child needs to get depends on the state he or she is in. On some occasions a few words from the mother serve as reassurance, and the child can go on quietly playing some distance away. Sometimes, if she or he is 'clingy', nothing but being carried everywhere can stop the child crying, tugging at the mother's skirts, and so on.

This description is very apt. Over the past two decades, many researchers have explored the complex relationship between children's exploration and play, and their need for a 'secure base' from which to do so, in the form of a person to whom they are attached (Parkes and Stevenson-Hinde, 1982). Interpreting the results is not simple, but there can be no doubt that there is a real relationship. There is tremendous value in the theory's emphasis on the need for physical contact and closeness, and how as children get older and their internal images of their parents and family and their knowledge about their place in the world become more developed, they can make do with less actual physical closeness and more symbols of it. The arm round the shoulder, the photo, postcard, phone call, can do the work of the hugs and cuddles of infancy (which is not to say that hugs and cuddles would not still be better). Psychoanalysts had already shown the importance of the baby's developing love for her or his carers. Bowlby and Ainsworth have narrowed the focus, concentrating on the visible signs of this love which we share with other mammals – physical closeness. It does seem likely that they are on to something, that the developing baby has a basic need for physical *closeness* to particular carers.

But on the evidence we cannot say much more than this. Children in residential homes who are usually deprived of long-term physical and loving relationships with particular carers are also usually deprived of much touching and carrying from *anyone* as babies. It is possible that if a society was more generally caring and more generous with physical affection, children might not have such a profound need for it from their particular carers.

Bowlby and Ainsworth go way beyond their own evidence when they try to use the findings of attachment theory to argue that the nuclear family, with mother as full-time carer, is the natural grouping for human beings. They see the child's programming as complemented by instinctive caring behaviour on the part of the biological mother, which is triggered by the hormones present in her body and the sight and feel of her new-born child. They agree that anyone who 'behaved in a mothering way towards a child' can become his or her attachment figure; but the difficulty is for the substitute, whom they assume will be female, to care with the same natural ease. The mother's natural caring response ensures that it is she whom the baby comes to know and later to whom he or she later becomes attached. The relationship between the pair developed '... in the environment of evolutionary adaptedness ... presumably the savannah environment in which the human species is believed to have first evolved' (Ainsworth *et al.*, 1971, p. 102). And what chance can modern reformers of family life have against the inheritance of that distant savannah?

But here the failure to take a cross-cultural approach trips up Bowlby and Ainsworth. Margaret Mead sums up their argument quite fairly (op. cit., p. 56): '... infants need the continuous presence of a mothering figure and Nature has provided a set of mechanisms which if permitted full play will establish just these conditions'. She goes on to show that such conditions are so unusual in primitive societies that such an inflexible outcome of human evolution would be disastrous. In fact, she says that only in societies 'which combine the production of food outside the home and the practice of contraception' is it possible for such an exclusive and continuous relationship between mother and infant to exist.

For under primitive conditions there are two situations which require a break in the continuity of mother–child care: (a) the need of the other children for care, and (b) the demands on the mother for food gathering, materials gathering, horticultural and other contributions to the food supply of the family group. The assumption that a mother–child pair relationship can be maintained without interruption until the child is two actually exposes the child to more traumata than if it is expected that several women can breast feed and care for the child, that a young girl or a grandmother or even a father can give it a dry breast for comfort, and that supplementary – premasticated – food can be made available to it at any time (loc. cit.).

Mead denies that there are any basic, programmed caring responses on the mother's part. Like babies, mothers are flexible, and different cultures handle birth and lactation differently:

> ... The mother may be required to do everything for herself – cut the cord and bathe the baby – or everything may be done for her; the father may be required to be present or rigorously banished; attendance at the birth may be limited to close relatives or women who have borne children, or birth may be in the midst of a chattering crowd. The infant may be placed at the mother's dry breast, fed at once by another woman, [or] kept without food until the mother has milk ... In short, the accumulated evidence from primitive societies suggests that at a very early stage in human history, traditional modes or behaviour were evolved which were related not to any immediate instinctive pattern or neo-natal mother–child relationship – such as has been described, for example, for goats and sheep and reindeer and moose – but rather to other parts of the learned behaviour of the particular people, their mode of life, means of transport, type of shelter, system of kinship organisation, methods of economic exchange and beliefs about the soul and the cosmos (ibid., p. 53).

More modern research in Britain and the USA has forced attachment theory to modify its claims. Many studies found that, even when the mother was the main carer, babies quickly became as attached, or even more attached, to fathers or other familiar adults. Typical was one Australian study, very carefully carried out, which looked at eighty two-year-old children, half of whom were in day care and half looked after at home. Interviewing the mother and father separately at the same time, to avoid bias, they asked to whom the child went if he or she was hurt, tired or frightened; they inquired how strongly preferred this person was over others, and just who could be accepted, and asked how the child behaved at parting and reunion. These were all two-parent families and almost all had a conventional division of labour. Unsurprisingly, most children first became attached to their mothers. One child was defined as 'unattached', but of the remaining seventy-nine there were seventeen exceptions. In eight cases the child had always seemed equally attached to both parents; in four the father was preferred; and in the other five cases it was other carers, including a grandfather who used to give the night feeds. By the time they were two, only fifty-six of the children were principally attached to their mothers, and, for most of these, father came a very close second (Gifford *et al.*, 1975). Attachment hierarchies are not as permanent as Bowlby and Ainsworth at first supposed. Sometimes children prefer one parent for one thing and the other for another. These preferences shift with experience. If you leave the children with their father for a weekend, on your return they may continue going to him first with their hurt knees, not to punish you, but simply because they have got into the habit of looking for comfort from him and finding it.

Increasingly psychologists are pointing out how ethnocentric attachment theory has been up to now. Yet ironically its reliance on Western societies does not always tend to support its conclusion. After all, these societies are organized in a way that encourages attachment to a single adult. If children do not appear to be 'monotropic' in such societies, monotropy cannot possibly be a basic human characteristic, as Bowlby and Ainsworth have supposed. All the evidence suggests that babies' attachments reflect their experience of care and interaction, as well as differences in their personalities. Babies who have been cared for by older children, by grandmothers, fathers, child minders and friends will have different relationships from those who have had a 'specialized' mother. Even when mother is at the top of the attachment tree and is *the* special person of all special people, it seems that the sort of satisfaction and comfort she offers is not unique, or does not remain unique for long. If necessary, children can get it from secondary attachment figures, always presuming that they are available and are capable of giving it. In the 'strange situation' tests devised by Ainsworth, toddlers used fathers as a base of safety and comfort in ways indistinguishable from the way they used their mothers. Whatever sort of start biological mothers may have, it is certain that non-mothers, including men, are also capable of giving young children the sort of care they need.

A HUMAN TENDENCY TO CARE?

We have emphasized the huge differences between various cultures in how babies and children are cared for. Despite these, in some respects all carers tend to behave towards young babies in the same sorts of ways. We exaggerate our facial expressions and keep them purer and more separate from each other than we would in interaction with older children or adults. In talking to babies we simplify syntax, use short sentences, talk more slowly and with a higher pitch. We change sounds and use nonsense sounds a lot. Games like 'peek-a-boo' are near universal. These care-giving responses are very effective in helping babies learn. In addition, there are responses on the carer's part that cannot be described on their own, because they represent a sensitivity to the baby's state. We have already described 'turn-taking' and imitation. In other ways as well, babies actively try to learn, express themselves through their pleasure in learning and, to a large extent, rely on their carers to put them in the way of new experiences by placing their chair, cot or rug where they can see things moving and happening, or by holding them in such a way, or by interacting with them directly. Carers usually respond to the baby's enthusiasm for various movements of the adult's face, voice or body by repeating them at different speeds and in slightly different ways, trying a variation when the baby's attention lapses. They also usually notice the baby's signals that he or she has had enough. The baby looks away, shows signs of sleepiness, and the carer reverses the process (Stern, 1977, Ch. 2).

Who does this? Not only biological mothers. Stern writes:

> Unlike some animal species, in man this specialized ability is extended to include almost all its members both male and female from middle childhood through old age. The implications of this arrangement are that we have enormous flexibility in instituting any number of social groupings to substitute for or, simply and more commonly, to add to the biological mother's role in providing appropriate social stimulation for infants in the first six months of life (ibid., p. 35).

Stern claims that the sort of behaviour described here is relatively independent of learning and experience with babies, as well as gender. Against those who believe that care-giving responses are specific to women and who see doll play among girls as resulting from the hormonal difference between them and boys rather than from socialization, Stern points out that these care-giving responses (exaggerated speech, expressions, etc.) are not seen in play with dolls but *are* seen in both boys and girls when they are interacting with a real baby.

Stern's work strongly suggests that the biological mother is not the only person with 'maternal instinct'. The presence of a helpless human infant can trigger caring responses in anyone. We all dislike intensely the sound of a baby crying. Physiological tests of amount of sweating, heart rate, blood pressure and so on have shown that children and adults of both sexes show signs of stress while watching a video recording of a baby crying (Frodi and

Lamb, 1982, p. 1183). A baby's smiles give pleasure to all humans. When you add to this the prevalence of the initially unlearnt behaviour described above, the slow, exaggerated pronunciation and so on, the case for a *human* propensity to care for babies is impressive. However, there is far more to mothering than this. We know that care by the biological mother is not essential to healthy development; we know that care by a single woman in her place is not essential; but we have not looked at the plausible-sounding argument that the biological mother is usually the best person to care, because her relationship to the child motivates her in a very special way.

Mothering and other caring do not just concern small babies. Children need different sorts of caring for years. Even if we concentrate on the care of babies, the question of who can best care for them, could be rephrased: 'Who will be willing to care for them?' A carer in the way mothers care is someone who takes on a commitment, whereas talking baby talk to the neighbour's child is an experience which can be terminated by walking away if the feelings it brings up are too uncomfortable. What makes carers care? Here there is some agreement between cognitive developmental psychology and psychoanalysis. Cognitive psychologists are concerned primarily with how children's thinking and their skills develop, and only indirectly with their emotional life which is central to the psychoanalytic approach. But both agree that the baby's love for the carer does not develop until about the middle of the first year, as we understand 'love' – meaning that the person who loves has an idea of him or herself as a separate person and an idea of the loved one as a person who exists even when not seen or heard. These sophisticated ideas are the result of much experience, which can only be acquired if there are not *too many* main carers. The baby has to be able to get to know the carer(s) in her or his many aspects (different clothing, different distance, in profile, etc.) and different moods, different ways of handling, and understand that these are all part of one person. Although the relationship is not fully understood, there is reason to believe that sensitive, caring handling of the baby, with respect for and insight into how she or he is feeling, is necessary for the baby to develop a strong concept of her or himself. If she or he is treated in a *totally* routine fashion, the baby will not come to feel that her or his needs and demands have any effect on the world.

Psychoanalysts and cognitive psychologists alike would say that this sort of care for a tiny creature is not easy to give. You have to be in a different state of mind from that in which we go about our daily business, and it is not a state of mind which many people can snap into and out of easily (although it can be done!). To care well for babies, far more than for older children, demands the ability to focus on small differences in their states which may be so slight that the carer talks of them (if at all) in terms of 'I just feel something's wrong', without being able to articulate exactly what is different. The slightly glazed look, the slowing down of responsiveness may indicate a coming cold. The rapid blinking and screwing up of the eyes may mean discomfort or impaired sight, or may mean the baby has just discovered a new thing that you can do with eyes. A baby might begin moving a leg again and again, holding the rest of the body uncharacteristically still. It takes some time to realize she or he has just discovered how to move one leg without the other pumping away in sympathy. Sometimes the baby goes bright red and looks intently in front, after a brief glance at the carer – a dirty nappy is coming. It is obviously not the right moment to run upstairs or to start washing up. The carer keeps still, holding the baby supported without any pressure on the bottom, and by temporarily waiting allows the baby to experience the bowel movement without distractions. Such sensitivity could not be taught as a set of rules. It is basically a matter of emotional sets of love, or at least commitment. It is here the biological mother is supposed to be in the best possible position to care.

EXPERIENCE AND COMMITMENT

Some psychologists and paediatricians (Klaus and Kennell, 1976) believe that there is a 'sensitive period' soon after the birth of a baby during which the 'bond' with its mother is formed. Separation of the two will prevent bonding and impair the future relationship, making psychological distance between them (and even physical abuse) more likely. Maternity hospitals and mid-wives are beginning to review the practice of separating mothers and babies soon after birth in the light of these claims. 'Nature' is coming into fashion in a certain trend of Western obstetrics, and many mothers these days long to hold their slippery new-born against their own naked skin, to put the baby straight to the breast and not to surrender it to be weighed, measured and otherwise 'tortured' in the 'nursery'. In a review of the literature on 'bonding', Martin Richards suggests that a mother like this, who may have heard about sensitive periods for bonding, who has looked forward to the sensation of holding her new baby and who has tried to avoid drugs lest they dull the experience, would be more upset by a separation of half an hour than a more conventionally passive mother would be by one lasting several hours. It would be possible for the distress itself to interfere with the new relationship. However, Richards concludes that there is no evidence that this close contact after birth is *necessary* for the typical attachment between mother and child to develop. Millions of mothers who had to endure the cruel and crazy practice of separating them from the babies that were so recently part of their bodies have come through to develop relationships with their children which are not discernibly different from those of mother–child pairs who remained together for the whole post-partum period (Richards, 1984).

Just as the mutual gazing and touching of new baby and mother, wonderful though it can be, is neither necessary nor sufficient for a good caring relationship between them later on, so the hormones present in the newly delivered mother's body are no guarantee that *her* caring responses will be stronger and more reliable than those of others. If these hormones were enough, there would be no 'rooming-in' mothers who choose to bottle feed from birth, or mothers who have their new babies handed to them on the delivery table and who feel a rush of despair instead of joy because they cannot see how to set about loving the small creature who now depends on them. If hormones were necessary, there would not be so many tender adoptive and foster mothers, and so many fathers able to enter the microcosmic world the baby inhabits.

When the baby is three or four days old, the mother's milk flows in response to her baby's cry. How she feels about this is another matter. She may be delighted, appalled or apprehensive. If she finds the whole thing repulsive, her feelings will act to stop the milk flowing – the 'let-down reflex' will be inhibited. As this illustration shows, the mother's experiences and feelings are more important than the hormonal levels which accompany them in their effect on the care she gives.

Feminists have rightly rebelled against the attempt to make women's reproductive capacity their whole destiny. The danger is of going to the other extreme and discounting the effects of biology. So says Janet Sayers in her book *Biological Politics*, and she draws on the work of the psychoanalyst Helen Deutsch to show that the same reproductive situation, such as pregnancy, will be experienced differently by different women, depending on their personality, life situation and feelings about motherhood. 'Consider, for instance, the biologically given fact that mother and foetus are physically united in pregnancy. Although this fact is constant for all pregnant women, Deutsch claims that women vary as to how they construe this biological constant. She argues that where women are psychologically unwilling to accept their pregnancy they may experience the embryo as a

parasite ...' (Sayers, 1982, p. 163); while for others: 'By tender identification, by perceiving the fruit of her body as part of herself, the pregnant
woman is able to transform the "parasite" into a beloved being' (Deutsch,
quoted loc. cit.). This insight can also be applied to breast feeding, and it is
easy to see why one woman may feel drained, exhausted, emptied where
another feels like an inexhaustible source of goodness.

Women's biological experiences of pregnancy, birth and the first contact
with the baby *do* matter. Very often it is a case of 'to them that have shall
be given'. If you feel good about yourself, about your situation and the
baby's coming, even a painful or complicated birth may be enjoyable.
Clumsy, thoughtless and humiliating hospital practices will cause distress,
but cannot ruin the experience. For a woman who is unsure, frightened,
with little support, such happenings may be the last straw, and actually
become more likely because she is less assertive or knowledgeable. The
biological mother is certainly intensely vulnerable to her experiences,
including the presence of the new-born, but this does not always make her
a better carer. Biological motherhood is rather like a drug, which sometimes
heightens your present mood and perceptions, and sometimes brings out
things previously unknown. Anyone taking it should be careful to have
support, because the effects are not completely predictable.

CULTURE AND EXPERIENCE

What it means to a woman to carry a child for nine months and then to
give birth to it will depend on her life, her personality, her circumstances,
but also on the society she lives in and how her culture interprets these
events. Material circumstances will affect this interpretation, too.

For instance, if many babies die in their first year and women have many
pregnancies but rear few children, this fact will affect the value the culture
puts on new babies and thence the woman's own feelings. If babies mean
an increase of poverty, or if they mean a future family worker, this will affect
the woman's attitude to her own pregnancy and birth. So will the kinship
system into which the baby is to be born. In some cultures, the bond
between the biological mother and child is expected to be of great significance to them both, in others less so. 'Amongst the Ndebele people of
Southern Rhodesia "mother" does not necessarily mean the woman who
gave birth to you. Mother, in the Western sense, plus all her sisters all go
under the term of mother ... the oldest of the sisters in any one family group
adopts the title ... "big mother" (Moyo, 1979, p. 180). The biological

mother and her female siblings are all 'little mothers', and the big mother is often the child's grandmother or some other older relation or friend. If a child is orphaned, 'big' and 'little' mothers are assigned from a friendly family. The 'big mother', not the biological mother, bears the overall responsibility for the child's bringing up, although the little mothers share the day-to-day work with her. This system of child care has its roots in the traditional Matabele economy, in which women do the farming while men go off to labouring jobs. Women of child-bearing years are at their strongest time of life, and cannot be spared from the heavy physical work. It is useful to have a system with redundancy built in, with alternative carers and home bases for every child.

> It is thought unnatural for the biological mother to show more interest in 'her' child than in those of her sisters and cousins. Nowadays this sometimes happens, because of European influence, but in theory this is not possible. In Si Ndabele you do not find a term which means 'child, my own biological child', and a different one meaning 'child, my cousin's child', the same term is used for both, 'my child' ... If a mother showed more interest in her 'own' children she would be badly thought of by the family and when her turn came to be 'big mother' she would be passed by. She would be regarded as a very selfish person ... (ibid.).

Despite Moyo's remark that it is because of European influence that the biological mother sometimes shows more interest in the child she gave birth to, it is more likely that the prohibition against doing this arose precisely because it sometimes happened spontaneously. It sounds very strange to us for such feelings to be condemned as selfish. If we want to imagine what it might be like to hold such a belief, a possible analogy from our own culture would be our disapproval of favouritism. It is inevitable that mothers should feel differently about their different children. Very often they will feel closer to one than to another. But there is a generally accepted rule that it is wrong to act on such feelings, and usually they should not even be verbalized. For the Ndebele mother, the specialness of her relationship with her biological child is suppressed rather than welcomed. Our society encourages us to feel that the child we gave birth to is 'ours' for all time, and builds a child care system on that commitment. The experience of pregnancy, birth and breast feeding can make a mother feel that all her love belongs to her own child. But it can work differently, to open her to a more generalized feeling for all children *as well as* this special love. Unfortunately our 'civilized' society does not build on this common response.

Mead writes (1962a, p. 52) of the *unreliability* of biological motherhood:

> We may ... consider whether the discoveries which have transformed the
> capacity which we share with other mammals to accept or reject our
> young into a capacity to preserve the lives of an increasing number of
> human infants may not actually be discoveries of *ways of overcoming the
> handicaps of the biologically given aspects of maternity* [our emphasis].
> Biological mothering is highly susceptible to conditions of pregnancy,
> whether the child was wanted or unwanted, its sex, the conditions of the
> mother's own childhood, relationships to the father, the nature of the
> delivery and the nature of the postnatal contact between mother and
> child, and finally the fit between the structure and functioning of the
> mother's breast and the infant's constitution ... Biological motherhood
> is a routine occurrence in the natural world; nursing – the responsible,
> devoted, conscious care of the young – is cultural and human.

Biological motherhood is limited, and may even result in the infant's death.
In societies where no artificial feeding is available, 'failure to produce milk
to nourish an infant which is demonstrating its non-viability by failing to
thrive on the breast milk its mother gives it is a biologically adequate
response on the part of the primitive mother' (ibid., p. 90). In those societies
as in ours, anxiety about feeding often makes matters worse – the milk
production falls. The result of that happening is quite different. In the society
where no artificial milk is available, the baby dies; in ours it is put on the
bottle. Biological motherhood has been supplemented by what Mead calls
'conscious nurturing'. She argues that shared breast feeding 'was the
beginning of this order of nurturing, continued in various forms of artificial
feeding, until men, as well as women, could share in the cultural nurturing
of an infant' (ibid., p. 52).

This does not mean that the biological mother should *not* care for her
child or that bottle feeding is preferable; the point is that if we uphold the
right of *every* child to good care, we cannot rely on 'natural' mechanisms
alone. The very experiences the biological mother has which can deepen
the relationship and commitment to the child can sometimes sabotage it.
We can never answer the question we posed – 'Is the biological mother the
best carer?' – without looking at the social setting in which she does it, what
support she has, whether there are other carers, and so on. These factors
may offset the unreliability of depending on one person's devotion – or not.

In a caring society, child care would be a common social project. Women
– and men – would be able to face their difficulties in parenting and talk

about them, without being labelled 'inadequate' to the next generation. There would be enough support for the group of people committed to a particular child's development for psychological 'cycles of deprivation' to have far less power than they have now, when mothers are on their own. Mothering would be available for the mother herself, so that she need not turn for it to her own child.

Biological motherhood, birth and lactation can seem to give the mother an 'unfair' start. We do not want to legislate this away, as in Marge Piercy's (1979) fantasy of the future where foetuses are grown and born in the laboratory and both men and women can breast feed. Despite this natural and well-known unfairness, there is also a less widely known general tendency for adults to want to care for babies and young children, and to know how to do so, which comes into play when they are given the responsibility. The *human* tendency to care for the young will certainly become stronger, once it is recognized and encouraged in men as well as in women. Future social arrangements to supplement the care of biological mothers or to replace them can draw on this potential.

In such a society, would the biological mother have a special part to play? Not in the sense of an essential part. At present the experiences biological mothers have in our society do not always make them mother well. But if the movement to give birth back to women were to succeed, and giving birth and breast feeding became a less alienating and stressful process, the basis would exist for shared parenting. Mothers would be less needy and more able to enjoy mothering without having to keep it to themselves. If biological motherhood was no longer a limiting, humiliating, powerless, second-class status, but entirely proud and positive, of course biological mothers would insist on the privilege of being one of their babies' main carers. It would still be true that her experiences would not guarantee that she would care any better than others. That would not matter, since there would be others to care both for her and for the child. Fathers and non-parents would also have been part of the movement to cherish new babies and young children, and to value their relationships with them. But whatever the sex of the carers, and whatever their relationship to the children, in order to care both for the children and for themselves, they will need working conditions very different from those which mothers have to accept today.

CHAPTER SEVEN

BEING MOTHER

COMPULSORY COMMITMENT

To become a mother is to make a lifelong commitment to another person. The strange thing about the commitment is that it *needs* to be entered into freely, but is in fact compulsory. Fathers can be more or less committed. If they are very committed, they are (usually) praised. For a mother to have only the degree of commitment considered normal for a father is to be thought of as unnatural and thoroughly wrong. These days, women have some choice about having children. The slogan of the women's movement, 'Women's right to choose', rests on the fact that the feelings you have about sex are quite distinct from how you feel about growing a baby in your body and looking after it in varying degrees for the next twenty years. The opposing slogan, 'The right to life', ignores the compulsory nature of the institution of motherhood. Women may be able to choose whether to have children (although social pressures are so great, contraception so chancy, and abortion facilities so patchy, that it is only a partial choice). But they do *not* choose the conditions under which children are cared for. When women become mothers, these conditions become their environment, which then usually prevents the full flowering of the commitment mothers can make to their children.

The way we institutionalise motherhood in our society – assigning sole responsibility for child care to the mother, cutting her off from the easy help of others, loving care, and making such care her exclusive activity – is not only new and unique, but not even a good way for either women or – if we accept as a criterion the amount of maternal warmth shown – for children. It may, in fact, be the worst. It is as though we had selected the worst features of all the ways motherhood is structured around the world and combined them to produce our current design (Bernard, 1975, p. 9).

In Chapter 1 we discussed the divorce of motherhood and power. Not everyone would see mothers' less powerful status as involving any depriva- tion. Economic dependence could be thought of as freedom – freedom from the *need* to work for money. It is quite true that a new mother who has to think about going back to work in a few weeks' time, whether to breast feed or not in the interim, who will look after the child, is under considerable strain. So is the woman who has to worry about where the next meal is coming from, who has no chance to take a holiday from pressing household concerns. That sort of motherhood is vividly described by the writers of *Letters from Working Women*, gathered by Margaret Llewellyn Davies at the beginning of this century:

> I am afraid I cannot tell you very much, because I worked too hard to think about how we lived. When my second baby came, I did not know how I was going to keep it. When the last one came, I had to do my own washing and baking before the weekend. Before three weeks I had to go out working, washing and cleaning and so I lost my milk and began with the bottle. Twice I worked to within 2 or 3 days of my confinement. I was a particularly strong woman when I married. There is not much strength left. But, Thanks be to God, I have not lost one. I have 2 girls and 3 boys, every one strong and healthy. The firm my husband worked for failed; then for most times he did not work; but I can truly say that for the most part of 25 years 17s. per week was the most I received from him (Davies, 1978, p. 111).

In complete contrast, in many two-parent homes in Britain today, the husband gets two weeks off work, the woman's mother or sister comes to stay, and there may be a temporary home help. Even when she is back in charge of the household, these full-time new mothers need not worry about breadwinning as well.

Donald Winnicott and many other psychoanalysts would argue that it is supremely helpful for the mother to be able to depend on the father's pay- packet as well as on his physical and emotional support. In this way she is free to experience 'primary maternal preoccupation', a state of intense identification with the child which allows her to know how he or she is feeling. This state, Winnicott says, gets the new relationship off to the best possible start. He calls it an 'extra-ordinary condition that is almost like an illness' (1964, p. 3). In this condition the mother may find it difficult to tell where she ends and the baby begins. She may find herself in the 'archer' position when she wakes up, or surprise herself sucking her own thumb. Her knowledge of the baby's needs is acquired in a way she cannot herself understand. For the time being, baby and carer are merged. According to this view, the mother's resumption of her outside interests should be timed to meet the baby's – and her own – gradually increasing needs for separation.

Not all mothers do become so preoccupied. Winnicott describes two ways in which things tend to misfire. If a mother's self-interests are 'too compulsive to be abandoned' (1965, p. 15), she may not be able to suspend them to such an extent. She may not get very close to the baby until he or she moves into the easier, more available phase of babyhood in the latter part of the first year. Other mothers who do become preoccupied with their babies never recover their self-interests. The state of identification with the baby, which is only advantageous if it is temporary, drags on and becomes pathological, hindering weaning and getting in the way of the baby's individualization and autonomy. Winnicott writes about these mothers as if their different reactions were a question of individual differences in personality and experience alone. To us, these two sorts of mothers represent the two aspects of the contradictory position in which all mothers find themselves placed.

Some mothers (with the 'compulsive' self-interest) are afraid to 'let themselves go' ... or perhaps would like to, but cannot. This is not surprising. The onset of the state of 'primary maternal preoccupation' can be alarming. Mothers often report that for the first few days they could not understand books or newspapers, or follow a talk on the radio. Nobody tells them that this state will pass or suggests that it is functional; or, if they do, references to 'you and your baby in a little intimate world' are so sickly sentimental that they bear no relation to the stormy passions of reality. In any case, these mothers' fears are well founded. They really are in danger of losing their 'self-interests' for good if, in their love for their babies, they find (as many do) either that they cannot bring themselves to go back to work and delegate the child's care to another (when their maternity leave is over) or that there is no longer a job to return to. For working mothers it is not exactly all or nothing, but all or very little. Few are lucky enough to have six months off work, or to return to a job with flexible hours.

The other mothers, the ones who never recover their self-interest, are also suffering from the restricted opportunities open to women in our society and the corresponding ways we think about ourselves. Perhaps they had their babies because they lacked enough self-interest and self-confidence in the first place. They look to their children to supply the meaning their lives lack, which in the short term children can do all too well. These mothers, who allow themselves to feel the joy of caring for babies and children, will sooner or later be forced to face the children's resentment and hostility, or find a way, in the end, to develop themselves.

Superficially our society might seem both to encourage new mothers to 'merge' with their babies and to provide the material support they need to be able to do so (men earning a 'family wage', health visitors, social and health services, maternity leave and pay). In fact, the lack of other parenting people, the isolation of mothers and the low status of child care make absorption in the baby a dangerous state of mind for women, which some dare not enter; while some others, who do, never recover, to their own and their children's ill-fortune. Because society makes it difficult for mothers to be anything else that is satisfying at the same time, it can be really difficult to let go as well as to give enough.

A Californian study based on 151 randomly selected people born in 1928 and 1929 in Berkeley illustrates these pressures which were particularly strong for mothers in nuclear families in the 1950s. One mother said:

> When the baby [third child] was just 6 months old, my husband was working extremely long hours, commuting to San Francisco and I saw relatively little of him. I was very tired and strained ... Anyhow the boy [Steven, now aged 8] said to me, 'I won't go to school today.' And when I asked him why ... he said 'I'm afraid to leave you alone.' I was horrified that he was carrying the load of my depression (quoted in Philipson, 1982, p. 36).

Another said:

> I'm crazy about the youngsters – get my love that way. He's [spouse] not demonstrative or affectionate with me. He works at night ... and part of the day. It's not a satisfactory life except for the children!

Philipson comments:

> ... the question remains as to whether it is satisfactory life for either mothers or children. In many cases the reality of children's needs is obscured because mothers are unable to disentangle their own feelings from those of their children (loc. cit.).

One further quotation shows the 'ambivalence about their children's autonomy' that Philipson says was common among mothers in the sample:

I was all wrapped up in her. I didn't go out much at all when I first had her ... Up till a month ago, I could never leave Melissa (she is 6½ years) ... I think seriously of separating myself from her sometimes. My sister wanted to take her this summer for a while, but I hesitated. They don't realise what it's like (ibid., p. 38).

Getting close to our children is one problem. There is also the danger of getting too close, so that we cannot distinguish our needs from our children's. Unless mothers have a clear knowledge of their own separateness, they will have difficulty in giving their children a strong feeling of *their* separate identity. This is particularly a problem for girls, since the mother is more likely to feel a boy-child as different from herself from the beginning; and, as he comes to know his gender, social pressures will push him towards taking men as his models (Chodorow, 1978, p. 109). But for both boys and girls, weaning (in the widest sense) is a problem for mothers whose children are their main purpose in life. The crisis the mother with adolescent children has to go through, as they leave home and leave her, to find new definitions of herself and her purpose (if she has not yet managed to do it) is rehearsed a million times as the baby and child assert their autonomy and independence.

The present way motherhood is organized does not help the carer to have both a well-defined self to 'merge' with the baby and also an awareness of their separateness. For some women there is no breathing space. Necessity, or their own needs, and the lack of support, make them more preoccupied with how to leave their babies than with the children themselves. Others, whom we have described as protected for a space, cocooned by relatives and husbands, are actually being prepared for their isolation as mothers. The 'family wage' ideal of the economically dependent biological mother does not so much protect her and the child in their mutual preoccupation as ensure that no one else enters the magic circle. 'Primary maternal preoccupation' need not be the monopoly of the biological mother. Her physical experiences often leave her weak but elated, open to new states of mind. But when 'primary maternal preoccupation' does happen, it is probably more the result of responsibility for the new-born. That responsibility itself opens the adult to new feelings or memories of old ones, if she or he is able to accept it. One father we know was not sure that his wife was going to be able to mother her new baby well enough. The first few nights the woman and baby were back at home, he slept very lightly and disturbed his wife by trying to turn her on to her side (as they had had the baby in the hospital), muttering 'You might choke on your back!' He obviously felt he had to mother them both. Once he was reassured that she could do it, he let the responsibility pass mainly to her.

Whoever the main carer or carers, he, she or they ideally need a period of partial withdrawal from the rest of the world: from business, material worries, politics and noise. It is nonsense to suggest that this can only be attained in a way which leaves the child carer socially handicapped for good, through her economic dependence and withdrawal from the labour market. As an obvious first step, parental leave for birth should be recognized as a priority. Both partners – or one, if only one was carrying on with paid work – could have a reduced work-load for many months. These arrangements need not be restricted to the nuclear family if the baby's main carers are not officially part of it, just as companions other than fathers are now beginning to be allowed into labour wards. As things are, the relationships between mothers and children are crucial because children are *made* uniquely dependent on this one special adult.

DEPRESSION: OCCUPATIONAL HAZARD

Depression is so common among mothers of young children that it could be called an occupational hazard. It is hard to give figures because it is difficult to draw a line between the debilitating depression, which clinicians would recognize as morbid, and 'normal' functioning, which in mothers often involves long periods of slight depression. It is possible to cope fairly well with depression which is like a cloud always present on your personal horizon, a sort of familiar which you can feel looking over your shoulder as you wash out the bottles, but which never becomes more tangible than a lack of zest and joy in relationships which could and should be full of pleasure and surprises. Many women realize they have been depressed only when the baby is weaned or becomes mobile, or when they go back to work or take some other step which reawakens their enthusiasm for living. All the same, some estimates put disabling depression at about a third of all mothers of babies, and the figure for working-class women is certainly higher (Welburn, 1980, p. 38). Some women never experience post-natal depression at all; for some, it is so bad that it causes a crisis for them, their children and entire families; while for some others, the depression that began sometime in the baby's first year drags on. Usually it gets slightly better, but it can go on for years until it becomes thought of as a part of the woman, as her habitual mood, as how she is.

Mothers of babies and young children should have no reason to be depressed. The pessimistic assumption that depression is normal and inevitable is often accompanied by the pretence that it is not happening or does not matter. Paradoxically, the notion that post-natal depression is 'normal' contributes to its often going unnoticed, even when serious. Welburn describes a woman whose state of mind went unquestioned until one day she burst into floods of tears during a conversation with her own mother. But by then, as the woman herself recognized, she was getting better.

... everything seemed futile you know. Nothing I did seemed to please the baby for a start. I felt helpless. It seemed like a project that I just couldn't get to the end of. I couldn't achieve anything. Every single thing that I did he bawled his head off at, he never smiled, was never happy ...

He seemed so desperate and then somehow I found myself getting more and more miserable ... And I went into a black pit.

For a start not a single thought went past my head. Nothing. Total blank, absolute blank ... Everything I was doing I was doing automatically, I had no mastery over it. I had no control over it at all.

After three weeks I went out of the flat. I couldn't leave the baby ... I don't know why, I was just terrified of leaving the baby. I took him out in the pram. I was walking and I crossed the street as though he wasn't in front of me. Because I remember, it was fascinating, fascinating to watch the cars go by so close to the pram. I just didn't have control over it. I saw it happening as if I wasn't there ... They must have gone by by centimetres ...

It never entered my head to ask for help ...

I remember thinking 'If only someone would take the baby off my hands for forty-eight hours, I'm sure I'd be able to cope' ... I felt responsible for him ... (Welburn, op. cit., p. 35).

An adoptive mother whose depression also went almost unnoticed came to the conclusion that the main cause was the great responsibility she had taken on.

Four years ago when my adopted daughter was tiny I spent hours of anguish that I felt I could not share. It is expected that a mother who has recently given birth will be tearful and depressed. This can safely be put down to hormone changes and the rigours of breast feeding. Adoptive mothers are less lucky.

When Anna arrived we were inundated with presents, cards and visitors, who wished to share our good fortune. They told me she was beautiful, I said she cried a lot and everyone laughed. I was frightened, tired and resentful, but to have voiced any doubt or complaint would have been as acceptable as a million pound pools winner complaining about the colour of the cheque ...

I felt I was living in a goldfish bowl with a rigidly fixed smile on my face (the *Guardian*, 2 May 1983).

This woman explained her tearfulness to her husband by tentatively referring to the difficulty of 'adjustment to a new member of the family'. She writes: 'If I had opened the floodgates, I knew I would have drowned.'

For her, as for the other woman quoted, there was no one to whom she felt it was safe to talk who asked her how she was. Both women smiled in their despair because they felt there was no one around who could bear to hear their feelings expressed without offering glib/frightened reassurances about hormones or adjustment. In other words, there was no one to do for them what they were trying to do for the baby. This common lack of supportive listeners is itself one of the avoidable causes of depression among mothers of young children. It also worsens the effects of the other causes.

Depression is depressing both to describe and to read about. We have to remind ourselves of the evidence that hormones or withdrawal of hormones could be only a slight contributing factor. This is good news: it means that maternal depression springs from the conditions in which children are cared for, not from motherhood itself. And these conditions can be changed.

The conditions of motherhood affect mothers differently. Some factors which often lead to depression only apply to some mothers. But underlying them all is the most general factor: the second-class status of women, which is part of the environment for all mothers. Self-esteem tends to be lower among women than men, and low self-esteem makes a person vulnerable to depression. Despite the rhetoric about the value of child care, mothers see recognition and rewards going only to people who achieve impersonal, measurable things, or who provide for some fantasy far removed from everyday caring. Women who are mothers are more likely to be cut off from participation in activities that bring status and recognition. The economic dependence of women is considered a normal state for them and is built into tax and social security legislation; it is even more common for mothers. It is difficult to feel like a strong adult and a full member of society if you are financially dependent on others. Various factors which each lower self-esteem by themselves have been found to make depression more likely among mothers of young children; they include being alone or without any close relationship, having lost your own mother as a child, having no job outside the home, and having several young children at home (Brown and Harris, 1978). In other words, those mothers with the least support, the most work, and the most unmet needs from the past to plague them are in the most vulnerable position.

It is ironic that the women who cope well with mothering are those who do not conform to the stereotypes of femininity. Having a low opinion of oneself and one's deserts is made more likely by becoming a mother – but it does not help mothers do the job. The most successful mothers are not at all passive. They have a realistic appreciation of themselves and the task, and a strong sense of themselves, and they do not even try to be perfect and selfless (Breen, 1975). The idea that motherhood should come naturally to women makes it harder to admit the difficulty of the task and ask for help. To need help almost seems to reflect on mothers' claims to womanhood, which are often surprisingly insecure. But to recognize the difficulty of the task is an essential step towards getting the support which can transform it.

The difficult task is partly a physical one, especially at the beginning. Night-shift workers are assumed to need daytime sleep. Sleep deprivation and interruption are well-known forms of torture. Yet in early motherhood (to some extent, parenthood) they are accepted as normal, although at the very least they slow down the mother's waking reactions, dull her thinking and make her more easily depressed. With more physical support and more sharing of the responsibility, there would be no reason for chronic exhaustion among mothers. It results solely from the organization of child care, and is a completely avoidable cause of much depression and child abuse.

When mothers have total responsibility, they are more likely to feel depressed. One study of forty-seven middle-class mothers with healthy babies found that although only a few would receive treatment, most of them felt depressed or anxious in the early weeks. Mothers who described their feelings like this were likely to smile less at their babies, were less attentive and less sensitive towards them, when observed every few weeks during the first three months. Not surprisingly, all these traits in the carer are known to affect babies' development. Most of the fathers were at home in the first two weeks, but fewer were available much by six weeks. If the father *was* often available and was actively caring for the baby when at home, the mother was less likely to be depressed or anxious.

By the time the infant was twelve weeks old, the amount of time ... spent with someone other than mother affected both mother and infant. The more time the infant spent with father, the less she cried when with mother, and the more time with a third party, the more she smiled at mother. This is obviously rewarding to the mother, as the more time the infant was out of her care the more responsive the mother was and the more she touched the infant affectionately (Antonelli, 1981)

So the most elementary and obvious forms of support have an immediately observable effect.

The difficulties of caring for children go beyond the physical work and the lack of relief. Mothers are expected to mother the entire family, not just their children.

Everyone has to roll over when a new baby is born. The baby pamphlets remind the mother to remember her husband's needs, to be understanding towards her displaced toddler. She is entrusted with 'making up for it' so that the other family members are compensated by keeping their places under the wide umbrella of her mothering. Who is going to make it all right for the mothers? When things go right, the baby can do it ... when things go right, she may not even feel any need for nurturance herself. She may be right there in her mothering, looking into the baby's grave eyes, feeling the suction pump of her toothless jaws on the breast. When things go wrong, it needs a strong woman, with a lot going for her, to manage to listen to hours of fretting or crying without feeling rejected, empty, hopeless, angry.

Mothers are trying to provide a loving environment for a new person who is both totally helpless and vociferous. Like all carers, to do this well they have to draw on their own experience. But as they open themselves to the memories of what it was like, they also remember how their own needs as children were not always met. This memory is very poignant because, as things are, mothers' immediate needs usually go unmet. They need mothering themselves; they need sleep; they need adult company and continuity with their old pre-baby selves, who played bridge or went to the pub or enjoyed long walks or making love. They need time and space to feel how their lives have changed, and people to listen to them. Above all, they need fellow-commitment and co-responsibility.

Mothers' needs are rarely met, yet they have to go on trying to meet the baby's needs. It can feel as if the baby or child is the powerful one, who allows or withholds sleep or love and approval. If there is no one else, mothers turn to their children for fulfilment of their own needs. Up to a point children can do this. Babies can give us the feeling of being loved, of emotional and physical closeness to another person, but only to the extent that we can give them what they need: there is no room for doubt, here, about who must come first. Adrienne Rich remembers (1977, p. 23) what it was like:

> ... my needs always balanced against those of a child and always losing. I could love so much better, I told myself, after even a quarter-hour of selfishness, of peace, of detachment from my children. A few minutes! But it was as if an invisible thread would pull taut between us and break, to the child's sense of inconsolable abandonment, if I moved – not even physically, but in spirit – into a reality beyond our tightly circumscribed life together. It was as if my placenta had begun to refuse him oxygen. Like so many women, I waited with impatience for the moment when their father would return from work, when for an hour or two at least the circle drawn around mother and children would grow looser, the intensity between us slacken, because there was another adult in the house.

Rich is describing here the legacy of 'primary maternal preoccupation' in a society which isolates mothers and children for much of the time without any other emotional and intellectual resources. As she goes on:

> I did not understand that this circle, this magnetic field in which we lived, was not a natural phenomenon ... because of this form – this microcosm in which my children and I formed a tiny, private emotional cluster, and in which (in bad weather or when someone was ill) we sometimes passed days at a time without seeing another adult except for their father – there *was* authentic need underlying my child's invented claims upon me when I seemed to be wandering away from him. He was reassuring himself that warmth, tenderness, continuity, solidity were still there for him, in my person. My singularity, my uniqueness in the world as his *mother* ... evoked a vaster need than any human being could satisfy, except by living continuously, unconditionally, from dawn to dark, and often in the middle of the night (op. cit., p. 24).

These are the psychological effects of the way motherhood is organized. The unique relationship evokes 'a vaster need then any human being could satisfy' for *both* mother and child.

The physical factors and the conflicts of past and present which we have described are common to all mothers. But in good material conditions, with no money worries and even the possibility of buying a little support or time off, mothers are less likely to become depressed as a result. If mothers are homeless, or in bad housing; if they are managing alone, or married to a man who is sick, unemployed or low paid; if the child is ill, or constantly sick, or cries all the time, the burden can simply become too great. Hannah Gavron, writing back in the 1960s, confirmed the truth of the cliché that middle-class mothers expect more of life than motherhood, while working-class women accept it as likely to be their main source of satisfaction. Yet, she says baldly (1968, p. 82):

> in some ways their ability to keep their heads above water as mothers appeared considerably less than that of their middle-class counterparts. The factors contributing to this situation include bad housing, lack of play facilities, lack of nursery schools, lack of babysitters, reduced contact with their extended families, and reduced earning capacities.

If you live in two rooms up two flights of stairs, and you have to try to keep the children quiet because the neighbour, who works nights, is asleep, all the ordinary problems of motherhood are terribly multiplied. The streets are unsafe, and much of the time there is nowhere to go. Play-groups and mother-and-toddler groups have slightly improved this situation since Gavron wrote. But these are far fewer on the ground in working-class areas than in middle-class ones. Working-class mothers have often either to shoulder the burden alone or, if they go out to work, to use child minders who are also working class, also isolated, and often also depressed.

Depression among mothers matters. Like all depression, it is a waste of life. But depression directly linked with motherhood is even more damaging, since the very conditions that make mothers likely to be depressed also make their children particularly vulnerable. Mothers are uniquely powerful over their children. It is easy to blame them, since theirs really are the hands which deal the blows as well as the arms that comfort. It is dangerous to make one person so special. The less her concentrated influence is diluted by other relationships, the more directly the mother's ups and downs affect her children. Child abuse is often a direct result of maternal depression. Less obvious forms of neglect often result, when mothers are apathetic and unresponsive rather than hostile and rejecting. If you have to drag yourself out of a pit of preoccupation with your own feelings, it is difficult to know what is really going on for your two-year-old.

The following history is described by Mills. One young mother who was deeply depressed spent most of her time reading, smoking and musing. She asked her little boy, who sat quietly gazing at her, to bring her an ashtray. He did, and she thanked him and stroked his hair. At this he began a search for ashtrays, which he piled up on the table next to his mother. She finally noticed, and lashed out at him. He returned to quiet, watchful play. A few minutes later his grandmother, who had been washing up, left the house to buy him some sweets. He asked his mother where granny was going. His mother said, 'She's going out because she's fed up with you.'

Some mothers who are depressed manage to remain responsive, but are quite unable to take control in any area. Their children may have to comfort them when they weep, and role reversal as early and as extreme as this must be a great strain for young children, although it is surprising how common it is. Whatever form maternal depression takes, and however acute or slight, it represents at least a difficulty for children faced with their own developmental tasks, and often a disaster. One study (Mills) of the processes of interaction between depressed and non-depressed mothers and young children concludes: 'What is apparent is that the modern practice of practically 24-hour care of very young children at home, without adequate physical or psychological supports, can be hazardous to the mental health of young mothers and often puts the development of their children in jeopardy.' Welburn (1980, p. 39) uses a picturesque comparison:

After we have given birth it is as if we wake up to discover that a mountain of sand has been deposited in front of the doors of our home. Some women get to work energetically to dig routes out. They have friends who come along and help. They work round the sand and over the sand; they find marvellously inventive ways to cope with the situation. Some women find one difficult route out and stick to that. Some try to dig a way through and get buried, others just look at it, feel defeated, retreat within their four walls and give up. Psychologists concern themselves with the reasons why some of us can be energetic and find routes out and others get buried or trapped. The latter are often called 'inadequate personalities' and ways to help them are suggested. This ignores the essential question of why the sand need be there in the first place. For the sand represents the ways in which the new mother is isolated from the outside world. This has little to do with her personal psychology. It is a matter of social organisation and social attitudes.

Welburn says the 'new mother', but it should be clear that there is no clear dividing line between post-natal depression and the depression mothers often suffer later on or go on suffering. The causes are similar and so are the remedies.

'GOOD' AND 'BAD' MOTHERS

Welburn pictures the conditions of mothering as a pile of sand at the mother's door. Until very recently, the question of the social context of mothering did not concern any school of psychology. They were engaged in trying to find out what children need, working out what sort of care could fulfil their needs, and judging mothers according to their capacity to give it. By that logic, only 'bad' mothers need be helped (or punished), and the actual system of individual mothering could remain unquestioned.

The doctrine that some mothers simply are 'bad' and others 'good' is plausible but false. It is an example of the sort of thinking which has become known as 'blaming the victim'. Such an approach emphasizes psychodynamics without looking at the social context of relationships. Individual mothers do their mothering in the context of their own personal histories and their own material circumstances, poor or rich. They have little control over the way in which they and their children are affected by the private forms of child care.

This is not to say that a mother's actions have no effect on her child. Since mothers are made so important a part of their children's environment, their behaviour assumes an awesome significance. In this century more stress has been laid on environment than on heredity. It is now understood that the child's inheritance is not fixed; it only takes shape in the interaction with its environment. This understanding has actually increased mothers' and parents' assumed responsibility. In the mid-1920s, the behaviourist psychologist Watson claimed to know how parents could produce useful citizens by the right style of child care.

A social renaissance was necessary, Watson announced, once mothers faced up to the implications of his research. 'Am I not almost wholly responsible for the way my child grows up?' a mother should ask herself. 'Isn't it just possible that almost nothing is given by heredity and practically the whole course of development of the child is due to the way I raise it?' If, on shouldering this burden, she staggered under the load, she was bound to ask: 'Where shall I find the light to guide my footsteps?' The answer was in the behaviourists' mapping out of 'infant culture'. The mother who mastered the essentials of behaviourism became 'a professional, not a sentimentalist masquerading under the name of Mother' (Hardiment, 1983, p. 173).

The modern approach would insist that sentiment is essential to further healthy child development, but with the same stress on the mothers' power. Thus Sroufe writes (1979, p. 840): 'To be sure, children have inborn differences in certain behaviour characteristics. These characteristics probably influence how we behave toward them (as should be the case if our care is sensitive and responsive). But we shape the persons they are.' Attachment theorists set out to predict how mothers shape their children. They arrange mothers on scales of sensitivity/insensitivity, acceptance/rejection, co-operation/interference and accessibility/ignoring (Ainsworth *et al.*, 1971). In a sample of 106 white middle-class American babies, 66 per cent of the babies were defined as 'securely attached': they explored actively when alone with their mothers, were upset by separation but readily comforted by getting physically close to their mothers on reunion. The other babies behaved differently, either avoiding physical contact or mixing attachment behaviour and avoidance. They were either very distressed or not distressed at all by separation. Ainsworth linked their behaviour directly to maternal behaviour. She judged their mothers to be either rejecting or insensitive (Ainsworth, 1982, p. 17).

> The mothers of 192 babies were not only highly insensitive but also inaccessible for prolonged periods. They were impatient with the role of housewife and mother, and found other activities to occupy them both at home and away from home. When at home they could go in and out of a room, preoccupied with other thoughts, and not even acknowledge the baby's existence ... The baby tended to be rejected along with the maternal role (Ainsworth *et al.*, 1971, p. 44).

Alas, Ainsworth may be right about her facts, but in the tone of this passage we can hear the ideological part psychology plays in bolstering up the status quo by blaming the mother. There are, after all, many women who are impatient with the role of housewife and mother but who are neither rejecting nor insensitive, and many men who are preoccupied in the way Ainsworth describes but who are not similarly blamed for the inadequacy of their child's attachment to them. Nor does Ainsworth ask whether these mothers have *reason* to be impatient with their role, and whether anything could be done about its limitations.

Ainsworth concludes: 'There is now a considerable body of evidence of continuity linking the organization of attachment to the mother at one year and the organization of social-emotional behaviour up to five years.' Other studies too have pinned down the inevitable influence of full-time mothers on their children's behaviour. But one study reports that 'mother–infant dyads of low socio-economic status' show less continuity. Where stress comes more from material circumstances than from the mother's present and past relationships, the quality of mothering cannot be so crudely presented as a personal characteristic of the mother. When family circumstances improve, so does the child's development (Vaughn et al., 1979, p. 971). Even within a middle-class sample, stress reduction noticeably affected the mother's behaviour to the baby and the baby's reaction to her (Ainsworth, 1982, p. 13).

Attachment theorists claim that the less diluted the bond between the child and the primary carer, the better for the child's development and ability to cope with stress in the future. But different societies have different ideas of healthy adult personalities and present different sorts of stress. The upbringing children need to become 'well adjusted' in the USSR is different from that required in the USA. Societies set children different developmental tasks. Some are basic, like learning to walk and talk. Others, like intellectual development, particular skills, and the sort of emotional development which fits in with the society's values, are more variable. People who live in crowded housing and work co-operatively had better not want to be alone. (See Bronfenbrenner, 1974.)

Faced with this sort of criticism, Ainsworth has retorted that societies are not all equally good. She would say that those which do not go in for exclusive mothering score lower on a criterion of mental health. She offers no evidence to back this up (Ainsworth, 1962, p. 147). In fact, as we have seen, mothers and children pay a high price for our system of mothering. Psychologists, like other people, have their prejudices. Kagan puts it well (1979, p. 890):

> The sacredness of the mother–infant bond may be one of the few transcendental ideas in modern American ideology that remains unsullied ... The number of books and articles on attachment and the importance of mother–infant contact during the early post-natal days seems to be generated by very strong emotion, suggesting that something more than scientific fact is monitoring the discussion. If the infant can be raised by any concerned adult one more sacred column will have fallen.

If this sacred column is to fall, it will need a push from mothers themselves. Mothers are often among the first to blame the victim – that is, themselves and other mothers.

Feelings of inadequacy and self-blame are extremely common among mothers. Mothers who do no paid work often feel inadequate as adult members of society and thus unworthy as mothers, while women who have paid employment feel guilty. Whichever choice they take, mothers tend to feel that their children's entire development is affected by their choice. In fact mothers often seem to feel that the good bits about their children are inborn aspects of their personalities, while the bad bits are their mothers' doing! Most mothers accept the myth of a possible perfect mother, whose children would effortlessly behave 'well' just because of *her* perfection. When a mother sées her children screaming in the supermarket for the sweets which the management has deliberately placed at eye level, or wetting their pants on auntie's best rug, she does not see them as separate people, but as little bits of herself, reflections of her mothering being judged and found wanting.

These feelings of total responsibility isolate mothers psychologically. Women often do not trust other mothers unless they go through a self-deprecating ritual and make it plain that they realize that their children have just as many problems and their mothering is just as imperfect. The mother who seems to cope wonderfully may find herself avoided, although she too may be a secret sufferer from self-doubt. Women who do not have such friendships with other mothers are in a more vulnerable state. But even between friends such competitive feelings, and defensive comparisons of children and practices, still go on (Eichenbaum and Orbach, 1984, Ch. 7).

Mothers do not invent the idea that they are totally responsible for their children's welfare. We have seen that they really are given an enormous amount of responsibility, and are left either almost alone or completely alone to carry it out. They may not have read Ainsworth, but psychologists and others keep repeating the message in the media, in popular literature and in education and the health service. For example, a well-known professor of child health said on television recently that the amount of stimulation and help a mother gives her baby in its first three years of life is invaluable and irreplaceable. He turned to his filing cards, picked one out and commented that this mother was a good mother who had done everything she should, including taking her child to all her appointments at the child health clinic. Watching mothers must have imagined their cards to be in his file.

Mothers differ in their confidence that they can shape their children. Middle-class women have been brought up to believe that they can affect their environment by their actions. They are likely to agonize over their decisions regarding their children and to blame themselves when even the smallest things go wrong. Working-class women, whose sphere of action is more limited, often seem more matter-of-fact and less guilt-ridden. But they are carrying a different burden. They feel generally powerless to change the conditions of life for themselves *or* their children. Their feelings of inadequacy are likely to be expressed more in resignation than in guilt. A working-class friend told us that she had decided to give up being 'mother'll fix it' for her teenage son, whom she saw as incapable of managing his life. 'After all,' she said, 'that's his personality. He was born with it. I can't do anything about it.' Similarly, many working-class women accept the schools' verdict that their children are simply not very bright. Despite the competitive feelings which divide them, and the paralysing effects of self-blame and hopelessness, from time to time mothers recognize how the system of blaming the victim works to turn them against one another. Their anger is rarely expressed. From their earliest experiences, women are trained to turn their anger inwards. Despite the awfulness of guilt feelings, they can seem less alarming than admitting that something is wrong and that it demands action. This might mean having to face up to difficulties in a marriage or other partnership, to relationships with the children themselves, or taking political action to try to change the situation of mothers. Motherhood as an institution is at once inside us and outside, and feels enormously powerful and all-encompassing. Mothers will find it easier to see through the myth of the perfect mother when non-mothers join with them to insist on better conditions for rearing children.

Support is now provided by some psychologists. Bronfenbrenner's approach is refreshing. He explains how misleading it is to concentrate on relationships between two people (mother and child), ignoring their social context. He points out that the nuclear family does not usually consist of only two people. 'The developmental potential of a setting depends on the extent to which third parties present in the setting support or undermine the activities of those actually engaged in interaction with the children' (Bronfenbrenner, 1979, p. 847). Our whole argument has been that the 'setting' of modern mothering is itself a powerful and unrecognized influence on mothers and children and their relationships. Bronfenbrenner also points out that research comparing home and day care has usually just crudely contrasted the child's experience in one setting with that of a 'matched' child in the other. Instead, it should study the interconnections and interaction between home and day care, and the ways in which these two settings could be made mutually supportive. Questions about the effect on children of mothers working outside the home

> ... cannot be answered by simple comparisons of children of working versus non-working mothers, or of youngsters enrolled in daycare versus those reared at home. What is needed is a systematic appraisal of the environmental stresses and supports experienced by families in our society and the effects of this experience on the family as a child rearing system ...

He concludes with a trumpet-blast against 'blaming the victim':

> Whatever the socio-economic level, ethnic group or type of family structure, we have yet to meet a parent who is not deeply committed to ensuring the well being of his or her child. Most families are doing the best they can under difficult circumstances; what we should try to do is to change the circumstances, not the families (ibid., p. 849).

CHAPTER EIGHT

THE CHANGING RULE
OF FATHERS

PATRIARCHY GOES PUBLIC

'The rule of fathers' is the literal meaning of patriarchy. Many feminists use the term to refer to *all* societies in which women are subordinate to men – that is, to all known societies. Adrienne Rich writes (1977, p. 57):

> Patriarchy is the power of the fathers: a familial-social, ideological, political system in which men – by force, direct pressure, or through ritual, tradition, law and language, customs, etiquette, education, and the division of labour, determine what part women shall or shall not play, and in which the female is everywhere subsumed under the male. It does not necessarily imply that no woman has power, or that all women in a given culture may not have certain powers ...

We don't argue with the picture Rich paints, but with the title she gives it. 'Patriarchy' has a specific historical meaning. Nowadays, in the UK, the USA, the USSR and other industrialized nations, men's greater power is unconnected with their fatherhood. It does not spring from their role in the family. Childless men are not necessarily *less* powerful than fathers. Kate Millett is one of those feminists who use 'patriarchy' in its widest sense; but she, too, distinguishes between 'traditional' patriarchy and its modern forms. 'Traditionally, patriarchy granted the father nearly total ownership over wife or wives and children, including the powers of physical abuse and often even those of murder and sale. Classically, as head of the family the father is both begetter and owner in a system in which kinship is property' (1971, p. 33). But nowadays, she adds, men's priority in law

... has recently been modified through the granting of divorce protection, citizenship and property to women. Their chattel status continues in their loss of name, their obligation to adopt the husband's domicile, and the general legal assumption that marriage involves an exchange of the female's domestic service and [sexual] consortium in return for financial support (ibid., p. 35).

Even these modern forms of chattel status are no longer the inevitable effects of marriage. The difference between most industrialized societies nowadays and 'traditional patriarchy' is not just one of reforms, however. As production has moved away from the family, the centre of male power has itself shifted away from fatherhood.

In many modern societies (in North Africa, for example) and for centuries of European history, the male head of the family controlled the wealth and labour power of all family members. Phyllis Chesler married into just such an Iranian family, and describes (1978, p. 157) how she saw her husband transformed from the independent liberal student she had married in the USA into a son dependent on his father's goodwill and power, when they went back to Iran:

Abdul Mohammed was his sons' favourite topic of conversation. His activities – and person – entranced them. They spent hours trying to outguess his next 'manoeuvre': it was the only control they had over it. *They* were their father's real wives. Despite their bouts of melancholy, self-pity, and bitterness, they still flushed with pleasure when their father openly favoured or complimented any one of them ... Their lives were totally in his hands.

It is important to remember that patriarchy in the literal sense does not just mean domination of women by men; it means that *some* men, *some* fathers, control *other* men and their family members, women and children, who are even less powerful than the weaker men and who will rise or fall with them. In *The Way of All Flesh*, Samuel Butler describes three generations of such a family. The English nineteenth-century upper classes remained a bastion of patriarchal families long after the wider society had ceased to be literally patriarchal. In Butler's novel, Mr Pontifex used to call in his sons 'for the fun of shaking his will at them' (p. 24). He got tremendous pleasure from the power game, pretending to cut his sons out of his will when he was annoyed with them, and leaving all his money to charity, then putting them back 'so that he might have the pleasure of cutting them out again next time he was in a passion'. Butler describes in horrific detail how one of the sons, Theobald Pontifex, grows up to become just as oppressive to his own sons and entire household as his father had been to him.

Kinship is central to the way wealth is distributed and controlled in patriarchal societies. Mario Puzo's novel *The Godfather*, set in New York in the 1940s, portrays the Mafia as a patriarchal island in a more modern, industrial society with different values. Don Vito Corleone is the patriarch (or 'Godfather') of the Corleone Family: one of several New York Mafia organizations. The Godfather uses his considerable power, his political connections and his right to the favours of those he has previously helped, to fix things for men who make a commitment to him in return, who promise to be his friends. His youngest son and future successor tries to explain to his all-American fiancée:

> My father is a business man trying to provide for his wife and children and those friends he might need someday in a time of trouble. He doesn't accept the rules of the society we live in because those rules would have condemned him to a life not suitable to a man like himself, a man of extraordinary force and character ... he operates on a code of ethics he considers far superior to the legal structures of society (Puzo, 1969, p. 367).

This 'code of ethics' is one which presumes a rigid separation between men and women. The world of business is for men. Michael Corleone is breaking the rules of his world in saying even this much to Kay Adams. Men control women, by money and violence, and a wife belongs to her husband. When the Godfather's daughter is regularly assaulted by her husband, her parents refuse to take her back because to do so would be to treat her husband with disrespect. Softness, compassion and grief are feelings that only a woman can indulge for long. The Family's adopted member and adviser, Hagen, had been kidnapped and released unexpectedly. His wife screamed out in joy:

> By the sofa Tom Hagen was holding Theresa close to him, his face embarrassed ... [he] disentangled himself from his wife's arms and lowered her back onto the sofa. He smiled at Michael grimly. 'Glad to see you Mike, really glad.' He strode into the office without another look at his still-sobbing wife. He hadn't lived with the Corleone Family for ten years for nothing, Michael thought with a queer flush of pride (ibid., p. 98).

Another novel, *The Chosen*, set in the same time and place shows patriarchy with a very different face. This patriarchal island in post-war New York is the community of Chassidic Jews, who continue to live as they had done in the Jewish townships of Eastern Europe in the eighteenth century. In the Corleone Family, men were respected for their ruthlessness, for their calculated killings – not for pleasure, but 'as a matter of business'. Among the Chassidim, men are respected for their piety, for their learning and knowledge of the Torah; and their ability to lead other men depends on these intellectual and spiritual qualities. The Chassidic rabbi had led his followers as refugees into the United States:

> 'No one lives forever. My father led his people before me, and my grand-father before him, and my great-grandfather before him ... Daniel will one day take my place.' His voice broke, and he stopped ... Then he went on, his voice a little hoarse now. 'My son is my most precious possession' (Potock, 1970, p. 166).

Despite the dramatic contrast in ideas of masculinity, the exclusion of women from the important, the male world, and women's general sub-ordination to men, despite their power within their own sphere, are very similar in both these patriarchal communities.

There could not be a society in which *all* fathers made up the ruling class. But in genuinely patriarchal societies, only men whose wives bear children (whose labour power they can control) have any hope of becoming patriarchs themselves. Of those who make it, the ruling-class patriarchs rule over society, while the lower-class patriarchs only rule their own house-holds. The 'rule of the fathers' can only hold sway when kinship is important to business, to buying, producing or selling, or when production is actually home-centred. As we have seen in Chapter 1, when it is possible and practical for women and grown sons to set up on their own, to live indepen-dently, the fathers' rule at home crumbles.

> The Old Order is patriarchal: authority over the family is vested in the older males, or male. He, the father, makes the decisions which control the family's work, purchases, marriages. Under the rule of the father, women have no complex choices to make, no questions as to their nature or their destiny: the rule is simply obedience ... The patriarchal order of the household is magnified in the governance of village, church, nation. At home was the father, in church was the priest or minister, at the top were the 'town fathers', the local nobility, or, as they put it in Puritan

society, 'the nursing fathers of the Commonwealth', and above all was 'God the Father'.

Thus the patriarchy of the Old Order was reinforced at every level ... Rebellious women might be beaten privately (with official approval) or punished publicly by the village 'fathers', and any woman who tried to survive on her own would be at the mercy of random male violence (Ehrenreich and English, 1979, p. 6).

Capitalist industrialization doomed patriarchy, although many great battles against it still had to be fought. Potentially liberating ideas of equality in citizenship were in the air. Bourgeois ideology sounds very grand, if you assume that 'men' includes women. 'Liberty, equality, fraternity' ... 'All men are created equal ...' The American Declaration of Independence can still lift hearts – and the struggle is still going on to fashion laws in its spirit. Women were inspired by such promissory notes to question the 'naturalness' of their submission to their fathers and husbands. Men could still

... claim the new public world of industry and commerce as their own. But ... as the production of necessary goods goes out of the home, the organic bonds holding together the family hierarchy are loosened. The father no longer commands the productive processes of the home: he is now a wage-earner, as might be his son, daughter or even wife. He may demand submission, may tyrannise his wife and children, may invoke the still-potent sanctions of patriarchal religion, but no matter how he blusters, now it is the corporation which brings in 'the fruits of the earth' and dictates the productive labour of the family (ibid., pp. 10–11).

As kinship diminished in importance in economic and political life, the system of male domination became more impersonal and fatherhood lost its potency. As we have seen, family relations have become 'private' affairs. Fathers' greater power in families results from men's greater power in society, not the other way round. To overstress the domestic tyrant nowadays would mean missing the main target: public authority, the state in all its forms.

MAKING MEN FATHERS

The notion of the 'rule of the father' still leaves us with a puzzle: where do fathers come from? Fatherhood is always defined in terms of a relationship between a man and a woman, the child's mother, rather than in terms of a *direct* relationship with a child. Sometimes the man who has 'paternal' rights and responsibilities is the child's mother's brother, more often her husband. Kate Millett cites the nineteenth-century anthropologist Malinowski who said that all societies ensure that '... no child should be brought into the world without a man – and one man at that – assuming the role of sociological father' (op. cit., p. 35). She sees this rule as a way in which '... patriarchy decrees that the status of both child and mother is primarily or ultimately dependent on the male' (loc. cit.). This rule is not as universal as Malinowski presumed. It is certainly breaking down in our society. Women are still punished (informally) for having children on their own, but the punishment is not working very well as a deterrent. Millett's basic point remains valid: that fathers are *constructed*, usually through marriage, and that the way in which this is done is very much part of the apparatus of male domination.

Men do not bear children. The direct biological connection between fathers and their offspring is hard to verify. A doctor in a labour ward said:

> ... he had often heard a father say to his baby, as he first held it, 'I'm your dad', yet he had never heard a mother say 'I'm your mum'. In this expression may be found, perhaps, an indication of the distance hitherto felt by many fathers between themselves and their unborn child and an attempt to express a physical and emotional relationship that had until the moment of birth been for him at one remove (Brown, 1982, p. 118).

Fathers have to introduce themselves to their babies because the direct biological connection is missing and our society makes that difference between men and women highly significant. For men that distant ejaculation (and who is to know which one?) is a tenuous link with the babies they are assigned. That is why the search for physical similarities with their children means more to men. In this sense, which our culture makes a very important one, all fathers are adoptive, or you might say fathers-in-law. Toby, Miki's son, stated that 'Daddy is really my Daddy-in-law because I didn't come from his tummy'.

Monogamous marriage was invented to construct a definite link between men and 'their' children. Marriage cannot be seen as simply a mutual commitment made by two equal partners. Historically, it has been one of the ways of restricting women and controlling their sexuality to ensure that men only father their own biological children. In most existing societies, inheritance passes down the male line. Over a century ago Engels described how patrilineal inheritance came to replace 'mother-right', in which kinship was traced through the female line, and he called this shift the 'world historic defeat of the female sex'.

Some societies today have matrilineal inheritance – not the full-fledged 'mother right', but a system where property passes from a man to his sister's children. Here men are still more powerful than women, but there is not such a need for strict control of women's sexuality to make sure there is no ambiguity about who fathers which child. The uncle/father knows the children were born of his sister, and that is all that matters. You don't have to agree with Engels' shakier anthropological speculations about matriarchy and mother-right to agree with him that monogamous marriage developed to control women's sexuality, so that men could be sure they were the social fathers only to children who were biologically their own. This is the root of the 'double standard', the reason why monogamy has always been more stringently enforced on women.

Engels writes that monogamous marriage

... was not in any way the fruit of individual sex love, with which it had absolutely nothing in common, for the marriages remained marriages of convenience, as before. It was the first form of the family based not on natural but on economic conditions, namely, on the victory of private property over original ... common ownership. The rule of the man in the family, the procreation of children who could only be his, destined to be the heirs of his wealth – these alone were frankly avowed by the Greeks as the exclusive aims of monogamy ... [which] appears as the subjection of one sex by the other (Engels, 1968, pp. 502–3).

Only among working people, Engels argued, could monogamy be voluntary and an expression of love. For since working-class people had no property to pass on, there was no motivation for enforcing the women's fidelity to ensure the husband's paternity.

The economic argument needs some supplementing here. Engels' rather romantic view of a proletariat free from sexism does not correspond with reality. Working men *work* for their children, even if they have no sizeable property to pass on to them. They are just as keen as upper-class men to know for whose kin they are making an economic investment. It is not that they are never willing to be social father to another man's child – rather that they like to know and decide.

Engels does not seem to think he need explain *why* men are so keen to ensure they do not wittingly father another man's (biological) child. In fact this obsession does need explaining. It could only arise in a culture which understood the mechanics of conception, and in which men's relationship to women and children was seen in terms of ownership. In such a culture, intimacy with women and children is problematic for men just because of the inequality in power. Women can justly feel, whatever happens, that the children they give birth to are flesh of their flesh. Men cannot. All societies have to *construct* a relationship between men and children that will allow them to get close. Monogamous marriage can be seen as a way of designating which children men can safely care about. As a system, it is ridden with anxiety. Men who fail to control their wives, to keep them 'pure', become that horned figure of fun, the cuckold, and the bastard children to whom they have lent spurious legitimacy are seen as parasitic cuckoos in their nests. The love and money they have spent on other men's children drain away their masculinity and leave them weak, out of control, less male. The entire complex of ideas here is based on property ownership and competition for limited resources, and the fears spring from guilt. Strindberg expresses this masculine anguish in *The Father*. The Captain's wife is financially and socially dependent on him, and he rigidly controls her life. With the manipulative skills of the oppressed she convinces others that he is going mad, and actually drives him crazy by suggesting to him that he is not his daughter's father. Strindberg, speaking through the Captain, sees women as immensely powerful (1949, p. 71):

CAPTAIN: Can you explain to me how it is that a grown man can be treated as if he were a child?

NURSE: I don't understand it, but it must be because you are all women's children, every man of you, great and small.

CAPTAIN: But no women are born of men. Yes, but I am Bertha's father. Tell me, Margret, don't you believe it? Don't you?

NURSE: Lord, how childish you are. Of course you are your own child's father.

It becomes clear that the Captain's conviction that women are untrustworthy comes from his own success in seducing other men's wives. He says to his wife:

I have worked and slaved for you, your child, your mother, your servants; I have sacrificed career and promotion; I have endured torture, flagellation, sleeplessness, unrest for your sake, until my hair has grown grey; and all in order that you might enjoy a life without care, and when you grow old, enjoy it over again in your child. I have borne it all without complaint, because I thought myself the father of the child (ibid., p. 82).

Unmoved, she continues her merciless course and gets him committed to a lunatic asylum by provoking him to violence. His old nurse herself puts the straitjacket on him. The dying Captain (it seems to be grief which conveniently finishes him off) says: 'A man has no children, it is only women who have children, and therefore the future is theirs, while we die childless' (ibid., p. 99). The moral seems to be that of so much Restoration drama, otherwise worlds apart from Strindberg's bleak austerity: watch your wives.

We also get a glimpse, in this painful play, of men's wish for a direct, known connection with the future. One man of thirty-six, who was an AID donor of sperms to lesbian would-be-mothers, described his motives: 'I'd reached a stage where I thought I might never get married. I might never sire children. This seemed a good opportunity.' If he knew he had 'fathered' babies '... it would fill me with a certain satisfaction – that life hadn't been a complete waste, that I had used it for a purpose' (Hanscombe and Forster, 1982, p. 102).

The direct biological connection with children has enormous symbolic importance for most men. *She* magazine recently had an article entitled 'Could a Man have a Baby?' It looked at the possibility of transplanting a 'test-tube' embryo into a man's abdominal cavity, of removing it at about twenty-four weeks' gestation, and completing the developmental process in an incubator. This procedure is so unlikely to succeed, and the whole idea of mimicking an ectopic pregnancy so devious, that you might wonder why anyone should feel a pull to think along those lines at all. The title 'Could a Man have a Baby?' provides the answer – a real seller (*She*, January 1983). It is central to the definition of a 'man' that he is someone who cannot, ever, have a baby. The possibility of contradicting that definition probably fascinates most people because we all feel some regret for the parts of ourselves that rigid sex roles have forced us to sacrifice. In men, this regret could be given a stronger name: womb envy.

WOMB ENVY AND THE CONTROL OF WOMEN

The evidence that men envy women their reproductive role has been gathered and written about, but remains controversial and difficult to assess. Anthropologists can tell us of the custom of the *couvade*, in which '... the husband shares in the birth by acting it out either at the same time or after his wife is in labour, or by sharing the lying-in period' (Kitzinger, 1978, p. 122). In *About Men* Phyllis Chesler has a section entitled 'Womb-less Men' which consists of a collage of words and pictures, with occasional poetic but disjointed statements from her own pen. The message which emerges is that a lot of religion is a man-made compensation for men's sterility.

> I was God, the Father, who gave birth to Adam, and Adam, the man, who gave birth to Eve, and God the Father who Created Christ (op. cit., p. 41).

> Michelangelo's 'Creation' and William Blake's 'Elohim Creating Adam' are both highly artistic expressions of male uterus envy ... Michelangelo's 'Creation' is so grand, so exquisite, so compelling, that no one ever wonders: 'How can a child be born without a woman being involved? In fact, where is that male God's mother?' (ibid., p. 43).

Psychoanalysts (and novelists) have shown that men's dreams and fantasies often involve a wish to be passive – a part of all of us that 'masculinity' prohibits. Some sorts of evidence are less contentious. A friend of ours has a boy of five who recently became very upset when a small girl friend of his told him categorically, 'You'll never have babies.' And some men are quite aware of their regret, as their new-born nuzzle their armpits.

One way of suppressing forbidden wishes is to control the people – women – whose way of being reminds men of what they cannot have and dare not consciously want. In most societies, female sexuality, menstruation and childbirth are considered dangerous to men. They risk the loss of male power by contamination. And this is true, in a way. Men can only get back their feminine selves by power-sharing. In most societies, the risk of emasculation is resisted by various rituals and by keeping men away from women at critical points. Women's sexuality is more heavily controlled than men's. Sometimes this is done in brutal and obvious ways, as in the still-widespread practices of clitoridectomy and infibulation. These mutilations ensure that women cannot enjoy sex, so are unlikely to seek it, and that they can only be enjoyed by the right men. The justification given is in terms of men's ownership and men's expectations of women's bodies.

Of course, the double standard still operates in Western societies which are quick to condemn 'barbaric practices'. 'Good' women a hundred years ago were supposed to see sex as a duty, which made adultery less likely. Sexual desire in women was only appropriate for non-wives whose children, if they had any, would not be entitled to the protection afforded by certain paternity. The new freedom for women to enjoy (hetero) sexuality, the 'science' of sexology and the endless manuals on giving and receiving pleasure do not really signal an end to the control of sexuality – just a new way of doing it. Now that women are not invariably economically dependent, marriage is less compulsory, so

> ... the sexologists do their best to make marriage sound more attractive by adding, as a bonus, the hope of multiple orgasms for the woman ... The woman who enjoys sex no longer risks being burnt at the stake ... on the contrary, she will be praised by *Cosmopolitan*. At the same time, the husband finds it difficult to honour all the clauses in the new property contract proposed to him (Reynaud, 1983, p. 95).

Reynaud lists some of the commonest metaphors used in pornographic writing, and some 'great' writing too, to describe sex between men and women as an assertion of male power. Woman is the violin, man the musician, or

> ... he can identify with the hunter, weapon in hand, confronting his most dangerous quarry, woman; the toreador in the bull-ring, feeling reassured by the presence of his sword, knowing he will soon deliver the final thrust; the sweating gymnast performing tirelessly until he has worn out his vaulting horse; the warrior after the siege, breaking down the drawbridge with his battering ram and forcing his way as victor into the conquered stronghold (ibid., pp. 44–5).

All very familiar stuff, and nothing to do with loving. The symbolic role of the sperm, which invades the 'conquered stronghold', is very clear, and when we think of unwanted pregnancies, all too accurate. If men cannot *have* wombs, they will control them.

Men's womblessness is arguably the source of their present greater power. Nevertheless, men also experience it as a deprivation. It represents the feminine side of themselves they have been obliged to give up or keep under firm control. One way of coping with the resulting conflict is to undervalue women's creativity through birth, and to stress other forms of creativity. Another is to control women's reproduction and decide the terms on which birth takes place.

In industrialized societies, the largely male medical profession controls women's access to birth control and abortions, and birth itself. Management of labour in these countries could be seen as a distorted expression of womb envy – by being present, men can share women's experience in imagination. It is partly a way of making sure men's womb envy and women's reproductive power do not get out of hand. Women's experience of birth is controlled, so that it becomes safe to a society based on female subordination: women are forbidden an active part in birth, kept subordinate in this area as in others. The womb is robbed of its power as a symbol by depersonalizing it – making the woman's body no longer her *private* parts but the legitimate territory of the largely male obstetric profession.

Kitzinger describes (op. cit., p. 146) how childbirth is a sort of initiation into motherhood for women.

> It involves separation from 'normal' people going about their everyday lives; taking over by agencies outside the women's own control; investigation and assessment involving exposure of the most intimate parts of the body to men and strangers . . . Only after these rites of separation and humiliation does society remake her as a mother.

In a different way, 'his' wife's subjection to these procedures is a sort of initiation for the man becoming a father. Other men do things to the sexual parts of *his* sexual partner. Kitzinger sees the shaving of the pubic hair as a ritual desexing of the woman, to make the obstetrician's invasion of the husband's rights acceptable. She points out that no medical purpose is served.

> The labouring woman is often covered from the waist down with sheeting. When an obstetrician isolates with drapes the lower half of a woman's body, it becomes *his* sterile field. But it is clearly neither his, nor, because of the juxtaposition of vagina and anus, sterile. It is a convenient fiction . . . by which he asserts his rights and insists that the woman keeps hands off her own body, which becomes out of bounds. This is another way in which the genital area is depersonalised . . . It provides an armour against his own feelings . . . not only disruptive of sexual emotions, but very often also those of tenderness, compassion, sympathy and friendship, in the doctor–patient relationship (ibid., p. 149).

In the face of massive evidence that intelligent, informed self-determination is the single biggest factor for a successful birth, obstetricians obstinately cling to their over-used armoury for intervention. One writes: 'The active management of labour necessitates that obstetricians take over, not just a single aspect of delivery but responsibility for the whole process or parturition. Our control of the situation must be complete' (quoted in Oakley and Richards, forthcoming). Later they quote a doctor saying to a patient who was unhappy about being induced, 'If we explained to everyone and everyone's husband, we'd spend all our time explaining. I think you've got to assume if you come here for medical attention that we make all the decisions' (ibid.). Thus birth, a great personal and social event, is taken away from *both* parents and becomes a pathology understood only by experts.

It is men, of course, who have recently been giving birth back to women. Leboyer and Odent are French obstetricians who emphasize quiet, natural births as best, even in conditions which most obstetricians would see as requiring intervention – such as a mother over thirty-five expecting her first baby, in the breech position. They benignly allow women to regain their power. But if you watch the film of a Leboyer birth, you will see that the new-born is first held by the obstetrician who delivers, massages and bathes the baby, instead of putting it straight into the mother's arms and to her breast. If you watch a film of Odent's deliveries, you will see that the mother is certainly a star (while the father is even more marginal than in a modern hospital birth), but the real superstar is Odent, who holds her in the 'supported squat' position and who, above all, *allows* her to be active. These men usher in motherhood: like the traditional obstetricians – although so unlike them – they are the midwives of motherhood and fatherhood. Not just a baby is born, but new relationships, new statuses, and the circumstances of their birth must encourage a proper respect for authority.

It is not fathers who control the process of birth. Their autonomy is even less than the woman's. The process of making the woman the patient, and the man the 'patient's husband' (whether or not they are married), allocates them both their roles in the hospital ward and the world outside.

On arrival with his wife, the father is treated as if he were 'invisible' ... In my research fathers recall their 'entrance trauma' (especially acute for the first birth) with anger. They describe their wives as being 'taken away' or 'disappearing'. The format is the same. The midwife approaches the couple, confirms the mother's identity, and the two go off. The father is left standing, often with no explanation, and remains so for some time. Fathers recognise their peripherality. Some see their wives as being reincorporated into a 'society of women' ... During labour/birth the father can be 'activated', but as a background prop, supportive of the main action ... at the lowest level possible – as an 'extra' with no predetermined part in the script. His mask (usually incorrectly worn) has no sterile function, but the emphasis on pollution and infection symbolises that this is a hospital rite and not a familial occasion (Richman, 1982, p. 102).

In wanting to share the experience of birth, men are already going against powerful social taboos. They *are* entering a woman's world, although one which is actually controlled by doctors (mainly men), and, in any case, not by the mothers who are made the objects of the process. It is ironic that, whereas in general husbands have considerable power over their wives, when they declare their wish to *support* their wives in labour and birth (not a particularly manly role), their willingness to witness the blood and pain, to share the tenderness, the devices through which *women* are made to feel powerless in that situation are extended to them. They, too, experience lack of respect, the feeling that you don't matter as an individual, that everyone except you is very busy on an important errand, so that you hardly even dare ask for the information you need and have a right to. Fathers enter the 'women's world' at their peril, even though it is *not* controlled by women. Their experience of subordination in it may well deter them from messing around with the conventional division of labour between mother and father when they get home.

In both areas, of sexuality and of childbirth, what we are witnessing is not simply male control over women. Men's sexuality is constrained as well by the power relations which it comes to reflect. It is not *natural* to men to get sexual pleasure from dominating women. In maternity hospitals men too are controlled by the rigid conventions that allot us our places in the soap opera of birth and child care. Before the mother and child leave the hospital, its staff will have tried to 'get the relationship established' between them. Mothers must learn to love their babies, to change nappies, bath and feed them. Fathers who try to do these things at visiting time are often discouraged, and the idea that they might need to hold their new-born is new. One father we know was told to 'stop bonding – it isn't fair on the mother'.

Male control of women's bodies is the dark side of womb envy. It has a gentle side, too. There are increasing numbers of men who are not afraid of being 'like women', of fathers who want to participate in *all* aspects of looking after children. The story of modern fatherhood is one of a movement from controlling to sharing, even though, without further institutional change, this process cannot get very far.

CHAPTER NINE

FATHERS TODAY

STEREOTYPICAL FATHERS

Once upon a time it was clear what a father was. When the dominance of men went almost unquestioned, the role of the father in the family seemed an essential aspect of civilization. Fathers represented the wider society, its claims and its morality. Mothers and children stood for the life of the instincts and the limited ethics of the home.

The traditional characteristics of the father can be traced back to patriarchy. Fathers were supposed to be powerful, authoritative figures, who provided for their families, thought about their welfare and protected them. Of course, many fathers fell short of this stereotype. Today the stereotype itself falls short. It is true that fathers who act the tyrant within their families are protected by legislation which takes it for granted that women and children are normally economically dependent, and by the reluctance of the law to interfere in violence within families. The general inequality of power between men and women will always throw up tin-pot patriarchs, but they no longer play an essential part in keeping the system going. It can dispense with them. The oppression of women could still go on, even if all men loved their wives and children and showed it all the time.

These changes are clearly reflected in the law affecting the custody of children when their parents get divorced. In Britain in the early eighteenth and nineteenth centuries a father would automatically get custody in any dispute, because '... a mother, as such, is entitled to no power, but only to reverence and respect' (Blackstone, quoted by Lowe, 1982, p. 26). Significantly, this way of settling things was often described as 'natural' in the cases of the day. Lowe quotes (ibid., p. 27) from a judgment in 1883: 'To neglect the natural jurisdiction of the father over the child until the age of twenty-one would be really to set aside the whole course and order of nature and ... the very foundation of family life.'

Of course it was the father's *authority*, not his participation in the child's daily care, which was here thought of as natural and as non-transferable. Any servant could do the caring. It would only be wealthy people, after all, whose custody cases would come to court.

One woman who fought for legal recognition of the importance of motherhood was Caroline Norton. She and her husband had been unhappily married; one day, when Caroline was visiting her sister, her husband took their three children to his cousin and refused his wife access to them. She discovered that as a married woman she was almost powerless in law. Her husband was legally allowed to keep the children from her, and to keep all the furniture and property she had brought to the marriage. When, in 1837, she began working with Talfourd, a Member of Parliament, on the Infants' Custody Bill,

> ... the *British and Foreign Review* published a long and insulting attack in which it called Mrs Norton a 'she devil' and coupled her name with Mr Talfourd's in a most impertinent way. Caroline, furious to the last degree, prepared to bring an action for libel, only to realise once more that, as a married women, she could not sue! 'I have learned the law respecting married women piecemeal, by suffering every one of its defects of protection,' poor Caroline wrote; it was but too true (Strachey, 1978, p. 38).

When the Bill hung in the balance in the House of Lords in 1838, Caroline Norton's pamphlet stating the case for it was published, under a male pseudonym so that it would carry more weight. The Act was passed in 1839. It laid down that '... a judge in equity might make an order allowing mothers against whom adultery was not proved to have the custody of their children under seven, with right of access to their elder children at stated times' (ibid., footnote, p. 39).

In the late nineteenth century, around the same time as this Act to allow married women to own property in their own right, other legislation was passed which made it easier for courts to give mothers custody – at their discretion. In 1925 the principle of paternal power was radically modified. It was then that the present principle – that the welfare of the child must be the chief consideration – first became law.

The shift in law to the notion of the mother as the caring (and therefore the essential) parent really came about through the Industrial Revolution. As Leonore Weitzman says (1981, p. 100), child care used to be '... perceived primarily as child training, and fathers were presumed to have superior skills and knowledge (especially where boys were concerned) for this vocationally oriented relationship'. When fathers left the home to work, when formal education and apprenticeship outside the family became the most common form of vocational training, 'education' and 'care' began to be seen as different processes, with education taking place outside the home and care within it.

As fathers moved off the farm into wage labour in factories and offices, women's maternal instincts were 'discovered', and mothers became increasingly associated with child care. Thus, it was only when women assumed the *de facto* full-time responsibility for child rearing that legislators and judges came to view the mother as the person 'naturally' responsible for children (loc. cit.).

This happened in the USA much as in Britain. So the notion of 'the child's best interests' is by no means a neutral one. How it is applied will depend on the ideas of courts of the behaviour suitable to men and women. Most states in the USA have sex-neutral statutes, but nevertheless it is almost always mothers who get custody, because the mother's care is believed to be in the child's best interests – unless it can be shown that she is 'unsuitable'. Adultery used to be considered evidence that a woman was an unsuitable mother. It no longer is, but conformity to standard ideas is still required. Lesbian mothers rarely get custody if there is a dispute. The courts' views of mothers' and fathers' roles remain stereotyped. Weitzman cites a case where a woman who had been awarded custody of her daughter lost it to the father when he applied to the court for a transfer, solely because the mother was working whereas the father's second wife was a full-time housewife (ibid., p. 116).

In family life, care is now legally recognized as more important than authority. The father has a chance of getting custody only if he can show that he can provide another woman to do the caring, or that he has a capacity for caring himself. His patriarchal authority, his moral leadership, count for nothing. In family life, fathers are officially dispensable, even though their absence is deplored. Men keep their greater power in society and in marriage, and therefore in family life, but they have lost their greater power *as parents*. Ironically, it is only when women leave their husbands, or threaten to leave them, that their increased power as mothers has any bite. It is still difficult for women with no income of their own and with dependent children to strike out on their own. If they leave without the children, their chances of getting custody may be affected. But unless they leave, they are not entitled to welfare benefits. Despite this problem, a small revolution has taken place. Women can choose to leave and can live alone, or with their children. The very possibility of being independent of any individual man, even if in poverty, has shifted the balance of power in marriage considerably.

In patriarchal days, paternal authority was a fact of life and one which could easily be justified in economic terms. The father controlled the family's income and resources, so he had a direct economic interest in bringing up his children as good workers and desirable marriage partners. Neither women nor children were full citizens with equal rights and responsibilities; it was the father's job to make sure they conformed. Authority distances, even though in patriarchal societies the father might well be physically present. The awesome respect considered a suitable feeling for children to have towards their fathers in pre-Second World War German middle-class families had a special name: *Ehrfucht*, meaning honour and fear.

The comic strips of the *Beano* still show Dad wandering about with his slipper to whack Dennis the Menace or Minnie the Minx. But are fathers really still the family hatchet-men? These days, they have no economic motivation to control their children. They are unlikely to benefit from their children's achievements. Few people in the developed countries plan to have children because they think of them as an investment, or because they depend on their help in old age. Most British and American couples would prefer to have a boy first, but there is not the same low relative value set on girls because they are a bad investment – they leave home when they marry – that sometimes leads to female infanticide in poor countries. Our culture strongly disapproves of thinking of children in economic terms – that is, in any economic terms other than our own treatment of them as objects of consumption. *Our* economic calculations are in terms of how many children we can *afford* to support. The Legal & General Insurance Company survey in 1983 calculated that the average working couple will spend £70,000 on their first child up to the age of sixteen. This includes the woman's loss of earnings, and other expenses on food, clothes, presents, holidays and pocket money.

David Owens (1982, p. 77) asked working-class men about their desire to become fathers, shortly after they or their wives had been to an infertility clinic.

> The men looked forward to having children who were viewed as likely to provide enjoyment, pleasure and companionship when older, and who as babies were essentially 'fun' ... reasons related to the continuation of

the family, or the desire for a son and heir were noticeably absent. Whilst this lack of interest in inheritance may be due to the class background of the men, it seems that there was a lack of a long-term perspective in general, since the men did not view children as providing a semblance of immortality, except in a few cases, nor did they seem concerned to have children as a means of achieving financial security or, contrary to Busfield's and Paddon's findings, as a source of companionship in their old age.

If men want to father children in order to enjoy their companionship, they are unlikely to want the distance and deference from their children which go along with authoritarian fatherhood. In fact we find two apparently contradictory things happening. In some families, father is ultimate authority, in line with the traditional concept we have been looking at: 'Wait till your father comes home.' Mothers do the hour-by-hour setting of standards, disciplining and punishing – if punishment is used. But father's authority is referred to, sometimes as an empty threat, sometimes as a real one. In families with fathers, in the USA at any rate, men are more often responsible for child assault. And child battering is the inevitable unacceptable face of 'legitimate' parental physical control and punishment of their children. In complete contrast – at first glance – is the image of the father as the gift-bearer, the soft option, the one who draws the night-wandering child on to his lap in front of the television while the mother shrugs impatiently, the one who excites the children when they should be getting sleepy, the one who buys them sweets. The contrast is not as complete as it may seem, for some fathers do both.

Whether fathers beat or treat has become more a matter of individual history and temperament than ever before ... because beating and treating are equally expressions of power. Fathers are no longer more powerful than mothers as parents, but they have not lost their superior power as men. Being the boss, the primary decision maker, is one way of showing it. Being the chief playmate and gift-bearer is another. Fathers can afford to enjoy being with their children without worrying about the effects of their behaviour, since they will usually be somewhere else. Being the gift-bearer, the one who spoils, is the direct consequence of being the parent with the most power over the family's resources – the provider. *This* stereotype still has some reality, however much male unemployment and mothers' paid employment complicate the picture.

Feminists have been cynical about the idea that men are acting as good fathers by providing for their families. The idea that paternal love can necessitate the absence of the father seems too reminiscent of old stories of man the hunter, woman the tidier of caves ... or woman as the centre, always waiting, the soul of the house where man can slough off the cares of the outside world. John Donne wrote about it 300 years ago (1960, p. 45), comparing himself and his woman to a compass:

> Thy soul, the fixed foot, makes no show
> To move, but doth, if th'other do.
> And though it in the centre sit
> Yet when the other far doth roam
> It leans, and hearkens after it ...

For feminists, to understand that men see themselves as working for their families means putting aside a lot of hurt and anger. We feel angry at the narrow choice open to people who want to be close to children: to be a 'mother' or a 'father'. More concretely, the working week is too long, part-time work too badly paid, houses are themselves designed to push us into cornflake-packet families, there is too little day care or other support for parents, and what there is is often bad. We can get so indignant about the situation within which men are expected to 'provide', and what it is like for women, that we fail to appreciate men's work as a direct expression of their affection for their families. Of course, many of the men feminists are close to are enjoying themselves bread-winning. They are in middle-class jobs that occupy their minds and give them good wages and high status, however much they complain about the demands and the routine of work. And many feminists, being highly educated women, are conscious that had they been men they would be in just such jobs, or they would be at a more senior level in their own work.

Class differences have contributed to the ghetto-ization of the women's movement. Working-class women's understanding of their men's work as a genuine contribution to the family (not a selfish absence) makes some feminist arguments seem nonsense to them. They know, because they see it every day, that working-class men are exploited and oppressed and have little power themselves, even though they have more than women. They know how hard they work. Even though they can see perfectly how women are unequal, how men are the dominant group, working-class women are very unlikely to see men as *the enemy* – even when they have been at the receiving end of male violence and selfishness.

When their children are young, most men work longer hours than at any other time in their working lives. Mr Parker, quoted in an Equal Opportunities Commission study, is a semi-skilled welder. 'Due to complications during Mrs Parker's pregnancy, and immediately after her discharge from the hospital, Mr Parker found it necessary to take six weeks in total off work – all of it unpaid' (Bell *et al.*, 1983, p. 53). He could get no *paid* leave because it all had to be taken at fixed times. He was asked if '... the birth of his son affected the number of hours he sought to work ...' 'Yes, I'd like to work more hours because of the money – because I have to, it's as simple as that. [I have] another mouth to feed' (loc. cit.).

In another study, a van driver was asked whether his family occupied his mind very much; his hobby is painting.

Most of it. They occupy it more than the work and ... the painting put together really ... The family matters most. That's what it's all about. Nothing would be worth doing if it was not for the family. If I hadn't got the family perhaps I wouldn't bother. I'd probably be on the dole – well I wouldn't be on the dole, but I'd feel I might as well be (Tolson, 1977, p. 69).

A study of 369 young fathers found:

Nearly half the men specifically mentioned their role as bread-winners as an aspect of their feelings of responsibility for their child ... 'Given me some motivation, something to work for.'

Some thought the effects on their work were negative:

'Now you're stuck ... I can't look round now, I've got to keep working' ...
'I had intended to continue what I was doing but left a 'good' technician's job to earn more money ... there's so much scope in technician's work, and you never stop learning – whereas the work I'm doing now, there's nothing more to learn ...' (Simms and Smith, 1982, p. 146).

Once you have others dependent on you, it becomes much harder to risk losing a steady income. It is harder to strike, harder to move house, harder to train for more skilled work, even if these changes would be in the long-term interests of the family. For many men, like the ex-technician quoted above, having children means saying good-bye to what opportunities there were for satisfying work. On the other hand, having children can give meaning to boring, alienated work. To spend forty or fifty hours a week making profit for someone else by lifting things from here to there or performing the same operation as car after car slides past, for the sake of a wage packet, is not an uplifting experience. But when men's children are dependent for their food, their shoes, their toys on that wage packet, working for money, for the sake of money, is so obviously a rational and right thing to do that the work loses some of its power to degrade. In this way, as in so many ways, men need their children.

All the qualities considered appropriate for fathers, all the things fathers typically do, spring from the way society is organized, not from the nature of the adult male. To take a rather laughable example:

> The father not only deals with activities of his job or the affairs of the day but also usually directs the family towards the pursuit of distant goals. In most families, for example, Father has the primary voice if not the final word on any major expenditure or major change: a new car or house, a move to a new location, a decision to save money or spend the savings, and so on. Thus he demonstrates to the family the art of planning, the disciplined pursuit of goals, and the delaying of immediate gratification in favour of ultimately more satisfying distant goals (Lynn, 1974, p. 104).

The trouble with mother is, she just can't wait. But to the extent that fathers really behave like this, it can only be because they are the family's main earners.

Fathers are often seen as the link between the family and the outside world. Two single parents who believe fathers play an essential role in child development argue that the father's part is universal and irreplaceable:

> ... the mother is the organic parent, bonded to the child through the fulfilment of its basic physical needs, the father has the social assignment to lead the child out of its dependency into an appropriate expression of independence ... The father must help his child become whatever the particular society expects. Thus while the content of 'mothering' – giving birth, feeding, cleaning and providing other physical care – has been universal, the content of fathering has depended on the particular social situation and historical time ... But the *dynamics* of the father–child relationship *are* universal. The father is the caring and involved adult who helps the child to separate from the mother, relieve the child of the guilt which might attend such a separation, and supports the fledgling autonomous self (Rosenthal and Keshet, 1981, p. 12).

Fathers are often linked to weaning, literally and symbolically. The father steps in with the bottle, when the mother wants to cut down breast feeding, because he cannot bear to hear the baby crying and is sure to give in. The father is firmer with the small figure that silently appears in the lounge when the adults are watching television. Or he is supposed to be. When he is, the child takes in the message that mother represents the original peace of union with her body and all its plenty, and father the demanding, chilly but exciting world outside her. But there is nothing timeless and inevitable about this. These are just aspects of parenthood, which are often split in our society and assigned to the father and mother. They do not have to be. Even as things are, mothers have to 'father' in this sense, even mothers who live with their children's father. They, too, represent society; they, too, have to help the child to independence and encourage their 'fledgling selves'. They have to do this although, as we saw in the chapters on motherhood, their own lack of independence makes it very difficult for them to do so in the conditions of nuclear family life. Many women are 'fathers' in the sense of being another caring and involved adult who is not the mother. Aunts, family friends, grandmothers may do this. So do teachers and play-group leaders. If men and women were socially equal, this aspect of fatherhood would no longer be seen as the particular province of men.

FATHERS AND SEX-ROLES

One characteristic of contemporary fathers is hard to explain in terms of their social position. All the research suggests that fathers play a greater part than mothers in encouraging the behaviour conventionally thought appropriate for boys or girls, and in discouraging deviations from it. Just one example: in one study, thirty pairs of American parents were asked to rate their babies on eighteen characteristics. The babies did not differ on average on such dimensions as length, weight, alertness or muscle tone. 'Parents, however, rated the girls as softer, finer featured, smaller, weaker and more delicate, and rated the boys as firmer, larger featured, better co-ordinated, more alert, stronger and hardier. Fathers were overall more extreme in their ratings than mothers' (McGuire, 1982, p. 103).

In McGuire's own research with two-year-olds in forty families, fathers were found to disapprove more than mothers of certain toys for boys. While mothers would reject dolls and push-chairs as suitable toys for boys, they were happy for their sons to play with dustpans and brushes, pots and pans and so on. Not so the fathers. She also found that fathers with sons described them in more positive terms than fathers with daughters. Even their mis-behaviour was described as 'mischievous – I wouldn't have him different'. In playing with their children, the fathers with boys would have mock fights and would tolerate a lot of real or acted aggression. The fathers of daughters played physically, but in a different way. They would let the little girls ride on their backs, throw themselves on to their fathers, tease them and express aggression up to a point, but then the father would be more likely to demonstrate how powerful and strong he was and subdue his daughter – all in fun. In general, these fathers were stricter with their girls' anger than the fathers of boys were with their sons (ibid., p. 118).

Fathers' main emphasis is on the need for their sons to learn to behave 'like men'. There seems to be considerable anxiety underlying this insistence. One nursery school teacher found himself

> ... angry at little boys who cried when they felt hurt or sad. His anger was so upsetting to him that he withdrew whenever little boys needed consolation or support. Under the careful and supportive probing of the head teacher in the school, who sensed his conflict, he exclaimed that 'I never was allowed to cry when I was little and they shouldn't either'. Further talking suggested that when little he had very much wanted to cry and be comforted and felt he rarely got what he needed from the grown-ups in his world, particularly his father (Fein, 1974, p. 60).

Caroline caught a glimpse of this anxiety when a little Australian boy who was visiting recently came into the kitchen in a long dress. For a split second his father looked panicky. Then he shifted into a heavy jokey routine: 'No son of mine is going to be a poofter.' Five minutes later the child was back in trousers. His mother had been unconcerned throughout.

The various research studies agree that fathers are less strict with girls who break the gender rules, although they usually encourage daughters in traditionally feminine activities. Fathers pay more attention to sons in most respects, but baby daughters come in for more cuddling (Parke, 1981, p. 58). Fathers' importance to girls is usually thought of in Freudian terms. Fathers are seen as their daughters' second love objects, and this transfer of loyalty, attraction and affection is thought essential to adult heterosexuality. A psychiatrist writes that an infant girl needs

> someone who can enjoy her beauty, her smile, her pretty dress, her first efforts at make-up and jewelry, [which] helps her gain the confidence that she can attract, charm and interest a man. A father who is made nervous by and ridicules her little feminine gestures, or who is always too tired or angry to be pleased by them, or who is absent too much, can cause his daughter to be insecure about her body and her inability to attract a man (Appleton, 1982, p. 13).

But here everything is back to front. Appleton is writing as if there were no need for fathers to help girls become feminine. He obviously believes girls are born with 'little feminine gestures' (perhaps a hand to her hair? or the motions of washing a floor?) and all the father has to do is respond to them – as a man.

Mothers certainly do treat boys and girls differently, and feel differently towards men. But they are probably less insistent than fathers on conformity to the external signs of gender. Perhaps they have a more realistic appraisal of the strength of the processes that will tame the tomboy and toughen the sissy. Why this difference? We suspect it is the insecurity and superficiality of the father's own imposed masculinity that makes him jump at his little son sweeping the floor with an apron round his waist. You could argue that the father encourages sex-role stereotyping because the power structure of male dominance is in his interests. But we believe that ultimately men are the losers as much as women, and their anxiety about sex roles partly reflects a wish to break the invisible strings that bind us.

Girls become women by becoming like their mothers. Boys become men by becoming *unlike* their mothers. Yet both are brought up by women and, for both, a woman was the first model as well as the first love. In male-dominated societies where women do most of the child rearing it is difficult to become a man. In many groups,

> The father ... actually takes the male child away from the mother at age seven or so and initiates him into the ways of men. In some cases the young son goes to live exclusively with men; in others, he undergoes rituals which separate him from his babyhood and identification with women, and serve to remind him of his adult destiny (Rosenthal and Keshet, op. cit., p. 12).

At a circumcision party in Turkey, about a hundred guests ate and drank and listened to singing and dancing to celebrate just such a transition. The victim, pale-faced, was wheeled in for ten minutes, to be congratulated. He was just seven years old. At that age, upper-class boys are still sent away to 'prep school'. But for those groups who have no *formal* movement for boys from the women's world to the men's, the process is more gradual, although difficult. We were told by a teacher that Miki's son and Caroline's daughter would probably drift apart, once they were at school. A year later their friendship is still going strong; but such attachments become rarer and rarer until, by age eight or nine, sex segregation is so marked that boy–girl friendships, if they survive, are usually surreptitious (Best, 1983). One fantasy (Allen, 1974, p. 5) about what it is like for boys to be inducted into masculinity deals with the visit of 'Uncle Macho' to the bedside of a five-year-old boy:

'Wake up, boy, the early bird gets the worm, you know!'

Mark rolled over and rubbed the sleep from his eyes, then he squinted up through the semi-darkness of the early morning at the figure standing beside the bed. Towering over Mark was a large man with a red face, a crew-cut, and a thick neck that bulged over his shirt collar.

'Strong silent type, eh?' the man observed. 'A real chip off the old block!'

Suddenly Mark became frightened by this strange man in his bedroom and he began to cry.

'Hey, cut that out, young fellow!' the man said, leaning over and snapping his fingers in front of Mark's face. 'Big boys don't cry.'

Mark noticed for the first time that the man had a brown leather briefcase in his hand, one just like his father carried to work in the morning and brought home at night. The man spoke again, this time in a very business-like tone of voice.

'I'm your fairy god-father, but you can call me Uncle Macho. We have some very important business to discuss, you and I, man to man.'

Mark swallowed hard and blinked.

'But I'm not a man yet. I'm just a little boy.'

'But you will be a man before long,' Uncle Macho replied, 'and you must begin preparing as soon as possible. You are five years old today and it's high time you began thinking about how to get a jump on the other guy and get ahead in this dog-eat-dog world.'

'Uncle Macho' gives Mark written instructions – with pictures – all he needs to know to 'become a man'. As his fairy godfather leaves, 'Mark saw through the window behind his rocking horse that the sun was just beginning to come up'. Uncle Macho promises to return when Mark is 'about thirteen'.

Girls can usually observe women every day, and have free access to the activities they are taught as part of womanhood; men are *normally* absent for a lot of the day, and the activities which mark them as male (not just putting out the dustbins) usually take place at work, where the boy cannot follow. 'Boys are taught to be masculine more consciously than girls are taught to be feminine', writes Nancy Chodorow. This is not, she goes on to say, because there is anything inherently more difficult in the roles boys have to learn. It is because the boy is

... parented by a woman ... Dependence on his mother, attachment to her and identification with her represent that which is not masculine: a boy must reject dependence and deny attachment and identification ... A boy represses those qualities he takes to be feminine inside himself, and rejects and devalues women and whatever he considers to be feminine in the social world (Chodorow, 1978, p. 181).

Masculinity is defined in negative terms – not so much 'like Dad' as 'unlike Mum'.

Boys know they must not be 'sissy', but it is often very unclear to them what being 'sissy' means. To be punished by people one loves for breaking subtle and unclear rules is an enormous strain. The resultant anxiety, one psychologist says, '... frequently expresses itself in overstraining to be masculine, in virtual panic at being caught doing anything traditionally defined as feminine, and in hostility toward anything even hinting at femininity, including females themselves' (Hartley, 1974, p. 8). Hartley found that boys had crude, overemphasized notions of sex roles compared with girls. The boys she talked with felt a lot was demanded of them: they had to be able to fight, to run, to be strong and clever much more than girls. They believe that men '... are usually in charge of things; they work very hard and they get tired a lot; they mostly do things for other people; they are supposed to be bolder and more restless, and have more courage than women. Like boys, they too mess up the house' (ibid., pp. 10–11). A man's lot according to these nine- to eleven-year-olds sounds hard; is it worth it? But their view of girls' and women's expected behaviour is 'reeking of limitation and restraint'.

Concerning adult women we are told: they are indecisive; they are afraid of many things; they make a fuss over things; they get tired a lot; they very often need someone to help them; they stay home most of the time; they are not as strong as men; they don't like adventure ... [they] are the ones who have to keep things neat and tidy and clean up household messes; they feel sad more often than men ... When he sees women as weak, easily damaged, lacking strength in mind and in body, able to perform only the tasks which take the least strength and are of the least importance, what boy in his right senses would not give his all to escape this alternative to the male role? For many, unfortunately ... The outward semblance of non-femininity is achieved at a tremendous cost of anxiety and self-alienation (ibid., p. 12).

It is this anxiety about masculinity which probably underlies most fathers' insistence on conformity to sex roles.

As we saw in Chapter 5, Chodorow and others see the system in which women do the early physical caring as self-perpetuating. Boys can go on loving women when they become men, even though they rejected their mother as a model. But the quality of this love has been adversely affected by their training in masculinity. Contempt and hostility are likely to be mixed in, so that

> ... women are seen not only as caring and supportive, but also as seductive, mysterious and dangerous ... Close supportive relationships are difficult to find amongst other men in the competitive work world, so men often become very dependent on wives. They try to recreate an adult version of the primary relationship with their mothers that they so long ago abandoned. At the same time they may be seeking reassurance in their masculine stance which can reproduce the old hostilities and contempt for their mother ... In addition, their long training in suppression of feelings can make men very unsatisfactory and demanding partners (Richards, 1982, p. 71).

If men are unsatisfactory, women turn to children. When men become fathers, their motives are very different. Mostly, they do not think of the relationship with their child as much as becoming a father. 'To have a child is to do as their father has done and it forms part of the stereotyped masculine identity they have accepted' (ibid., p. 70). So theoretically there seems little hope that fatherhood can break this circle.

In real life, the circle is breaking. We see all around us fathers whose love of their babies recreates their own infancy, fathers who 'mother'. Chodorow has offered an element of the explanation of how the sexual division of labour keeps going from generation to generation. But her account underestimates the inbuilt conflict. Even the anxiety with which some men cling on to masculinity is a sign of its fragility. More and more men are wanting far more from fatherhood than their own fathers experienced.

FATHERS AS CARERS

All the evidence is that fathers *can* 'mother'. Like women, even before they have children, men can distinguish different kinds of infants' cries, the pain cry, the hunger cry and so on. When they first meet their new-born, fathers are deeply moved. Like mothers, they touch and explore them. 'In my studies of fathers and newborns I have consistently found that fathers are just as responsive as mothers to infant signals such as sounds and mouth movements' (Parke, 1981, p. 44). Parke goes on to ask whether

> ... fathers are secondary caregivers because they are less talented at child care than mothers? When Douglas Sawin and I tested this hypothesis, it turned out to be wrong. We observed mothers and fathers feeding their babies and measured the amount of milk consumed. The babies took almost the same amount from fathers as from mothers. But of course there is more to being a competent caregiver than merely getting food into a baby ... parental competence is best measured by how sensitively parents interpret and respond to infants' cues and signals ... By behaviours such as sucking, pausing, coughing or spitting up, infants indicate whether the feeding is going smoothly ... fathers were just as sensitive to these signals as mothers (op. cit., pp. 48–9).

Yet these were fathers who fed their babies *less* often than the mothers.

From the baby's earliest days, participant fathers tend to be playmates rather than nappy-changers. Changing nappies is presented to us as such an integral part of motherhood that no researcher would ever ask a woman how often she did it – and had she ever changed a *dirty* one? For fathers, even those with relatively egalitarian views, it is still seen as an *option*. Women often find they cannot bear to stand back and let the man 'make a mess of it' – 'Let me do it!' Her feeling that she is more competent in this area, his (partly welcome) feeling of helplessness, and the future division of labour between the two are often set up by the end of the baby's first week of life. But *playing* with the baby is something else. Even fathers who do little else tend to play with their babies. Their style of play differs from mothers':

> Father picks up seven-month-old Nathan, tosses him in the air, and throws his head back so that he and Nathan are face to face. As Nathan giggles and chortles, father lowers him, shakes him, and tosses him up in the air again. Mother sits ten-month-old Lisa on her lap and pulls out her favourite toy, a green donkey that brays when you squeeze it. Lisa smiles, and for the next few minutes mother moves the donkey in front of Lisa's eyes, makes it bray, and talks and sings to her daughter. Lisa watches intently, smiles, and occasionally reaches for her donkey (ibid., p. 56).

Fathers who were their babies' main carers smiled more at them and imitated them more, but their style of play remained very physical. Mothers who went out to work played more with their children than mothers at home, but still in the old, more verbal, 'feminine' way. Of course, this does not mean that these differences in style of play are necessarily biologically based. After all, we spend a long time learning and living our gender roles before we reach the state of parenthood, so even if at that stage fathers become the primary carers, by then they will be already formed in habits and outlook by their experiences as men.

Fathers who do look after their children get some of the rewards that usually go to mothers. Seventy-one Australian fathers who looked after their children for, on average, twenty-six hours a week were compared with the fathers of 145 'conventional' families. Mothers and fathers were asked separately how their shared care giving had affected the father–child relationship. Two-thirds replied that it had become closer or better. Perhaps they felt such a reply was expected, but '... there was a better balance between mother– and father–child relationships. They felt this had occurred because fathers were now much more involved in the day-to-day problems ... rather than simply being the 'fun person' who played with children after a 'hard day at work' (Russell, 1983, p. 121).

When fathers were asked what they enjoyed about looking after children, 97 per cent of the highly participant fathers (but only 58 per cent of conventional fathers) gave the sort of answers mothers typically give: '... that they enjoyed the love and affection they shared with their children, the stimulation and fun they experienced, and the satisfaction they derived from watching their children grow' (loc. cit.).

The intimacy that is common between mothers and children develops through the unspectacular hours together.

> You need intimate contact with a child, not understanding from a distance. If there is any lesson I've learned, it is that I have to spend time with Mary Ann and Lena. Time, that's what I've needed. Not going to the museum and making little journeys to the park, but just kind of hanging out. And through this hanging out, I've become responsible. I've gotten to learn what I'm like and what they are like as people (Boston Women's Health Book Collective, 1981, p. 226).

Some fathers have been surprised at the depth of their feelings: 'There is a bond between me and Luke which transcends our being together. I feel this bond especially when I am not with him. It's been so important to me to discover that I can love someone so deeply' (ibid., p. 227). A study of shared parenting found fathers who '... have gone 'ga-ga' over their children. In contrast, not one mother described her relationship with her child in comparable terms. She would talk about her attachment, her endearing feelings, her sense of closeness to the child, but never in the discourse of a love affair' (Ehrensaft, 1983).

These fathers, professionals in their thirties and forties, came to the relationship hungry for intimacy and found it easier to get close to a child, who is less powerful, than to an adult woman. This produced considerable jealousy from the women Ehrensaft talked with. The fathers talk in a lover-like way because heterosexual love is their most available model for close relationships. They have never got that close to a man, not even their fathers. They were mothered by women, and it is difficult for them to see themselves as mothers. 'I'm absolutely in love with her. Just passionately in love with her. On occasion that's almost frightening' ... 'Now my favourite activity in the world is staying home with Michael. I do it every time I get a chance. I cancel appointments so I can have a whole day with him' (ibid.). We note, though, that it was only appointments this man cancelled – not his job.

Not everyone feels such strong emotion. In any case, intimacy is threatening as well as rewarding. One man friend of ours was a 'sharing parent' when he and his partner were both out of work. Then he got a job:

I really believe, and I believed then, that the work I was doing in this company was not at all important, compared with raising children. It wasn't even *interesting*. I was much more interested in Tom and Emily. But when I left the house in the morning I always felt a sense of relief at being on my own, at not having to think, at least not about anyone else, at everything being impersonal and emotionally undemanding until I got home.

Men have been taught to feel incompetent about child care and house-work. They feel inadequate and they tolerate it badly. For most of them, the appropriate feelings towards the children well up when they find themselves solely responsible and, as they come to succeed, their self-confidence and practical skills increase. For men on their own, the difficulty is often to believe in themselves: 'It's when she cried and I didn't know what to do for her; I didn't understand it. So I would try to figure it out by trial and error. Did I do something bad? ... It took a while but I finally learned how to figure out what's bothering her' (Rosenthal and Keshet, op. cit., p. 123).

Fathers seem to feel least competent in dealing with their children's emotions: 'My wife is different. What she does is just somehow intuit what's upsetting our son. Or sometimes she will just say "You feel sad," and not need to know the reason but just deal with the sadness. I don't know if I can do that. I have to understand what is wrong' (ibid.). The empathy involved in caring for children is certainly easier for women. But as we saw when we discussed motherhood, the drawback that goes along with women's ease in personal relationships is their difficulty knowing where they end and the children begin. For fathers, who as babies themselves were seen quite early on as different by their own mothers and who are therefore surer of the boundaries of their separate selves, it may be easier to keep a sense of the child as a loved but separate person.

Whether fathers are at ease 'mothering' has nothing to do with how 'feminine' or 'masculine' they are. It is connected, not surprisingly, with how rigid their ideas are about sex-appropriate behaviour (Russell, 1983, p. 59). However, it does make a difference to fathers' feelings whether they look after their children *by choice*.

About one in nine single-parent families has a lone father. Sometimes the father took over because he and his wife agreed this would be best. These are usually men who did a lot of the caring before the marriage broke down. One study found that men like these

> enjoyed looking after children and, in comparison with the two other groups, were less likely to believe that children were really a mother's concern. As one father commented: 'You come out with all these clichés about the softness of women but we can be equally soft and sensitive. The stereotype of a man being aggressive and not being able to relate to things that are gentle is just untrue.' They themselves felt little conflict between their gender identity and their position as primary caregiver, but it was reactions from others that often caused disquiet ... (O'Brien, 1982b, p. 190).

One man remarked that people seemed to feel '... that there is something rather peculiar about a man who can cook and look after a house and kids and so on'.

The second group in O'Brien's study was men who were angry with their wives, and whose fight for custody had been partly to punish them. The third group was men whose wives had walked out and who had had little choice about the child care arrangements, at least at the beginning. These fathers felt most conflict about their position, and tended to deny that a father could care as well as a mother. 'A father cannot provide all the child's needs, there's no way you can. A child must have a good loving mother' ... 'I've got to be strict and stern or I've got to be loving and warm. I haven't got the right shape to give them the cuddles they like' (ibid., p. 194). These men, who felt hurt and let down, would probably not realize that women themselves often feel *they* cannot 'mother'. Lone fathers did better if they felt they had *chosen* to be their children's main carers. No doubt mothers would too, if such a choice were offered.

Enough fathers care for children to prove that men *can* nurture as well as women, despite their upbringing. But if the women are around, they rarely do it. For the last twenty years or so, there has been a lot of talk about 'symmetrical families'. Ironically, the 1950s were presented as a period of *liberation* for women.

> Marriage today is ideally envisaged as a partnership in which husband and wife share each other's interests and worries, and face all major decisions jointly ... to most younger husbands, washing up is no longer a sign of henpeckery, but something to be taken for granted. Thus the emancipation of women in one generation has been followed by the domestication of husbands in the next ... (Newson and Newson, 1963, p. 133).

The Newsons interviewed 709 mothers of one-year-olds in Nottingham in 1959. They found fathers feeding babies (only 22 per cent never did it), changing them (20 per cent often, 37 per cent sometimes and 43 per cent never), putting them to bed and taking them out. They concluded: 'At a time when he has more money in his pocket, and more leisure on which to spend it, than ever before, the head of the household chooses to sit at his own fireside, a baby on his knee and a feeding bottle in his hand: the modern father's place is in the home' (ibid., p. 147).

According to a recent article by Lewis and the Newsons, based on interviews in Nottingham of parents of one-year-olds in 1979, this trend continues. Twenty years on, the proportion of fathers who have never changed a nappy was down from 43 per cent to 11 per cent, and the percentage who never bath a baby went down from 61 per cent to 46 per cent (Lewis *et al.*, 1982, p. 175).

All the same, to call these 'symmetrical families' suggests an odd idea of symmetry. It is rather like a see-saw with one end in the air. We are told that before, say, 1945 the angle was even steeper. Others deny this. Whether or not things used to be worse, there is certainly little symmetry, even during the time fathers *are* at home.

There *has* been a shift in attitudes. Men no longer jeer at other men who push their babies in prams or carry them in slings. There is not so much a change in what is done – for some independent men always took part in baby care – as in what people think about it. One study found a class difference between middle-class and working-class married men with children. The middle-class men often brought work home and did far less than their share of domestic work and child care, even when they were at home with their wives. Most of them felt guilty because they were doing so little. The working-class married men were doing more in the house, especially those whose wives had outside work. But they felt resentful rather than guilty – they felt they should not have to do housework and child care as well as paid work (O'Brien, 1982a).

It seems that the only real change is that bread-winning and caring for young children are increasingly seen as compatible. However, this only means that men 'help' more, often picking up the bits of child care they like the look of and leaving the dirty nappies for the mothers, like Simon Shaw in a case-study of father's participation.

Simon Shaw, postgraduate student, and Evan Crawley, British Rail guard, came out on the physical caretaking scales as participating very little in the routine handling of their babies. They have never bathed the baby, rarely fed the baby, seldom attend to the baby in the night. Yet ... on the one hand, Simon Shaw has carved out a very distinctive educational and intellectual role for himself (reading to the baby, talking to him, offering him unusual toys, food) and has taken this aspect of fatherhood very seriously. He has read extensively about babies both for personal and academic reasons and is highly engaged in assessing the minutiae of the baby's life. At eleven weeks *post partum* he is keeping a detailed journal of the baby's progress. On the other hand, Evan Crawley sees his role in early infancy as minimal, is rarely at home – working long hours and relaxing after work with his friends – has not read anything about babies or infant care and does not know what the baby's daily routines are because of his absence from the home (McKee, 1982, p. 126).

Families are joint projects. If women become convinced that they make a far larger contribution and feel resentful, family life becomes less pleasant and smooth-running. Some couples keep up the belief that the father *would* do anything, if necessary. This makes it less galling that he actually does little. Often researchers who conclude that highly participant fathers are widespread are just asking questions which trigger the father or mother into displaying the father's symbolic contribution, the token of his goodwill.

Fathers do not actually have to do much to earn their wives' gratitude and stave off resentment:

> ... in order to maintain belief in the father as mother substitute he needed only to deputise for *part* of the mother's usual activities. The main requirement was simply to mind the children. Some wives made elaborate arrangements, such as preparing food in advance ... domestic activities additional to the childminding were usually defined as a welcome extra ... wives, even in their absence, retained overall responsibility and knowledge (Backett, 1982, p. 211).

Or as one father in this study put it:

> 'I mean if you've got children, that's it, it's non-stop work. I mean *I* participate when I feel like it, but if I feel like burying my head in the newspaper *I do*, or if I feel like ignoring the disturbances that are going on, then I can do it' (ibid., p. 108).

DO WE NEED FATHERS?

Some feminists believe they should not let men into their stronghold until they have more power in the outside world. They remember divorce cases in which the man's shared parenting has led to his getting care and control of the child, so that he has ended up with mothering, the final feather in his cap, and the woman vainly looking for work. In reaction, some men feel bitter about women's power at home.

The author of a new novel, interviewed in the *Guardian*, said: 'Too many fathers, like Hooper [the hero of the novel] only wake to realise what they have missed when they are out of the family or their children have grown up. Men often have their hands tied within the family where women and children combine to contain or marginalise them, leaving them either to wreak havoc or to concur submissively' (*Guardian*, 26 September 1983). You can practically hear the violins. This man feels that women are very powerful. Lacking women's training in accepting subordination, he feels bitter and resentful about them having more power in the area of child care – completely ignoring all the areas in which men have more power. Old battle-lines are drawn up yet again.

We now have the anomalous situation in the family where the father is the more powerful adult, as a man, especially if he is the bread-winner, but the woman has more rights over the children. While they remain married, how equal they are in terms of decision making and use of household resources depends mainly on *him*. If he likes, the woman may not be conscious of his power to withhold money (where he is the bread-winner), to insist on sexual relations she does not want and to get away with a degree of violence that would not be tolerated by the law outside the haven of the home. The equality of the 'equal' marriage depends on the man's refusal to use the power society gives him. Making husband and wife equal in practice in an individual marriage is not impossible, but it demands a lot of effort – rather like running on the spot. And the husband still has more *potential* power. Once the woman leaves, the situation is transformed. Sole custody is usually awarded to the mother, together with care and control, and the father is given 'reasonable access'. The woman is likely to be poor, but she usually has the children. The man is probably better off financially, but he hasn't.

The courts are supposed to decide on custody according to the best interests of the child, but these interests are interpreted according to two principles. One is that the status quo, the way things are, should not be disturbed, on the grounds that that would itself upset the children. The other is that children are in general best off with their mother. The status quo is more likely to be changed if it is a father who has the children, as this case illustrates:

> The parties married in March 1979, and a child was born in May 1980. In February 1981 the mother left, leaving the father with his daughter. He looked after her, first with the help of relatives and later with his intended second wife, who moved into the matrimonial home. The mother lived elsewhere with her new partner, and saw her child regularly. The Magistrates granted interim custody to the father. After a year and a half the child was moved to the mother by a High Court decision, on the grounds that a child ought to be with a mother when other things are more or less equal. The decision was upheld on appeal (Families Need Fathers *Newsletter*, Summer 1983, p. 12).

'Families Need Fathers', the British organization for non-custodial parents, demonstrates in London every Fathers' Day. Like conciliation services throughout Britain, they argue for joint custody in all cases, for enforcement of access if the parent with care and control of the child does not allow it, for conciliation as part of divorce proceedings and, in the long run, for an end to the adversarial divorce system where the parties are presumed to be at war. They estimate that within two years of divorce, 40 per cent of children have lost contact with their non-custodial parent (Benians *et al.*, 1983, p. 15). Very often the parents are both bitter, hurt and angry. They cannot think clearly about their children's needs. It is difficult for each to believe that the children can really receive the love and consistent nurturing they need from the other parent who, they feel, has let them themselves down. The custodial parent, usually the mother, finds the other parent inconsistent and unreliable in his attitude to the children: 'He refuses to make definite arrangements. I want him to visit once a month and take our son out for a whole day, but he just won't commit himself' ... 'He often arranges to see the children and then doesn't turn up, so I have to cope with the disappointments' ... 'My husband lavishes outings and presents on the children and they eat out in expensive restaurants, which makes it difficult for me when they come back' (Gingerbread and Families Need Fathers, 1982, pp. 23–4).

The other parent may not be able to get access at all. From being part of the child's daily family life, the father becomes more like a visiting uncle whose rights depend on the mother's agreement. 'My access order has twice been defined by the courts. The latest one states that I should see the children for 5 hours twice a month, plus 14 days staying access during the summer holidays. However, my ex sabotages these arrangements continually' (ibid., p. 16).

Even when access arrangements work, it is not easy to fit a close relationship into these rigid timescales, which take no account of the way the child and parent are feeling that particular day. As the minutes and hours tick away, the father searches for some meaningful act or gesture that symbolizes his feeling for the child (such as the presents or meals out that annoy the other parent so much!). Just being together doesn't seem enough, especially if there is no real home where the father can take the child and they are meeting in museums, parks or cafés. It is easy to understand the distress of those fathers whom FNF represents, as well as the hurt suffered by the custodial mothers who feel the children blame them for the loss of their father. It is easy to understand the men who shut themselves off from the whole situation by breaking contact very early on, by moving away and pretending they never had children at all. It is also easy to understand the deep anger of the wives of these men. 'The children [11 and 12] often ask about their father. I don't know what to say. He only lives fifteen miles away, but we haven't seen him for years. I've written to him, but he doesn't reply. Perhaps he's moved. It's hard to tell the kids that their dad isn't interested' (ibid., p. 17).

Although they have a few non-custodial mothers as members, and are formally an organization for all non-custodial parents, FNF is primarily a group of fathers trying to combat their powerlessness as parents. They maintain that both parents have equal rights as well as equal responsibilities. It is on these grounds that they think both parents should have custody, and there should be no legal prior assumption that mothers are the right people to have care and control. But Families Need Fathers and equivalent organizations will never succeed in uniting women and men on this programme until they give more thought to equal rights in *marriage*. The reason why so many women are willing to become lone mothers, to exist for years and years on supplementary benefit or insecure maintenance payments, to take on all the responsibility and the work of looking after a child on their own, is because – for so many of them – it was rather like that *before* the marriage broke down. At least afterwards they have some independence, to think, to live as they please, even with little money and babysitting problems. As one one parent said to us: 'Before he went I used to spend a lot of time with him negotiating about who should do what and resenting it because he did less than his share. Now I don't stop to think – I know I have to do everything. But I feel a lot freer because I don't waste any time resenting it.'

For many mothers, the father's providing for the family by going out to work does not seem as much a contribution to their welfare as her greater or full-time emotional and physical commitment. After all, if they had no children, he would still be going out to work – and so would she. Once the marriage has broken down, it seems to many women much too late for the father to discover the everyday joys of parenthood.

Women's greater power as a parent in custody cases is just the other side of the sexism which *makes* us have the primary responsibility for children when there is no dispute. It is because we are *pressured* into being the primary parent, by economic pressures, by the way the law is framed, by public opinion created by the media and the whole education system, that, when these cases come to court, we are considered the *suitable* parent. It would be fine to have equal rights in custody cases, if we did equal amounts of parenting *before* marriages break down. To unite women and men in favour of the rights of fathers necessitates taking on the *whole* struggle against women's subordination.

Do children need fathers? And if so, what sort of fathers? The loss of a father through death or separation is a terrible event for children. It can affect their deepest feelings about themselves. A study of divorcing families in California showed that even if the parents had been getting on badly for years, the decision to divorce came as an unwelcome shock to the children. They felt rejected by the father who left, even those who were old enough to know that they were not to blame. Their self-esteem suffered and, the younger they were, the worse the effect (Wallerstein and Kelly, 1980).

Our family is part of whom we are. When it breaks up, everything else feels threatened too. For a few years children often feel they must be careful to avoid losing their mother as well. When fathers lose contact with children, the sense of rejection is even stronger and, for pre-school children, so-called 'reasonable access' of fortnightly visits is nothing like enough to keep the link vital for them, and to stop them feeling abandoned. The worse the hostility between the parents, the more the children suffer. Small wonder that study after study of children who have lost their fathers through divorce or separation shows them emotionally disturbed, getting on less well with others, not playing so imaginatively, withdrawn and often doing worse at school. The children who did best in Wallerstein and Kelly's five-year follow-up were those for whom the divorce made sense – which is not to say that *they* wanted it. They could see that it had improved life for their mother, sometimes for both parents. The other children who were least disturbed were those who never really lost their father, because they continued to have a close relationship with him on a different basis.

All this tells us little about children's needs for fathers. The studies on divorce show what we already knew: that when a child makes a close relationship with an adult it is distressing and damaging to have it severed or threatened. Until very recently it was almost always the father who left the child, so we have no comparable data for children who lose their mothers through divorce. We know that it hurts more to lose contact with a father through divorce than through death.

If children have no fathers, what do they lack? We were appalled to hear the children of an inner-city nursery school where about half the children came from lone-parent families, singing at a Christmas concert

> I'm sorry for that laddie
> He hasn't got a daddy,
> The little boy that Santa Claus forgot.

The child without a daddy won't usually be forgotten by Father Christmas but, until there is more research about children of lone mothers who have never had any relationship with their fathers, we will have little idea. One lack is obvious: the lack of more than one active, responsible parent.

'Children with more than one caretaker have "all of their eggs in one basket". If the child knows only one person to be trustworthy, and if that person is tired, worried, angry or irritable, the child has no other resource and must suffer the consequences of the adult's temporary and quite normal inability to provide appropriate care' (Boston Women's Health Book Collective, 1981, p. 243).

But why stop at two parents? And need the other carer or carers be a father? The traditional literature (Lamb, 1976) assumes that children need both a male and a female parent in order to become confident, heterosexual masculine men and feminine women. How will boys learn to be men without their dads to copy? But, as we have seen, most of boys' sex-role learning comes from the media, from other boys, and involves dissociating themselves from mother more than copying father, because so many fathers are normally absent on a daily basis. Superficially, there is no problem. All the same, some of our deepest attitudes to men and women are laid down in our childhood. It can affect us all our lives to have or to lack early intimacy with a man who loves us. Many children *are* better off without their fathers, because they are violent or abuse them sexually. These sorts of behaviour are simply extreme forms of what is considered normal behaviour for men. Children do not need traditional fathers, authority figures or gift-bearers, or teachers of sex roles. They *do* need fathers as carers.

Men need to share in looking after children to reclaim their tender, caring selves. Far from needing fathers to teach them how to be 'proper' boys and girls, children need fathers who are fully human, who have not denied their 'feminine' side, to model for them how loving and gentle men can be without giving up their strength and confidence. If we were cared for from birth by men as well as women, boys and girls would not develop such divergent personalities. Girls would have less trouble becoming separate beings, and boys would not be obliged to repress their soft sides in order to identify with men. As adults, we would not fit so neatly into the system that oppresses women and limits men.

We cannot change society simply by 'shared parenting' or the 'new fatherhood'. For families without fathers inside or outside the home it has little relevance. The inequality of women at work makes it a practical impossibility for many. Basically it is no more than another form of private child care, another way of handling the contradictions in the nuclear family, and we have seen that it can bring its own new contradictions. It can become a system of bureaucratic shift-changes in which the children feel like parcels handed from one reluctant parent to the other. Or it can be good. Like all parenting within small families, it '... rests on the accidents of individual solutions, of individual goodwill: to make of child care such a hostage to fortune is to depart a long way from socialist aspirations to democratically accessible community services' (Riley, 1983, p. 152). So it is and, as Riley says, there is a real danger in the present tortoise-like climate that individual solutions will be accepted *instead of* 'social' campaigns. However, for most people social campaigns would have to succeed before shared parenting would be possible.

The most obvious obstacle to shared parenting or swapping roles is the inequality of women at work. Role swaps usually happen in cases where women have more earning power than their partner – it is only in this unusual case that the question gets raised at all as to who would rather stay at home. Couples who share parenting have either unusual or very flexible jobs, or perhaps job share or both work part-time. To earn enough money like this, they have to be professional or self-employed. As unemployment increases, some men are being pushed into role swaps or sharing parenting against their will. The learning and unlearning they need to do is made more difficult by the blow to their self-esteem that they have already received. And to go against standard notions of masculinity really needs commitment.

To make shared parenting possible for more than a few, we need more child care provision, shorter working days, paternity leave and leave for either parent when children are ill. We need the state to guarantee children's economic welfare, so that it is completely separate from the vagaries of their parents' sexual relationships. All these struggles in the 'wide world' for concrete social reforms are usually seen as part of the fight to end the oppression of women. They would actually ease the position of lone mothers and women together with children. They could just as accurately be seen as struggles to allow equality in parenting, and a future for fatherhood. They would also provide a basis for extending commitments to children outside the nuclear family. Shared parenting is no *solution*, but it is an elementary step to take towards a better way of living. Whenever men and women live together with children, if they can both or all have close relationships with the children without being debarred from other work and commitments, this is in all their interests.

CHILDREN'S CARE

In Part Three we focus on challenges to the conventional system of private family care. We look at a few of the many projects which effectively contradict widely accepted notions about children's needs and capacities.

Pre-school children, especially under-threes, are supposed to be too young to be cared for with others of the same age and away from their mothers. We turn this assumption on its head and argue that young children need to be together, as much as they need to be with adults. Together with Pam Calder, we use a review of the mainly psychological literature to show that there is plenty of evidence that day care can enrich children's lives. Yet much of this evidence is ignored in the conventional view that the most we can hope for from non-maternal care is that it do no harm.

Community nurseries go even further and challenge the philosophy and practices that have grown up in the nursery world itself. They begin to question the divisions between parents and professionals, between trained and untrained workers, and open possibilities for the sharing of care and commitment between parents and others. Audrey Maynard discusses the community nursery movement in Britain and looks at two contrasting nurseries in some detail, the Children's Community Centre which is twelve years old, and the newer Ackroyd. In different ways, they each undermine accepted ideas about the division of responsibility between parents and workers, and between home and out-of-home activities.

The co-operative crèche described by Jonathan Trustram goes against reliance on the one-to-one relationship between mother and baby. It brought together 5 very young children who came to know each other in ways not usually experienced by such youngsters (not even siblings, who are usually wider apart in age). Through their co-operation, the parents also came to feel close to each other's children in ways non-parents rarely experience, so that categories of 'your' and 'my' children lost some of their relevance.

The children's workshop challenges conventional ideas about children's capacities and bridges the gap between play and work. Wiebke Wüstenberg and Stephen Castles set up a workshop for schoolchildren after school and in the holidays. The workshop demonstrated that children can enjoy themselves, gain self-confidence and respect for themselves and their community, by working with tools usually reserved for adults and making things in ways they choose for themselves.

Even at second-hand, with all their faults and their limitations, these experiences stretch our notions of what is possible.

CHAPTER TEN

CHILDREN IN NURSERIES
by Pamela Calder

CHILDREN TOGETHER

This chapter focuses on nursery care. Nurseries are different from the other sorts of care we have discussed. This is partly because they look after pre-school children, for whom home care is conventionally considered most necessary, and partly because they cannot easily be thought of as family-substitutes or mother-substitutes, but have to be discussed on their own terms.

There is no shortage of critical literature claiming to show that nurseries are bad for young children. Recently there has been a swell of research showing that *good* nurseries 'do no harm' – a relatively modest claim. Both aggressive and defensive arguments have something in common: they both take private child care by mother at home as the normal type and, although they may use it as a 'control', they rarely investigate it. Yet there is no single type of home where a certain sort of care is offered. Homes differ even more than nurseries, and we shall show how difficult it is to generalize about nurseries as we found for homes in Chapter 2.

We want to reverse the assumptions generally made. Instead of assuming that children at nurseries are deprived of mother's care, we shall assume that children at home are deprived of other children's company. For although it is difficult to pin down essential features of nursery care, we do know that in all nurseries, bad and good, children are together. This is our starting point. We can tentatively think of a good nursery as one in which young children can *benefit* from being together. We know little about children's relationships with each other. Western industrialized societies attempt to organize children's lives so that adults are the main influence on their development. All the same, it is generally recognized that children enjoy being together, that being able to form friendships with other children is an important part of growing up, and that children who are isolated for any reason are likely to be lonely and often socially disabled as adults.

Many readers of Michael Deakin's book *The Children on the Hill* felt uneasy at his account of the care and attention lavished on two brothers and a sister by their mother and father, in an isolated cottage in Wales. Deakin wrote (1973, p. 25) of this system of education: 'It demands first and foremost a total and long-lasting dedication to the children, an almost mystical dedication of their mother's life to their upbringing ...' The children grew up excelling in music and mathematics, cut off from their own age group.

Deakin's book could be seen as a caricature of the middle-class professional belief that, for children to develop optimally, adults should devote total attention to them to develop their curiosity and give them access to the best of adult culture. Attempts to do this are constantly interrupted by the behaviour of children themselves. From an early age, if given the opportunity, children will form their own groups or alliances, independent of any adults. Certain sorts of children's fiction, such as the school story or adventure stories, are probably popular because in these the children are in control, with other children, in a world that they create for themselves, and the adults are mere cardboard figures.

The degree of control adults exercise over children's relationships with each other varies today by class and by geographical location. Where children have more freedom from adult supervision, even young children may be able to form autonomous groups of friends. In many places, whatever adults' attitudes are, the way family and village space is organized allows even tiny children to make contact with one another. But in our motorized society today, traffic often makes even rural villages unsafe. Many children have little control over their own friendships with others until they go to school. Their parents decide whom they see and how often, especially in middle-class homes.

Most adults feel ambivalent about children's friendships. We are alarmed by groups of older children who are obviously enjoying being without adults. At the same time, we believe that the capacity for making friends is a social skill our own children should acquire. We have contradictory feelings: we know that children enjoy being with each other, but we fear that the loyalties they have to each other and the influence they have on each other may lead to the loss of adult control over them. One source of this ambivalence is the way in which children are oppressed. As part of a general tendency to treat them with less respect, their friendships are not usually granted as much significance as those of adults.

The priority put on children's relationships with *adults* is reflected in child care policy. Children are educated together in groups when they reach the age of five or six, not because they will enjoy it better, but because this is an efficient way to use adult time to introduce them to adult culture. Of course, parents know that one reason children put up with boring lessons is that, whatever the quality of the teaching, school is one place they can meet their friends.

Before school age, children are considered *cognitively* unready for formal education. What they are thought to need as pre-schoolers is not education but care, care at home with perhaps a little group care and opportunity to make friends at a few play-group sessions. We have already pointed out how absurd it is to split 'care' and 'education'. This split in practice corresponds to a theoretical split in psychology itself, between learning and emotions, between the 'cognitive' and the 'affective'. The theoretical split is as artificial as its practical mirror image. Psychologists such as Piaget have studied children's intellectual development while paying scant attention to their emotional life. Psychologists like Bowlby and Ainsworth have studied children's emotional needs and have had little to say about their intellectual needs, their need to learn.

Children's friendships have been marginal to both traditions. Bowlby and his co-workers, and psychoanalysts of various schools, have stressed parent–child dynamics as the ones which matter. Lasting relationships between under-threes which are emotionally important to the children are a little suspect from a psychoanalytic point of view. Many psychoanalysts would fear that such friendships had been formed to compensate for the lack of adequate relationships with adults. Burlingham and Freud, for example, wrote (1943, p. 39) that: 'Under ordinary conditions friendships of long duration are ... very rare among young children. Lasting attachments are formed to grown-ups or to older children; playmates of the same age are used for purposes of play only, and friendships fall apart when the momentary reason for them (the play) has ended.' They did observe real friendships in their residential nursery, but they saw these as abnormal, as a sign of the way in which toddlers in groups are forced 'to become social at an age when it is normal to be asocial' (p. 23). They go to some pains to point out that the apparently altruistic behaviour of infants who comfort each other, restrain each other or help each other is actually 'egoistic', for 'there is little difference between comforting another child and comforting oneself' (p. 32).

Children are learning about others in their early social behaviour, and certainly they do so by identifying with others. But it is absurd to suggest that their feelings and actions are invalid or unreal because they are still developing. It would also be quite wrong to think that because children need loving relationships with adults *as well*, that somehow means they do not *really* need each other.

THE EGOCENTRIC CHILD

Until recently, many cognitive psychologists thought young children could not 'have fun' with each other because they did not recognize each other as social beings. Following Piaget, children were thought to be 'egocentric'; that is, to see the world from their own point of view and to find it difficult to imagine themselves in the position of others until they were nine or ten years old.

Margaret Donaldson is one of a growing number of psychologists who are challenging Piaget. She reports a number of experiments which contradict his view of egocentrism. It is *because* the children are trying to take the adult's point of view into account, and to make sense of the task, that they make mistakes. For example, in one experiment when the adults asked the same question twice, the children obediently changed their answer, picking up the implication that their first answer must have been wrong. One of Piaget's demonstrations is known as the Three-Mountain Task. A child sits at one side of a table on which is placed a three-dimensional model of three mountains, on which are a church, a house, and a tree. Children are able to pick out a picture that corresponds to their own view of the model, but cannot choose a picture corresponding to the view a doll would have if it were placed on a chair on the other side of the table.

Piaget had shown that children could only succeed in this task when they were about nine years old, and used this as evidence for their continuing egocentrism. Martin Hughes, one of Donaldson's colleagues, has shown that even four-year-olds can succeed at a task which makes similar demands on children's logical capacity but is presented differently. He used material which meant something to the children. Each child was presented with a model of a 'naughty boy' and asked to hide the model so that it could not be seen by either of two models of policemen. Children as young as four years old had 90 per cent success, showing themselves far from 'egocentric' (Donaldson, 1978).

In practice, in the nursery school movement, in nursery nurse training and in the Pre-School Play-Groups Association, the idea that young children are 'egocentric' is linked with the notion of 'parallel play'. This concept was introduced by Parten in 1932. It has been used to suggest that children under the age of three gain nothing by being together – that they may play beside each other but each at their own activity, with none of the co-operative play they will show later. It is true that the way children typically play together changes as they get older, but they can and do play co-operatively at well under three. A friend remembers an occasion when she had momentarily left her own fourteen-month baby together with the ten-month-old child she regularly minded, and had gone into the kitchen to put the kettle on. Suddenly she heard uproarious laughter, and ran into the next room to find the older baby feeding the younger one with an empty plastic spoon, and the two of them stopping after each spoonful and laughing just as older children do, looking at each other and spurring each other on. Even in 'parallel play', when each child is concerned with his or her own activities, the quality of their play changes and becomes more complex when they play in the presence of other children (Becker, 1979; Rubenstein and Howes, 1979).

THE SOCIAL RELATIONSHIPS
OF BABIES AND TODDLERS

Cognitive psychologists now realize that they have seriously underestimated babies and young children. It is only recently that young babies' remarkable capacities to understand their surroundings through sight, sound, smell and touch have been recognized. And now in addition, psychologists are coming to recognize that babies as well as young children can relate to people in various complex ways.

Until recently most British research focused on the baby's relationships with a single adult – in practice the mother. This relationship was taken as the basic form of all adult-to-child, and child-to-adult, two-person 'dyadic' relationships. All the developmental issues that interested psychologists could be studied within this early relationship: the development of the child's intelligence, learning, attachment and social behaviour. This meant psychologists were uncritically accepting 'common-sense' traditional views about the roles of men and women. In practice they were also ignoring the importance of the other relationships children make, or simply assuming that these are similar to the one with the mother.

Thus, recent research on mother–child relationships has recognized that there are *two people* involved, both of whom contribute to what happens between them. Either may make the first move, to which the other responds. This way of looking at things is an advance on the earlier conception of the adult as the only powerful agent and as the sole moulder of the child's values and character. All the same, the narrow focusing on the child's relationship with just one adult has told us little about the nature or extent of relationships that children form with others.

The focus of inquiry is now widening to an interest in babies' relationships with other adults, such as fathers, and to their relationships with other children. American psychologists (Bronson, 1975; Mueller and Brenner, 1977; Becker, 1979) have recently carried out empirical studies that have established to their own satisfaction that babies *can* engage in social interactions. Many of the experiments on toddlers' 'peer group interactions' have brought children who do not know each other to a room in the research centre where they are observed together. This research has given us some information about how children behave in these temporary situations and has convinced psychologists that babies *can* respond socially to other children. But it has little to say about young children's longer-term relationships or friendships.

A few of the American studies (Mueller and Brenner, 1977) have gone beyond the situation where one child meets another child stranger in an unfamiliar laboratory. They have begun to admit that whether the children are familiar with each other might be an important factor in how well they get on and how they behave together. The very fact that experimenters have found it possible to research into toddlers' sociability without thinking that it might make a difference if they knew each other suggests that they had decided in advance that young children do not have friends as older people do. Even within the behaviourist tradition which disregards the subject's own view of the situation, it would have been hard to ignore the relevance of friendship and acquaintance if the subjects had been adults.

Typical of recent studies is one by Doyle, Connolly and Rivest (1980) on sixteen children between three and four years old. Not too surprisingly, when these children played with another child whom they had met several times before, their play was more 'socially active, socially competent and cognitively mature' than when they were with another child they had not previously met. Becker (1979) showed similar differences with a group of nine-month-old babies. As they got to know one another, they interacted more often and in a more complex way. Once gained, these social skills were extended to other non-familiar children. Becker also noticed that the babies paid more attention to their playmates while they were in their own home than when they were in the other child's home. Most studies of infant peer-group behaviour have been in laboratories, and may have underestimated the extent of babies' sociability which is so easy to see in everyday life at home.

Most parents will have stories like Miki, whose sixteen-month-old son had been looked after with another boy of the same age once a week for several months. On one occasion Graham, the visiting child, was sitting rather withdrawn and ignoring Toby. For a whole hour, while his mother breast fed the new baby, Toby tried to get Graham's attention, to entertain him in play. Finally, in exasperation, he went to the hall where Graham's coat was, brought it back and put it on Graham's head. It was quite clear what he expected from his social relationship.

Caroline's little girl, Debbie, had been cared for, together with another child of the same age, for two or three mornings a week ever since they were four months old. Before they were one year old they used to play games in which one would start doing something, such as banging on a stool with a cup, then stop and look expectantly at the other, who would do the same thing, then stop, and this would be repeated over and over while both babies laughed. When they were fifteen months old, Debbie went away for three months. Ruth used to ask after her often at first. After a couple of weeks, she stopped asking and was fairly unresponsive to postcards from Debbie's family. A week before Debbie's return, Ruth's mother told Ruth that Debbie would be 'back soon'. Ruth started asking for Debbie so incessantly that her mother regretted having mentioned it. When they met again, the two babies stared at each other for a few minutes and then seemed delighted to be reunited. For some months after that, Ruth used 'soon' to mean 'in a long time', and was a little anxious if Debbie had a cold or went on holiday so they couldn't be together.

Recently, controlled observational research had backed up parents' views of their children as sophisticated psychological beings. Dunn and Kendrick's study (1982) of forty children over a period of fourteen months sensitively observed the changes in the children during and after the birth of a sibling. They wanted to find out to what extent young siblings can understand and communicate with each other. They found that the first-born children often commented on what the baby wanted or intended. Children under three did this as often as the older ones, often remarking on actions of the baby that the mother had not noticed, for example 'Sue H.: He wants to go out ... James R.: Dawn wants cakey, Mum ... Jill J.: Kenny want bit meat'. Many of the elder children who showed such empathy with their baby siblings were themselves under eighteen months. By the time the younger siblings were just over one year old, they in their turn were beginning to show signs of understanding the older siblings' wishes. Dunn and Kendrick reported (op. cit., p. 140) 'even $2\frac{1}{2}$-year-olds changed their speed when talking to their baby siblings'. Parents and others who spend a lot of time with children would say that it is not only brothers and sisters who can be so sensitive and responsive to each other, as long as they have the chance to get to know each other well.

Children not only understand each other, they are also mutually attracted from the first months. Some psychologists (Brookes and Lewis, 1976), studying the relationships of young children, have noticed that infants and young children are very interested in each other, and would rather approach other children than adults. This confirms Pam's experience. She remembers her eleven-month-old out in a pushchair in a street market using the opportunity to turn and look around at other children as they passed. A friend has a similar account. 'Baby' was one of the few words her fifteen-months-old daughter knew, and she used it extensively. When out for a walk, she would look into all the prams and point at the baby, and also (embarrassingly) point at other young children older than she, if they were being carried, saying excitedly 'Baby, baby!' At thirteen months old, two days after Pam's daughter learnt to walk she was using her new-found skill to join the end of a line of other young children, all strangers to her, who were running together around a pub garden while their respective parents were sitting at tables having their drinks.

It may seem obvious that children like approaching other children, but this view conflicts with the other accounts we are given of young children's responses to strangers. Psychoanalysts first formulated the view that, from about seven or eight months old, babies begin to react to strangers with fear or anxiety. Cognitive psychologists have tried to pin down this phenomenon. In one laboratory experiment where an unsmiling stranger approaches a baby in a high chair, and then picks her up, about half the babies of nine months or older who were tested became sober, stopped playing, whimpered or burst out crying, or looked or turned away as the stranger got nearer (Waters, Matas and Sroufe, 1975).

This sort of reaction is usually explained as the counterpart of the baby's becoming attached to her carers. It can be seen as a clear sign that the baby no longer sees all people as equivalent and avoids those she does not know (Schaffer, 1971b). It seems from other experiments that this reaction is not so often triggered by the approach of a strange *child*, and this difference has raised problems for psychologists who wanted to explain it simply in terms of fear of strangeness, of unfamiliarity itself (Brookes and Lewis, op. cit., p. 323). We have to remember that not all babies show such an avoidance reaction, and that those who do on one test may react differently a month later. In any case, a stranger in the laboratory may be the last straw for the baby. Babies' reactions to strangers on their own territory may be quite different (especially to strangers who smile). Many issues are confounded here.

There are several possible reasons why babies might react differently to child strangers. In the laboratory experiments, the children have no control over the approach of the stranger and no clear idea of his or her intentions. In more ordinary situations, young children do sometimes decide to go up to adult strangers, even ask to be picked up by them. In general (like adults), children seem to feel less anxiety when they are in control of a situation. With other children, even strange ones, they are more often in a position to take the initiative and more often free to leave if the situation does not suit them. Another related possibility is that babies are apprehensive of strange adults because they know they are likely to attempt to 'look after' them – to tickle them, pick them up, change their clothes: attentions which are not welcome from strangers. Children do take liberties with each other, but they are easier to stop and they do not go to the lengths of changing babies' nappies.

Bower (1982) has suggested another type of analysis. He argues that the baby's anxiety is not a response to loss of the mother, but to the different and difficult communication problem a new adult presents. A strange adult will know too little about the young child to interpret his or her necessarily limited repertoire of gesture and vocalization, and will herself or himself talk differently and do things differently from the child's own familiar communication partners. Perhaps because children and babies are nearer in age than adults and babies, it is easier for a baby to interpret an unfamiliar child's signals than to interpret the actions of an unfamiliar adult. Whatever the reason, young children's interest in each other, and in older children, is more than just the absence of anxiety and avoidance. It has the quality of delighted recognition: another person like me!

THE EFFECTS OF DAY CARE

As we have seen, children can and do form strong relationships with one another. This has implications for our organization of child care, but implications that have hardly been recognized by most existing research. Mainstream psychological research into child care has on the whole been directed at answering two rather different questions: 'Does day care enhance or retard intellectual development?' and 'Does day care enhance or retard children's emotional development?'

These questions are very narrow. They reflect the split in psychology between the 'cognitive' and 'affective' (thought and feelings). They are asked partly because they correspond to important psychological theories. How children learn, and under what conditions they learn best, is a central theme in the study of child development. It is also easier to measure than more subtle questions such as how happy children are. The measures of intelligence, of vocabulary, and so on, make some sort of sense and have some stability. It is equally certain that they leave all sorts of things out. They do not include social learning: children learning how to negotiate, how to communicate, how to lead. Nor do they tap how children learn to think of themselves, their self-image and degree of self-esteem, nor what they expect for themselves.

Measures of emotional development are usually derived from 'attachment theory', which we discussed in Chapter 6. The child's emotional development is usually judged by whether he or she remains 'attached' to mother and other family members. Attachment theory has laid down an outline of normal emotional development and ways of measuring whether a particular child *is* 'normally attached' (for instance, by observation in the 'Strange Situation'). In most of this research there is a glaring omission: there is hardly ever any investigation of the types of relationship the child has in day care and what sort of emotional experience *day care* is. Another missing link is an investigation not just into whether children in nurseries are still attached to their mothers, but how the mother–child relationship is affected by the child's absence.

For the time being, we have to make do with the answers to these rather narrow questions. The answers do not tell us *enough*, but they are still interesting and indicative.

In her recent review of research into day care, Clarke-Stewart reports that more than thirty different studies carried out in the last fifteen years support the conclusion that 'decent day care has no apparent detrimental effects on children's intellectual development' (op. cit.).

Studies of the emotional bond between child and mother, measured in terms of the 'strange situation', reached a similar conclusion: that decent day care seemed to have no ill effects. These studies indicate unequivocally that children in day care are indeed attached to their mothers and that this feeling is not displaced by their feelings for their daytime care givers (Anderson *et al.*, 1981).

Many of the early studies were accounts of day care intervention programmes directed at ghetto children, but it has recently been shown that these conclusions hold as true for the children of middle-class and professional parents as for the children of poor parents (Rubenstein and Howes, 1979 and 1981; Carew, 1980).

In Carew's longitudinal study, observations were made of children and their carers in their own environments at home and in day care in the USA. The home care sample were twenty-five white children from a range of social classes; the day care sample were children from highly educated families. Her study is particularly interesting because she looked in some detail at the actual interactions between children and their carers, both at home and in the day care centres. She tried to pin down which practices lead to children's intellectual development and which have no apparent effect. Both the home study and the day care study showed the importance of experiences which helped language development. Children whose carers took the initiative in helping them master language, for instance by teaching them a new word, were likely to have higher IQ scores. In contrast, the intellectual experiences children create in solitary play, either at home or in the day care sample, were shown to have little effect on IQ scores.

Carew believes her study shows the important role the carer has in creating and structuring experiences for the child, not just in responding to the child's initiatives. She writes (op. cit., p. 66): 'Casual observation reveals that one outstanding aspect of the behaviour of many effective caregivers is its frequent educationally provocative nature. Without a tinge of embarrassment such a caregiver will label "rhinoceros" and "elephant" for a one-year-old who may barely understand "doggie" and "kitty".' Carew also observed that in this study 'children in day care received almost three times as many language mastery experiences from their caregivers at all ages than children in home care'.

Other commentators are loath to accept these conclusions and continue to look for more subtle differences between the language development of home-reared children and those in day care. Barbara Tizard (1975) has looked at nursery education in Britain. She argues that children get much wider and different experience of language use in the family than they do in a nursery education. The nursery school staff cannot know enough about the children's life outside the school to be able to sustain the conversation with them that their parents can. This argument has been used by others to suggest that nursery schools are failing in their aims and to exonerate the government's failure to implement the promise that nursery education would eventually be provided for all children over three whose parents want them to have it.

We do not have to accept this argument. We can agree with Barbara Tizard that where nursery schools, like schools in general, are separated from the children's lives at home and there is little communication between parents and school then there will inevitably be differences between the conversations children can have with their teachers and in the family. But not all these differences are necessarily negative. One of the skills of conversation the child needs to learn is to take into account what the person they are talking to (in this case their teacher) does or does not know. It is also true that nursery schools need not be as segregated from the children's home environment as they usually are.

Some studies have begun to look at other aspects of group care. Rubenstein and Howes, for instance, have looked at the relationships that the children form with each other. They compared young children (seventeen to twenty months old) in day care with a matched group reared entirely at home. In their study they found that the infants in day care smiled more, seemed happier, wandered about less and played at a higher developmental level than did the infants reared at home. They suggested two reasons for these differences: one was that the mothers at home gave more reprimands, directions, orders, prohibitions and intruded more into their play than did the carers in the centres; the other was that, in the presence of other young children of a similar age, the children played in more complex ways with toys and other objects and played with each other for almost a quarter of their time. This contrasted with the home-reared sample, only a few of whom had regular contact with other familiar young children.

All research in this area that attempts to compare 'home' and 'day care' comes up against the perennial problem we have been emphasizing – that there are *enormous* variations within each group. If you find that *as things are*, mothers tend to shout at their children more than nursery workers, this need not mean that they shout *because they are mothers*. They may well shout more because of bad housing and other material problems, and because they suffer from their isolation and low status as mothers. If you find that *as things are*, carers in many nurseries keep a 'professional' distance from the children, this does not mean that relationships in nurseries are *inevitably* emotionally distant. With different organizations, as we shall see, they are closer and more informal. The most hopeful research developments are those studies, like Rubenstein and Howes, which look at the detailed behaviour of carers and children in both nursery centres *and* homes. To do this intelligently means laying aside the prejudice that full-time care at home in our current system of private child care is the normal and desirable way of bringing up pre-school children, and no longer ignoring the importance of young children's relationships with each other.

NURSERY PHILOSOPHY AND ORGANIZATION

Some of the most detailed information that we have about nurseries in this country comes from the series of studies carried out in Oxfordshire under the direction of Jerome Bruner. These studies show that nurseries differ enormously, even when they are of similar size and take in children from similar backgrounds. Sylva and Roy point out that the different names for different kinds of provision for the under-fives actually obscure the differences within each kind of provision. They found that not only are there differences between nursery schools, nursery classes and play-groups, but also that the differences within each grouping may be as great as the differences between the groups. They found striking differences in the Oxfordshire provision for under-fives, and then compared it with pre-school provision in Miami, in the USA. In their turn, the Miami centres had a different philosophy from those in Oxfordshire: there were different kinds of toys; there were fewer shared outdoor toys; there was less free choice indoors for the children – more was organized for them.

These are among the issues that need to be explored if we want to know what kind of day care to provide. The focus of earlier research on the question of how day care affects IQ and whether or not it harms children's relationships with their mothers was far too narrow. We need to take into account the reasons why nurseries are set up, the values of the staff and how they are organized. As Garland and White say (1980, pp. 108–9):

... nursery life is not like family life: on the whole nurseries do behave as though they had some end in view, as though a definable goal were expected of them. We do not ask mothers what their aims and objectives are as they sit in the park with their offspring, perhaps because (having no choice in the matter) we trust them to be sufficiently well-disposed to their children and to know them sufficiently well to be the best judge of their needs at any one moment. But nurseries cannot deal with one child at a time ... the nursery has to make some decisions about priorities, and hence programmes.

In their critical account of one local authority day nursery, Bain and Barnett (1980) recognize the importance of nurseries' philosophies and organization. They argue that day nurseries are unconsciously organized to prevent 'intimacy between nurse and child', and suggest factors which they think lead to the prevention of intimacy:

– an emphasis on domestic duties, physical care and appearance (with a corresponding emphasis on the Matron's rule);

– the structure of multiple, indiscriminate care;

– treating children as a group rather than as individuals, and as though they have identical needs;

– the ordering and regimentation of the children;

– the denial of the importance of attachment;

– the attitude that nurses are the same and easily replaceable;

– the splitting of nursery care from parental care.

Thus they identify a number of issues which can be related to the staff's values, to their training, and to a hierarchical system of staff relationships.

But Bain and Barnett use their analysis based on one day nursery to criticize nurseries in general. There is no evidence that all nurseries are the same in these respects. How sensitive the staff are, and how much intimacy they create between themselves and the children, differs from nursery to nursery. It is true that there is probably less variation between local authority day nurseries than between the various community nurseries and workplace nurseries. Some of these issues have been discussed on short courses which Pam has been organizing for workers from various kinds of nurseries.

Community nurseries have often been set up with aims that deliberately challenge the practice of other existing nurseries, so that anti-racist and anti-sexist objectives are explicit and written down. Some also challenge traditional hierarchical systems of organization by working as a collective, paying all staff equally and sharing all the responsibility. Community nurseries recruit their children largely on a residential basis. In contrast, the staff in local authority day nurseries know that, at some stage in the allocation of children from a long waiting list to the few available places, these children's circumstances have been judged so poor that they will gain through being in a nursery. Thus the staff know that they are considered more suitable and more able to cope with children in their care than the mothers themselves. Staff relationships with the parents cannot be one of partnership. Even if they are newly trained, younger than the mothers, and with (so far) little experience of children, they are expected by the authority that employs them to guide, encourage and educate mothers in the appropriate care of their children. In practice, the staff often have minimal links with parents, and indeed they often complain about them. One complaint was that a mother dressed her child in her best clothes and then wanted the staff to stop her playing with the sand and water in case she got her clothes dirty. The staff responded to this request by taking off the little girl's clothes while she played with the sand and water without telling the mother. Another worker from a different nursery complained about a mother who brought her child to the nursery unwashed and in the same dirty clothes day after day. The staff believed this was because they used to send the child home in clean clothes, and this meant that her mother could avoid doing the washing. They believed they had now thwarted this behaviour by washing the child on arrival and putting him into clean clothes in the nursery, but changing him back into the clothes he had come in before they sent him home.

Both these examples show how nursery staff can see mothers as inadequate and their own role as manipulating or educating them. This view is now being institutionalized by some local authorities (as we saw in Chapter 2), in the transformation of some day nurseries into family centres. Family centres are no longer expected to replace the mother for part of the day; their function is to provide an educational setting for child and mother, where they can both learn different ways of responding to other people and to each other. The idea is that when this re-education has succeeded, the nursery place can be given to another child and family. The patronizing philosophy underlying such practices must affect the kind of relationship the staff can have with the parents, even if it is not made explicit.

In contrast, in many of the nurseries set up by voluntary groups, the parents do feel that they are partners, with the staff, in the care of their children. In many cases, some mothers or fathers are on the management committee or have representatives on the management committee and can influence decisions about how the nursery is run. Often, the workers in the nursery also participate in the management committee or have representatives on it, and this gives them a feeling of control in their work.

A price does have to be paid for such autonomy. Much of the workers' time may be taken up organizing, campaigning and applying for grants and continued funding in order to keep the nursery and their own jobs going.

They may have to take on many clerical, financial and management tasks that other people would do for them if they were working in local authority nurseries. But despite such stressful working conditions, this involvement can mean that nursery staff gain a sense of their own worth – which Bain and Barnett found lacking in the staff of the nursery they studied. How the staff feel about themselves affects the children: people who feel they are doing important work well are much better able to give the children they care for the feeling that they are special. These conditions also make it easier for staff and parents to see their different responsibilities to the children as related. Parents are more likely to be welcomed as helpers in the nursery. Staff and parents are more likely to discuss the children together and to see themselves as involved in a joint enterprise.

A study on children in residential care carried out by Jack and Barbara Tizard (1975) confirms the importance of organization of day care. They found that, in children's homes where staff had some autonomy and could make their own decisions, the children were given more freedom and wider experiences, such as excursions, shopping, going to cafés, and on trains and buses. In nurseries where all decision-making power resided with the nursery matron and other staff had little authority, the children's lives were far more restricted. In the more autonomously organized groups, the staff interacted more with the children, talking, reading and playing with them; and observers saw the children active rather than passive. The quality of their talk differed too. 'Staff in nursery groups which had most autonomy offered more informative talk, spoke in longer sentences, gave fewer negative comments, and were more likely to explain themselves when they told the child to do something, than were those in the institutionally oriented groups' (Tizard, 1975, p. 123).

Bronfenbrenner has shown that what effect day care has on children depends on the values of the carers in the centre, the culture from which those values come and the specific programme it inspires. His account of day care in the USSR and the USA showed how in each country the children in day care conformed to prevalent adult values: in the Soviet Union, the children were conformist and co-operative; in the United States, independent and individualist. Some commentators on day care in the USA have noticed increased aggression among children in nurseries. This could be the result of the culture's individualistic and competitive values transmitted through day care, rather than of day care itself.

Children at home learn the dominant culture, of course; but if their families are nonconformist in any way, they probably learn it more slowly at home than in group care where it is often formally transmitted, at least through toys, books and play materials and often by what is said and done by nurses and teachers. One anthropologist who studied Polynesian and European-run play centres in New Zealand reported that at the Polynesian centre the children were encouraged to play together, were served their snack collectively, and did a lot of collective singing and dancing. At the European centre each child helped him or herself to a snack, and it was the individual work which received praise while the collective work (like a joint tower building project) was more likely to be ignored (Rubin p. 129). Day care is collective by definition, but that need not mean it encourages children to co-operate with others, to recognize other children's strong points, to help them when they need help. In the USA and Britain, these co-operative values *are* expressed in nurseries, but there is far more stress on doing better than others and doing it all by yourself.

INSIDE THE NURSERY: HIGH QUALITY CARE

We have seen that nurseries differ in overall structure and that in different nurseries the staff have different ideas about why the children are there. Different nurseries also have different ways of programming the children's days and different ideas about how rigidly or flexibly their programmes should be applied. Garland and White studied ten British nurseries, seven private and three local-authority ones. They found the basic pattern of the day was similar.

> The first couple of hours in the morning before milk-time were spent in free play (though what was meant by free play differed from one institution to another . . .). The range of equipment offered to the children in all the nurseries included sand, water, paint and clay or dough; puzzles, drawing materials, constructional games and lego, a wendy house or home corner; a climbing frame; and bicycles or scooters and balls for outdoor play . . . At mid-morning the children would all be given milk and biscuits. Once a group of children were together in this way, the nursery staff often took the opportunity to read a story, sing some songs and nursery rhymes or talk about a topic of special interest . . .
>
> The second part of the morning was often used for more directed activity. Sometimes this consisted of setting out a particular craft activity on one table, but sometimes it was organized more formally. At Wilber-force, the children had a twenty-minute music and movement session

before being divided into age/ability groups for the next hour, when each group used the same materials as in the free play session – for example, using the water tray to discuss sinking and floating, or hot and cold ... Two other nurseries ... used a different system: a teacher ... or a play-leader ... would be available in a small room to which groups of two or three children could go at a time ... The supervision of meal-times was often left to the least qualified staff ... One nursery ... was unusual in this respect in that they regarded meal-times as a special event in the day ...

A rest period was compulsory for the children at all but one of the private nurseries, but none of the State nurseries insisted that all their children should rest ...

In the afternoon the children tended to be taken out for a walk or to play outside if the weather was fine ... Outside visits, and visitors to the nursery, provided some variety ... [Most of the] nurseries took their children out quite often, either in twos and threes, when a member of staff wanted to go shopping or to the bank, or in small groups to the local park, play-group, library or swimming pool; or occasionally on more organised outings to a farm or a museum ...

At every nursery ... activities tended to tail off towards the end of the day when both staff and children were tired ... (Garland and White, 1980, pp. 41–2).

Within this basic framework, Garland and White found enormous differences in emphasis and in quality of care. In one nursery 'free play' was understood by the staff as a free time for them, too. In others, play was seen as central to children's development and either structured, facilitated or built upon, in considered ways. There were big differences, too, in the amount of control children had over what they did. Some nurseries' programmes reflected the basic belief that adults know best what children need, whereas others had a child-centred approach and a more democratic style of management. There were also contrasts between the warm, caring approach of some adults and the regimented discipline of others. As Garland and White say:

It is more difficult to define when things are going well (and even more so to see the reasons for it) than it is to determine when things are amiss. When an adult threatens a child with violence, or hurls its comforter in its face with a contemptuous remark, it is plain that something has gone wrong; but the outward signs of things going well may be no more perhaps, than the expression on a face, or a particular quality to the noise in a room (ibid., p. 10).

No wonder researchers have found it difficult to pin down this quality and to find particular forms of structure or particular programmes that make things 'go well'. But since all the claims for benefits from nursery care specify 'decent' or 'high quality' day care, it is important to have an idea of what definable qualities make for a good nursery.

Some nurseries would not be seen as 'high quality' by anyone's standards. Some are overcrowded places where the ratio of staff to children is so high that the children never get individual attention or special consideration, where the staff are dissatisfied and turnover and absenteeism are high, where the children are regimented and the structure of the day is rigidly predetermined, with cleaning and cleaning-up given higher priority than play. Other nurseries will be considered 'high quality' by some people and not by others. In what follows, of necessity we express our values.

(a) Staff, Organization and Training

How a nursery is organized and the values and training of the staff probably outweigh all the other features that can contribute to a good nursery. We know that the physical setting, the amount of space available, the quantity of materials and toys present all have an effect on the children's social and intellectual development. But it is the way in which space is organized, the size of the groups that the children are in and the decisions that the staff make about what materials should be available and what activities should take place that determine the nature of the nursery – in other words, the nursery's philosophy and organization.

If the staff and management committee are not committed to opposing racism and sexism, then these oppressive features of the wider society will inevitably find their way into the nursery. Clearly there is a distinction between nurseries in which staff are *themselves* racist and sexist in their attitudes, however unconsciously, and ones in which they are simply resigned to 'reality' and do not believe they can do anything other than tell children who call a little Indian boy a 'Paki' that it isn't a nice thing to say. But resignation changes nothing. When four-year-old Anna went to pre-school in Australia, she was not allowed to go on the slide by a group of bigger boys, who had decided that this was a spaceship banned to girls. The nursery teacher's idea of handling the situation was to lead Anna towards the wendy house, because 'you can't change personalities. These are some of our more boisterous children.'

A study of nursery school children showed that when they wanted to be friendly with another child or join in his or her play, the way they behaved depended on their sex and the sex of the others. Boys approaching boys were often aggressive or challenging. Boys approaching girls would give orders ('Hold this swing for me'), or simply join in their play without speaking. Girls approaching girls often asked questions ('What are you doing') or challenged them ('Bet you can't do this'). Girls approaching boys were more likely to offer to do something for them or with them or to offer information. The researchers concluded: 'both boys and girls see boys as occupying a superior position that allows them to make demands and implies that they should be addressed more indirectly and politely' (Phinney and Rotheram, 1983).

Nurseries are in a unique position to work to undo the effects of racism and sexism on their charges – or to reinforce them by collusion or in action. We would include a commitment to countering racism and sexism as a feature of high quality care, although much more exchange of information is needed about how to do this. Rubin reports a study which shows that what nursery workers say does make a difference. Whenever they saw a boy and a girl or a mixed-sex group playing together, the teacher would comment approvingly about what they were doing. Over two weeks '... the rate of cross-sex co-operative play increased dramatically' without the children playing any *less* with playmates of their own sex (op. cit., p. 101). Most nursery workers would not think of trying anything like this because their training does not make them aware of the need and the possibilities.

We would also advocate a democratic staff structure. This principle may well be difficult to reconcile with opposition to racism and sexism, until workers' training is improved so that it can give them a sense of how much they can achieve and why it matters. In general, a democratic staff structure will provide better staff–staff, staff–child and staff–parent relationships than a hierarchically organized structure. Some nurseries are organized so that staff are effectively isolated and have no chance to discuss what they are doing or give each other any feedback. One worker in a local authority nursery had been talking about her view of the relationships between nursery workers and the children they care for. When asked whether the other workers in her nursery shared her views, she said she had no idea since she only saw the other staff in the garden. In contrast, one of the community nursery workers said that in her nursery discussions take place every day, with staff meetings once a week, and on the whole she believed there was agreement in her nursery.

The workers' training matters too: 'With more training in child development, studies consistently find, pre-school and day care teachers and day care home providers are more interactive, helpful, talkative, playful, positive and affectionate with the children in their care (and the children are more involved, co-operative, persistent and learn more)' (Clarke-Stewart, 1982, p. 99). In Britain, the training that nursery teachers get is better in this respect than the nursery nurses' training which emphasizes domestic rather than cognitive skills.

(b) Grouping the Children

We have emphasized the potential nurseries have for fostering children's friendships. How the children are grouped within the nursery is a decision which the staff or management committee make, which can affect the children's relationships. The children may be organized in family groups, age groups, or not divided into groups at all. They may all be in one room, or in several. Where several rooms are available, the choice may be between putting the babies in one room, toddlers in another and nursery school-age children in a third, or to have a group of children of mixed age in each of the rooms – 'family grouped'. Nurseries which organize the children into 'family groups' probably do so because they see their role as a substitute for the child's own family. Others, which organize children into age groups, are probably following implicitly the other ordering principle of our society, which equates age and development level and assumes children of the same age can be taught efficiently together. Both these principles have stultified thinking in this area.

If babies are segregated, they may get to know their carers well; but any relief staff, who have to replace the familiar ones if these are absent, will be strangers. When the babies are old enough to move on to another room, some of the children will be strange to them. On the other hand, the youngest children in 'family groups' may have to compete with older ones for attention and their needs may get overlooked. There are also disadvantages for the older ones. The answer is probably found in each case by using resources flexibly to meet certain aims, rather than by following abstract principles and copying either schools or families. Children need stable groups of children to be with, as well as a choice of playmates at their own developmental level, which may not be the same as their chronological age.

When two children are of approximately the same age and degree of competence, neither can be assumed to be the leader or authority in their interactions. Instead, they start at an equal level, with distinctions of status emerging only as a result of the children's own negotiations and discoveries about themselves. The potential for intimacy ... seems likely to be greatest among children who can identify with each other as equals (Rubin, 1980, p. 113).

Some good relationships may also form between older and younger children, and can be especially valuable for children who find difficulty making friends with their age mates. One rather competitive boy was helped by

> The day care centre's ... switch to mixed age grouping [which] gave John an opportunity to exercise leadership more gently and approximately. Whereas John's competitive encounters with children of his own age were often disapproved of, he was admired by the younger children he helped and praised by adults. The result was to increase John's sense of competence and, ultimately, to facilitate his relationship with children of his own age as well (ibid., p. 114).

For some activities it is appropriate to group children according to their developmental level. That does not mean they have to be permanently segregated with their 'equals'.

(c) Staff–Children Relationships

Another dimension along which nurseries differ is the extent to which particular staff members are given responsibility for particular children. In some nurseries, children have their 'special' carer, while in others all staff are responsible for all the little ones.

On one of Pam's courses, nursery workers from both local authority day nurseries and community nurseries were asked to discuss the questions: What do you think the relationship between the nursery workers and the children should be?

Do you think other nursery workers/the other workers in your nursery agree with you?

Depending on your answer to the first question, how do you think your nursery should be organized so that the kind of relationship you believe there should be, can take place?

They broke up into small groups of three or four; each group included both workers in local authority day nurseries and workers from other kinds of nursery.

A number of interesting issues arose from their discussions. It was clear that various ways of organizing were represented. One nursery had all their thirty children in one room. Another had three rooms where the staff were interchangeable. In each case the nursery workers did not want to change their system. A third day nursery, run by a local authority, had children 'family grouped' in different rooms with two members of staff in each room. The staff member from this nursery would have liked the children to be able to move between rooms.

In answer to the question about the kind of relationship that staff should have to children, two groups said spontaneously that there should be no favouritism; and in one of the other groups, the nursery workers said that children should not get too attached to any one member of staff. This does sound a bit like the avoidance of intimacy which Bain and Barnett criticized. But, interestingly, this group consisted of two women who worked for local authorities and only one who worked in a community nursery. The community nursery worker disagreed to some extent and added: 'If a child is insecure then it should be allowed to identify with one member of staff if it chooses to,' and also said she thought it important that staff should have 'time to listen and get to know the child and parent'.

Is it 'favouritism' if a professional carer has strong feelings about a particular child or children? A predictable, high standard of considerate behaviour should be expected from nursery workers, and this must include listening to children so as to get to know them well. One of the advantages of nursery care can be that the relative detachment of the staff makes them better able to be consistently caring and predictably 'there'. This need not preclude a degree of intimacy, but there seems to be an idea that, because it is easier for a particular worker to get closer to some children than to others, it will be fairer if she does not get close to any of them.

Nursery workers are sometimes criticized as carers because they cannot be committed in the way that a mother is. The argument runs that commitment to a child means that even the less pleasant side of child care, such as cleaning babies' bottoms, becomes a form of physical intimacy if the person doing it cares about the person they are cleaning up. Mothers will coo, talk, play and smile at their babies while they change their nappies. Can nursery workers feel the same? With the best will in the world, not if they have six babies to look after, all demanding their attention at the same time. But in principle the answer is, yes. How one feels about the physical intimacy involved in caring for a baby probably depends on whether one has enough time to get to know that baby as a person. The commitment follows from the knowledge and the responsibility; given the appropriate circumstances, carers other than mothers can have similar feelings.

(d) Toys and Play Materials

The setting of the nursery does matter, but apparently unpromising premises can have unexpected advantages, as Pam saw during a visit to a community nursery, housed in a converted building. Three thirteen-month-old babies were all having a finger-painting session in which they used their hands and feet to make marks on large sheets of paper. They finished the session with a very enjoyable communal bath in a paddling pool. This activity was possible because the rooms were kept warm enough, winter and summer, for the children to take their clothes off without getting cold, and the bathing took place in a room that used to be a bathroom – perfect for wet activities.

Although children *can* play with sticks and stones, their play is certainly affected by the surroundings and what is provided. If toy guns are available, they are more likely to play warlike games. If there are hardly any toys, they become more likely to quarrel, or wander aimlessly about. If there is too little space (less than twenty-five square feet per child) they become more aggressive with one another and more destructive with the toys. If there is space and equipment outdoors, children will be less aggressive, more co-operative and sociable with one another.

Different kinds of play materials encourage different sorts of play and a different role for the teacher or nursery worker. Dressing-up clothes encourage children to do things together. With constructional toys they tend to concentrate on what they are doing and talk less, while with paint and puzzles they tend to run to the teacher for help or suggestions. Some play is complex, like an elaborate game of fire-engines and firemen; some play is simpler – like watching sand pour through a funnel, over and over again. Some play is creative – like making clay animals; some, like puzzles, develops problem-solving skills. We have to assume that all play is valuable if it seems to satisfy children, and we expect a high quality nursery to provide materials and a place in the programme for each sort of play.

(e) Programmes

The programmes of good nurseries can differ enormously. Miki's daughter Charlotte has been to nurseries in Bristol and Toronto. There are about twenty-four children at a time in the British nursery, and the day is fairly structured. This does not necessarily mean that the children feel restricted.

If the structured activities are appropriate and there is day-to-day flexibility, they *can* feel more in control because they know what is going to happen next. Charlotte enjoys going upstairs with some of the older children, to work with numbers or on projects, learn poems and other intellectually demanding activities; while the younger ones have their own painting, sticking or model-making activities in the downstairs room. Lunch is eaten socially at mixed-age-group tables, and in the afternoon again there is a time for indoor or outdoor 'free play' and a time for such organized activities as cooking, dancing or drawing. In contrast, the Canadian nursery was much bigger – about sixty children – and there were fewer structured activities and more outdoor play. (There was a compulsory rest after lunch, however!) The 'feel' was entirely different. There was less stress on group activities like painting murals, and more on individual activities; and the workers saw themselves more as resources for the children than as organizers. Charlotte's favourite song from the summer spent in that nursery was:

> Swimming, swimming in the swimming pool,
> When days are hot
> When days are cool in the swimming pool.
> Breast stroke, side stroke,
> Fancy diving too
> Don't you wish you never had
> Anything else to do?
> But ...

Such relatively unstructured programmes and larger groups make it more important for the children to have their own friends. In a smaller group or with a more structured programme, children can do without their own 'best friends' if necessary. That may be good for some who find it hard to make friends, but only good in the sense that it delays their social learning further – puts the problem off. Different programmes seem to suit different children and serve different aims, so this decision is very much an expression of the nursery's philosophy.

(f) Hours in Day Care

We know much less about how long a nursery day children of various ages can benefit from. Staff who work in local authority day nurseries often complain that the day is too long for both them and the children. Because they are open from eight in the morning till six at night (a ten-hour day), the staff usually work a shift system. This means that a child who spends the whole day in the nursery will not have been greeted at the beginning of the day by the same person who says good-bye. By the same token, the mother will not be able to compare notes with the same staff member. Of course, that the nurseries are open for ten hours a day does not mean the children have to be there for that long, and many will be brought later or collected earlier, especially in community-based nurseries.

It is impossible to lay down hard and fast rules about how long children should spend in nurseries; it depends on the nurseries and on the children. For one child, four hours will be too long at a certain stage in his or her life – leaving aside questions of familiarity and 'settling in'. Yet others, like Miki's four-year-old Charlotte, often do not want to go home after an eight-hour day. Perhaps in another nursery Charlotte would not want to stay. If nurseries have enough settled staff to allow the children to get to know and trust them ... if they are flexible enough to encompass the opposites of flopping passively on cushions in front of a TV as well as using all the child's skill and imagination in some activity ... if they have space and time for both noise and quiet ... young children may be happy there for long hours. The way work is currently organized means that nurseries have to accommodate the standard working day instead of the needs of children and parents. If the length of the working day were changed, children's nursery carers could be responsive to their varying needs at different points in their childhood.

CHILDREN TOGETHER

Children need each other as well as caring adults. Perhaps we do not understand the significance of their friendships because we have not asked questions about them. Brown and Harris's research (1978) showed that a close and intimate relationship with another person seemed to be a major factor in preventing depression in women. Intimacy between children may well have a similar protective effect. In a moving letter quoted by Hartup (1978), one man looked back on his life as a child, and concluded that his friendless state then had had a far-reaching and devastating effect on the rest of his life.

... I am an only child, now 57 years old and I want to tell you some things about my life. Not only was I an only child but I grew up in the country where there were no nearby children to play with. My mother did not want children around. She used to say I don't want my kid to bother anybody and I don't want nobody's kids bothering me.

From the first year of school I was teased and made fun of. For example, in about third or fourth grade I dreaded to get on the school bus to go to school because the other children on the bus called me Mommy's baby. In about the second grade I heard the boys use a vulgar word. I asked what it meant and they made fun of me. So I learned a lesson: don't ask questions. This can lead to a lot of confusion to hear talk one doesn't understand and not be able to learn what it means ...

I never went out with a girl while I was in school – in fact I hardly talked to them. In our school the boys and girls did not play together.

I could tell you a lot more but the important thing is I have never married or had any children. I have not been very successful in an occupation or vocation. I believe my troubles are not all due to being an only child, but I do believe you are right in recommending playmates for pre-school children and I will add playmates for the school-ages and not have them strictly supervised by adults. I believe I confirm the experiments with monkeys in being overly timid sometimes and overly aggressive sometimes. Parents of only children should make special efforts to provide playmates for their children.

Sincerely yours

In our society the extent to which young children are in a position to meet other children varies considerably. Dunn and Kendrick's research in Cambridge shows that many of the children there did meet other children regularly two or three times every week, while the London study carried out by Brown and Harris suggested that many mothers and young children spent the week in virtual isolation with each other, perhaps until the father returned at night. The child's only companion would often be the mother as he or she would be in bed by the time the father came home. The Brown and Harris research focused on the mothers and their depression. If the research had focused on the child, we could have found miserable, grizzly children.

Because we give children little autonomy, we unthinkingly break up the friendships they do form; we believe they have short memories and will soon form new relationships, but our own memories may prompt us to different conclusions. As a child herself, Pam moved from Britain to Iran at the age of seven; for three years, until they returned to England, in her dreams Pam's friends from England were still playing with her. She still remembers the three friends she had for the one year she spent as a seven-year-old in Abadan until they moved to Tehran when she was eight. The focus on mother–child relationships has blinkered us all and limited our vision of the enduring importance of children's friendships.

We have shown that many aspects of group care need more investigation. Although day care has been studied more systematically than care at home, it has been looked at only within narrow terms of reference, based on the assumption that maternal care at home normally fulfils all young children's needs. Researchers have noted that the child's relationship with a nursery carer is different from the relationship with mother, and that it does not substantially affect the mother–child relationship. But they have not asked what the relationship with the nursery carer is like, or what it could be like, and what it is like for children to be cared for by people who have quite different expectations of them from those held out by their mothers and other carers at home.

Despite the limitations of the research, it is clear that nursery care must not be dismissed from the child's point of view and seen as no more than a convenience for the mother. The effect of group care on children depends on the aims and practices of the nurseries they go to, not simply on the hours they spend out of the house. The view that day care is inevitably second best is self-fulfilling. We have seen that children can benefit both socially and intellectually from group care in nurseries. For that to happen, they need a stable group of children as well as a stable group of adults. We assume it is important for children to be with adults who are not hassled, hurried, frustrated or isolated. The carers in group care can have more support from other adults then mothers at home usually have, and the use of group care for part of the time may improve the quality of care at home.

CHAPTER ELEVEN

COMMUNITY NURSERIES

by Audrey Marnard

1. THE COMMUNITY NURSERY PHILOSOPHY

Community nurseries first began to emerge thirteen years ago. Right from the start they attracted enthusiastic interest as they seemed to offer an alternative approach to child care. There has always been debate around the issue of just what a community nursery is but, through all the differences of approach and emphasis, four principles consistently emerge.

To begin with, admission to community nurseries is based on a waiting list of children living in the area immediately surrounding the nursery. A fundamental tenet of community nurseries is that child care is a *right* which should be available to all parents and children. In the current system, parents who can't prove themselves sufficiently desperate or who can't afford to pay the high price of a private nursery are unlikely to find a nursery place for their child. Thus, access to child care is either a privilege awarded to those with sufficient resources to pay for it, or a sign of failure indicating a family's inability to cope with their child.

Basing admissions on a waiting list restricted to local children is one important way community nurseries integrate themselves with neighbourhood life. When children live near the place where they are cared for, it is easier both for them and for their parents to get to know each other outside the nursery. Many community nurseries see these friendships outside the nursery as a valuable part of their work.

The second policy common to community nurseries is their commitment to be open five days a week from eight in the morning to five or five-thirty in the evening. These hours allow parents to work full-time while their children remain in one setting for the entire day. This prevents the fragmentation of a child's day which often results when working parents have to juggle child minders, siblings and nursery classes to care for young children while they are at work. Here again, community nurseries challenge the prevailing assumptions about children and child care. The reason most often given to explain the short hours of most nursery schools is that such hours are in the best interests of the child. Those involved with community nurseries wonder if that is necessarily the case. So often the needs of working parents are portrayed as in opposition to the needs of their children. But if children are in cosy, intimate surroundings in which activity is paced intelligently, no conflicting interests need develop. No nursery *requires* children to attend all day, but it is an important *option* for parents to have.

The third common policy of community nurseries is that they involve parents in the *management* of the nursery. Though the degree of involvement and responsibility may vary between nurseries, parental involvement is universally recognized as an essential ingredient in any good programme. When parents and staff co-operate, it is possible to develop an environment in which both groups feel confident and powerful. In some nurseries, parents are the largest group on the management committee and they effectively *control* its workings. In other nurseries, parents are not in the majority and these are run more democratically, with the power shared equally between parents, workers and the occasional interested person from the neighbourhood.

Fourth, and finally, all community nurseries are linked by their efforts to integrate 'caring' and 'educational' functions. Children's daily activities at the nursery usually combine the traditional sorts of play one expects with an added home-like dimension such as visiting neighbourhood shops or helping prepare the food. Nursery teachers visiting various community nurseries would probably be struck by the degree to which these centres operate as a new sort of extended family. There is often considerable warmth and affection between children and workers which is expressed more openly than in traditional nurseries.

The policies which have been outlined here – democratic admission, flexible hours, extensive parental involvement or control, and the integration of 'education' and 'care' – all challenge prevailing assumptions about child care. Taken together, they amount to a new philosophy of child care, which is not always consciously held or expressed by the workers in community nurseries but which sees the task of child rearing as the shared responsibility of parents and professionals.

In London in 1977, interest in community nurseries reached a peak. Several nurseries held a series of meetings and organized a workshop on

Community Child Care. Their purpose was to discuss the issues and ideas involved in community nurseries and to explore the possibility of setting up a community child care organization which would link existing community nurseries and act as a pressure group on local and central government.

After six months of discussion, the idea of a central organization fell out of favour. Many people believed that there was a 'contradiction in the idea of having a centralized/national mouthpiece for community-based child care', as the minutes of one meeting put it. They feared that a central organization with such a relatively narrow focus would compete with broader-based local child care campaigns and result in counter-productive factionalism. In retrospect, it seems a pity that some of these initiatives were not continued. Workshops in particular could have served a useful role in providing a forum for various groups to discuss ideas such as problems of shared parenting, management structures, or how to handle children's aggression. The one workshop that was held was very popular, with nearly a hundred people attending.

The years since that groundswell of interest and communication in 1977 have been increasingly fraught with isolation and financial difficulties. Because of these problems, most nurseries have focused less on the wider ideological and philosophical levels of the politics of child care. Instead, the struggle has been to keep the nursery doors open. Doing that has often had to involve making compromises which depart from some of the generally accepted principles we have sketched out. In many nurseries there is now a gap between what is thought of as ideal, and what is in fact practicable.

The two nurseries described in this chapter have been chosen because they provide contrasting insights into new ways of organizing child care. The Children's Community Centre in Camden Town, London, opened in 1971. The people who were involved in the nursery at the beginning wanted to see if they could overcome the isolation and frustration they felt as parents. They worked as a group to create an environment in the nursery which was supportive for adults as well as for children. In effect, Children's Community Centre has become a community of parents and workers who share the burdens and pleasures involved in caring for young children. Ackroyd Nursery in south-east London provides an interesting contrast with the Children's Community Centre. Ackroyd was opened in 1980, not by the parents but by a group of individuals concerned about the lack of child care in their community. What goes on at Ackroyd has less to do with shared parenting but is more concerned with bringing children both out of the home and out of the nursery and into the world at large. The community is seen as a resource for the nursery and one of the best places for children to learn.

Both these nurseries are 'community nurseries' in terms of the basic criteria we have outlined. But because community nurseries are a grass-roots phenomenon, there is much variety between them. No one nursery can be said to embody a community nursery 'ideal'.

2. THE CHILDREN'S COMMUNITY CENTRE

(a) Origins of the Nursery

The spirit and philosophy which guided the opening of the Children's Community Centre was very much in keeping with the political and social critiques of the day. In the late 1960s and early '70s, a fairly steady stream of political and sociological writings appeared, attacking the nuclear family and arguing for a thoroughgoing restructuring of family relations. At the time, nurseries were seen as one of many ways of altering living arrangements, to make them compatible with egalitarian relationships. A group of women involved with the women's liberation movement decided to try and put their ideas into practice by setting up a nursery for their own children. This nursery became the Children's Community Centre (CCC). From the start it was committed to a collective and alternative orientation. Those involved with starting the nursery had high hopes. They wanted the experience of caring for children collectively to ease some of the contradictions of family life. They also hoped that the children who attended would develop a 'new consciousness', so they wanted the environment to be as 'liberating' as possible. From the beginning, there were debates in the women's movement generally, as well as among the women who started the CCC, about how it could achieve these aims.

The first few years of the nursery's existence were fairly tense as parents tried to find ways of resisting stereotyped sex roles, aggression and competition between children. In an early report on the nursery they wrote:

> We refuse to believe that competition, individualism, hierarchies and authorities are all part of 'human nature' and believe that it is possible to rear different kinds of people: people who can work together, who support and care for each other and who are sensitive to each other's needs. How do we do it? How can we begin to change things?

Although absolute answers to those questions are unlikely (and indeed, in the conservative climate of the '80s, people at CCC and elsewhere are less inclined to ask them), the concerns that underlay such questions can still be felt at the Children's Community Centre.

(b) Building that collective feeling: Management of CCC

One of the challenges that faced the founding parents at CCC was how to *run* a nursery along lines consistent with their principles. What management structures did they need to develop? How would they establish a rapport with the community? What were the best ways of fostering the kind of alternative family atmosphere they hoped to establish? In order to nurture the kind of collective environment they wanted, they had to decide what forms of organization to set up.

Eighteen months after the nursery opened, the parents and workers put together a pamphlet on their experiences in collective child care. One section deals with the problems of working collectively. This section, entitled 'Working together', makes the point that people are simply not used to trying to share responsibility for child care: 'We are all so used to the intense privacy of the family, and caring for our young children throws up such deep-seated feelings that it is hard to bring this private world into public'. The principal mechanism that evolved at CCC to ensure a shared or collective feeling of responsibility for the children was the weekly meeting.

While *every* community nursery has management committee meetings at more or less regular intervals, the approach at CCC is different. At most community nurseries, the management committee restricts itself to dealing with issues affecting the running of the nursery, such as salaries, building maintenance, worker contracts, etc. At CCC, the primary focus is group discussion of children's progress and behaviour and the nursery's atmosphere. All parents were encouraged to attend Sunday meetings, for a joint review of some of the children. The following quotation from the pamphlet describes this process and explains the reasoning behind it:

> Our aim is to discuss one or two children each week – but only if their parent(s) are there. This is always useful to parents and workers as it makes the crucial link between the home and the Centre: does the child behave differently in each place? Is she treated differently? Does the parent act in the same way in both places? How do people on the rota react to the child? In this way important issues are raised about the attitudes to childcare, and discussions can take place not, as it were, between a lone parent and a group of professionals, but among a group of people who know and care for each other's children, and who can share their

problems and learn from each other (Children's Community Centre, 1972, p. 19).

This principle of joint public discussion of individual children amongst parents and workers is probably the most radical and revealing element of the philosophy of CCC. They hoped these meetings would result in parents and workers sharing responsibility for all the children: a new sort of extended family.

One essential element in this plan was the parents' weekly rota in the nursery. For a number of parents, especially those in working-class jobs, the rota requirement was always an inconvenience. But it is obviously the only way that parents could get enough information about the children's behaviour in the nursery to enable them to play a full part in the weekly meeting. For this reason, and because it would be so expensive to hire another worker, the rota requirement still exists at CCC.

(c) Premises: A House is a 'Home'

Since it opened in December 1971, the Children's Community Centre has moved twice. It is now in a spacious three-storey house in Lawton Road, owned by Camden Council. For the nursery to have an entire house to itself has an enormous impact both on the general atmosphere and on the way it permits the children's activities to unfold. In addition, the house has a well-designed back garden which is the envy of most who have seen it.

The plan of the nursery is quite straightforward. On the ground floor, there are two playrooms, one of which opens into the garden and a kitchen. On the first floor, there are two big playrooms equipped with jumping mattresses and a wendy house. On the top floor, there is a reading room, a meeting room for adults (fitted with comfortable chairs) and a small 'children only' room into which adults are not allowed. The garden is divided in half: one half contains a magnificently designed tree house and an intricate system of green knowles giving children a little grassy privacy; the other half of the garden is partially terraced and has tables for outdoor activities in the summertime. The whole house is painted throughout in the most exuberant colours, while the furnishings are sturdy and strictly 'jumble sale' in style.

Though the location of a nursery in a given community, and the building (or part of a building) used to house it, are often matters in which the individuals involved have little choice, these factors have an enormous effect on what sort of nursery it becomes. For example, if a nursery is some distance from shops, children are less likely to be able to do 'errands' for the nursery. Geography has a powerful effect, especially when the plans include the unsteady legs of a group of two-year-olds. Similarly, the design and number of rooms in a nursery deserve considerable attention. If there are large numbers of children in one big room, adults will have to be very organized to prevent outbreaks of total chaos.

The children at the Children's Community Centre are lucky to have a house for themselves. People tend to feel at ease quite naturally in houses, while in other, more institutional settings it takes considerable design and planning to create the same result.

(d) CCC Today

In the fourteen years since the nursery first opened, the insistence on the development of collective feelings has lessened. The founding parents and their children have moved on and their replacements have not necessarily shared or understood their vision. These changes reflect the more conservative trends of society in recent years. The two main areas of concession and change have been the weekly meeting and the rota shift requirement.

Today, nursery meetings at CCC are held once every two weeks, while the ever more controversial rota requirement has been eased so that those shifts are covered by friends and ex-parents more regularly than by current parents. This means the nursery can meet the needs of working parents more effectively. The individual behaviour of children is still discussed at meetings, but with more of an eye towards maintaining communication and less expectation of collective *responsibility*. Despite these changes, the nursery continues to function very much as a community in and of itself. The children and their parents have considerable contact with each other inside and outside the nursery. For example, children very often spend weekends at each other's houses or go on holidays together. In 1982, many children and parents went to Glastonbury together for a CND festival. The result of these contacts is that the parents as well as the children become friends, loyal to each other and to the nursery. Ex-parents' children and workers frequently return to visit.

CCC is still committed to many of the values it began with. Workers still try not to restrict children unless they have to, and to counteract racism and sexism. On one visit in summer I found most of the children in the back garden, some quite naked and others in various states of undress, around a large paddling pool, while a worker showed yet others how to thread beads on to a string. These boys and girls proudly displayed their necklaces to me.

In general, the girls at CCC are encouraged to be physically adventurous. In one of the upstairs rooms there is a wooden platform four feet high from which the children jump and tumble on to mattresses or into their carer's arms. At any time parents and ex-parents are likely to be working in the nursery and it would not be easy for an outsider to tell who was a worker and who a member of staff, because the workers are very informal in their management of the children. While activities are planned for the day, children are quite free to do something else. The seventeen children range in age from two to five years, but right from the start they are given full access to all activities. Adults supervise and occasionally join in activities, but the children are given the option of doing things independently or of being on their own or together. There is a small children's room at the top of the house, its walls dominated by a mural of an underwater scene, with one mattress for furniture, where adults are not supposed to go during nursery hours.

In general, CCC workers still believe children should be allowed to work things out for themselves with the minimum of adult interference. Obviously, not all children can manage this sort of freedom, but workers do try to encourage them in this direction. The workers at CCC are a collective; there is no one person in charge. Because parents feel it is very important for children to see men in non-traditional nurturing roles, they have gone out of their way to find suitable men to employ in the nursery.

The nursery hires three people full-time, one of whom is a man, to care for seventeen children and depends on others to fill the rota. There is increasing support for hiring a fourth worker and doing away with the rota altogether, which would effectively be a retreat from the radical attempt to break down the division between parents and professionals. CCC is up against the rigidity of the standard working day and working week, and the segregation of home and work. In sheer practical terms, a fourth worker would mean an increase in the rates that parents would pay. Current fees (1982) are £20 a week, and parents are, not surprisingly, reluctant to put them up.

(e) CCC and the Community

From the children's point of view as well as that of the adults, CCC exists as a world unto itself. As a whole, however, the nursery has been somewhat isolated from the local community. Some local people have been uneasy at the amount of freedom the children are allowed. Efforts are being made to improve the relationship with the neighbourhood. CCC would like to make its premises available to local groups to use in the evenings. In addition they are encouraging more of the parents living nearest to enrol their children on the waiting list. Even if these moves succeed, CCC will probably remain more inward-looking, more self-searching in atmosphere, than many other community nurseries.

In the meantime, during its ten-year history CCC has evolved an unusual form of nursery provision. It is a tightly knit community and membership is not automatic, so the following entry by a parent in the nursery journal stresses:

> 7 May 1982. It is very difficult to find the time on your own to write in this journal – quite apart from the fact that you probably have to have been here for 3 months before you can summon up the courage to put pen to lined paper!
>
> A lovely quiet time today now that Emmanuel, Matthew and Sam are asleep and I am in a quiet room. I must admit that I was very hesitant at first [about the nursery] – it feels like it takes a very long time to feel at home but once you do start feeling at home it's worth the long wait. Kids staying at night at other kids' homes is wonderful. It allows you to do so much more and it's nice.

Not many parents would ever speak of feeling 'at home' in their child's nursery. More than anything else, this seems to summarize the unique aspect of the atmosphere at CCC.

3. ACKROYD

(a) Origins of the Nursery

In the decade between the opening of the Children's Community Centre and the opening of Ackroyd Nursery in 1981, popular attitudes towards the family underwent an enormous shift. During the 1960s it was common to hear many of society's ills being put down to the nuclear family and its alienating effect on the individual. People tried to develop alternatives to the nuclear family, of which collective child care was just one. Such was the atmosphere in which the Children's Community Centre was founded. Recently a totally different attitude towards the family has surfaced in the popular imagination. The family has become, once again, a 'haven in a heartless world' (Lasch, 1977). These days it is thought to be under unbearable stress and badly in need of support. These changes in perceptions have resulted in different approaches to child care. Thus, while many nurseries founded in the 1970s were dedicated to providing a creative alternative to and for families, the nurseries which have been opening in the '80s have tended to see their main function as supporting families. Although the concept of support sounds particularly paternalistic, Ackroyd nursery accomplishes its self-appointed task in an extremely graceful way. Ackroyd has been open for only a couple of years, but it has much to offer those looking for new ways of making a nursery *work*.

(b) *Bringing the Nursery to Life: You Too Could Start a Nursery*
Ackroyd is a small seventeen-place nursery in south-east London. It opened with an urban aid grant in 1981. It employs two full-time and four part-time workers. Parents pay a weekly fee of £20 (1982).

Plans to open a nursery in the Crofton Park area began in 1979. Jean, a local resident with nursery nurse training, observed that in this largely working-class area there was a serious shortage of all-day child care provision for under-fives. While holiday schemes were regularly set up for schoolchildren, there were few resources for working parents with young children. Jean's first step was to contact a responsible local council community worker. Next they filed an application for an urban aid grant, while support for the project was growing in the local community. A public meeting was held to discuss the nursery and this was followed up by a series of informal gatherings in the homes of local people, open to anyone interested. Eventually, over a period of a couple of months, a steering group was formed. These people made contacts with other nurseries and organizations for under-fives, and in the process clarified their own ideas about what they wanted the nursery to be like.

In time, the priorities of the nursery-to-be emerged. The steering committee wanted to provide all-day care for local children, and to integrate the nursery into community life as much as possible. Jean commented, during one discussion of the nursery practices, that she didn't want it to be hidden away from the rest of the world, adding to the isolation of women and children. These attitudes naturally shaped the decisions to be made in the second stage of planning: where to locate the nursery and whom to employ to work there.

When the steering committee for Ackroyd Nursery began looking for premises for their programme, they were excited by the offer of the entire first floor of the local community centre. Two rooms were available, with space to create a small room with toilets and sinks. This location would guarantee that the children and staff would not be isolated. The community centre was a base for a pensioners' scheme, a mother-and-toddler group and a teen club. There was, however, one drawback: the rooms would have to be cleaned every night so that other groups could use them in the evenings, which meant nursery workers having to reorganize play equipment every day. The steering committee decided that the advantages of the situation outweighed the inconveniences, and began renovating the rooms. By January 1980, the rooms had been transformed into a nursery play-space.

Just as the priority for location of the nursery had been easy access to the community groups and activities, so the steering group was committed to hiring people who lived locally to work in the nursery. As at CCC experience with children was viewed as being just as important a qualification as an NNEB or teacher training. Advertisements for the position were placed in the local paper and in shop windows. There are four part-time positions and two full-time. By organizing shifts in this way, the steering committee hoped to create employment opportunities for local people. Unlike at CCC, the staff at Ackroyd do have supervisors. But the small size of the nursery allows considerable flexibility and co-operation in decision-making, and the super-visors themselves work with the children, side by side with the other staff.

Having organized the premises and hired the workers, the last things to slip into place were the children. Notices were placed in shop windows and local papers. Parents quickly applied for places. Of those, fourteen were taken off the waiting list and five were admitted from the social services. Of those, two were part-time places.

(c) Management

The management at Ackroyd differs in a crucial way from that at CCC. The difference is between parent control and parent involvement. All parents at Children's Community Centre are expected to be present at those meetings where major decisions are taken. Thus the parents inevitably form a clear majority and effectively control the management of the nursery. In such a structure the workers do not have much power, which frequently causes conflict when issues such as financing are discussed. For example, at CCC, when the workers want a pay rise, they must persuade the parents to increase their salary; as the funds for such increases must usually come from the parents' pockets, this task is not easily accomplished. By contrast, the management committee at Ackroyd is composed of two parent representa-tives, two workers and one person from the community centre which houses the nursery, and two representatives from the Crofton Park area.

Parents are encouraged to attend the monthly management committee meetings, but it is the committee which takes the decisions. The parents' point of view is represented but does not necessarily determine the decisions taken about the nursery. Ackroyd Nursery does not share CCC's aim of fostering a collective feeling for the children among the parents. Most parents at Ackroyd work full-time. What they want is a nursery for their children where they can be involved without having to be responsible for running it. They want a place where they are comfortable and feel free to participate, without having to control the management. Most important is that their children are happy while they are away.

(d) *Premises and Programme:*
Towards Developing a Community Nursery Curriculum
From the street, Ackroyd Nursery has a somewhat forbidding atmosphere. Its dark brick walls and barred windows belie the liveliness of the activities within. Two rings of the bell will summon one of the Ackroyd nursery staff to lead you upstairs to the young children's domain. In the main playroom one finds all the standard nursery equipment. There are table toys such as puzzles and lego placed on mobile shelves or on the child-sized tables. Costumes, Fisher-Price toys, playdough and paints are also available – although not all activities are brought 'out' on a given day. The smaller room is usually more of a quiet room used for naps and story times. Anyone who has worked with children knows that trying to keep harmony between seventeen children in a mixed age group in two rooms day after day is a difficult task. Fortunately the staff at Ackroyd have a number of ways they can diversify their daily routine.

To begin with the day is divided by the lunch break. Children go downstairs and take their dinner in the community centre's main dining-room. During this meal some of the pensioners may join the children. After lunch the younger children will often take a nap while the older ones go out for an expedition to either a local shop or perhaps (even better!) one of the staff's homes. Mid-afternoon, the children usually go into the nursery's back garden. If it rains, children can use the large hall on the ground floor of the centre. It is big enough for ball games as well as tricycles. This variety of settings in which children can play and talk to various adults is one of the more unusual aspects of this nursery. In most nurseries there is a sense of being *rooted* to the premises; in particular, any trip out into the neighbourhood is considered a major expedition. By contrast, the children and staff at Ackroyd are fairly mobile. The children enjoy being able to go to shops or staff homes, and many parents feel they benefit from the neighbourly atmosphere. Ackroyd does *not* feel like an institution.

If Ackroyd were any larger it would be a completely different place. Its small size is certainly a major factor in allowing this flexibility and mobility. There are only fifteen full-time places; the children range in age from twenty months to five years. With these small numbers the mixed age grouping works quite well. However, if the nursery were to expand, many organizational changes would have to occur. If the parents at Ackroyd appreciate the relaxed atmosphere, they are also aware of the ways that the children are being prepared for school. Two members of staff have teacher training and the children's activities certainly have educational content. The children there *learn* a great many things but in an environment that feels distinctly more like a home than like a school. The style at Ackroyd (and indeed at most community nurseries) combines the educational and caring functions which historically have been divided in state-organized pre-school provision. More research needs to be done on the best ways of doing this, but community nurseries have begun the task. The carers' relationships with the children they look after and the nursery's place in community life should all be consciously recognized as part of what the nursery has to offer.

(e) Bringing Children into the Adult World: the Community Nursery Role

In the previous section we gave a rough outline of how the day is organized for the children, that is, when they go where. But that tells us little about what the children are doing or how they might be feeling. Inevitably, caring for children collectively requires considerable structure and organization. Many adults who are aware of this regimentation of behaviour are consequently wary of the idea of collective care, especially for young children. At Ackroyd, one senses that the structure and organization work *with* the child rather than against him or her. The children take part in a good many 'adult' activities (in the shops, at the laundry and so on), as well as in the child's world (playing with toys and books). But because Ackroyd is a nursery rather than a home, the workers can afford to allow the children to set the pace, something which can cause mothers at home with their young children acute frustration (as we saw in Chapter 7). Small community nurseries, like Ackroyd, may be able to avoid isolating children in a specially designed children's environment. A trip to a store or launderette, which is routine to an adult, is potentially of great interest to a child. Young children love to act out what they see of the adult world. The keys, the money, shopping bags, fruits and vegetables – all these are props through which children begin to make sense of the world around them. A nursery curriculum based in part on children's participation in the life of the world around them would have much to offer.

4. COMMUNITY CHILD CARE

The two community nurseries we have described illustrate two different approaches to child care, and ultimately to the question of what sort of society we want. The CCC approach stressed the need for a collective sense of responsibility for the new generation. Taken to its logical extreme, this would mean that responsibility for individual children would fall from the shoulders of individual parents, and instead be shared by all the adults running the nursery. In our society today parents *are* ultimately responsible, whatever their political ideals, but CCC is able to give them comfort and advice, to share concern, and to decrease their feeling of isolation and insecurity. Ackroyd's approach seems more modest in terms of its implications for social change, but in day-to-day life its contribution is considerable. Only the *nursery* staff, not the parents, are seen as having a *collective* responsibility, but the daily tasks involved in caring for the individual children are shared between the nursery carers and the children's own parents. The emphasis is on making child care part of the fabric of neighbourhood daily life, so that children are not confined to a world segregated by age, but still have the advantages of activities and equipment designed specially for them.

There has only been room here to give an idea of two community nurseries out of the twenty visited, which all made their own special contributions and offered different contrasts and a sense of many possibilities. Study of community nurseries might well show why so many local authority day nurseries are considered unsatisfactory for children by the staff who work in them, as well as by outsiders. The difficulties these nurseries face are well known. Children with problems (their own or their families') are concentrated in special nurseries and, as a result, the environment is often stressful for both children and adults. Children do not have the option of leaving (where would they go? Back to their 'difficult homes'?). Staff do. Turnover is high and stress is a big factor. For instance, in one local authority nursery with a good reputation, the children present in the nursery when it was studied turned out to have had between six and seventeen 'major caretakers' each (i.e. nurses who had stayed more than a month). The staff had high sickness rates, and few stayed in the job more than a few months (Bain and Barnett, 1980, p. 28). Parent involvement is another perennially difficult area. Communication with families is not easy, and the large size of the nursery can make it harder. It is precisely in these difficult areas that the strengths of community nurseries can be seen most clearly.

To begin with, community nurseries have exceptionally consistent carers. Contrary to what one would expect in such low-paying jobs (with a salary of between £3,000 and £5,000 p.a.), most staff stayed a year or more. It was common in the nurseries we visited to find one staff member who had been there for four or five years, while others had been a bit more transient. This kind of consistency is extremely important to children. One reason for the lower turnover in community nurseries is probably their size: none had more than twenty-five children enrolled. This is a manageable number, and allows day-to-day flexibility in planning, instead of the rigid adherence to a daily routine which can become a fetish and distance the staff from the children's actual needs and states of mind, and their own ability to respond to these.

Another reason, related to size, is that there tend to be less hierarchical structures and more co-operation. Workers we spoke to frequently mentioned how they enjoyed sharing skills with each other and the whole process of working together. Parents as well as workers appreciated the less formal and more home-like atmosphere and, from the parents' point of view, these nurseries are satisfying. In interviews, parents stressed the positive relationships between them and the workers. Although all nurseries go through bad patches, communication tends to be very open at community nurseries. What particularly pleased most parents was the flexibility with which the nurseries tried to meet the children's needs. Appreciation from parents who have the space to express it must itself be a factor in the job satisfaction of the staff, which is probably considerably greater than for staff at state-run nurseries. Despite the low pay, community nurseries' staff have a sense of the value of their work – which is often lacking in the discouraging conditions at many local authority nurseries.

Finally, from the children's point of view these nurseries seem to *work*. While not much is known about children in groups, it seems logical to conclude that bringing together children who live near one another is a principle that makes better sense than selecting the most difficult children and placing them in a playroom. There are difficult children at every nursery – that is inevitable – but the current practice in state nurseries makes little sense. Community nurseries have much to offer besides play partners: they have the potential to offer a wider range of activities than one could find in most households and a group of sympathetic adults who tend to see themselves equally as carers, friends and teachers.

There is no inherent reason why community nurseries should not become an increasingly important part of total provision and be set up all over the country. The majority of the present community nurseries are in urban settings, where the demand is great – in York, Glasgow, Leeds, Reading, Manchester, Bristol and Birmingham, as well as in London. Tiverton in Devon is one exception: a co-operative crèche is developing there in a local shopping centre. Several community centres had been providing crèches while parents did errands. Over time these crèches combined and began caring for particular children at a set price. There is no obvious reason why rural community nurseries could not be set up wherever enough children are living, or in centres where parents go to work or shop.

Unfortunately, the reason why community nurseries *are* likely to become more important is a negative one. The current Conservative Government's cuts in state services have affected day nurseries and nursery schools. If current trends continue, the only funding available for community nurseries will be from charities and other large voluntary organizations, or from progressive local authorities, both of which are coming under increasing pressure as government cuts bite deep. Community nurseries cannot be self-financing if they are to serve the communities, which need them, and pay their workers even a low living wage. Local authority financial aid is the obvious solution. The trouble is that the conditions local authorities impose may push the nursery nearer to the models offered by their own day nurseries or nursery schools. For example, one nursery which had council funding was pressurized to move towards an explicitly educational programme. The children were re-grouped according to age to make this easier. The debate about whether it is best to group children in mixed-age or same-age groups is a complex one. It tends to reflect the sterile split between 'care' and 'education'. Mixed-age groupings are justified as 'natural' and 'family-like', same-age groupings as facilitating formal learning. Community nurseries have the potential to challenge this simplistic dichotomy, if their financial backers will allow them, but this will not happen automatically. Since the 'care' and 'education' split determines the sort of training carers have, and their pay and working hours and conditions afterwards, once local authority funds are involved, workers are likely to be classified as nurses or teachers and paid accordingly. Nurseries which try to resist falling into one or other category may be forced, in the end, to combine the two. The authors of *Nurseries Now* say of combined centres: '... all the old traditions and divides of nursery school and day nursery are simply being maintained in a new setting – indeed, by putting them side by side the anomalies in admissions, cost, equipment, staff pay and conditions are made even more glaring' (Hughes *et al.*, 1980, p. 152). Alternatively, in an attempt to avoid staff grievances about pay differences, all are paid on the nursery nurse scales, and any teacher employed is therefore under-paid in relation to her colleagues in nursery schools.

Councils which help fund community nurseries often do so as a cheap way of providing day care, not because they understand and support the principle behind their organization. Egalitarian and collective ways of making decisions are often anathema to many local councillors. Nurseries trying to forge closer links with councils need sophisticated management committees prepared to do battle for their ideals. Similarly, community nurseries which get some funding from social services sometimes find that, if referrals become too big a proportion of their intake, the character of the nursery has to change to cope with the specific problems of those children. Many of the problems of community nurseries stem from financial worries. Continual hassles over costs, salaries, and child–teacher ratios do not help develop a relaxed, confident atmosphere. But the solution to the problem often brings new problems which threaten those very principles through which, we have argued, community nurseries can make such a valuable contribution to our thinking about child care.

The argument developed in this book is that the current system of privatized child rearing operates at a high cost to both children and parents. Another point needs to be made, however. As long as the ideology of motherhood and privatized child care remains unchanged, there can be no 'good' system of community child care. Nurseries will always be seen as second best. The nurseries discussed in this chapter are imperfect manifesta-tions of a desire to develop a new form of child care which meets the basic needs of humans – adult and child – for community and support.

CHAPTER TWELVE

A CO-OPERATIVE CRÈCHE
by Jonathan Trustram

*'We need each other to make caring for children
the pleasure that it can be, not the chore it so often becomes.'*

(Rob, one of the fathers)

WHAT WE ARE

Our co-operative crèche consists of five small children whose parents have got together for two years now to co-operate in their care. When we began, only one child had reached her first birthday, now the youngest is nearly two and a half. Every morning, the children are looked after for four hours by the crèche worker, the writer of this chapter, who is also one of the fathers. A different parent works with him each day of the week. We meet every six to eight weeks to talk about practical matters and about ourselves and our children. The crèche is based in one of our homes and moves on every six weeks. It costs about £15 a week for each child, adjusted slightly according to parents' means.

WHO WE ARE

List of Characters

ROB, part-time osteopath, thirty-one, always used to do a morning, and CLARE, part-time but for the first nine months of the crèche full-time GP, now does Thursdays, the parents of KATE, three years and two months.

CLAIRE, part-time teacher, thirty-one, does Fridays, and ANDREW, full-time teacher, thirty-five, the parents of KATHERINE, nearly three (and now of Matthew, a few weeks).

JONATHAN, part-time crèche worker, thirty-six, and SHEILA, part-time to full-time feminist therapist, forty-one, does Tuesdays, the parents of ROSIE, nearly three. (Sheila also has two daughters, aged eleven and fifteen.)

JO, part-time feminist therapist and writer, forty-one, does Wednesdays, the mother of CASEY, two years and ten months.

JESSICA, until recently part-time student counsellor, thirty-eight, does Mondays, and JOHN, full-time teacher, thirty-five, the parents of MARTHA, nearly two and a half.

First things first – as is fairly obvious from the list of characters, we are all middle class. Except for Jessica, who has recently given up her job, we are all employees of the state or, in a sense, would like to be. Here I refer to the therapists and the osteopath who would like the National Health Service to cover their work but who, at the moment, find themselves in that grey area sometimes known as 'private practice' or 'alternative medicine'. The crèche itself of course is either 'private' or 'alternative', depending how you look at it; and I too would like to see my kind of work given local authority or government support.

We are all paid 'adequately' to 'very well' – those of us whose pay is merely adequate (Rob, Jo and myself) being bolstered by our class position, by living in shared houses and, (except in Jo's case) by our co-parents. Except for the full-time teachers, we have part-time jobs with reasonably flexible hours, allowing us to do our morning at the crèche and to provide emergency cover. We all have houses big enough to accommodate the crèche, some of us living in couples, some in shared houses, and some in couples within shared houses. We all have gardens and cars.

Secondly, we are socialists and feminists. (The crèche could be seen as a mixture of the socialist, the feminist and the bourgeois.) The political organizations we are individually currently active in (as well as organizations of radical teachers and doctors) are the Labour Party and CND.

We are four couples and one single parent. Four of the five children are first children and the fifth is my first though not her mother's. The youngest parent is twenty-nine. Most of us, women as much as men, have spent years working. We didn't have the same acute *personal* need to get away from our children that a lot of parents–mothers – have, cut off at eighteen or nineteen from a world they have scarcely begun to enter. For most of us, to have or not to have children was a burning or quietly smouldering issue all through the 1970s. It took some of us years to make up our minds that (a) we were emotionally able to be parents, and (b) the world was still not too dreadful a place to bring children into. Doubts remain about ourselves and the world which make us *protective* parents, but also anxious to *enjoy* our children while we can, while they are still young, for some of us will probably have only – and who would have thought the 'only' would come so soon? – one child. The children were finally conceived round about the time that Thatcher came to power, and all born in 1980, the year of the baby boom.

We all had collectives – working collectives and/or living collectives – in the background, or the middle ground (and now the crèche itself, of course, in the foreground). Some of us, though our lives have become more 'nuclear', though mortgages are a reality and not a joke, still have a strong emotional and political attachment to collectives or to the idea of a collective, in spite of the failure of earlier utopias in which we attempted to abolish jealousy, possessiveness (including the possession of children by their parents), loneliness, competitiveness, the nuclear family, sexism. These idealistic attempts at deep, sudden, personal changes were made, at least in my case, with no idea of the resistance to such change that we would meet from within ourselves, or of how to help others to change. We now approach child care with the understanding that ideological change cannot be imposed, that we cannot compel children to co-operate, for example, and that false optimism leads only to cynicism.

We read the book, *The Death of the Family*, or we meant to read it, but the family did not die. We are recreating it. But we still have doubts about our new isolation. When a child is born, the isolation of a couple, especially the woman, becomes more pronounced and more critical. We wanted, not just to get someone else to look after the children, however well, but to share child care, to share the experiences of parenting, and we wanted our children to share their lives with each other. We didn't see why that couldn't happen when they were still babies.

We weren't sure how much we wanted the crèche for ourselves, and how much we wanted it for the children. Rob thought it would be great for the children to be with each other, but found that, in fact, they often snatched and quarrelled for a lot of the morning; but, on the other hand, that the crèche was vital for him, as a place where *he* could share. And that even if you discovered a child minder who was like a cross between playschool, grandma and Father Christmas, there still wouldn't be anything in it for the parents.

Getting together was a long, slow process. Rob and Clare talked to people they knew, including some parents who had already set up a nursery, the model for ours, with a similar structure (except that the worker was not a parent). They advertised for other interested parents, and the first meeting was held in early March 1981. The crèche did not begin until late May. In the early meetings in Jessica's words,

> we talked through our disparate needs: for full- and part-time care, for babies with ages ranging from six to fifteen months, in the morning or afternoon, and so on. We began to talk about what kind of care we wanted. For example, we wanted to be involved in and have control over what happened to our children, and we wanted both children and parents to develop close relationships with each other through a small and regular group. We believed in a non-authoritarian, non-sexist approach where the emotional needs of the children were regarded as most important. We also expressed some of our anxieties about not knowing each other, and the need to build up a sense of trust before committing ourselves.

Clearly it is possible for people to agree on the need for a non-authoritarian, non-sexist approach to child care and yet not like one another. A sense of trust, of just getting on with each other, was obviously vital for the later success of the group. Jessica also writes: 'Although practical things filled the agenda of our meetings, at the same time we were testing out our feelings and were able to make compromises about the practical issues, once we were sure of each other.' For example, at one point Andrew and Claire dropped out of the group because they thought they lived too far away from the others, and they wanted the crèche to start earlier in the morning than most other people. But finally, feeling good about the people in it and really wanting to have Katherine in something like the crèche, they came back in. The extra travelling has never been too much of a problem, and Katherine has usually been left early with the parent who was working in the crèche that morning.

Some people dropped out of the group, uneasy about the high level of commitment needed to get the project going and maintain it – coming to lots of meetings, giving your home over to the crèche, sharing your feelings about children, or because they had incompatible practical needs ... And maybe also feelings that they did not 'belong' to the group.

The worker. They began to look for a worker, wanting someone who would not only be good with the kids, but would be able to 'deal with' (in Jessica's words) the parents. The other crèche had had a first worker who dropped out after a week. They finally found me through personal contact, and so the problems of selection were side-stepped. Fitting in with the parents has never been a real problem – since I am of course one of them – but it can be hard, working with a different parent each day. The dynamics of the group are constantly changing, chiefly because the child whose parent is 'on' often behaves very differently, affecting her relationships with the other children as well as with me.

I came to London five years ago after four years in a country commune, learning and sometimes failing to live and work collectively, working (slowly) towards a non-sexist division of labour, and sharing responsibility for children within a framework of primary care from their parents ... learning to see everybody's point of view, with the consequent risk of becoming confused and indecisive. Then I was a home help for two years, mostly looking after very isolated old people. I had a child, who will probably be my only one, and, wanting to get the most out of her first few years, the job more or less fell into my lap, just when I was ready for a move from the very old to the very young. I get embarrassed when people react in an extravagant way to the fact that I have always looked after Rosie as much as Sheila has and that I work in child care. This seems to me fairly ordinary, if not strictly speaking 'normal', though not without difficulties of course. I feel it is vital for men to be more closely involved in child care if patriarchy and male violence is to begin to crumble. And that, however bleak our immediate political prospects, one thing that *can* happen now, is that men can change. The other parents were glad they had found a male worker – Rob having wanted it, for example – but had thought it very unlikely that they would find one. Sheila was pleased for me to be doing the job, but also worried that she didn't see enough of Rosie. On the other hand, if she had had to be the main parent, she would not have had a third child.

Dalston

Three of the children live very close together, in Dalston, so that is where the crèche usually happens. (Katherine lives a mile and a half away, in Stoke Newington, a similar district, and Rosie lives in Holloway, three and a half miles away, in the only house the crèche never uses.)

Dalston is a part of the London Borough of Hackney, whose population has dropped from 257,000 in 1961 to 180,000 in 1981. As the working-class whites left for Stevenage, Harlow and Swindon, West Indians, Turkish Cypriots and the white 'trendies, lefties and weirdos' moved in – and so did the cars and lorries. Dalston's main shopping street, running north–south, must be one of the most poisonous and uncomfortable in Europe, with pedestrians crammed in and fenced off from the road, and children in buggies on a level with the exhausts. At the southern end of the high street, at a crossroads with no pedestrian crossings, is its junction with a narrow main road which marks the southern boundary of Dalston, carrying much of the heavy traffic between Europe and Britain and Ireland. (My personal favourite of the moment is The Halal Meat Packers of Ballyhaunis, Co. Mayo, carrying Irish beef slaughtered according to Moslem dietary laws to the Middle East.) Close to this crossroads is Dalston Junction station on the North London line, which carries us to Kew and Hampstead Heath, and nuclear waste from Sizewell to Windscale. Also close by is Ridley Road Market, with reggae booming out from record stalls, where some mornings there is enough room for the kids now to wander safely along, looking at mangoes and bananas and clothes-pegs and ridiculous frilly dresses, and collecting things like wooden garlic boxes from Spain. There are no tower blocks or very big estates. The side streets of Dalston are fairly peaceful, late-Victorian terraces, some of mean proportions, others more generous, with improved or dilapidated houses, cracked pavements, Asian corner shops, cats sitting about, dandelions to pick, some roses to admire. There are two parks close by, with children's playgrounds. There's a baby bounce, two mornings a week, at the local sports centre. The Dalston Children's Centre runs a drop-in, every morning. Hackney Under Fives have a mini-bus which we use with the other crèche. Having no premises of our own, our environment is vitally important. Dalston is both a rich and a poor environment ... on the whole, of course, with unemployment at 20 per cent, rich for the rich and poor for the poor. It is part of the social power of being middle class that we make the best use of even the free and cheap facilities, including the crumbs that the new inner-city crusade throws Hackney's way. Means of transport are vital – we all have cars; and now that the kids are old enough to be able to sit in the back with just one adult, we use them quite a lot. Moreover, we can afford to use the (still excellent) train services. Probably the most important way in which we have been materially affected by the present economic and political situation is in the amazing number of burglaries we have had between us.

THE CRÈCHE ITSELF

It's a volatile little institution – moving on to another house every six weeks, with a different parent each day – with an awkward and contradictory nature. It's a fairly daring trip into collective child care which at the same time has *built into it*, through the daily presence of myself and one other parent, the primacy of parent–child relationships, a primacy asserted by both children and parents. It has often been hard for children to let go of their parents (and also sometimes for parents to let go of their children), but it has often been harder for the children to have their parents in the crèche and yet not have them, because they have to share them. The child who, on Monday has learnt to do without her parents in the crèche, has her mother there on Tuesday, and maybe will fight not to have to share her, and be aggressive to the other children or lose interest in them. So Monday's autonomous toddler is turned into Tuesday's anxious, clinging infant, and her parents may not often see her at her crèche best. And we, the parents, have to cope with seeing our little darlings learn to bite and snatch. We need to trust each other, for as parents we are very exposed to each other, we see each other anxious, angry, lethargic, depressed. And we have to deal with those awkward little stirrings of envy and competitiveness when, for example, Katherine began to sleep dry through the night while Rosie and Casey, after a premature enthusiasm for the potty, were back in nappies, night and day. It's easy to see why nursery workers are often impatient for parents to leave (though they can also accuse them of just 'dumping' the kids). But they don't have to cope with the child who, having been 'good' all day in the nursery, is a furious little beast when she or he gets home again. In the early days of the crèche, two of the children in particular were often good, withdrawn, as if already trained by their first birthdays to be model schoolchildren. But gradually they all came to express their anger and fear. And there's lots of it.

A clear picture is difficult because little children don't stay still long enough to be described (or sometimes even photographed), especially if you write as slowly as I do. More than half the youngest child's life has gone by since we had our first 'writing' meeting and I began, with Rob and Jessica, to tell the story of the crèche and how we feel about it and what we think it means for the children. Our feelings about it all change fast, too. (It's nearly a year since I wrote the first version of this passage and they're still changing.) Is it 'good' for them? Can they cope with it all? Children's highs and lows are extreme, and so is the experience of looking after them: the good times fill you with optimism and love, the bad times are so depressing ...

They like to do things together. The magical moment on the very first day, when none of them before had sat on a little chair at a little table, was when they all, except Martha, who was still in a high chair, sat down to dinner. They seemed to like it, and the adults – there were quite a lot of adults around for the first few days – were delighted. There they were, side by side, with their yellow plastic bibs and their yellow stick-on bowls, not throwing their dinner on the floor, not smearing it all in each other's hair, but simply sitting there, eating it. Casey did fall off his chair two or three times in the next few weeks (we had to remember to box him in), and so, later, did Martha. But basically, lunchtime was a great social success, and the babies round the table the first image of happy collectivity. Visitors in the first few months were always greatly impressed by it, and again, not so much by the eating as the sitting. Maybe it was also the yellow uniform. (In the structure of the crèche's morning, meals and, until recently, sleep have always been the most important elements: elevenses and lunch, with eating in between discouraged.) The first time we went on the North London line to Parliament Hill (on a day when for some reason there were four, not five, babies, so the trip was easier) they sat facing each other, their feet barely poking over the edge of the seat, but they wanted to sit independently, not on knees, and Katie grinned delightedly and said, 'I like it!' and Rosie, who was sitting opposite her said, 'I like it!' and they all laughed. By the time Rosie, Katherine and Casey were coming up to two, their sense of doing things together extended to one of the older ones, for example pointing out that Martha didn't have her hat on when we were getting ready to go out, and to the concept of turns: 'It's Casey's turn' ... 'It's my go'. And a crude sense of fairness or equality, from which, however, envy and competitiveness cannot be disentangled. If Katherine had penguin with her in the buggy, then maybe Rosie wants Snoopy. Or maybe she wants penguin, too. Or maybe she wants anything except what's on offer. And they all liked to put on funny clothes, bounce together on a mattress and all go on the swings together ... although, on the other hand, Casey often chose quite often, quite early, to be an outsider. One of the first things they did together, when only Kate was yet two, was to play ring-a-ring-o'-roses and here we go round the mulberry bush. They loved those games. But then again, it's always your privilege to walk out of the ring, leaving the others going round in a circle holding hands, while you go off and do something by yourself in a corner. And the circle's usually there to come back to. And they began to sit round the table, all of them or some of them, with playdough, and things to stick in it and cut it with, and a little flour to dust on it, and *play* with quiet concentration ... each absorbed in her or his own game, yet getting ideas from each other as well as from the adults, and co-operating with each other. They would share things, sometimes with a great show of giving, sometimes casually. They snatched things from each other, and sometimes, after clutching it to demonstrate their power and possession, would give it back, graciously, with a 'here you are'.

Going out. The children's need for sleep, as I have already said, was a big factor in the structure of the morning. We quickly developed a routine of taking them out with back-packs and buggies, and would go out every morning in all but the worst weather, if only to give them a sleep. And we were sometimes driven out of the house just because the outside world became a sanctuary, during the first autumn and the following famous winter of 1981–2, from their possessiveness and jealousy. Out in the park we were more of a homogeneous little group, it was us and the outside world, we could relax.

A Walk in the cemetery (written in May 1982 when the children were around two).

I nearly always carry the back-pack, usually with Rosie in it, because although she's the heaviest, she's used to it, and she likes it, and I'm used to carrying her. She's my child, and being in the back-pack is one way of not sharing me with everybody else. And she's used to sleeping in it, and stays asleep when I take her off my back and prop up the back with cushions. Back-pack was the third word she spoke. Other parents sometimes carry a back-pack too. But none as much as me, and the back-pack has definitely become a key element in my style of child care. It began before the crèche started – carrying was a form of care and comfort which, when Rosie was still little, I used, I think, in competition with the breast. Increasingly as she grew older, I would carry the others too, particularly Casey and Martha. Perhaps it has become a macho style of child care, especially as among the parents there are, as well as an osteopath, two bad backs. Anyway, I carry the back-pack and push the two reclining buggies joined together with three buggy clips which I believe are now almost impossible to find, and the other parent pushes the double buggy (non-reclining). Hanging from the handles are our plastic bags, with food and drink, spare nappies (but now more and more spare knickers), coats, buckets and spades for the sand pit, maybe a ball; while the children sometimes each have a doll or a teddy or penguin or rubber teddy or a clown to cling to or drop. We don't travel lightly but we do travel. We are a small, independent, mobile unit ... They all like being on the move, and they like being outside, and swings and roundabouts, and dogs and ducks, and the bright green gravel on the graves in the overgrown cemetery, and the snow, and the paddling pool. We were in the cemetery this morning, and when we got to the war memorial, which has a flight of steps leading up to a large platform with a low wall all around it good for walking on, we found a whole lot of three-year-olds, another nursery. There were two tired women sitting on a bench, obviously workers, the kids were swarming round, I counted ten, counted again and there were twelve, counted again and there were fifteen, and not much older than most of ours. When we started, five babies between two of us was as much as we could cope with. Only one of them could walk. But now three of them (almost) are two, and four of them (almost) are out of nappies during the day. Most of the difficulties we have now are to do with them being insecure or aggressive, or tired but not wanting to sleep, or hurting themselves as they become more ambitious. It is becoming increasingly clear that our luxurious $2\frac{1}{2}$: 1 ratio is still necessary because both adults are parents. On a bad day I feel that I could more easily look after five children on my own if none of them were Rosie. There in the cemetery, watching that other nursery, suddenly I felt our privilege again. The two nursery workers sat on the bench and shouted out when someone went too far away. They looked too tired to move. I was holding Casey's hand as he walked along the wall. We can allow the children to do dangerous things, and to do different things at once, because we're not each trying to look after six children, although again on the other hand, the presence of two parents can make our kids *less* adventurous, more babyish and clinging. So the kids on the war memorial swarmed all over us, not being used to adults who actually *play* with children, and of course especially all over me, because I'm a man. When we left, Rosie and Katherine, fascinated by the bigger children, wanted to stay behind, and some of them followed us down the grassy path between the graves, and had to be fetched back.

The difference between that nursery and our little crèche was already comparable to the difference between the local comprehensive and an expensive private school.

Anger, violence, aggression

> My father groaned, my mother wept
> Into the dangerous world I leapt.

In a way, looking after nice little babies is easier. Even when they're not nice
we don't get angry with them in the way we can do with slightly older
children, whom we begin to treat as moral beings. When a child is persis-
tently naughty or violent it can create tension between the adults as well
as the children. I hesitate to use the word 'violent' at all, but it is inevitable,
and the difficulty of the word suggests the difficulty of the change from the
innocent world of babies. The children's aggression towards each other is
one of the hardest things to take, especially if they are the first or one and
only, and especially if you make the mistake, as we tended to do at times,
of investing in them your political hopes, your hopes for the future of the
human race (the myth of the baby as redeemer). It seemed like a mockery
of our ideals, a confirmation of our fears: jealousy, possessiveness, snatching, hair-pulling, biting – everyday reality in the co-operative crèche. But
after a while of course, you realize that the devil is not in them, that they
come through it, that it is an inevitable part of growing up out of a world
of safety and dependence towards autonomy, but that, yes, our children are
not perfect.

It began during the crèche's first winter (the famous winter of 1981–2,
when Kate and Martha were ill a lot) with snatching and snatching's
partner, holding on. That is to say, the holding on could be as aggressive
as the snatching, and fear inseparable from anger. It was a complicated
business: a child might take something he or she really wanted to play with
and had been waiting for, from someone who was holding it, not playing
with it. Or they might snatch something that was being played with, just
to interrupt another's game. (Games had begun to get complicated,
involving lots of little objects, vulnerable to raids.) Or a child might cling
to something for comfort, and we would say, 'Can Rosie play with that,
Casey? You're not using it.' It could well end up that, in an absurd pursuit
of justice, half of the snatching was being done by the adults, who were
restoring to their previous user objects to which they were in fact indifferent.
Is snatching snatching if the victim doesn't appear to care? Or if the victim
is holding on aggressively to stop others from playing? And how can the
victim develop his or her autonomy if constantly protected from the
dominant ones? If the objects themselves are not the real point of the
conflict, it is not helpful for the adults to play judges, and get everybody even

more fixated on the disputed objects. It makes more sense to try to get the passive victim involved in something he or she enjoys, and to play a lively game with the ebullient aggressor, or to encourage the children to divide up in different parts of the house, with different activities – or to take them all out to the swings.

Clearly, *property* is a closely related issue. The children would sometimes bring their own things to the crèche, to share or to cling to. None of them had fixed comfort objects; it could be anything at any minute. We generally accepted that a child had the right to her or his own things. After all, we have given them a clear sense of mine and yours, ours and theirs, a picture of property in which some things are collectively owned and others privately owned though generally shared, and still other things which are specially private. Special toys of the child whose house we were in would be put safely away.

We entered a complex world of things acquired, clutched, discarded, rejected – of holding on and letting go, which I feel was closely related to the potty-training which began with the spring in 1982, though I have to admit to only the sketchiest grasp of the psychoanalytic theories involved. Along with aggression, caring and sharing began to develop. Sometimes the most special, private toys would be got out and everybody be allowed to play with them. Sometimes the child whose house was in use would take some or all of the children up to her or his room, and in the midst of a period of fighting and anger they would achieve a space of calm autonomy with the adults right out of the way.

More direct aggression, chiefly biting, came after snatching. Biting seemed irresistible, expression of so much power and strength. It is the only way a two-year-old can make an adult, never mind another child, cry out with pain. One of the greatest difficulties about this new phase of aggression was that it forced the adults – and chiefly me – to confront the anger and violence within ourselves. 'Mothering' was relatively easy. Coping with the children's violence returned me to the male stereotypes. As much as any-thing, we were helped by the children themselves, by the speed with which the victim recovered from the attack, the way two children could be hating each other one minute, loving each other the next. Mostly, what was needed was simply to be patient and protective of the aggressor as well as the victim. But, particularly with biting, a clear 'No' is necessary and we had occasion-ally to pull a child off another, without also being violent ourselves. I learnt that there is no clear dividing line between restraint and violence. The crisis of teeth in flesh has sometimes caused me to separate two children more roughly than was necessary. Several times I have slapped a child – lightly, but with the feeling that I wasn't in control of what I was doing. It was unnerving to feel, at times, that I was being provoked and tested, with the same child persisting in attacking the others, despite every possible type of verbal prohibition – pleading, soothing, reasoning, scolding, shouting, expressing all the shock, distress and outrage I felt. How angry would I get? How much could they trust me? How adequate a substitute for parental authority and love was I?

Sheila had thought that the children's aggression would put a great strain on relationships between the parents, who tend to be angriest both at their own children when they are violent, and at other children for hurting their own, because of the demands we make on our own children and our protective feelings towards them. Here, our meetings were very helpful, for we kept in touch with our feelings about it all, even if we didn't come up with a 'policy' for dealing with it. It was good to acknowledge how difficult and painful it all was, and to agree that, at its worst, it was really a question of weathering the storm, continuing to be loving even if we were very angry at times, and we would come through. It seems to be something they all have to go through (although of course in many different ways), and this is highlighted by the fact that when Kate began to be occasionally angry and violent we were almost *glad*, because it was part of a dramatic move for her out of a period of insecurity, passivity, clinging to her parents when they were around.

Separation worried us. Even those of us who had not encountered any alarming theories on the subject had experienced, and even enjoyed, our babies' total dependence on us. (It creates a reciprocal dependence.) In spite of sickness and sleepless nights we were all very excited about our babies. Our relationships with them continue to be (though not, of course, exclusively so) fierce, romantic and possessive. We had expected our children to be upset at being left in the crèche, and made it one of our aims in the crèche to allow full expression to their feelings of sadness or anger (although that is obviously not possible when the expression is violent) and to comfort them whenever they wanted comfort.

When the crèche started, none of the children except Kate appeared to mind being left. Casey, in particular, who was nine months old at the beginning, never seemed at all bothered when Jo left. But more than that, when he was fifteen months old he still refused to acknowledge her leaving and would steadfastly ignore her when she said goodbye to him (although in different situations he was by this time very much into goodbyes and waving). Then suddenly one day, when she left, he cried and cried. This show of feeling was greeted by us with the same relief that we felt on Kate becoming aggressive. Katherine and Martha went through something similar, though not so dramatically as Casey, getting upset at their parents' leaving long after they were settled and happy in the crèche. (But only crying for, at the most, a few minutes, and usually stopping the moment their parent was out of the door.) Kate and Katherine sometimes expressed their distress, not by crying but by being very withdrawn and pliant, sometimes just staring into space for a while. Again, when they had a good scream it was a relief to us as well as them. They would all occasionally cry bitterly and cling to their parents when they came back – when it was safe to cry – after being apparently contented all morning. And they have all needed at times to assert their private, exclusive relationship with their mother or father when it was their day 'on'. When I first left Rosie with Jo for the afternoon, a few months after the crèche began, I was anxious. And when I came back to get her I was greeted with the same airy reassurance that I had given out hundreds of times already: 'Oh, she was fine!' And I projected or thought I heard the implicit: 'What makes you think she needs you so much?' Looking back over the two years of the crèche, I have a sense that, for little children, in spite of all the difficulties, parting from their parents can be sweet.

Some Notes on Sex, Sexism and Heterosexism

An interesting group dynamic: the fathers all have daughters, the only boy in the crèche does not have a 'real' father (he sees his father about once a month), and Jo, his mother, is a lesbian and the only single parent. Is it in part due to the avoidance of certain controversial issues that the crèche has been a good place for Casey? We have been very tolerant of each other. Jo is left with some ambivalent feelings about her own position in it, but the crèche has been a secure place for Casey. Has the mother, once again, paid a price for her child's well-being? Jo writes:

> The crèche has definitely been a safe and rich place for Casey, despite the difficult periods he has been through, and always having to share Jonathan who is particularly important to him. The important aspect of it for me has been the collectivity and the growing relationships between the children, as well as the shared understanding of children's feelings

– especially about dependency, separation, and being upset. The balance we have between adults' and children's needs has particularly suited me – and is something I didn't feel confident of finding elsewhere. But the crèche has also been quite a compromise for me – I have felt isolated as the only single parent and only lesbian. It would have been much easier for me if there had been other parents more committed to living outside of heterosexual nuclear couples, and more discussion and validation of this in relation to the children. Our anti-sexism, such as it is, hasn't extended to opposing heterosexism, and the rest of my life has felt quite invisible at times – a problem lesbians are very familiar with. And I'm sure it will be good for Casey to get to know other children with situations more like his own.

Though a slightly premature baby, and still a rather small and skinny child, not very adventurous physically, Casey was always the best at throwing. And threw with a passion. Almost as soon as the children began to do things together, he would sometimes take on the role of outsider, and later, when lego and all sorts of bits and pieces were set out on a table for the kids to play with, he would express his feelings by rushing up and sweeping everything to the ground. He has nearly always been the least violent of the children. He has consistently been much less interested in dolls and soft toys. He doesn't like dressing up. He has a passion for trains – watching them, riding in them, playing with them. These stubborn little facts, the love of throwing, of trains – what do they mean? Jo is sometimes fearful, for no good reason, but because we are always on the look-out for such things in boys, that when he is about six, and at school, he will get into playing with guns and become violent and aggressive. (There is evidence for the idea that it is harder for boys not to conform at school to sexist stereotypes than it is for girls.) There are times at the crèche when I give the children rides, when they stand on my shoulders, or I make little structures out of bricks and planks for them to climb on, and they may be drawn to this activity, or they may join the other parent, who is sitting reading a story to her daughter. Only if this were to become a regular pattern would it be 'sexist'. Being 'physical' with the children, in a comforting way through carrying, as well as playing, has always been an important part of my child care. Again, it can only be sexist if it contributes towards the children forming a picture of men as much stronger and more physically energetic than women. To some extent, this has happened, for example, as Claire, the most 'physical' of mothers, has become gradually less mobile during her pregnancy. But then, what *does* follow from the fact that, on the whole, men *are* stronger than women? Not necessarily very much at all, for they don't have to be more acrobatic, or more inventive of physical games or physically more adventurous than women. In fact, one way in which I *have* been stereotypically male is in favouring games in which I swing the children around, so that I am active and they are passive, whereas some of the parents encourage the children towards games, such as bouncing on a mattress or doing somersaults, where they become adventurous and develop their own power and skill.

Our commitment as a group to opposing sexism fits uneasily with the traditional division of labour in two of the families where the fathers work full-time at the moment. This has meant that in the crèche, as well as at home, the mothers have been the responsible and involved parents. Despite this, Martha and Katherine are less likely to associate men with absence, and with activities away from home and children, because I am the crèche worker and Rob used regularly to do a morning. But what does it mean for Rosie, that she sees less of her mother than any of the other children? Although Sheila was glad that I decided to work at the crèche, she is looking forward to a more 'equal' relationship with Rosie when the crèche comes to an end. Recently Rosie, like Katherine and Kate, was missing her mother more, sometimes getting upset when, for example, we arrived home from the crèche and Sheila was still out at work.

A father's view (written by Rob in June 1982, when Kate was 2¼). What a delight when Kate has slept well and wakes in a good mood: she's a joy to be with. So much easier too when I start work at ten – I'm sure she often responds to the chaos around her as Clare and I battle and fret about getting to work. She does genuinely want to go to the crèche – we tell her that's where she's going and she tells everyone else who's there to listen: 'Going to the crèche, Katherine's house, see Rosie,' nodding her head in affirmation, 'Daddy going to the crèche?'

'No, Clare's taking you in the car – I'm going off to work.'

'Bye-bye.' 'Bye-bye.' Waves, smiles, kisses, protest, tears in response to that gesture – different every day – who can say why? In the car, on the bike, in the buggy on the way – often chattering, often quiet. Arriving, sometimes she rushes off and gets involved in something, oblivious to me, until she suddenly remembers. Other times she clings tight, buries her head – 'don't like Casey ... Katie wants it, Katie wants it, no, no ... ! Katie's, Katie's.' Our parting ritual – a kiss, 'Bye-bye, Katie, I'm going now, you go to Jonathan,' he lifts her up. We all agreed to make it an issue, acknowledge the separation and not pretend it's easy. Still it hurts, almost as much as it ever did, when she cries – (only once did I wait outside the door and listen to see if she stopped). I thought it was a phase that simply passed, but it's not. One day she waves me willingly good-bye, the next she seems mortified with grief. I know that she will be comforted and that she won't be denied the chance to express her sadness, and that people will tell me how she's been, even if I don't ask, but still, there is a moment of doubt: what are we doing to her? Are we asking too much? It is when there is tension and upset at home that Kate finds the crèche hardest. Is all the coming and going, the disorder in her mother and father's lives compounded by the five other adults that she meets at the crèche?

We've all had these anxieties, and more: tears for the biggest, for the smallest, for the youngest, for the oldest, for the only boy. Katherine, physically a three-year-old at eighteen months, but with the vulnerability of her age, still needing at times to be a baby. Rosie, a year ago always needing to be where the action was, a steamroller – how different she is now, how quickly things change, and how unchanging they seem at the time. Casey, for months not outwardly acknowledging Jo's leaving. Martha, the youngest, still crawling when the others could all walk, struggling to keep up, sometimes not noticed when she needed special attention. Kate, oh Kate, we all think our own kids are the most difficult, and are harder on them than on the others. Picking her up from the crèche, she often starts moaning at me as soon as she sees me. She's wonderful, a delight, with others, but miserable with me. I find myself wishing she were tougher, less complaining, even *bigger* (she's the oldest but nearly the smallest) – then I wouldn't feel so upset by her crying.

I've had some dreadful times in the crèche when it's been my morning on. Kate has been clinging pitifully to my legs while I've tried to cook the lunch or comfort another child. And if Jonathan tried to comfort her she would become even more upset and angry. It went on for about three months – long enough to make me feel it wasn't worth it. That period coincided with the worst period of collective illness. They struggled over toys but had no difficulty sharing their colds. Often at that time I completely missed the fact that Kate was ill and thought her so demanding 'simply' through emotional distress, through anxieties about separation.

I've had a recent experience of just how important the crèche is in my life. The crèche is in the middle of a month's holiday – the month of August – it suits most of us, but Kate's mother and I have had to go on working and take a holiday later. It's meant alternating work with child care the whole time. The conflict of interests between me and Kate has been pressing and immediate, and yet I only have to work part-time and as yet only have one child. I need the crèche for the time and space it gives me, free from Kate. At its best it leaves us both energetic and eager to spend time together. At its most prosaic, she is very well looked after: I have enormous confidence in the other adults. We've been very fortunate in that we share a commitment to the children's emotional well-being and a willingness to let them express their feelings in safety. Without that confidence in those looking after my child, I think I would find it difficult to be free from anxiety when I was away, which would inevitably affect Kate's experience of the crèche. It's lovely too to know the other children so well, and to look after them at other times.

Kate has always talked about the other children. (For all of them, the others' names were among their first words.) She's recited their names as we travelled to the crèche, loved looking at photographs of them all and asked at weekends, 'Are we going to the crèche?' She plays in a different way with the other children than with me or Clare – it's more animated, more inventive, often less harmonious, but more expressive of her developing autonomy.

When I see her with the other children, I think of the concessions she has to make to my limitations as an adult! Being a parent involves endless contradictions. Since having Kate I've felt a lot of joy and, at the risk of sounding trite, a profound opening out of my soul and a real connectedness with the world. I've also felt constrained and restricted, bored and angry, and longed for the freedom of the days before she was born.

Being a child, particularly in an inner city in the 1980s, is often painful, full of conflict around freedom and boundaries, assertion and vulnerability, contact and separation. The more I meet my own needs, the more I have to give to Kate that which is truly for her. I know I can't begin to do that without help. We need each other to make caring for children the pleasure it can be, not the chore it so often becomes.

TOWARDS A CONCLUSION

We're white, middle class, with houses and gardens and access to cars. We know or we find out about the toy museum, the times of the trains to Hampstead Heath, the swimming pool, the baby bounce. We have the money to employ a worker. We have had enough in common as parents to give a pattern and security to our child care. More than that, partly because we are nearly all first-time parents, we came to do things together; the crèche actually influenced the kind of parents we have become, so that it has often worked as a natural extension of home life. And in between home and the crèche there has developed a system of 'swaps' (I have your child on a Tuesday, you have mine on a Wednesday). In many ways, what we have now is like an extended family. So we're very privileged. The question we have asked ourselves for a long time now is, how relevant is the model of our crèche to other, poorer, less socially powerful people? Does our privilege make the whole thing possible, or is it the icing on the cake? After all, our crèche is not so very much dearer than a child minding service. But even in those few local authorities 'loony' enough to make child care and women's rights a priority, professional help and resources are strictly limited, the more so as those councils have been penalized for 'overspending'. When it comes to dealing with the council bureaucracy in less important matters, we have occasionally found ourselves powerless. Nobody, for example, has any idea why the new helter-skelter in the playground at Clissold Park has sat untouched for nine months, while someone looks for the missing bolt. It's actually getting rusty now so, when they finally do fix it, they'll probably have to paint it again before anyone can use it. When we were planning to merge with the 'other crèche', we thought of using a one-o'clock club in the park before one-o'clock, but the council officer who arranged to meet us there, to talk the idea over with the workers, failed to turn up (twice), and the workers never knew anything about the idea or the meeting there with us. (And, anyway, they thought it was impossible for two groups to share the same premises.) Even in an area full of schools with falling rolls, bankrupt businesses, boarded-up shops and warehouses, short-life houses, empty churches and chapels and synagogues, looking for premises was a barren business. On the other hand, there is now a possibility that after the summer, when the crèche finishes and some of the children go to nursery, others will join up with the other crèche in a hall in a disused synagogue which is being turned into a community centre with £90,000 of Inner City Partnership money. Some of the crumbs are cakes.

THE CHILDREN NOW (May 1983)

There should be a special place for KATE in the conclusion, although it may be that I am speaking too soon. There is a passage in Erikson's *Childhood and Society* which reminds me of her at the moment:

There is in every child at every stage a new miracle of vigorous unfolding, which constitutes a new hope and a new responsibility for all ... a crisis, more or less beset with fumbling and fear, is resolved, in that the child suddenly seems to 'grow together' both in her person and in her body. She appears 'more herself', more loving, relaxed and brighter in her judgement, more activated and activating (Erikson, 1965, p. 246).

Some of the circumstances that have coincided in Kate's new vibrant and contented state are: the crèche has moved from her house to Casey's house; we have by now got together more equipment and initiate more games and activities; we have a new style, more stimulating for older children; the other children are ready for the creative, fantasy games which she often initiates; she has taken on a new identity, insisting consistently that she is not Katie but Meg, Meg the witch, occasionally wicked Meg (the others being Mogs and Owls). She has come through her winter illnesses, which included a frightening asthma attack, a lessening of what Rob called 'the disorder in her mother and father's lives', and spring is here, albeit the wettest on record. She treats me somehow more like a friend and guide, less like a parent substitute. She is no longer troubled by the fact that I am an unsafe source of comfort because there is so much competition for comfort. Having to give less, emotionally, I can give more, imaginatively. (But also, I *can* give her comfort when she needs it because it is for a specific reason; it is a finite thing she needs, not the impossible, all-embracing thing she wants when totally miserable.) I like to think also that when Kate first decided that she was going to be Meg, tolerance in the crèche of her new identity (and a sort of sharing in the joke, for she usually likes to be humorous about it) helped to overcome Rob and Clare's intolerance of it, that we helped them to see that there was no point in fighting it. Kate's happiness at the moment is particularly pleasing because it is her parents (and she) who came closest to despairing of the crèche, during several periods of misery and illness.

KATHERINE is also much happier in the crèche now than she was through the winter, and the kind of change that has taken place in my relationship with Kate has happened with her, more dramatically, more painfully. Claire, her mother, had a baby at the beginning of April of this year, and for Katherine her mother's pregnancy was a difficult time. She became obsessed with babies and families. (One day, looking into the toilet, she told me that she had done a mummy shit, a daddy shit and a little tiny baby shit.) Since Christmas, 'Away in a manger' has been her favourite song. She was often solicitous and maternal towards the other children. She was also at times very aggressive towards them. And she could easily collapse into being a baby herself. She grew increasingly upset at being left by Claire in the crèche. I found it difficult to cope with her aggression, particularly as she became withdrawn from me, frequently ignoring me completely when I spoke to her. When the children were younger, they almost always welcomed comfort if they were upset at being left in the morning; but now included in Katherine's unhappiness were feelings of hostility towards me. She almost always preferred the parent who was 'on' to me. And since at that time Clare, rather than Rob, did Thursdays, and Katherine always preferred a mother to me, I felt a distinct loss of power and security. So far, it seems that Katherine went through most of her extreme fears and extreme excitement *before* her brother was born. Now that she has a real brother she is less of a baby, less of a mother, less of a bully. In the crèche she is more able to share and co-operate and create with the other children. She no longer seems to blame me for taking her away from her mother. Like Kate, less desperate for comfort, she is more able to seek it. One day at the beginning of May she hurt herself while I was at the sink, washing paint pots and brushes. I told her that when I'd finished ('just a second' ... 'in a minute' being constant refrains – played back to us now, of course, by the children) I would sit down with her and look after her. Rosie intervened, wanting something, and Katherine said crossly to her, 'No, your daddy's going to sit down with *me* and look after me.' It felt wonderful to me that she was again able to know what she wanted, and able to make use of what was offered to her, instead of being locked in fear and anger. In the end, I was able to sit down and read a story to both Rosie and Katherine. Although Katherine is now once again able to trust me and get comfort from me, I think this takes place in the context of actually *needing* me less.

CASEY too is freer and happier now. In the last few weeks he has finally, and with a great sense of excitement and confidence, begun to pee independently in the toilet, instead of spraying it around aggressively. For quite a long time, about four months, the older girls had ganged up against him, said they didn't like him sometimes. He withdrew from their games more than before, and from many of the activities the adults initiated, and sometimes made himself a victim for their aggression. He was in the process of finding his sexual identity – which was made more difficult by all the other children being girls. His close relationships with Rosie and Kate outside the crèche did not hold up inside, in the face of the overwhelming group dynamics at that time. At times he clung desperately to me, seemed to glory in dirtiness (with spit, snot, pee and food) to the growing discomfiture of the older girls who were acquiring a new sense of 'clean' and 'dirty'. One day a couple of weeks ago I was reading *Where The Wild Things Are*; we had got to the wild rumpus and I suggested that we had one. Casey said, 'But I don't know how to rumpus.' He was able to admit that he wanted to join in, but didn't know how to. So I showed him and we all had a good rumpus. Now he joins much more in the fantasy games and clings to me less; he is more social and more independent, more integrated with the others as the pattern of relationships in the group has shifted. Though Casey treats me like a father in some ways (recently, as he was coming out of that last phase of struggle, he threatened several times to cut off my nose), Jo says he is no longer obsessed with the nuclear family model of Sheila, Rosie and myself. I used to wonder whether, appearing and disappearing regularly, never being quite close enough or available enough, I was becoming only too much like a real father.

For ROSIE, this is maybe the most difficult time. She is now the most aggressive of the children (though still often sunny and contented). Is it hard for Rosie to share me all the time? That is the question I've been asked dozens of times, and I'm still not sure. She has never clung to me very much – no more than anyone else – and has rarely reacted jealously when I have been comforting another child, and would usually, if she made a choice, prefer the company of the other parent present to mine. But she has sometimes struck at the basis of the crèche by breaking up games I have been initiating, telling me not to sing a song and so on. And she certainly used to love the times when we were 'alone together'. (So did I.) She would often prefer me to Sheila when we were both at home. Maybe her current aggression is highlighted by the fact that the others are more content. But if one thing that is happening for the children at the moment is the discovery of their autonomy, then this is surely more difficult for her. I worry about what it will be like for her to go to a nursery, after being used to having me for so long, and being so close to the other children in the crèche; but, at the same time, I think she is ready for a change.

MARTHA ... The other day in the churchyard opposite Jo's house (an area of grass, dandelions, chickweed and ragwort inside a belt of lime trees, undercarpeted with masses of bluebells) we were playing in the sand left by the builders who came to stop the tower from falling down, and picking daisies and dandelions; Martha sat quietly, filling a plastic beaker with sand, patting the sand down with a spoon, filling it till it spilled over, then piling on more sand, sometimes a few grains at a time, sometimes a spoonful – while the others buzzed around her with their social fantasy games – doing just what she wanted to do, absorbed, peaceful, separate. She is also, at two years and five months, old enough now to join in the fantasy games if she wants to, the favourite one of the moment being the trip to Coconut Island in a boat or plane constructed from chairs, blankets and cardboard boxes, powered by a vacuum cleaner. Along the way there are songs, fights, monsters, feasts and face paints. (One result of the structure of the crèche has been that I have learnt things from all my co-workers, and here I would like to say that Claire in particular initiated this kind of game, which was both creative and collective, and stunningly expressed the children's developing powers. But it was I who thought of the vacuum cleaner. Of course, Claire got the idea from Kate, who dreamed it up after her trip last Christmas to stay with relations in New Zealand.)

But it is still true that it is at times easy to ignore Martha, because the other children are being more vocal or more aggressive or more pathetic – but often when being 'ignored' she is simply playing happily. On the other hand, she recently began to play an absurd game with food which seemed designed to attract attention, asking for a peanut butter sandwich, then saying no to it and asking for marmite, throwing away the marmite and demanding peanut butter instead, etc. Often treated benevolently as a little one by the other children, she is never excluded as such, or bullied. In a struggle over something with one of the big ones, she can be fierce. In a sense, the ending of the crèche is saddest for her, because if she was too young for it when it began, she will certainly be too young to leave it when it ends. She is in no danger, unlike the others, of being bored in the crèche, nor is she oppressed as much by all the sibling-like rivalries and jealousies.

POSTSCRIPT (July 1983)

Of course the way we have done it is not the only way; reading this account, you might not realize how flexible the 'co-operative crèche' structure can be. 'Tiddlers', up to now referred to as 'the other crèche', who gave us the idea and the inspiration, have the same structure, with the big difference that they had never had a worker who was a parent as well. They have been going for about three and a half years now, and have no plans for closing down. Whereas we have been a tight, secure and unchanging group, they have been through a lot of changes. They now have a whole new generation of tiddlers, including the sisters of two of their originals. Though at one time they found the problem of being in their own houses worse than we did, they now find it much easier again, with younger children, and meet in a different house each morning: the house of the parent who is on. 'Tiddlers' is more of a social institution in its own right, the more so as their workers have not been parents, whereas our crèche has been more like an extension of the family, and some of our problems and strengths stem from this.

For instance, we have found no permanent answer to the problems of child–parent relationships within the crèche. The children continue to lurch from a state of pathetic dependence to one of vigorous independence and back again. Legless Casey one minute ... then ready, steady, go! he's sprinting and wobbling down the road. Maybe it's a misleading snapshot, but seeing a dozen children from a nursery at the paddling pool the other day they seemed strong, happy, equable, independent – and the adults with them were having a good time as well. (That picture stands out in contrast to the group we met at the cemetery.)

We partly planned to end the crèche now because we thought they would all be ready for a change, for the stimulation and variety of a proper nursery, and for independence from their parents and the sometimes incestuous intensity of the crèche. Besides this, I needed a change, and Rosie needed to make friends in her own area. And the parents – and children, too – wanted their houses back. All this remains true, but not exclusively so. As ever, there are good days and bad days, and the way we view the ending of the crèche changes with daily experience. The children are looking forward to their nurseries, but do they realize that it's the end of the crèche? We plan to try a regular weekday afternoon and Saturday morning together next term, so it won't be a total break. Unfortunately, none of the children will be going to the same nursery, and there are doubts about just how stimulating and exciting their nurseries will be. Child care is passing out of our hands, the state is taking over, they will be eased or forced from nursery to primary school to secondary school to ... ? Goodbye, babies.

CHAPTER THIRTEEN

TOTTERDOWN CHILDREN'S WORKSHOP

by Wiebke Wüstenberg and Stephen Castles

Totterdown Children's Workshop was set up in 1979 to provide afternoon and holiday care, combined with community education, for five- to twelve-year-old children.

1. THE COMMUNITY

Totterdown is a working-class neighbourhood, just across the river Avon from Bristol's flashy commercial centre. Rows of nineteenth-century terraced cottages teeter on astonishingly steep ridges – some streets have gradients of one in four. The housing is often in bad repair and therefore fairly cheap – a factor which has attracted low-income families of various ethnic groups: Irish, Poles, Turks, West Indians, Pakistanis and Bangla Deshis. People like living in Totterdown, despite poor housing and lack of amenities – the area has a feeling of openness and community. People stop and talk to you in the street, and the newcomer can make friends quickly.

These good community feelings are all the more surprising in view of the fact that the planning authorities have been doing their best to destroy Totterdown for the last ten years. The area is sliced by the Bath Road and the Wells Road – both major commuter roads. In order to build a multilevel interchange to cope with the daily traffic jams, the County Council pulled down the whole core area of Totterdown in the early 1970s; about a quarter of the inhabitants had to move to new estates on the outskirts of Bristol. What was left was a gaping hole – a field of rubble, which reminded older Bristolians of the blitz – until royalty came on a visit and grass was hastily put down. Mind you, there is a nice view, right over to Clifton and the suspension bridge ... The county council soon got cold feet – the planned interchange was too expensive. While they dithered about what to do, Totterdown stagnated, for no rebuilding was possible until road plans had been finalized.

Local people reacted by setting up the Totterdown Action Group, which protested about the planning blight and took positive steps to improve conditions. A variety of local groups, including social clubs, political party branches and churches, played an active part in this. They managed to get Totterdown declared a Housing Action Area, which meant that various loans and grants became available. At the same time, a number of people from both Totterdown and other parts of Bristol got together with the intention of providing shopping and social facilities to replace those which had been demolished. On the edge of the 'hole' they were able to obtain use of a large building which had previously housed a high-class drapery store. In spring 1979, the Totterdown Shopping, Community Action and Exhibition Centre was ceremonially opened by the local MP, Mr Tony Benn. The Centre housed a vegetarian café, stalls selling everything from old clothes to groceries, an exhibition area, artists' studios, a bicycle workshop and space for children's activities.

2. DEVELOPMENT OF THE WORKSHOP

Totterdown has a large number of one-parent families and families in which both parents have to work. There is therefore considerable demand for care facilities, both for pre-school children and for schoolchildren after school and during holidays. There is little public provision of pre-school care and none at all for schoolchildren. Local churches and associations have done their best through voluntary efforts for years, but provision of mother-and-toddler groups and holiday play-schemes is only a marginal help for many families. Totterdown Centre therefore aimed to provide additional care and play facilities for local children.

We came to Totterdown early in 1979, and were offered the opportunity of setting up a scheme for children in the Centre. Before coming to Bristol, we had both been involved in various children's projects at a college in West Germany. There is a great need for after-school care in West Germany, because school takes place only in the mornings – from half-past seven or eight to about one o'clock. Indeed, in the first years of primary education, children often only have between two and four periods, with a different timetable each day – an impossible situation for working parents. There are many latch-key children, and play and care facilities for them are far from adequate, both in quantity and in quality. Official after-school facilities, provided by local authorities, are called *Hort*; they are available for only one per cent of all schoolchildren. The *Hort* is designed to care for children before and after school (from seven in the morning until half-past five), to provide a warm lunch, to assist with homework (which even primary school-children have to do) and to provide supervised play facilities. There are long waiting lists, and priority is given to children from one-parent households or from households where both parents work. However, provision is very far from adequate even for these children. In many places over 40 per cent of children in the *Hort* are from families of immigrant workers.

In most of these out-of-school care facilities there is a serious lack of staff and the groups are too big. The situation is worsened by the stress which overflows into the *Hort* from school (need to do homework, aggression and need for movement and play after sitting in the classroom) and by the rigid legal requirements concerning supervision. This makes it very difficult for *Hort* workers to adopt flexible ways of working which respond to children's needs and allow links with the community. Children who have to go to the *Hort* are split up from their friends after school. They are not allowed to decide for themselves what to play and when to do their homework, but have to conform to the timetable imposed by the *Hort*. Many children regard it almost as a punishment to have to attend the *Hort*; others look down upon them for it. The *Hort* has the stigma of a 'total institution'.

Because of all this, various attempts have been made to set up open 'children's houses'. These are community projects where children can come and go as they please, without being registered by parents. They are staffed by specially trained social workers, who try to provide a stimulating play environment and give help with homework and other problems as required. On the whole, such models have proved successful, especially in attracting children who might otherwise be on the streets. The current crisis of municipal finances has unfortunately led to considerable restrictions in this field. We had helped plan such projects and train staff for them, and were interested in applying our experience in Totterdown. The idea was to set up a children's workshop in the form of an open club, where children could come and go as they wished. As the name implies, the emphasis was on practical work – making and repairing things – and the underlying educational aim was to help children understand the community they live in through learning about work. We shall describe these aims in more detail below.

The plan was to set up the project in such a way as to encourage community participation in all aspects of the Workshop, and to give children a large amount of self-determination. So we contacted local associations and held meetings to form a committee to run the Workshop. But participation was low, and those few people who did turn up were sceptical. We came to realize that Totterdown people were justifiably mistrustful of middle-class people who came into the area with grandiose plans: they had heard it all before, and the reality they saw was the destruction of the neighbourhood. So we went ahead, together with the people who had set up the Centre, hoping that attitudes would change once things got off the ground.

The Centre provided a large basement room for a workshop and two smaller rooms as play space. The rooms had been boarded up for years and were damp, filthy and in poor repair. They needed plastering, redecorating and rewiring, but little finance was available. At first, the Manpower Services Commission had held out hopes of funds for three workers; then came the 1979 election and Thatcher put paid to that. Work started on a shoestring, with small grants from various charities such as the National Playing Fields Association. Lack of money meant doing everything ourselves, but we soon came to realize that this was to some extent a blessing in disguise: as local people saw what was going on, they began to take an interest and to help. One day, a man turned up with a whole carload of paint, hinting that it was better not to ask where it had come from. A builder who lived next door watched our inept attempts at plastering, then took the trowel and showed us how to do it. When we had to remove a massive stone threshold, the men repairing the road outside came in and chopped it out with their pneumatic drill. Soon people were bringing in wood, old tools and carefully washed jam-jars, plastic containers and the like.

The Workshop first opened its doors in August 1979 as part of the Totterdown Summer Play-scheme. We offered projects lasting a morning or an afternoon to give children a chance to get to know the Workshop: making stilts, constructing musical instruments and then playing them, making boats with rubber-band motors, and so on. The children enjoyed it very much, and so did the helpers who were sent down by the play-scheme. Children teetered home on their stilts and showed them to their parents with great pride. We sent round a leaflet, announcing that the Workshop would reopen as a club when term started, providing play facilities three afternoons a week. Parents had to give written consent for their children to join, and we decided to charge a fee of 15p per month (later increased to 25p). This only made a modest contribution to running costs, but would, we hoped, help to give the children the feeling that they were paying for the Workshop and that it belonged to them.

The Workshop quickly became known: fifteen to twenty-five children came in every afternoon, and we soon had over a hundred members. Children were trying out this new play opportunity – most children living within walking distance came in at least once. But soon a regular membership developed: certain cliques decided to make the Workshop their regular meeting-place, while others rejected it. The few children of middle-class families did not stay. The children who did were a mixture of ages and ethnic groups. As the children took possession of the Workshop and made it part of their social life, grown-ups started to accept it and to participate as well. Local people aged from fifteen to seventy came in to help. The project's emphasis on learning through work helped workers and housewives to realize that they had the ability to teach, even though they had not had any educational training. Totterdown people are workers, and they are happy to pass on their skill and knowledge to children, and to help children realize what work means to the community. As more and more people took an interest in the Workshop, it became possible to establish a proper management committee, and to register the Workshop as a charity.

3. AN AFTERNOON IN THE WORKSHOP

An account of a reasonably typical afternoon gives an idea of the way children use the Workshop. At about two o'clock we arrive to get things ready – today we have decided to offer leatherwork, as a mother who works in a corset factory has brought in a bag of leather offcuts. The two helpers (Ted, a social work student on placement from the local polytechnic, and Marion, an out-of-work mother) come in soon after, and help get tools and materials sorted out. We put out boxes containing leather punches, needles, eyelets, thread, rivets and so on. Marion mixes up powder paints in the smaller playroom for children who prefer to do painting.

Shortly after half-past three, there is a loud rapping at the door and the first children arrive: Ian and Jill from across the road. They have got their three-year-old brother Tim with them, because their mum has to go out. Various children drift in over the next hour. Some come straight from school, others go home first and tell their mums they are going down to the Workshop. Some of the younger children are brought in by parents who often stay and chat a while. There are likely to be a lot of children today, for it is a damp autumn afternoon, and the icy Bristol wind howls up the hill, making it too cold to play outside for long. If the children could not come to the Workshop, they would be huddled up in front of the TV in living-rooms which are too small to play in.

Most of the children want to do leather work – it is a favourite activity, perhaps because attractive and useful things can be made quickly. Several decide to make 'rocker wristbands' – leather bracelets, studded with rivets. Others make little purses, embroidered with beads. Jane and Betty want to continue with the plywood bookshelves they started a few days ago. Two new boys come in – Peter and Ron. We suggest they start off by making wooden sandals – this is our standard starting project, as it is fairly easy and gives children something useful to take home to show their parents quickly, while giving us a chance to assess their ability with tools. But they want to do leather work too, and start making wristbands. Three or four children do not want to make anything and sit in the little room chatting and looking at comics. Marion is helping some girls with painting. After a while, a few of the younger children get fed up with leatherwork and join them.

A gang of mini-skins – ten years old but already in jeans, braces and boots – bursts in noisily at about half-past four. They are all fairly regular Workshop users. Today they rush around, making disparaging remarks about the efforts of other children. 'I'll show you how to do it,' says one, taking the leather punch from Ron's hand. He makes a few holes in the wrong place, and then moves on to 'help' Anita, who tells him to clear off. An argument flares up, the children all rush around, shouting, and chaos is imminent. This is the moment when we yearn for an outside area, where one of us could get a football game going, until the boys have used up enough energy to be able to do something else. We suggest a game of table tennis in the yard, but that only occupies four children, and not for long.

Another helper, John, a pensioner, comes in and tells us about his bad feet, before settling down to help some of the younger children with their purses. He is very kind and patient, and the children like working with him. The painting group has got fed up with art, and are now 'putting on a play' for everyone. All the children come and watch, but soon drift away again. The plays are always the same: drunken father, helpless mother and children who are beaten and not allowed to do anything. Deprived of an audience, the actors start stripping off and painting one another. Ted tells them to stop, for fear of a conflict with the parents. Now the children find it even more fun to annoy Ted, and start playing him up, in the hope of making him lose his temper. Three-year-old Tim is almost completely covered in paint by now, and roams around the workshop, so that we have to keep sharp leather tools out of his reach. Children under five are really not allowed in, but when other children have to look after smaller brothers and sisters you have to let them in. Although we find it noisy and hectic, most of the twenty or so children go about their tasks with quiet concentration, and seem to be enjoying themselves.

By half-past five a number of purses and wristbands are finished, and their proud makers run around showing them to everyone. At six it is time to clear up. Some children want more time to finish their work, but others make a bee-line for the door, in order to avoid helping. I stand there and try to explain that everybody should take a part. All my anti-authoritarian principles start sliding at this point, and I feel like locking them in until the task is done. As usual, some children – mainly girls – are willing to help and get the job done, while those who don't want to help stand there arguing until nothing is left to do. At half-past six, the children have gone, and we all collapse into a heap while someone makes tea.

It all sounds rather chaotic and aimless, and a long way away from our high-sounding pedagogical aims, doesn't it? But of course there are connections, however contradictory.

4. AIMS AND CONTRADICTIONS OF THE WORKSHOP

(a) Community Education

One of our main aims is to help children learn about the community they live in, through productive work, through bringing local people in as educators, through dealing with local problems, and through visiting workplaces. Most local people who know about the project have a positive attitude towards it: they know how restricted play facilities are in Totterdown, and can relate to the idea of learning through work. Yet – initially at least – it was not *their* project, but something initiated by outsiders. We wanted democratic structures: a steering committee representing parents, Workshop workers and other local people; children's meetings to make decisions about activities, club rules, opening times, purchases, etc. We wanted open decision-making and discussion about problems like overcrowding of the Workshop, the situation of girls, age limits, clearing-up. But people show relatively little interest in participating in such decision-making structures. They seem to prefer to leave such matters to the Workshop workers and to a few active, usually middle-class people, who can be relied on to get things done. Perhaps parents of Workshop children just do not have the time to take an active part (although they do find time when practical help is needed), or they are used to leaving educational matters to others.

(b) Linking Care and Education

The Workshop is designed to place equal emphasis on care and learning, for we feel that school, with its abstract and formal curriculum, does little to help children understand the community they grow up in. We therefore did not want to provide 'registered care' (where parents register their children with the project, which then acts *in loco parentis* for a fixed time). We feel that this can have negative consequences through splitting children up into those who have someone at home to look after them after school, and those who do not and therefore *have* to join an after-school scheme. Such care might be seen as discriminatory. Above all, it splits up children's friendships and spontaneous groupings. The Workshop was conceived as a children's open club, where children can come and go as they wish. This makes it possible for children to stay together with their friends, to make their own plans and decisions, and to use the Workshop as they want, rather than coming because they have to. This open structure is the precondition for self-determination and indeed for the other aims of the project.

This structure may not always be appropriate – but it works in Totterdown because the closely knit community structure makes it possible for children to play on the street and to come and go without danger. However, as regular groups developed, the Workshop certainly did take on a care function for many families. But, of course, the Workshop is not as open and available to the children as we would like: initially it was only open three afternoons a week, and it is not open at the weekend. There are age limits, and the restricted space available probably deters many children from coming.

(c) Self-determination

The socialization of most children, both at home and at school, is designed to make them do as they are told rather than developing their own ideas and initiative. Attempts to shape their own environment and make their own decisions are often stopped and punished. The Workshop aims to counter this by giving the widest possible scope for decision-making by the children. This applies both in the formal field of deciding on activities, solving conflicts and so on, and in day-to-day play and work. Clearly, there are a lot of potential conflicts implicit in this aim. The Workshop is very different from the children's own homes, where other forms of discipline and decision-making prevail, and its approach contrasts with that of the school, and of other community organizations, such as sports clubs. Indeed, this approach is not totally consistent in the Workshop itself. Various helpers have quite different attitudes and ways of relating to children, who in turn quickly realize what is expected of them and behave accordingly – a form of adaptation which may involve considerable self-conscious strain. Self-determination is also problematic in situations of conflict between children. When should grown-ups intervene in disputes? If one acts too quickly, the children do not learn how to solve the problem; if too late, the dispute may escalate and the weaker person may get the worst of things, and become demoralized. And what does an anti-militarist Workshop worker do if the children want help in making guns and swords?

(d) Having Fun

Children come to the Workshop because they enjoy being there. If it ceases to be fun, they stay away. The various grown-ups enjoy it too (most of the time, anyway) – indeed the voluntary helpers come because they find it satisfying to relate to children in a stimulating environment. The Workshop has an important social function for some helpers – particularly pensioners, unemployed persons and mothers of young children. It is important to see 'having fun' as a major aim of the Workshop. Any formal learning programme that stops children having fun has no place in this type of project. However, there need be no contradiction between having fun and informal learning about work, social relationships, and the like. Having fun is not just a question of offering exciting activities and interesting materials, but of creating an atmosphere in which children can develop and express their interests and feelings. It means responding to children's emotional needs and wishes, and giving them a sense of being accepted. Of course, there are no recipes for this – it depends on the sensitivity of the Workshop workers, and on having time and space to communicate adequately. Although the atmosphere in the Workshop is generally cheerful, friendly and supportive, it is often also too hectic and crowded to give individuals the attention they need.

(e) Questioning Sex Roles

In the Workshop, girls and boys have the same opportunities of doing woodwork or leatherwork, repairing toys or bikes, painting, acting or playing. Women helpers are just as likely as men to show children how to saw, plane or drill wood. For children – and for parents – this is unusual at first. Children tend to seek assistance from the men when doing woodwork, and to go to women when they want to do painting or dressing-up. But these barriers are quickly broken down. We find that girls enjoy doing what are generally regarded as male tasks as much as the boys. Although girls are often less used to using tools when they first come, they soon catch up, and are often more patient and persistent in their work. The main problem with sex roles in the Workshop has been in connection with Bangla Deshi girls. At first they found it strange to work with tools, but then came to enjoy it very much. However, several fathers stopped their daughters from coming when they discovered that they were in mixed-sex groups. That was why it was decided to have a girls-only afternoon, once it became possible to open five afternoons a week.

(f) Play as Work and Research

Through play, children take possession of their environment, come to understand the material properties of the objects of daily use, and get a grasp of the social relationships of their community. Lack of play facilities slows this process, but so do scientifically thought-out playgrounds, which pre-form play activities. In Totterdown, lack of playgrounds, traffic congestion, cramped housing and too much television hold back children's under-standing of the world. Hence the need to provide an open environment with tools and materials, and grown-ups who take children's ideas seriously. For play to become a research process, grown-ups have to learn to take on the role of helper and adviser, rather than that of formal teacher. There is no point in giving a formal course in joinery, however competent the teacher. An example: Ann, nine years old, wants to make 'a box I can lock up'. The helper must find out what it is for, what size it needs to be, what ideas Ann has about materials and appearance. The best thing is to let her look around and find suitable wood, hinges, etc. Then the methods can be discussed. Ann may not want to make it the way we would. Perhaps she wants to experi-ment and try things out. On the other hand, we have to try to judge what she is able to do, in order to prevent her getting frustrated and having a feeling of failure. But what is failure or success? It varies widely for different children, or even for the same child at different times. The grown-ups are often astonished by children's endurance at long, tedious tasks. Moreover, children often discover ways of doing things which we would not have thought of, and which are creative and useful. Perhaps after Ann has worked on her jewellery box for two or three afternoons, it may have turned into something quite different – 'a money box for my little brother' – but she is quite satisfied with it. Children plan, work and judge their results differently from grown-ups. Some children want results immediately, and give up at the first bent-over nail. Others work patiently for hours, but do not necessarily seek the quickest and most effective way of doing things. Others again *do* want to learn proper joinery. This possibility of self-determined work and play is especially important for children who have been labelled failures at school. In the informal Workshop situation, where there is no compulsion to carry out a predetermined activity in a pre-determined space of time, such children often discover creativity and ability, which gives them a new self-confidence.

(g) Learning as a Co-operative Process

In school, children are given the impression that learning should be taken like medicine: in prescribed doses, at fixed times. In reality, of course, they learn more from their parents, siblings, friends, from the media and the community than from school – but this is often not recognized as real learning. The Workshop aims to develop a style of work in which learning can be understood as a co-operative process. That means that ideas, methods and techniques are not just handed down from grown-ups to children, but are developed together, according to the task on hand. Children can learn from each other or from grown-ups, but grown-ups can also learn from children. This principle also gives a vital role to parents and other local people who are not professional educators but whose knowledge and abilities are vital in the Workshop. This informal, open type of learning has worked well in this project. It helps both grown-ups and children to question the way their life is dominated by experts, and to re-learn how to do things for themselves. After a while, grown-ups started coming into the Workshop when they wanted to make something, or when, say, a vacuum-cleaner had gone on strike. Obviously, none of us had the specialized knowledge necessary for such tasks, but grown-ups and children were often able to solve the problem together.

(h) Anti-consumerism

Questioning the role of experts also means examining the way our life is dominated by factory-made goods which we cannot repair or modify. In this respect, the provisional and impoverished nature of the Workshop actually has a good side: if we had ample funds to buy tools and materials, we would not learn to improvise, to beg, borrow and adapt things regarded by factories as rubbish. The recycling and creative use of all sorts of unusual objects and materials is not a pedagogical trick for us, but is vital for our survival. The children and grown-ups associated with the Workshop have learnt how to obtain things – from workshops, factories, stores, skips – how to change them and redefine their use. They have learnt how to improvise and do things for themselves, rather than depending on ready-made industrial products or on officially provided services.

5. THE FUTURE OF THE WORKSHOP

We left Bristol in late 1980, mainly in order to find work which paid us a living wage. Until then, the Workshop had been run almost entirely by unpaid workers. The project continued, thanks to the efforts of the Totterdown Centre which provided funds to employ a part-time leader, as well as a lot of support of other kinds: rent-free premises, free electricity for heating and organizational assistance. By 1982 the financial situation had improved somewhat: two people were employed on a Community Enterprise scheme and one on a Youth Opportunities scheme. It became possible to open five afternoons a week, and to provide full-time holiday play-schemes. As the project became better known locally, donations became more frequent, permitting the organization of outings and holidays for local children. The Workshop seemed to be becoming an important and accepted aspect of social life for many Totterdown children and parents. But the financial situation was never secure. Volunteers remained essential for the running of the Workshop – although this has its advantages too: the large number of helpers of all ages were an important link with the community, and they benefited too. Most people found working with children in the Workshop a very valuable experience. As this book goes to press, however, it appears that the strains of working continually on a shoestring have become too great. We understand that the Workshop no longer functions regularly; the premises seem to be in use as a Women's Workshop. Perhaps this reflects a shift in the priorities of the local community.

CHAPTER FOURTEEN

MORE THAN WOMEN'S BUSINESS

1. VISION

Child rearing does not have to be the way it is at present. Mothers' depression, paternal distance, and child abuse are all spin-offs of our current arrangements. These side-effects occur as predictably as the intended effects of healthy child development. The basic problem with the system is the amount of responsibility and the lack of support given to parents. Bronfenbrenner argues that when the social environment undermines parents' efforts, child abuse often results. Parents' personalities, lack of education, and children's 'provocative' behaviour, in an unsupportive system, all become powerful factors in producing child abuse. The solution, we believe, is to change child rearing, not simply to offer selective help to those who have succumbed to pressures which all parents have to face. It must be assumed that 'coping' parents and their children are also affected by the lack of support for child rearing.

We cannot solve these problems by tinkering at the margins. We need a vision of a radically better future, but such visions are hard to come by. Politicians do not offer them and most feminists have little to say about daily life for and with children. Eichenbaum and Orbach (1984) are the only feminists we have come across who begin to sketch such a vision. Their emphasis is 'to alleviate the imbalances that women and men experience in their psychological development' (p. 176). Like us, they feel that most people have avoided confronting such questions, preferring to demand 'a broad economic revolution that in its wake will usher in the equality of men, women and children' (p. 179). But generally, there is a hopelessness about radical change which comes through the old promises and the old demands. Kibbutzim are often cited as proving the enduring attraction of the nuclear family, because in some of them the children now sleep with their parents

instead of in children's houses. The communal experiments of the 1960s
are unfashionable. We have to turn to thinkers in the tradition of Butler's
Erewhon, creators of political utopias, to find any discussion of some important and pressing questions of child care.

Herland was Charlotte Perkins Gilman's vision, her utopia. She envisaged
a society of mothers. Men had all been killed in a war between the sexes
two thousand years before, and women bore daughters by parthenogenesis.
The narrator is a sociologist in a scientific expedition which strays into the
country of women.

'... you separate mother and child!' I cried in cold horror ...

'Not usually,' she patiently explained. 'You see, almost every woman
values her maternity above everything else ... child-rearing has come to
be with us a culture so profoundly studied, practised with such subtlety
and skill, that the more we love our children the less we are willing to
trust that process to unskilled hands – even our own.'

'But a mother's love,' I ventured ...

'You told us about your dentists,' she said, at length, 'those quaintly
specialised persons who spend their lives filling little holes in other
persons' teeth – even in children's teeth sometimes.'

'Yes?' I said, not getting her drift.

'Does mother love urge mothers – with you – to fill their own children's
teeth? Or to wish to?'

'Why no – of course not,' I protested. 'But that is a highly specialised
craft. Surely the care of babies is open to any woman – any mother.'

'We do not think so,' she gently replied. 'Those of us who are the most
highly competent fulfil that office; and a majority of our girls eagerly try
for it – I assure you we have the very best.'

'But the poor mother – bereaved of her baby –'

'Oh no!' she earnestly assured me. 'Not in the least bereaved. It is her
baby still – it is with her – she has not lost it. But she is not the only one
to care for it' (Gilman, 1979, p. 83).

Later the narrator described the Herland child facing life:

They found themselves in a big, bright lovely world, full of the most
interesting and enchanting things to learn about and to do. The people
everywhere were friendly and polite. No Herland child ever met the over-
bearing rudeness we so commonly show to children. They were People,
too, from the first; the most precious part of the nation (ibid., p. 100).

Imaginary societies are powerful devices for getting us to *see* patterns that have been taken for granted. Some feminist writers (in the tradition of science fiction rather than of Plato's *Republic* or More's *Utopia*) introduce thought-provoking ideas into their ordinary fantasy. Ursula Le Guin writes of an anarchistic planet, Anarres, where the family household only exists for a brief space until the weaned child takes up permanent residence in the nursery of children's dormitories and the parents become mere visitors.

> As a child, if you slept alone in a single it meant you had bothered the others in the dormitory until they wouldn't tolerate you ... Solitude equalled disgrace. In adult terms, the principal referent for single rooms was a sexual one. Every domicile had a number of singles, and a couple that wanted to copulate used one of these free singles for a night ... or as long as they liked. A couple undertaking partnership took a double room ... Aside from sexual pairing there was no reason for not sleeping in a dormitory. You could choose a small one or a large one, and if you didn't like your roommates you could move to another dormitory. Everybody had the workshop, laboratory, studio, barn or office that he needed for his work; one could be as private or as public as one chose in the baths; sexual privacy was freely available and socially expected; and beyond that privacy was not functional (Le Guin, 1975, p. 97).

Susy Charnas (1981) describes a society of women who live in a damaged world after a nuclear war. Here, too, there is the familiar device of imagining a women-only society where women bear daughters without male help. Groups of women become 'share-mothers' to particular children, and share breast feeding as well as responsibility for their care. In *Woman on the Edge of Time* Piercy (1979) imagines a future in which 'test-tube babies' are developed to term and live birth is abolished, so that both men and women can mother. She, too, raises some important questions in this bizarre packaging, such as whether adolescents want mothering, and whether lovers should co-parent.

The trouble with fantastic worlds is that their makers are not obliged to commit themselves about what is possible and what is not. *Useful* visions are grounded in reality. We don't want to write science fiction in this chapter, but to sketch a perfectly possible way of organizing child care, which would need radical political change to bring it about. It is only one of many possible directions. Its value is to embody a critique of the way things are and to set us thinking about how they might be.

When we assess the practicality of our vision, or of any conception of the

future, we have to take the *actual* state of affairs as our starting point, not
an imaginary ideal. Recent changes in family life have been so dramatic that
the New Right's recipe for a return to the conventional nuclear family is
as utopian as the feminist dreams we have just quoted. We noted earlier that
the supposedly typical family of a married couple with dependent children
constitutes less than a third of all families. Even in these, many of the women
will be in paid employment, since 56 per cent of mothers with dependent
children work for money (Martin and Roberts, 1984). People seem to be
taking the fact of marriage less seriously, since more men and women now
live together without it. Most people still get married, but one in every three
marriages ends in divorce. Almost 60 per cent of divorces involve dependent
children, a quarter of whom are under five. One and a half million children
in Britain lived in one-parent families in 1980; many others had a period
in such a family during their childhood. Many then moved into reconstituted families, since 80 per cent of those who divorce under the age of
thirty remarry within five years . . . and often become divorced again (Study
Commission on the Family, 1983).

In 1982 about a third (29,000) of all illegitimate births in England and
Wales were to mothers aged under twenty. For the first time (at least in the
recent past), illegitimate births actually outnumbered legitimate births
(27,000) to mothers in this age group. Many of these illegitimate births
are jointly registered by both parents . . . (Social Trends 14, 1984, p. 38).

In fact, almost half of these young unmarried mothers registered the child
in the father's name too.

The trends are complex and apparently contradictory: mothers tend to
bear fewer children; and more families consist of a single adult with a child
or a couple of children and the consequently intense relationships. Yet there
are more family 'corporations', combines or networks of step-parents, step-
siblings, half-siblings and so on, as well as more likelihood that great-
grandparents and grandparents are involved in the family circle. As Eichler
(1983, p. 26) puts it: 'These changes are touching the very basis of our
definitions of self and others.'

Obviously the system of private child care is even less suitable for these
shifting times than when the conventional (static) nuclear family was the
usual form. In fact, it is partly *because* of the system of private child care that
relationships between men and women are so fragile. Many people marry
young because the woman is pregnant, and they believe that children need
two parents. These couples often split up while the child is still a baby. But

at all ages and stages the uneven burdens of parenthood make for divisions and resentment between men and women. People don't give up: they continue to work at being parents and step-parents, and they re-commit themselves in second and even third marriages. The increase in both divorces and remarriages cannot be attributed to our system of private child care alone. But there is no doubt that the effect of marriage breakdown on children is made worse by this system. It is no better suited to support very young mothers, single mothers and fathers and complex reconstituted families.

For many years, women have remained in unhappy marriages for the children's sake. (So have men, but the big change seems to be coming from women.) Now this duty does not seem so plain. Obviously, some women leave violent marriages for the children's sake as well as for their own, and others feel it is in the children's interests for them to be strong and independent. Yet others feel that it is fine to do what they need to, whatever the effect on the children. There is often a real conflict of interests here.

The conflict of interests between men and women is old hat. The conflict of interests between adults and children is equally clear, but less often admitted. Women have been made the main parties in that conflict, so that it can look as if women's freedom is *necessarily* threatening to children, while children's care *necessarily* requires women to set their personal sights low. The PPA expresses this received wisdom in advocating mother-and-toddler clubs: 'The mothers gain in understanding. They come to terms with the state of parenthood in which the needs of another small but ultra-demanding being ... take precedence over their own.' That is how many women actually experience their lives.

A woman writes:

> I am not obsessed with my children – I want to live my life too. I do *love* them, I want to live with them – and the reality is that I *must* live with them and take responsibility for them, whatever the weather, the state of the nation, or my temper. Having had children I must settle on my bed because hardly anyone is going to share that responsibility without asking a very high price (letter to *Trouble and Strife*, No. 3, 1984, p. 5).

Sacrificing women to children is no answer. It is not really in children's interests to have mothers who are discontented or whose motto is 'you can't have everything'. The opposite answer, that children should be sacrificed to women, is rarely put forward, but it is often implied in the impatience feminists express with prolonged consideration of children's needs: 'Oh, no.

Not children again. I've come to this meeting to get away from children.
I have to think about mine all day. I want to talk about ME.'

Shulamith Firestone is one of the few feminists to recognize that children
are themselves oppressed.

Children ... are not freer than adults. They are burdened ... with an
unpleasant sense of their own physical inadequacy ... ; with constant
shame about their dependence, economic or otherwise ('Mother, may I?');
and humiliation concerning their natural ignorance of practical affairs
(1979, p. 101).

She argues that feminists must include children in their strategies for
change:

I say this knowing full well that many women are sick and tired of being
lumped together with children (ibid., p. 102).

Her remedy is sweeping.

People have forgotten what history has proven: that 'raising' a child is
tantamount to retarding his development. The best way to raise a child
is to LAY OFF (ibid., p. 90).

All institutions that segregate the sexes, or bar children from adult
society, must be destroyed. (Down with school!) ... (ibid., p. 195).

In her visionary society ('cybernetic communism'):

The concept of childhood has been abolished, children having full
political, economic and sexual rights, their education/work activities no
different from those of adults. During the few years of their infancy we
have replaced the psychologically destructive genetic 'parenthood' of one
or two arbitrary adults with a diffusion of the responsibility for physical
welfare over a larger number of people. The child would still form
intimate love relationships ... with people of his [sic] own choosing, of
whatever age or sex. Thus all adult–child relationships will have been
mutually chosen – equal, intimate relationships free of material dependencies (ibid., p. 222).

Our visionary society is more accessible than Shulamith Firestone's, and
need not await the coming of so-called 'cybernetic communism'. Even if it
made technological sense to eliminate drudgery in affluent countries, it
would not automatically make economic sense. And what sort of a vision

is it that excludes the Third World? It is easy to sidestep the real conflicts we live with and dream of a world in which relationships are trouble-free because 'freely chosen'. This butterfly approach might well result in the need for special emotional provision for the unchosen.

Up to now our own recommendations have been piecemeal. In the rest of this chapter we bring these together, first of all in our own vision of a different way of caring for children, and then in discussing the concrete steps we can take now.

2. GETTING WHAT WE WANT

Any vision of how children should be cared for has to be ambitious to be worth having at all. For children's care to be a public priority, the relationships between men and women, men and children, women and children (as well as relationships within each of these groups) have all to be transformed. We want a society publicly committed to children, to the future. In such a context, personal commitment to children would flourish, too. But there are massive obstacles in the way of achieving such a collective commitment: obstacles reflected in our minds, for the very idea barely makes sense to us through the spectacles of a capitalist economy.

In 'free-enterprise societies' the production of wealth is the great measure of what is worth doing. Activities are divided into those which produce wealth or further its production, and those which use it up. Some sectors of the economy, like manufacturing and marketing, are obviously wealth-producing; in a less obvious way so are some aspects of children's care. Children's health has to be attended to, or there would be no new labour-force. They have to be taught, because modern technology requires a high level of literacy and sophistication. But from a capitalist point of view, these necessities quickly become luxuries. Under certain conditions, capitalism can provide decent nursery care, but not in a way that challenges the way work is divided between men and women. It is still women who care when the nurseries are closed or the child is too sick to go. As Rowbotham puts it:

> To admit that child care in reality extends and interconnects throughout the fabric of economic and social life – that, like thinking, caring has to be a boundaryless activity – would mean recognising that thorough and fundamental changes are needed in capitalism if these basic human needs are to be justly met and time and labour are to be more equitably divided (Rowbotham, 1984).

Child care under capitalism serves the needs of the market. To spend money on ensuring that children's lives are enjoyable and fulfilling comes into the realm of luxury, along with art, libraries and conservation. To conserve the environment enough to satisfy public opinion makes capitalist sense, but to invest money into the future without clear expectation of a return for the corporation, rather than for humanity, lacks a political and economic rationale. The state has a less narrow view than the corporation, but governments are also blinkered by the short time-scale of capitalist economics and political rivalries. For all these reasons, we cannot expect capitalist societies to change in relation to women and children, unless they are forced to by popular insistence. Although Lady Howe recognizes the problem as we see it, she is optimistic that the solution will just happen: 'We urgently need a 'renegotiation' of work and family. There will be disagreement on the particulars. But once there is general acceptance that caring and domestic life are the equal *practical* responsibilities of men and women, then work patterns and policy, and much else, will fall into place' (Howe, 1984).

Socialists sometimes reject the importance of the 'quality of life' on the grounds that the day-to-day concerns of working people are more basic. This is misleading. It is true that many people do not have the time or liberty to think about some of the issues we have discussed. If there is no day nursery and you are forced to work, your immediate worry is provision rather than quality. But it does not follow that our concerns are unimportant or 'middle class'. It is rather that enormous groups of people have been cut off from crucial areas of decision-making and potential enjoyment. As the song says, the struggle is not only for bread:

> As we come marching, marching, unnumbered women dead
> Go crying through our singing their ancient song of 'Bread'
> Small art and love and beauty their drudging spirits knew.
> Yes, it is bread we fight for, but we fight for Roses too!
>
> As we come marching, marching, we bring the greater days,
> For the rising of the women is the rising of the class:
> No more the drudge and idler, ten that toil where one reposes
> But a sharing of life's glories, Bread and Roses, Bread and Roses.

Resources exist to nourish the whole world. The problem is that present methods of producing food and necessities and sharing them out threaten our environment and ignore the needs of millions of people. These issues of survival are not separate from the question of how children in more affluent countries should be cared for. If, out of guilt for the Third World, we accept low standards for our own children, we just contribute to the general hopelessness the system breeds and depends on. Besides, our children are going to need their wits about them to put things right. Those of us who want to change the world cannot possibly afford to accept the present ways in which children are brought up. Most present arrangements not only hold back the women who do most of the caring, they also aim at making children into submissive citizens or, failing that, into cynical, hopeless rebels. We need to study how to help children control their lives, become independent, learn to think and trust their own thinking, become aware of their own importance. So far, most socialists, as well as supporters of capitalism, lay greatest emphasis on children being 'good' – i.e. conformist or submissive – and getting them to subordinate their thinking to that of others.

We cannot wait for a sparkling new socialist society to produce new people with a higher consciousness. The new people are needed *now* to bring such a society about and ensure that it does consider these questions. That is why the experiments in child care our contributors have described are so important. They explore ways of empowering children as well as their parents. These projects give us a glimpse of possible forms of democratic, decentralized/socialist welfare. Local efforts like this are just as important as attempts to have a direct effect on the central state. They create a basis for the more obviously 'political' campaigning, by strengthening the local people involved and raising their expectations. Deacon calls such local projects 'prefigurative'. He warns (1983, pp. 245–6) that they often

> become no more than a new form of provision capable of being co-opted into, or permitted to run alongside, the predominant state welfare form of service. (An example here might be a Well Woman Clinic that supplements but does not challenge local patriarchal medicine.) ... Capitalist welfare is a highly centralised system, backed up by an efficient oppressive arm of the state. Much socialist theory and experience in other countries suggests that a high degree of nationally co-ordinated strategy is necessary to defeat it, and that this may impose requirements very different from those of prefigurative struggle (which may need to be experimental and tentative).

The co-operative crèche, community nurseries and the Totterdown Children's Workshop pose no direct threat to the state. But such experi-

ments may affect the children and their parents and challenge our pre-
conceptions about what is possible. Through this sort of work we discover
that children can do things we did not know, they could do, that we adults,
women and men, can also do things and enjoy things we had not previously
thought of.

In *Hidden Hands*, Anne Phillips shows that women have nothing to gain
from socialist attempts to put the economy right *first* and promises to think
about ending women's subordination *later*. Nor have children; nor, in the
last analysis, have any of us. For to try to put *this* economy right, resting
as it does on women's unpaid work and sex segregation in work, is to resign
ourselves to this state of affairs going on and on and on ...

> The important thing is to say what we want, not tailor our demands to
> the meagre prospects of today. The old labourist demands – a job and a
> decent wage (in brackets read, for men) – are no longer enough. We want
> equality between men and women, and that means equal hours of labour
> at home and at work (Phillips, 1983, p. 73).

For this to become a widespread possibility,

> We have to adapt work to fit in with the rest of life, and particularly adapt
> it to fit with children. For the present, the adaptation is done by women,
> the price of having children is paid by mothers. Why not a new approach?
> If the needs of children do not fit with the demands of full-time work, then
> the jobs must be changed (ibid., p. 5).

Work (in a wider sense than just jobs), child care and parenthood all need
to be changed. All our proposals are interrelated. Basically we are advocating putting the relationship between work and family responsibilities on
its head, so that family responsibilities take pride of place in our social
arrangements. At the same time, these responsibilities will be shared out
amongst a wider network than at present, in a way which will start to break
down the separation between work and child care.

3. WORK

We don't want to exchange current working conditions for a situation in
which some women, as well as some men, work fifty or sixty hours a week,
year in and year out, and others are involuntarily on permanent 'holiday'.
A shorter standard working day for all is a precondition for getting men
involved in child care. The difficulties of combining work and child care are

also reduced at a stroke if we work a six-hour day. Such a working day would give people time to relax together. But this shorter working day has to become the standard for *all* forms of employment to be fully effective. If it applied only to those categories of workers with special needs – such as mothers of dependent children or women with dependent elderly or handicapped relatives – present job inequalities would continue. An even shorter day might be an appropriate *temporary* option for some people, so long as it was paid at the rate for the six-hour day, and did not further fix *women* in the caring role.

The demand for a shorter working day has not been popular with male trade unionists. In Britain, when hours have been under discussion at all, men are on record as preferring a longer weekend and *women* a shorter working day (Phillips, op. cit., p. 59). But in the current recession, there are signs that men too are seeing the absurdity of *relying* on overtime earnings, when so many are unemployed. In West Germany the metalworkers' union, IGM, is (at the time of writing) on strike for a 35-hour week, to create jobs and make their own jobs more secure. In Britain, TASS at Westland Helicopter negotiated a 32½-hour week as part of a deal over new technology and consequent shifts. The AUEW as a whole is demanding a 37-hour week from some employers. The NUR recently asked for a shorter working day – but did not get it. The motives given by union negotiators do not include transforming the sexual division of labour at home and at work – far from it. These moves only show a growing together of what men and women feel is in their interests. Unless the shorter working day is demanded with the conscious declared intention of changing responsibilities *at home*, its achievement will be modest. In any case, legal restrictions on overtime would be needed as well, to avoid reproducing the old patterns where men work longer and earn more. At present, manual workers tend to work the longest hours when they have young children. Because of the current structure of careers so do professional and managerial workers, partly for financial reasons, and partly because promotional prospects are age-related.

Although it has been vigorously argued that success in a job is related to age, specific ability and aptitude, the arguments ring rather hollow. This present convention discriminates against women in employment and effectively ensures that the wives of professional and business men will have little help with the children when they most need it. If rewards for work were related to skill and effort rather than to some fanciful notion of responsibility, and if careers were restructured so that they did not conflict with domestic commitments, then men would be able to share the child care and women's careers would be comparable with men's. In any event, the traditional notion of career advancement through an age hierarchy is being eroded by changes in technology and the material conditions of employment.

At a time when the structure of work is in flux because of the combined effects of the recession and technological change, it makes sense to ask what we really want, and how we want to organize our lives. The three-day week, which is currently offered to some 'community project' workers funded by the Manpower Services Commission in Britain, sounds very attractive – if you discount the pittance presently paid. Similarly, flexitime and job-sharing or job-splitting represent a new willingness to break free of dogmatism about the 40-hour week. The trouble is, this new flexibility has benefited the government (who can pretend a half-job is a job for statistical purposes but not for pay) and the employers.

> Of course, many women welcomed it – it helped that delicate balancing act between work and home. But it still left *them* with this problem, releasing not only the men, but the employer, too. Flexible hours are desirable, but at present they ... can strengthen the convention that private life must not interfere with work. Instead of making employers accountable for our needs outside, flexitime can provide the perfect excuse for ignoring these needs (Phillips, ibid., p. 59).

As we saw in the case of the shorter working day, our proposals are more than possible – they are actually happening. At present the workers are paying for these changes – one way or another. There *is* a price to be paid. It has long been an honourable principle of trade unions that if you want to equalize, you fight to bring the worse-off up to the standard of the better-off, not vice versa. This is the right direction to aim in. It means trying to get capital, rather than labour, to pay for the reforms. But a capitalist society could not finance a shorter standard working day for all, and restricted overtime, without redistribution that involved *some* people taking home less pay, even though their basic rates, and even household income, might not suffer. The general pattern would be redistribution from richer to poorer, and from men to women: lessening differentials and abolishing the family wage. This would mean that some households with only one adult member would be worse off than at present, and households with several adults better off, assuming they would either all work or be eligible for benefits.

Phillips argues (ibid., p. 103) that feminist socialists must appeal to people's wish for equality and fairness and get trade unionism out of its rut.

When Barbara Castle introduced equal pay legislation, she shocked the labour movement by declaring that the easiest way to equal pay for women would be if the men agreed to stand still. But is it not more shocking that seven million workers get less than what the TUC considers a minimum wage? Or that in the same hospital some workers earn £63 a week and others £333?

She argues that both policy changes and trade union methods are essential. Trade unions' priorities would have to change, but that is not impossible.

The trade unions have been male organisations, there is no doubt. But they are, by definition, workers' organisations and are not inherently or intrinsically male ... They can change and they are already changing as ... women make themselves felt (Weir and McIntosh, 1982, p. 18).

Even if everyone worked a regular six-hour day, paid leave for childbirth and the temporary care of sick children and other dependent people would still be essential. As in Sweden, these must be *parent* entitlements, not just for mothers. The Swedish policy is to integrate work and family life: 'Sweden has clearly begun to move in this direction but it reports that it has a long way to go. Most men work full time, while most women work part time. Parent insurance and the temporary care allowance continue to be used largely by women ...' (Kamerman and Kahn, 1981, p. 52). All the same, in the years since 1974, more men are steadily taking up these options. A high percentage of women do work, and '... the very fact of male entitlement helps prevent discrimination against women in the labour market (at least in part) and works towards the long-term goal of full sexual equality, at home and at work' (ibid., p. 52).

No other country has such a comprehensive system of social benefits aiming at full sexual equality. In the US, as recently as 1976 Supreme Court judges ruled that if employers did not give women disability benefits when they were pregnant this did not constitute sex discrimination, on the grounds that if men were pregnant they would be treated in the same way. As if men could be! After a two-year legislative battle, a change in the law made pregnant women eligible for whatever sick leave benefits her employer would ordinarily provide.

The United States has the distinction of being the *only* major industrialized country in the world that lacks a national insurance plan covering medical expenses for childbirth and is one of the few governments in industrialized nations that does not provide any cash benefits to working women to compensate for lost earnings (Adams and Winston, 1980, p. 33).

Maternity and paternity leave are at the discretion of individual employers. In the UK, where maternity leave, benefit and pay are more generous, only seventy-six employers are known to provide paid paternity leave (Bell *et al.*, 1983, p. 74).

An adequate system of paid parental leave after childbirth would give women or men up to a year off work with the guarantee of job reinstatement. A resolution passed at the NALGO 1979 Conference demands:

> The right of both parents to attend – without deduction of pay – ante-natal and child-care clinics, and the right of the father to attend the birth on full pay.
>
> A maximum parental leave of 45 weeks on full pay, to commence 7 weeks after the birth to be taken by either parent. Paternity leave on full pay for 6 weeks to be taken at any time during the 18 weeks. Parents' entitlement to sick leave when their child is ill (NALGO Negotiating Kit, cited in Bell *et al.*, op. cit., p. 73).

If the term 'parent' is extended to include other adults who have made a parental commitment, this resolution offers a good model. More recently, a House of Lords Select Committee has recommended legislation, in line with the draft European Commission directive on parental leave. It seems absurd to treat children as hiccups in our real working lives. Being temporarily 'home based' in the new society, we envisage, would not be isolated and isolating. There would be no financial penalty. Help with child care would be available and there would be far more public places to go to and resources to use near at hand. Above all, the decision to take up parental leave would not condemn one to lead a second-class life indefinitely.

4. PARENTHOOD

So far, we have taken it for granted that parents are necessary and will remain so. But is this true? Children do need reliable relationships which combine intimacy, attention, nurturance and responsibility with long-term partisan commitment (love). At present, if these qualities *are* found together it is almost always in parents. People who are currently called non-parents could make such relationships with children, if they had a chance. In our vision, parenting in this sense would be an opportunity available to non-biological parents too, and so would less intense and long-term relationships with children.

Home is no more dispensable than parenthood. Like parenthood, it should not be confined to the family household. Creating a physical base for a group of people who share their own culture, jokes, rituals and intimacies is a pleasure which need not be restricted to biological parents and children. In kibbutzim, peer groups are at least as important as nuclear families in giving that 'sense of belonging'. Even as things are, the same feeling sometimes exists in schools, in day care and in work, as well as in the houses we call our homes. There are many possible ways of living, but our speculations need not take us far at the moment. We can see that in the future if children live together they will still need committed adults with them, who are able to value them all without being drawn into the children's own relationships with each other. They will also need adults who give them individual attention and commitment, even if they do not share a roof. For us now it makes more sense to think about how existing forms of living could be transformed.

Child care is too important to be put at the mercy of the financial and sexual relationship between the parents. Monogamous marriage is conventionally the 'right' context for child rearing. We have already argued that it cannot be good for children to be brought up by women who are financially dependent and socially subordinate. Inequality in such a close relationship as marriage is itself a constant source of strain. When marriages break up, children's financial dependence means they are often plunged into poverty. At the moment, sexual relationships intrude upon children's upbringing more than we often realize. When a violent quarrel erupts between mother and father, one or other or both will often think about splitting up and the question of who would get 'care and control'. If co-operating did not depend on the parents' sexual relationship, quarrels between them would be less threatening.

A sexual partnership which is reasonably harmonious *can* be a good basis for child rearing, but it is not a necessary one. People who decide to live together and make a common home for children need not be permanent sexual partners, and might even never have a sexual relationship. Parents could live together while their children needed them to, and be free to separate later without bitterness, and to have other sexual relationships even while living with co-parents.

If children always had a third or fourth parent as well, they would be less vulnerable to the ups and downs of an intense relationship between any two parents. There would be more close adults to think about the children's needs. It would be much easier for parents to concentrate their full attention on the children when they were together, if they were assured of support and time to themselves.

Accepting monogamous marriage as *the* background for child care effectively bans homosexuals and celibate people from parenting. but even so, lesbians and gay men are using AID to become parents, without official sanction and often without medical help. This is a proper use of AID, just as proper as its use by infertile heterosexual women who want to become mothers. If co-parenting contracts replaced marriage, celibate women and lesbians could use AID to become mothers or, like gay or celibate men, could become co-parents by joining up with a group which included a child-bearing woman. It would even be possible for a group of people to adopt a child with whom none of them had a biological relationship. We simply do not accept the view that the quality of parenting depends on biology.

> Western society supplies marriage as a custom to accommodate and regulate the primary biological needs and encourages the married pair to rear their offspring in the home ... There is a kind of chain reaction. The biological relationship demands a special intimacy and cohabitation reinforces special psychological needs for love and affection. Your own flesh and blood are necessarily rather special ... The biological relationship gives each of you a special preferment to love and affection from the other ... (Townsend, 1963, p. 252).

New customs can be forged – it is already happening – and new sorts of relationships which feel just as mysteriously 'special'.

The ban on gay parents is supposed to be in children's interests, to protect them from homosexuality. As a result, many children actually grow up to fear physical intimacy with members of their own sex. What really matters is whether the adults close to children are seen to treat each other with respect, not whether their love is 'unnatural'. It is ironic that *lack* of love between parents is considered harmless for children, as long as it is a lack of *heterosexual* love!

The other, more plausible arguments against gay couples parenting has been that children need a parent of each sex as models and to allow their own sexual development to proceed 'normally'. Millions of children who have been reared by single parents are just as 'feminine' or 'masculine' as children from two-parent families, and just as likely to be heterosexual. But we think that ideally children *do* need physically close, lasting relationships with both men and women from their earliest days, and are likely to yearn for a mother or a father if they have not got one. Co-parents' groups could be required to include at least one woman and at least one man. Co-parenting contracts could exist alongside marriage.

When the family wage is abolished, and along with it all tax and social security legislation that assume that women are normally dependent, marriage will no longer exist as an economic state. Everyone will be entitled to their own income, from wages where work is available, from benefits when it is not. People might still want to make their commitment to their sexual partners public, to have a party and celebrate their vows. Marriage might continue in this weak form, for homosexual as well as for hetero-sexual couples. But from a public point of view, how parents get on with their children matters more than how adults who are not parenting get on with each other. It is far more appropriate to have contracts for co-parents. When children are born, the names of their co-parents would be registered. They would promise to look after the children, to think about and act in their interests, to keep close links if they do not actually live together and to love and cherish each other *as co-parents*. This would be understood to mean that co-parenting must go on, whatever else happens between the adults.

Even with a universal and free system of child care to support them, co-parents would sometimes need help. Counsellors and conciliators would be available when co-parents felt stuck in a rut with each other, not only when they were about to abuse or neglect their children or when the co-parenting relationship actually broke down. If co-parents actually mistreated children, this would not be just a private matter. It would have to be prevented.

In Chapter 2 we saw parents as often victims of state intervention: the iron hand in the velvet glove of 'support'. But in any society, children must be protected from abuse and neglect, and parents themselves need to be protected from behaving like that. If child care had never been a purely private business, intervention would not be so stigmatizing and would not threaten a sudden transformation of the parents' status from all to nothing.

At the moment, since parents bear most of the work and costs of bringing up children, they expect to have the right to decide how they shall be brought up, and many see this as a natural feature of parenthood. Increases in social control are seen as interventions in private life, and indeed this is the form they currently take. The social services depart-ments of local authorities, the health visitors, the school welfare officers, are scarcely the agencies that socialists have in mind when we call for greater social responsibility for children. Nevertheless, we must refuse to accept the easy logic of parents' rights and must work towards greater social care and support of children and greater social, rather than individual, control (Barrett and McIntosh, 1983, p. 137).

If parenthood was freely chosen, there would be less child abuse and neglect. In our future society, the pressures on young adults to produce grandchildren for their own parents would not be as strong as they are today, because kinship would be only one among several ways of getting close to individual children. It would be much easier and more pleasurable to be a parent than it is today. All the same, some cases of abuse, neglect and mistreatment would occur. Whether we trust or mistrust the social workers or other state employees who step in depends on whose interests state policies seem to serve. 'Caring agencies' are trusted when they show that they value people while firmly putting a stop to their harmful behaviour, when they aim to help people take charge of their lives, and are free from sexist, racist and class stereotypes about how they should do it. At present, such attitudes are unusual and constantly frustrated.

One other key reform would make sure that children's material well-being was independent of their parents' economic fortunes. Child benefit must cover the *real* cost of child rearing, as it was originally meant to do. It would be paid to the co-parents with whom the child lived, and adjusted according to children's ages. Some people, like Penelope Leach and Mia Kellmer Pringle, want an increased child benefit to act as a sort of payment to a stay-at-home parent. We think the parent's income should be separate from the child's. Child benefit would not need to include any allowance for child *care*, if child care outside the home were free and universally available, and if parents were each entitled to money from wages or benefits in their own rights. As Eichler says, '... women's liberation should not be carried out on the backs of children'. We want the decision to care for a child at home to be made only when it is in the *child's* interests, not to find ways of making it in the *parents'* interests. The same objection applies to Eichler's 'modest' proposal for a monthly payment to the mothers of pre-school children corresponding 'to the average cost of a day care space'. This payment would be proportionately reduced when the child went to school, but would still cover the cost of care out of school hours until the child was fourteen.

The payment would be made to every mother, whether or not she held a paying job. If she was at home (or if the father stayed at home), the payments would be retained by the stay-at-home parent while they would presumably be utilized to defray the costs of day care in case both parents (or the one parent in a one-parent household) worked. The Child Care Tax Credit would be fully taxable, thus ensuring that the plan would be progressive (Eichler, 1983, p. 332).

Proposals like this have been echoed by other socialist feminists who see them as allowing 'choice' (e.g. Barrett and McIntosh, op. cit., p. 151). We think this sort of child care allowance accepts the idea of private child care, and just extends the idea of *parental* choice between private and state schools to a younger age group. Instead, we should be going against the notion that parents own their children, by giving children incomes of their own which their parents administer *as a trust*, and by demanding state-funded, public provision of free child care. Eichler realizes the importance of ending children's financial dependence. Her more radical proposal is for a taxable state-provided income to be transferred to every individual: woman, man or child. 'This measure would with one swoop eliminate total dependency of wives on husbands, and eliminate children growing up in poverty ... It would replace all social welfare programmes ...' (loc. cit.). But we do not want to keep child care a private business and simply provide individuals with the money to pay for it. How our children are looked after is a matter for us all, not just parents and 'experts'. Much sharing of information and experience on a basis of mutual respect would be needed to create a democratically run system of child care. In the next section we describe what such a system *might* look like.

5. CHILD CARE

Children's community centres provided for all children, from babyhood up to adolescence, are essential to our vision. These children's centres would not be exactly like current day care nor the same as nursery and infant schools, since they would integrate care and education. Like schools, they would be *universally* available and free to *all* children in the community or neighbourhood. Workplace nurseries, provided as they are on the say-so of particular employers, cannot be the model. They smack too much of the tied-cottage syndrome: a job for the life of a pre-school child. Local authority nurseries, with their selective intake, would no longer have any role. Playgroups, private nurseries, nursery schools would all be replaced by the Children's Centres.

The children's community centres would be like schools in another respect. Their daily *hours* of opening would match the new standard working day, which would be about the length of the present school day in Britain. We do not support present-day moves to shorten school hours, like some contemporary experiments with the 'continental day' – opening earlier and ending before lunch to avoid having to provide 'day care' through lunch hours and school meals. In the present situation this means some education authorities are hardening rather than softening the distinction between 'care' and 'education', and seeing their role as entirely educative. In contrast, we want to increase rather than decrease the mixture of care and education within the six-hour day.

Our children's community centres would *not* be much like schools, in terms of what they had on offer by way of formal schooling. We cannot specify their programmes in detail, but they would certainly have a wider understanding of how children learn than we see in schools today. Learning would be less desk-based, less classroom-based and even less based in the building. Children would probably go out frequently, to workplaces to meet the workers and have a go at pressing the switches, trying on the hats and even doing some of the actual work tasks. In the centre itself they would regularly be responsible for some real work: gardening, preparing the meals, helping construct climbing frames, cleaning and tidying up, servicing the electronic apparatus. They would also be involved in some administrative work, as well as taking part in making the decisions that affect their daily lives.

In our children's primary school the infants have been forbidden to play with mud and earth. The possibility of a sandpit at some time in the future has been mentioned as a compensation for this rule. Our children report this wistfully: it does not occur to them that they have any right to insist on the sandpit actually being provided. The teachers are right to protect the classrooms and equipment from the mud that used to collect before the ban. The parents were not consulted, but most of them would be reluctant to have the extra washing. What is wrong is not so much the ban on mud play as the insensitivity to the children's needs and failure to encourage them to speak up for their own interests. In the new children's centres, such an issue would be dealt with by debate within and between groups, and all sorts of solutions would be discussed. The children themselves would take part in implementing whatever was decided. Of course this would take longer in the first place, but since management would be part of learning, there is no question of wasted time.

Physical activities like swimming and creative arts are currently seen as marginal to education. Many schools rely on parents to teach children to swim or buy them music, singing or dancing lessons. The child's right to education is not really seen as including these: they are seen as perks. In the new children's centres drama, art and music and varieties of sports and games would be used for their own sakes and as a tool of learning. It is when teachers allow children self-determination in projects, experiments and demonstrations that the children blossom and show real enthusiasm. At present teachers are hide-bound by lack of resources and support. They feel they are working in the dark. They get little recognition of their extra work and thought, so there is a constant temptation to fall back on what the books say and what worked reasonably well last year. In our children's centres, there would be times set aside for children and parents and staff to give each other feedback, with the emphasis always on the good things that are achieved or attempted. There would also be more varied resources: more use of models, exhibitions, drama, as well as video tapes, television and computers.

The children's centres could dispense with the rigid age hierarchy, age of entry, and age grading, such as exists at present within all schools and even between types of school: nursery, infant, junior. The centres would be open to *all* children, regardless of age, ability or capability. On the other hand, children's development does occur in stages, so there would be some flexible grouping.

Special provision will have to be made for older children, as well as for adults' continuing need for formal learning. We can think of the children's community centres as catering for pre-adolescent children, roughly speaking. That does not mean adolescents would be excluded. Throughout the children's time at the centres, they would be involved in helping and teaching each other, and the older children might want to continue doing this. In any case, the children's centres would be part of or linked to wider community centres providing facilities for old people, mentally handicapped and disabled people and everyone else. Health care, cafeterias, laundries, as well as recreational facilities such as toy, book, film and video libraries, swimming pools, sports halls, meeting rooms, saunas, cinemas and theatres, would all be part of the wider community centres.

Community centres would be funded by central government, but local authorities and the centres' governing bodies would have discretion about the actual disbursement of funds, within guidelines setting out national standards. In this system, local authorities would be closely involved in developing and implementing the national standards. Sheila Rowbotham expresses the dilemma that socialists and feminists got into by accepting that power over local services should belong to the central state:

> When many social services were shifted from local to central government in the late nineteenth and early twentieth century, the socialists and liberals who campaigned for this transition saw State planning as a neutral force. The Fabian women for example regarded the State as a benign guardian of children. Many socialists and feminists have learned to be less optimistic now because we live in a welfare state. But nonetheless we continue to hand over our capacity to devise how to live to planners and policy makers. Their confidence and professional expertise is then experienced as an alien and arbitrary force over our lives ... The solution cannot be that we all take part in interminable committees and hearings on drains and damp. For with the best will to democracy in the world most of us have neither time nor inclination. The flesh is after all mortal and we have only one life, and who is left holding the baby? ...
>
> The balancing of direct democratic power and the delegation of aspects of control is something which a renewal of socialism has to take on. For our own failure to date means that we have abdicated a crucial zone of power, access to the very process of co-ordinating lived experience (Rowbotham, op. cit., p. 10).

We need *both* central and local democracy. The special quality of democracy is that it can be vitally connected with our daily lives and experiences. Local government – if it *were* truly local – could fulfil many of our fundamental needs. At the moment, local governments are a limited form of direct democracy. They have the potential to respond to the local diversity of needs, cultures and situations.

Child care activists are divided between two ideals. One is the resurrection of the street community, without its old deprivations. For instance, in some suburban areas of North America a system of neighbourliness has been created for the motorized society. Street hoardings advertise the Block Parent Community, an area in which people undertake to care for any local children in an emergency. The ideal of the street community is usually symbolized by the neighbourhood centre. In such centres everyone would know everyone else, and there would be more chance for integration of different ages and types of people and for direct democracy. This nostalgic picture is inviting to some and terrifying to others. In high-density neighbourhoods this may be possible. But in many places children's centres would have to be further than walking distance for most users, if they were to serve enough people to allow such resources to be provided. Even in high-density neighbourhoods, traffic makes walking hazardous, especially for children.

The other ideal is of larger-scale centres altogether. This poses the usual problems of scale but does allow better use of resources. After all, not all communities are based on residence nowadays. In Australia and the USA especially, some schools and day care are based as much on communities of interest or areas where many people work. With a combination of co-parents and freely available community centres in every town and city, commuting parents would be able to find and choose suitable services, in which they could still be closely involved. Such centres might even be based on groups of friends, rather than on residential community. Local authorities would be responsible for deciding on the location of community centres and, if necessary, on who was able to use the more popular ones. The centres themselves could make decisions about their own design, management and day-to-day affairs.

The National Child Care Campaign (NCCC) in Britain is trying to build a mass campaign for child care facilities which share some of the qualities of our children's centres. It demands 'flexible, free, democratically controlled child care facilities funded by the State, thus recognizing that child care provision is necessary to meet the needs of children and parents'. It believes that it is possible to achieve some of these aims by negotiating with current central governments.

> We call on central government to co-ordinate services centrally. Central government should make available sufficient resources to enable local authorities to provide a free childcare service based on the local community's own assessment of its childcare needs. Furthermore, local authorities should be mandated to provide childcare services based on such an assessment.

Our rather grand vision has its roots in immediate, practical possibilities. For the moment, the NCCC is aiming at integrating and extending day care, without challenging the split between care and education. The NCCC chooses to call its objective 'local nursery centres', since at present it aims to build up comprehensive, free services for all pre-school children, combined with 'facilities for the local community such as after-school provision, toy libraries and drop-in centres'. These local nursery centres would be run much as we envisage the management of children's community centres.

'They would be democratically controlled, giving staff, parents, local people and local groups the chance to participate in the management and running of the centre ... The funding and accommodation for such centres would be the responsibility of local authorities.' In some respects, such a managing group would be similar to the government bodies already mandatory for schools. The extent of parental representation on these is currently being increased. Present Tory philosophy is expressed in its Green Paper (Department of Education and Science 1984), on *Parental Influence at School*.

For the Tories, consumerism is the chief reason for giving parents more say. For different reasons altogether, we would also want a strong influence for parents, including the non-biological parents, in organizing the centres to meet children's needs. Contrary to Tory logic, we would also want staff, as the children's carers, to have an equal say. There would also be elected representation of the other users of the linked community centre – children themselves, elderly people, handicapped people and so on – as well as other staff, such as health workers and peripatetic carers (more on this later).

At the moment, social services are provided in separate places for special categories of people, who are segregated according to their age, ability and needs. This division of services is arbitrary and not at all in the users' interests. Why do we need separate political and administrative systems for each of the welfare services – the National Health Service, education, and the personal social services including nurseries? Of course, to bring together all these local services under one roof or on one site poses its own problems. We have already mentioned the most obvious: that of size and complexity. A community centre catering for all ages and stages could be most intimidating and awesome for little ones. Yet within the centres there could be special provisions for children so that, when appropriate, they could be separate from adults and adolescents. Rooms or buildings could be set aside especially for them, with sharing negotiable.

We see the children's centres as something like contemporary health centres, at which you are expected to be registered with a doctor. Instead of a doctor, all children would be registered with an 'adviser' at a particular centre. The centres would deal with routine health care as well as with the rest of the children's everyday lives. The children's parents would get together with the adviser to decide how soon children should start coming to the centre regularly, and for how long. They might decide that particular children should stay at home with a 'home carer', and only use the centre as a drop-in facility. Or they might decide that some combination of individual and group care was best for a particular child. Over time, the adviser and the other paid carers would come to know the child well. Like the parents, the advisers would undertake to think about the children and their particular needs. Sometimes they would disagree, just as sometimes the parents would disagree among themselves. Usually, such disagreements could be solved by agreeing to try a course of action, and to review it after some time. Sometimes they would go deeper, and the governing body of the children's centre would have to adjudicate, with appeal, if necessary, to a more distant, independent judiciary.

Although all new-born children would be registered at centres, in the first months of life babies would probably visit the centres with a parent. Nobody would ever *have* to be alone with a child or children. Knowing that a child-centred place with supportive staff was always available would free parents on maternity or paternity leave to enjoy the hours spent alone with their children.

The new society would still need child minders and nannies because not all children's needs could be met in centre care. There could be a new type of job which brought together the qualities of both: a position called a 'home-carer'. The home-carer would be employed by the centre but could work in his or her own home, or in the child's home, or in both, combined with spending some time at the children's centre. Some home-carers could also be peripatetic, and work as carers for sick children, 'baby-sitting', for emergency care when none of the co-parents was available. These peripatetic carers would have come to know the children through their involvement in the centre. In some ways, they would be a variant of the health visitor or pre-school home (or education) visitor, an important and regular partner in children's lives. The current reliance on young girls' need for money or the reciprocal goodwill formed through the baby-sitting circle is at best a precarious stopgap, typical of our contemporary commitment to private care for children. Witness an advert in a newsagent's window: 'Wanted: babysitter for two children of 3 and 5 years old: be paid to watch a colour TV for 3 or 4 hours, with your boyfriend.' What lack of respect for children this reflects!

Our carers, whether home-based, centre-based or peripatetic, would of course be well paid. They are not to be guests or visitors on whose goodwill and friendship we are forced to rely. The job of being a carer, combining the various skills of contemporary mothers as carers and educators as well as health professionals, will be recognized as highly skilled and responsible work – not dismissed as women's work and the old 'labour of love'. Carers would be *less* professional in the sense of 'distant'. Ordinary skills of getting on with people would be clearly relevant, and the changes in parenthood would also mean such skills were more widespread. Carers would be rather analogous to co-parents, combining intimacy, attention, nurturance and responsibility, but the relationships would usually be less intense because less long term. In this type of work as in all others, the current distinctions between home and work, unpaid and paid employment, between family and work would begin to disappear.

6. AND FOR NOW?

Our vision has led us into the future. What can we do *now* to ensure a better deal for parents and children, at work, in care and education, and at home? We have already pointed out some links between the present and our vision. There are several current campaigns by trade unions and the labour movement, by pressure groups such as the National Child Care Campaign, and the Women's Rights Unit of the National Council for Civil Liberties, that give us ample opportunities to bring this future nearer.

At work, we can struggle with our trade unions to get out of the rut of economism, and demand changes that will make work fit our family responsibilities, rather than vice versa. We can build up the campaign for shorter hours, especially for the shorter conventional working day. We can point out that the potential effects of a shorter working week would be far less useful to women. Alongside that, we need to keep up the pressure for better maternity leave and benefits, for paternity leave on the Swedish model, with its parental leave for sick children, too. The recognition of the need for time off with pay for expectant and newly delivered mothers is a vital and hard-won gain. It is a chink in the armour of the state's social and economic policies, since it means that motherhood and work can go together. It opens the door to extending leave and benefits to mothers with older children, and to fathers too. The battle to demonstrate the justice of this principle still has to be won. As recently as 1975, the well-known Fabian socialist Peter Townsend republished a series of essays in which he argued against giving women credit for a period of child rearing in the calculation of their retirement pensions.

It is obviously right to waive normal contributions during a person's sickness or unemployment and to credit him for the spell of work. In assessing his pension, his work-span should not be reduced by these periods off work. Such periods in a person's life are periods of adversity, which he *avoids* if given a choice. The years of motherhood are plainly not comparable. Few women choose to avoid them. The State can be expected to compensate people for time off work only when what is clearly an adversity is imposed on them against their wishes (pp. 245–6).

Motherhood is clearly not adversity, but it is not just a private choice as Townsend implies. We need social policies that recognize it as a contribution to the public good.

The labour movement as a whole also needs to be pressed into action on these matters. Without a *national* system of parental entitlements, parents whose bosses do provide parental leaves will be tied to their jobs for the life of their dependent children. In its last manifesto, the Labour Party paid lip-service to these questions. Women's votes matter to them. We must keep the pressure up. We also need more realistic child benefits which actually meet the costs of rearing children. The Child Poverty Action Group (CPAG) has been tireless in keeping this matter in the public eye. Yet again, in the present token benefits lie the seeds of growth. In its system of social benefits, Britain half-heartedly admits that parenthood costs money. The US federal government only compensates parents through the tax system. The effect of the child care tax credit for working parents (liberalized in 1981) is to encourage 'capital to move into child care services'. Child care is still seen as 'a personal expense' rather than 'as a responsibility to be shared between business and government' (Card, 1984, p. 19). These measures encourage employers to provide 'on-site child care', deducting the costs from wages and salaries. The result will be patchy, primarily helping middle-income people. Nevertheless, in one respect it is better than the attitudes of the British tax system (David, 1985b).

In a typically punitive move, the British Inland Revenue has declared that employment-based child care is a perk, not a legitimate expense. Any direct subsidies to parents' child care costs by employers are taxed – back-dated, too! The EOC, along with the NCCC and the Women's Rights Unit of the NCCL, has mounted a campaign to demand a reversal of the principle only just publicized. Cathy Itzin has also been fighting the Inland Revenue for some time, arguing that it should recognize child care expenses as work-related and give tax relief. It is important to get this principle recognized, even though women are so clustered in low-paid jobs that, for many, tax is not very significant.

The National Child Care Campaign provides the obvious umbrella for our struggles to get decent child care for pre-school children and, along with the Out-of-School Alliance, day care for children after school hours and in school holidays. It has already done useful work in supporting local campaigns to get community nurseries established and to fight closures. The cuts and the recession do not mean we can postpone thinking about the quality of day care, but they do mean that existing nurseries are essential for parents who have to work. Even if a nursery is not ideal, it would rarely be in the children's interests for it to close.

The National Child Care Campaign supports initiatives in the voluntary sector, like community nurseries, even if they are not in receipt of local authority help. It is essential to support self-help efforts. For one thing, there is so little state provision that people are forced to help themselves and need support to do it. Of course we run into the old dilemma that, while people will meet their own needs, it is easier for the state to ignore them, even if the people involved wear themselves into the ground and have no time left for their own children.

Self-help schemes, with their imagination, their flexible thinking and community involvement, give us an invaluable glimpse of possible futures. The trouble is that while parents are so unsupported they really want a break from child care, not to do more of it. For this reason, entirely parent-run schemes, like the University Nursery in Bristol, are not ideal, either now or in the future. As soon as someone supplies a child care arrangement, many parents become quite passive. Their lives with jobs and children have little room for managing nurseries and play-schemes. The few parents who are left holding the collective baby can become overworked, resentful or contemptuous. Self-help schemes need the resources to employ professionals, and have to keep their sights set on getting public funding without losing community control. When this happens, parents and others have the chance to negotiate with the staff about the philosophy and quality of the nursery, without having to shoulder entire responsibility. But even if our children go to local authority nurseries, we can be involved. We can make a point of saying what we appreciate and letting the staff know what we think is good for the children.

Child minders are now organized in a National Association. It is true that at the moment child minding depends on women's own dependency, on their responsibility for most of the unpaid work in the home. Child minders are usually women who *have* to be at home. It would be as absurd to try to abolish child minding now as it is to oppose part-time work or job-sharing and put down the women who have to turn to these short-term solutions. The more visible and the better organized child minding becomes, the higher its standards will be. Salaried child minding schemes are the way forward because they make child minding more public. They can allow minders to use common resources like toy libraries and minder-and-toddler groups, so that minding becomes more sociable for the children and the adults.

What about play-groups? Play-groups themselves are a welcome development, cheerful, informal places for children to get together. What needs to be altered is the rigidity of the ban on under-threes, the insistence (where it exists) on parents working on the rota, the common disapproval of working mothers, of nurseries and the acceptance of nominal payment for play-group workers. Play-groups are patchily provided, like child minders and community nurseries: they cannot be a substitute for a co-ordinated, free and universal service. But we should not underestimate their present importance to children and parents.

Despite the lack of provision for pre-school children, mothers of that age group feel they are in control. When children go to school, mothers feel that they have to submit to some distant authority. Should we support current campaigns for parent participation in schools? There are many different reasons offered for getting parents involved, only some of which we support.

First, the democratic argument that parents should have a say in the running of schools. Parents are citizens and also, in a sense, users of the schools, since they are indirectly affected by whatever affects their children. For this reason, rather than because they have special information or special rights, they should be able to participate. The 1980 Education Act in England and Wales aimed to create a political position for parents in the system of running schools. All state and voluntary schools are to have their own governing body, and not just a collective one for several schools as in the past, nor the almost powerless 'managers' of primary schools. To have two elected parent representatives and an elected teacher representative on these bodies is clearly a progressive step, although suggestions for the participation of pupils on governing bodies were rejected. We do not accept the government position that children are not citizens and that parents can be their proxies. Nevertheless, parents should be on governing bodies, and we would support the latest Tory proposal to increase the number of parent representatives, but not at the expense of teachers.

Up to now, governing bodies have had little control over what happens in schools. They have nothing to do with the curriculum, and little control over resources. They do have some power over teacher appointments and school discipline; but most of the power is still in the hands of the head-master or headmistress. A parent 'manager' in a relatively progressive area wrote to the *Guardian*, saying that their suggestions were listened to as 'from an amateur to a professional: they were politely received and ignored'. Few parents went to meetings to elect governors: '... This is hardly surprising when they are selecting from candidates they probably know nothing about for a job of unspecified duties and responsibilities' (*Guardian*, 25 October 1983, p. 13). In fact most teachers feel threatened by involved parents, and prefer them to spend their energies on fund-raising.

In some other countries, parents have more rights, but usually on the presumption that they possess their children. In both the USA and Canada, schools are not run by the local authorities but by special bodies of elected citizens, school boards in the USA, school board trustees in Canada. Running for office for school boards is taken very seriously. A mix of people as governors, as on the British model, is preferable to this degree of parental control, as long as governing bodies really do have some control over the day-to-day and long-term running of the schools' affairs.

Another version of parental involvement stresses that co-operation and better communication help both parents and teachers. This is obviously true. We should press for our schools to increase chances for sharing information, letting parents into the schools to talk with the children, run clubs, share skills. Down with the situation where the parents may not pass the gates! But what about the actual teaching? Our children's primary school boasts '51 parental helpers', according to the head. When pressed, he admitted that these were all mothers. (In contrast, both the outgoing Chairman of the PTA and the incoming one were fathers.) As the education cuts bite, more and more schools are relying on the unpaid voluntary help of a small number of mothers to actually *teach* reading and maths, as well as cookery, playing the recorder, laminating and selling books. Is this amount of involvement really exploitation – of women cut off from the world of employment? But do we, at the same time, whatever the cost, improve the daily lives of some of our children?

Within schools, mothers' help may modify social inequalities, although it does pit working mother against helping mother. It also means that in middle-class areas where a good many stay-at-home mothers are teacher trained or otherwise qualified, the school is getting skilled unpaid helpers. In such areas, where PTA funds are probably used to buy extra textbooks and materials, the cuts have less effect than in an inner-city area where less maternal help is available and the mothers who can help are less skilled. This goes against the whole idea of universal education. Inevitably in some cases the children of helping mothers are treated differently. We have heard of cases where younger siblings were offered an early place in school, of others where the 'star' children in the annual play had 'helping' mothers. Helping mothers cannot bring their younger children into school, yet they are not offered expenses to pay for child care. If we accept this situation, delighted to have a chance to peep into the world that holds our child for six hours a day, we are actually helping to cushion the effects of the education cuts (David, 1985a).

A third version of parental involvement is that parents sit on governing bodies as proxies for their children. The people who currently have most understanding of the individual children are certainly likely to be their parents. But how can parent representatives speak for *all* children? Or why should they have any more right to do so than, say, teachers? *Children* should have more say in their care, at every level, not necessarily always by electing their representatives on to committees but often by being listened to carefully by adults when they talk about their experiences.

What about home? What can we do in our own everyday lives to make them more satisfying for our children and ourselves? For couples, shared parenting is one obvious, and (for some) relatively easy, solution, despite its limitations: '... "Shared parenting" cannot take over a great deal of rhetorical space in feminist socialist ambitions for the future of the family ... it rests on private goodwill; but private goodwill cannot be relied on to sustain a whole politics...' (Riley, 1983, pp. 152–5). Of course Riley is right to point to the inadequacies of the slogan 'shared parenting', especially for mothers on their own by force or by choice. But goodwill, whether private or public, is a precondition of good child care arrangements.

Besides, shared parenting need not be restricted to mothers and fathers. Even today it is possible to enlist the help and commitment of friends, relatives, cohabitees and lovers. A lot of the isolation and burdens of parenthood are self-inflicted. The practical problems are real enough, but once we realize how impossible a task is given to parents, especially to mothers, some of our guilt evaporates. We realize that we need help, not because *we* are inadequate but because only one or two parents are not enough for one child, let alone for several children. We can begin to see how well we do, all things considered. We can help our friends see how well *they* do. We can stop being apologetic about working, or needing time to ourselves, since it is not in the least our fault that the way society is organized brings our needs into conflict with our children's. Once we realize that we are not alone, we are in a strong position to create a world in which parents are appreciated and supported to care for the children's sake.

REFERENCES

Adams, C. and Winston, K., 1980, *Mothers at Work*, Longman.

Adams, P., 1981, 'Social Control or Social Wage: On the Political Economy of the Welfare State', in Dale, R. *et al.* (eds.), *Education and the State*: Vol. 2: *Politics, Patriarchy and Practice*, Falmer Press.

Ainsworth, M. D. S., 1962, 'The Effects of Maternal Deprivation: A Review', in *Deprivation of Maternal Care*, World Health Organization.

Ainsworth, M. D. S., 1973, 'The Development of Infant-Mother Attachment', in Caldwell, B. M. and Ricceleh, S. (eds.), *Review of Child Development Research*, Vol. 13, University of Chicago.

Ainsworth, M. D. S., 1982, 'Attachment, Retrospect and Prospect', in Parkes and Stevenson-Hinde (eds.) (*vide infra*).

Ainsworth, M. D. S., Bell, S. M. and Stayton, D. J., 1971, 'Individual Differences in Strange Situation Behaviour of One Year Olds', in Schaffer (ed.) (*vide infra*).

Ainsworth, M. D. S., Bell, S. M. and Stayton, D. J., 1974, 'Infant-mother attachment and social development', in Richards (ed.) (*vide infra*).

Ainsworth, M. D. S., Blehar, M., Waters, E. and Wall, S., 1978, *Patterns of Attachment*, Embaum.

Ainsworth, M. D. S. and Wittig, B. A. (1969), ' Attachment and Exploratory Behaviour of One-Year-Olds in a Strange Situation', in Foss, B. M. (ed.), *Determinants of Infant Behaviour*, Vol. 4, Methuen.

Allen, B. 1974, 'A Visit from Uncle Macho', in Pleck and Sawyer (eds.) (*vide infra*).

Anderson, C. W., Nagle, R. J., Roberts, W. A. and Smith, J. W., 1981, 'Attachment to Substitute Caregivers as a Function of Center Quality and Caregiver Involvement', in *Child Development*, 52, 53–61.

Antonelli, A., 1981, 'Cognitive Development in the Home Environment' (unpublished paper).

Appleton, W. S., 1982, *Fathers and Daughters*, Papermac.

Arnold, S., 'A Tale of Nine Nannies', *The Observer*, 8 May 1983.

Ashford, N., 1981, 'The Neo-Conservatives', in *Government and Opposition*, 16, 3.

Association of County Councils, 1984, Memorandum in *Children in Care*, Vol. II, by Social Services Committee, HMSO.

Backett, K., 1982, *Mothers and Fathers*, Macmillan.

Bain, A. and Barnett, L., 1980, *The Design of a day care system in a nursery setting for children under five*, Tavistock.

Balbo, L., 1981, 'Crazy Quilts: Rethinking the Welfare State' (unpublished paper).

Bamburger, J., 1974, 'The Myth of Matriarchy', in Rosaldo, M. Z. and Lamphere, L. (eds.), *Woman, Culture and Society*, Stanford University Press.

Barclay, P. M. (Report of a working party chaired by), 1982, *Social Workers: Their Role and Tasks*, Bedford Square Press and NCVO.

Barker, D. L. and Allen, S. (eds.), 1976, *Sexual Divisions and Society: Process and Change*, Heinemann.

Barrett, M. and McIntosh, M., 1983, *The Anti-Social Family*, Verso Books.

Beaile N. and McGuire, J. (eds.), 1982, *Fatherhood: Psychological Perspectives*, Junction Books.

Becker, J. M. T., 1977, 'A Learning Analysis of the Development of Peer-Oriented Behaviour in Nine-Month-old Infants', *Developmental Psychology* 13, 481–91.

Bell, C., McKee, L. and Priestly, K., 1983, *Fathers, Childbirth and Work*, Manchester, EOC.

Belsky, J. and Steinberg, L. D., 1978, 'The Effects of Day Care: A Critical Review', *Child Development* 19, 929–49.

Benians, R., Berry, T., Conling, D. and Johnson, P., 1983, *Children and Family Breakdown*, Families Need Fathers.

Bernard, J., 1975, *The Future of Motherhood*, Penguin.

Bernard, J., 1983, 'Ground Rules for Marriage', in Horner, M., Nadelson, C. C. and Notman, M. T. (eds.), *The Challenge of Change*, Plenum Press.

Best, R., 1983, *We've All Got Scars*, Indiana University Press.

Bezveselny, S. F. and Grinberg, D. Y. (eds.), 1968, *They Knew Lenin*, Moscow Progress Publishers.

Blatchford, P., Battle, S. and Mays, J., 1982, *The First Transition*, NFER Nelson, Guildford.

Blehar, M., 1974, 'Anxious Attachment and Defensive Reactions Associated with Day Care', *Child Development* 45, 683–92.

Bone, M., 1977, *Preschool Children and the Need for Day Care*, OPCS, HMSO.

Boston Women's Health Book Collective, 1981, *Ourselves and Our Children*, Penguin.

Boulton, M. G., 1983, *On being a Mother: A Study of Women with Preschool children*, Tavistock, London.

Bower, T. G. R., 1982, *Development in Infancy*, W. H. Freeman and Co.

Bowlby, J., 1951, *Maternal Care and Mental Health*, World Health Organization.

Bowlby, J., 1953, *Child Care and the Growth of Love*, Penguin.

Bowlby, J., 1971, *Attachment*, Penguin.

Bowlby, J., 1979, *The Making and Breaking of Affectional Bonds*, Tavistock.

Breen, D., 1975, *The birth of a first child*, Tavistock.

Brimblecombe, F. S. W., Richards, M. P. M. and Robertson, N. R. C., 1978, *Separation and Special Care Baby Units*, Spastics International Medical Publications.

Bristol Women's Studies Group, 1979, *Half The Sky: an introduction to Women's Studies*, Virago (reprinted 1984).

Bronfenbrenner, U., 1974, *The Two Worlds of Childhood*, Penguin.

Bronfenbrenner, U., 1977, 'Towards an Experimental Ecology of Human Development', *American Psychologist* 32, 513–31.

Bronfenbrenner, U., 1979, 'Context of Child-Rearing', *American Psychologist* 34, 847.

Bronson, W., 1975, 'Peer-peer interactions in the Second Year of Life', in Lewis, M. and Rosenblum, L. A. (eds.), *The Origins of Behaviour: Friendship and Peer Relations*, Wiley.

Brookes, J. and Lewis, M., 1976, 'Infants' Responses to Strangers, Midget, Adult and Child', in *Child Development* 47, 323–31.

Brown, A., 1982, 'Fathers in the Labour Ward' in McKee and O'Brien (eds.) (*vide infra*).

Brown, G. W. and Harris, T., 1978, *Social Origins of Depression*, Tavistock.

Bruner, J., 1980, *Under Five in Britain*, Grant McIntyre.

Bryant, B., Harris, M. and Newton, D., 1980, *Children and Minders*, Grant McIntyre.

Burlingham, D. and Freud, A., 1943, *Infants without Families*, Allen and Unwin.

Butler, S., 1971, *The Way of All Flesh*, Penguin.

Card, E., 1984, 'Tax Breaks for Child Care', *Ms Magazine*, March 1984.

Carew, J. V., 1980, 'Experience and the Development of Intelligence in Young Children at Home and in Day Care', *Monographs of the Society for Research in Child Development*, 45 (6–9, Serial No. 189).

Central Policy Review Staff and Central Statistical Office, 1980, *People and their Families*, HMSO.

Centre for Educational Research and Innovation (CERI), 1982, *Caring for Children*, OECD.

Charnas, S. McKee, 1981, *Motherlines*, Hodder & Stoughton.

Chesler, P., 1978, *About Men*, Simon and Schuster.

Chodorow, N., 1978, *The Reproduction of Mothering*, University of California Press.

Clarke-Stewart, A., 1982, *Day Care*, Fontana.

Clarke-Stewart, A., forthcoming, *The Chicago Study of Child Care and Development*.

Clarke-Stewart, A. and Fein, G., in press, 'Programs for Young Children, Day Care and Early Education', in Nassen, P., Hath, M. and Compos J. (eds.), *Carmichael's Manual of Child Psychology*, Wiley.

Comer, L., 1974, *Wedlocked Women*, Feminist Books, Leeds.

Coote, A. and Campbell, B., 1982, *Sweet Freedom*, Picador.

Crine, S., 1979, *The Hidden Army*, Low Pay Unit.

Croll, E., 1974, *The Women's Movement in China*, Anglo-Chinese Educational Institute.

Dahlberg, F. (ed.), 1981, *Woman The Gatherer*, Yale UP.

Dale, R. *et al*. (eds.), 1981, *Education and the State*: Vol. 2: *Politics, Patriarchy and Practice*, Falmer Press.

Dally, A., 1982, *Inventing Motherhood*, Hutchinson/Burnett.

Daly, M., 1979, *Gyn/ecology*, The Women's Press.

David, M. E., 1980, *The State, the Family and Education*, Routledge & Kegan Paul.

David, M. E., 1983a, 'The New Right in Britain and the USA: a new anti-feminist moral economy', *Critical Social Policy*, Vol. 2, No. 3.

David, M. E., 1983b, 'Sex Education and Social Policy: A New Moral Economy?', in Walker, S. and Barton, L. (eds.), *Gender, Class and Education*, Falmer Press.

David, M. E., 1984, 'Women, Family and Education', in Acker, S. *et al*. (eds.), *World Yearbook of Education 1984: Women and Education*, Kogan Page.

David, M. E., 1985a, 'Motherhood and Social Policy: a matter of education?', *Critical Social Policy* 12.

David, M. E., 1985b, 'Moral and Maternal: The Family in the Right', in Levitas, R. (ed.), *Markets and Morals*, Polity Press.

David, M. E., 1985c, 'Teaching motherhood formally and informally', in Deem, R. and Whyte, J. (eds.), *Girl Friendly Schooling*, Methuen.

Davies, M. L., 1978, *Maternity: Letters from Working Women*, Virago (introduction by Gloden Dallas) reprint of 1918 edition.

Davis, L., 1983, 'Now You See It: Now You Don't', *Australian and New Zealand Journal of Sociology*, Vol. 19, No. 1, March, pp. 79–95.

Deacon, B., 1983, *Social Policy and Socialism*, Pluto Press.

Deakin, M., 1973, *The Children on the Hill*, Quartet.

Department of Education and Science (Green Paper), 1984, *Parental Influence at School*, Cmnd 9242, HMSO.

Donne, J., 1960, *The Poems of John Donne*, OUP.

Downick, S. and Grundberg, S. (eds.), 1980, *Why Children?*, The Women's Press.

Doyle, A., Connolly, J. and Rivest, L. P., 1980, 'The Effect of Playmate Familiarity on the Social Interactions of Young Children', *Child Development* 51, 219–23.

Doyle, A. and Somers, K., 1978, 'The Effects of Group and Family Day Care on Infant Attachment Behaviour', *Canadian Journal of Behavioural Science* 10, 38–45.

Dunn, J. and Kendrick, C., 1982, *Siblings*, Grant McIntyre.

Dunn, L., *Peabody Picture Vocabulary Test*, American Guidance Services, Circle Pines, Minnesota.

Eckelaar, J. M. and Katz, S. N. (eds.), 1978, *Family Violence*, Butterworth.

Ehrenreich, B. and English, D., 1979, *For Her Own Good*, Pluto Press.

Ehrenreich, B., 1983, *The Hearts of Men*, Doubleday.

Ehrensaft, D., 1981, 'When Women and Men Mother', in *Politics and Power Three*, Routledge & Kegan Paul.

Ehrensaft, D., 1983, *Dual Parenting and the Duel of Intimacy* (unpublished paper, presented at American Sociological Association annual meeting, in New York).

Eichenbaum, L. and Orbach, S., 1982, *Outside In Inside Out*, Penguin.

Eichenbaum, L. and Orbach, S., 1984, *What Do Women Want?* Fontana/Collins.

Eichler, M., 1983, *Families in Canada Today*, Gage Publishing.

Eisenstein, H., 1984, *Contemporary Feminist Thought*, Counterpoint.

Eisenstein, Z., 1982, 'The Sexual Politics of the New Right: on understanding the crisis of liberalism for the 1980s', *Signs: Journal of Women and Culture* Vol. 7, 3.

Engels, F., 1962, 'The Condition of the Working Class in England', in *Marx and Engels on Britain*, Foreign Languages Publishing House, Moscow.

Engels, F., 1968, 'The Origin of the Family, Private Property and the State', in *Karl Marx and Frederick Engels: Selected Works*, Lawrence and Wishart.

Equality for Children, 1983, *Keeping Kids Out of Care ...*, a review of evidence given to the House of Commons Social Services Select Committee on Children in Care 1982/83.

Erikson, E., 1965, *Childhood and Society*, Penguin.

Fein, R. A., 1974, 'Men and Young Children', in Pleck and Sawyer (eds.) (*vide infra*).

Ferri, E., *et al.*, 1981, *Combined Nursery Centres*, National Children's Bureau.

Finch, J., 1983, 'Dividing the rough and the respectable: working class women and preschool playgroups', in Garmanikov E. *et al.* (eds.), *The Public and the Private*, Heinemann.

Finch, J., 1984a, 'The Deceit of Self Help: Preschool Playgroups and Working Class Mothers', *Journal of Social Policy*, Vol. 13, part 1.

Finch, J., 1984b, 'Community Care: Developing non-sexist alternatives', *Critical Social Policy* 9.

Finch, J. and Groves, D. (eds.), 1983, *A Labour of Love*, Routledge & Kegan Paul.

Firestone, S., 1979, *The Dialectic of Sex*, The Women's Press.

Fowler, W., and Khan, 1974, *The Later Effects of Infant Group Care: A Follow-up study*, Ontario Institute for Studies in Education.

Fowler, W., 1978, *Day Care and Its Effects on Early Development: a Study of Group and Home Care in Multi-Ethnic Working-Class Families*, Ontario Institute for Studies in Education.

Freeman, C., 1982, 'The Understanding Employer', in West, J. (ed.), *Work, Women and the Labour Market*, Routledge & Kegan Paul.

French, M., 1978, *The Women's Room*, Sphere.

Friedl, E., 1975, *Women and Men*, Holt, Reinhart & Winston.

Frodi, A. M. and Lamb, M. E., 1982, 'Sex Differences in Responsiveness to Infants', *Child Development* 49, 1182–8.

Garland, C. and White, S., 1980, *Children and Day Nurseries*, Grant McIntyre.

Gavron, H., 1968, *The Captive Wife*, Penguin.

Gifford, J., Collins, C., Hambly, M., Nairn, R., Webbs, S. and Wilkinson, W., 1975, *A Comparative Study of Attachment Patterns in Creche and Home-Reared Two Year Olds* (original full unpublished report).

Gilder, G., 1982, *Wealth and Poverty*, Buchan and Enright.

Gilman, C. Perkins, 1972, *The Home: Its Work and Influence*, University of Illinois Press, a reprint of the 1903 edition.

Gilman, C. Perkins, 1979, *Herland*, The Women's Press.

Gingerbread and Families Need Fathers, 1982, *Divided Children*, Gingerbread and Families Need Fathers.

Glazer, N. and Moynihan, D. P., 1963, *Beyond the Melting Pot*, MIT Press.

Golden, M. *et al.*, 1978, *The New York City Infant Day Care Study*, Medical and Health Research Association of New York City.

Goldfarb, W., 1955, 'Emotional and Intellectual Consequences of Psychological Deprivation in Infancy: a Re-evaluation', in Hock, P. H. and Zubin, J. (eds.), *Psychopathology in Childhood*, Grune and Statton.

Gough, K., 1975, 'Origins of the Family', in Reiter (ed.) (*vide infra*).

Graham, H., 1983, 'Caring: a labour of love', in Finch and Groves (eds.) (*vide supra*).

Graham, H., 1984, *Women, Health and the Family*, Harvester Press.

Griffin, A. E. and Griffin, P. B., 1981, 'Woman the Hunter', in Dahlberg (ed.) (*vide supra*).

Hanscombe, G. E. and Forster, J., 1982, *Rocking the Cradle: Lesbian Mothers*, Sheba Feminist Publishers.

Hardiment, C., 1983, *Dream Babies*, Cape.

Harris, M., 1978, *Cows, Pigs, Wars and Witches*, Fontana.

Hartley, R., 1974, 'Sex Role Pressures and the Socialisation of the Male Child', in Pleck and Sawyer (eds.) (*vide infra*).

Hartup, W. W., 1978, 'Children and their Friends', in McGurk (ed.) (*vide infra*).

Hayden, D., 1981, *The Grand Domestic Revolution: A History of Feminist Designs for American Homes, Neighbourhoods and Cities*, MIT Press, Cambridge, Mass., and London.

Hewitt, M., 1958, *Wives and Mothers in Victorian Industry*, Rockliff.

Hoggett, B., 1977, *Parents and Children*, Sweet and Maxwell.

Holman, R., 1980, *Inequality in Child Care*, Child Poverty Action Group and Family Rights Group.

Howe, E., 1984, 'Towards More Choice for Women', *New Society*, 24 May 1984.

Hughes, M., Mayall, B., Moss, P., Perry, J., Petrie, P. and Pinkerton, G., 1980, *Nurseries Now*, Penguin.

Illich, I., 1983, *Gender*, Marion Boyars.

Jackson, B. and Jackson, S., 1981, *Child Minder*, Penguin.

Jackson, S., 1982, *Childhood and Sexuality*, Fontana.

Janis, M. G., 1964, *A Two Year Old Goes to Nursery School*, Tavistock.

Johnson, L. and Dineen, J., 1981, *The Kin Trade: The Day Care Crisis in Canada*, McGraw, Hill Ryerson.

Kagan, J., 1976, 'Emergent Themes in Human Development', *American Scientist* 64, 186–96.

Kagan, J., Kearsley, R. P. and Selazo, P. R., 1978, *Infancy: Its Place in Human Development*, Harvard UP.

Kagan, J., 1979, 'Family Experience and the Child's Development', *American Psychologist* 34, No. 10.

Katz, S., 1971, *When Parents Fail*, Beacon Press.

Kamerman, S. and Kahn, A., 1981, *Child Care, Family Benefits and Working Parents*, Columbia UP.

Kirsch, C., 1979, 'On the Origin of the Inequality between Men and Women', in Turner, D. H. and Smith, G. A. (eds.), *Challenging Anthropology*, McGraw-Hill, Canada.

Kitzinger, S., 1978, *Women as Mothers*, Fontana.

Klaus, M. H. and Kennell, J. H., 1976, *Maternal Infant Bonding*, C. V. Mosby.

Kollontai, A., 1977, *Selected Writings*, Allison & Busby.

Lamb, M. E. (ed.), 1976, *The Role of the Father in Child Development*, John Wiley and Sons.

Land, H., 1976, 'Women: Supporters or Supported?', in Barker, D. L. and Allen, S., *Sexual Divisions and Society: Process and Change*, Tavistock.

Land, H., 1980, 'The Family Wage', *Feminist Review* 6.

Land, H., 1981, *Parity begins at Home*, EOC, Manchester.

Land, H., 1983, 'Poverty and Gender: The Distribution of Resources within the Family', in Brown, M. (ed.), *The Structure of Disadvantage*, Heinemann.

Land, H., 1984, 'Changing Women's Claims to Maintenance', in Freeman, M. D. A. (ed.), *State, Law and the Family*, Tavistock.

Lasch, C., 1977, *Haven in a Heartless World*, Basic Books.

Le Guin, U., 1975, *The Dispossessed*, Granada.

Leach, P., 1979a, *Who Cares?*, Penguin.

Leach, P., 1979b, *Babyhood*, Penguin.

Leacock, E. G. (ed.), 1981, *Myths of Male Dominance*, Monthly Review Press.

Lessing, D., 1969, 'The Antheap', in *Five*, Panther.

Lewis, E., Newson, E. and Newson, J., 1982, 'Father participation through childhood and its relation with career aspirations and delinquency', in Beaile and McGuire (eds.) (*vide supra*).

Lightfoot, S. L., 1977, 'Family-School Interactions: The Cultural Image of Mothers and Teachers', *Signs: Journal of Women and Culture*, Vol. 5, No. 2.

Lightfoot, S. L., 1978, *Worlds Apart*, Basic Books.

Lowe, N., 1982, 'The Legal Status of Fathers, past and present', in McKee and O'Brien (eds.) (*vide infra*).

Lynn, D. B., 1974, *The Father, His Role in Child Development*, Wadsworth.

Manicom, A., 1984, 'Feminist Frameworks and Teacher Education', *Journal of Education*, 166, No. 1, pp. 77–89.

Martin, J. and Roberts, C., 1984, *Women and Employment: A Lifelong Perspective*, HMSO.

Marx, Karl, *Capital*, Vol. 1, Everyman.

Marx, K. and Engels, F., 1962, *On Britain*, Foreign Languages Publishing House, Moscow.

Mayall, B. and Petrie, P., 1977, *Minder, Mother and Child*, London Institute of Education.

MacFarlane, A., 1977, *The Psychology of Childbirth*, Harvard UP.

McGuire, J., 1982, 'Gender-Specific Differences in Early Childhood, The Impact of the Father', in Beaile and McGuire (eds.) (*vide supra*).

McGurk, H., 1978, *Issues in Childhood Social Development*, Methuen.

McKee, L., 1982, 'Fathers' Participation in Infant Care: a critique', in McKee and O'Brien (eds.) (*vide infra*).

McKee, L. and O'Brien, M. (eds.), 1982, *The Father Figure*, Tavistock.

Mead, M., 1962(a), *Deprivation of Maternal Care: a Reassessment of its Effects*, World Health Organization.

Mead, M., 1962(b), *Male and Female*, Penguin.

Melville, J., 1983, in *New Society*, 17 March.

Millett, K., 1971, *Sexual Politics*, Hart Davis.

Mills, M. (unpublished paper), 'Towards an Understanding of the Process of Maternal Interaction with Young Children'.

Moskowitz, D. S., Schwarz, J. C. and Corsini, D. A., 1977, 'Initiating Day Care at Three Years of Age: Effects on Attachment', *Child Development* 48, 1271–6.

Mount, F., 1983, *The Subversive Family*, Counterpoint.

Moyo, E., 1979, 'Big Mother and Little Mother in Matabeleland', in Bristol Women's Studies Group (*vide supra*).

Mueller, E. and Brenner, J., 1977, 'The Origins of Social Skills and Interaction among Playgroup Toddlers', *Child Development*, 45, 854–61.

NSPCC Battered Child Research Team, 1976, *At Risk*, Routledge & Kegan Paul.

Nava, M., 1983, 'From Utopian to Scientific Feminism . . .' in Segal (ed.) (*vide infra*).

Nelson, K., 1984, 'Towards a Feminist Strategy for Social Policy' (unpublished paper, presented at Critical Social Policy annual conference).

Newell, P., 1983, 'One law for parents, another for children?', *Guardian*, 5 October.

Newson, J. and Newson, E., 1963, *Patterns of Infant Care in an Urban Community*, Penguin.

Newson, J. and Newson, E., 1968, *Four Years Old in an Urban Community*, Penguin.

Oakley, A., 1974a, *The Sociology of Housework*, Martin Robertson.

Oakley, A., 1974b, *Housewife*, Penguin.

Oakley, A., 1979, *From Here to Maternity*, Penguin.

Oakley, A. and Richards, M. P. M. (forthcoming), 'Parents' attitudes to elective delivery', in Chalmers, I., Anderson, A. and Turnbull, A. (eds.), *Elective Delivery in Obstetric Practice*, OUP.

O'Brien, M., 1982a, 'The Working Father', in Beaile and McGuire (eds.) (*vide supra*).

O'Brien, M., 1982b, 'Becoming a Lone Father', in McKee and O'Brien (eds.) (*vide supra*).

Oliver, J., 1983, 'The Caring Wife', in Finch and Groves (eds.) (*vide supra*).

Olmesdahl, M. C. J., 1978, 'Paternal Power and Child Abuse', in Eckelaar and Katz (eds.) (*vide supra*).

Owens, D., 1982, 'The Desire to Father', in McKee and O'Brien (eds.) (*vide supra*).

Parker, R. D., 1981, *Fathering*, Fontana.

Parker, R., 1984, in *Children in Care*, Annex C171, Committee on Social Services, HMSO, London.

Parkes, C. M. and Stevenson-Hinde, J. (eds.), 1982, *The Place of Attachment in Human Behaviour*, Tavistock.

Parten, N. B., 1932, 'Social Participation among Pre-school Children', in *Journal of Abnormal Social Psychology*, 27, 243–69.

Pawlby, S. J., 1977, 'Imitative Interaction', in Schaffer H. F. (ed.), *Studies in Mother-Infant Interaction*, Academic Press.

Peaslee, M. V., 1976, *The Development of Competency in Two-year old Infants in Day Care and Home-Reared Environments*, doctoral dissertation, Florida State University.

Peckman, J. A. (ed.), 1981, *Setting National Priorities*, Brookings Institution.

Philipson, I., 1982, 'Narcissism and Mothering: the 1950s Reconsidered', *Women's Studies International Forum*, 5.

Phillips, A., 1983, *Hidden Hands: Women and Economics*, Pluto Press.

Phinney, J. and Rotheram, M. J., 1983, 'Same Sex differences in Social Overtures Between Same-sex and Cross-sex preschool pairs', *Child Study Journal* 12, 64.

Piercy, M., 1979, *Woman on the Edge of Time*, The Women's Press.

Pleck, J. H. and Sawyer, J. (eds.), *Men and Masculinity*, Prentice Hall.

Popay, J., Rimmer, L. and Rossiter, C., 1983, *One parent families: parents, children and public policy*, Study Commission on the Family.

Potock, C., 1970, *The Chosen*, Penguin.

Pringle, M. K., 1980, *The Needs of Children*, Hutchinson.

Puzo, M., 1969, *The Godfather*, Pan.

Ragozin, A. S., 1980, 'Attachment Behaviour of Day Care Children: Naturalistic and Laboratory Observation', *Child Development*, 51, 409–15.

Ramey, C. T. and Mills, P. J., 1977, 'Social and Intellectual Consequences of Day Care for High Risk Infants', in R. A. Webb (ed.), *Social Development in Childhood, Day Care Programs and Research*, Johns Hopkins UP.

Rappaport, R., Rappaport, R. N. and Strelitz, Z., 1977, *Fathers, Mothers and Others*, Routledge & Kegan Paul.

Reiter, R. (ed.), 1975, *Towards an Anthropology of Women*, Monthly Review Press.

Reynaud, E., 1983, *Holy Virility*, Pluto Press.

Rich, A., 1977, *Of Woman Born*, Virago.

Richards, M. P. M. (ed.), 1974, *The Integration of the Child into a Social World*, CUP.

Richards, M. P. M., 1982, 'How Should we approach the Study of Fathers?', in McKee and O'Brien (eds.) (*vide supra*).

Richards, M. P. M., 1984, 'The Myth of Bonding', in McFarlane J. A. (ed.), *Progress in Child Health* Vol. 1, Churchill Livingstone.

Richman, J., 1982, 'Men's Experiences of Pregnancy and Childbirth', in McKee and O'Brien (eds.) (*vide supra*).

Riley, D., 1983, 'The Serious Burdens of Love', in Segal (*vide infra*).

Rimmer, L. and Popay, J., 1982, *Employment Trends and the Family*, Study Commission on the Family.

Robinson, H. B. and Robinson, N. M., 1971, 'Longitudinal Development of Very Young Children in a Comprehensive Day Care Program: The First Two Years', *Child Development* 42, 1673–83.

Rosenthal, K. M. and Keshet, H. F., 1981, *Fathers Without Partners*, Rowman and Littlefield.

Rowbotham, S., 1984, in *New Statesman*, 13 January, p. 10.

Rubenstein, J. and Howes, C., 1979, 'Caregiving and Infant Behaviour in Day Care and at Home', in *Developmental Psychology* 15, 1–24.

Rubenstein, J., Howes, C. and Boyle, P., 1981, 'A Two Year Follow Up of Infants in Community based Day Care', *Journal of Child Psychology and Psychiatry*, 22, 209–18.

Rubin, Z., 1980, *Children's Friendships*, Fontana.

Russell, G., 1983, *The Changing Role of Fathers*, Open UP.

Rutter, M., 1972, *Maternal Deprivation Reassessed*, Penguin.

Ryan, W., 1976, *Blaming the Victim*, Vintage Books, New York.

Sayers, J., 1981, *Biological Politics*, Tavistock.

Schaffer, H. R. (ed.), 1971a, *The Origins of Human Social Relations*, Academic Press.

Schaffer, H. R., 1971b, *The Growth of Sociability*, Penguin.

Schaffer, H. R., 1977, *Mothering*, Fontana.

Schaffer, H. R. and Crook, C. K., 1978, 'The Role of the Mother in Early Social Development', in McGurk (ed.) (*vide supra*).

Segal, L. (ed.), 1983, *What is to be Done about the Family?*, Penguin.

Sharp, R. and Green, A., 1975, *Education and Social Control*, Routledge & Kegan Paul.

Sharpe, S., 1984, *Double Identity*, Penguin.

Shaw, J., 1981, 'In Loco Parentis: A relationship between Parent, State and Child', in Dale *et al.* (eds.) (*vide supra*).

Simms, M. and Smith, C., 1982, 'Young Fathers: Attitudes to Marriage and Family Life', in McKee and O'Brien (eds.) (*vide supra*).

Smith, D., 1983, 'Women's work as Mothers: a new look at the relation of class, family and school achievement' (unpublished paper).

Social Services Committee, 1984, *Children in Care*, HMSO, March.

Social Trends 14, 1984, HMSO.

Solnitt, A. J., 1978, 'Child Abuse: The Problem', in Eckelaar and Katz (eds.) (*vide supra*).

Squibb, B., 1980, *Family Day Care: How to Provide it in your own home*, Harvard Common Press.

Sroufe, L. A., 1979, The Coherence of Individual Development', *American Psychologist* 34, 10.

Steinfels, M. O'B., 1976, *Who's Minding the Children?*, Harper Torchbooks.

Stern, D., 1977, *The First Relationship: Infant and Mother*, Fontana.

Strachey, R., 1978, *The Cause*, Virago.

Strindberg, A., 1949, *Eight Famous Plays*, Duckworth and Co.

Study Commission on the Family, 1983, *Families in the Future*, Study Commission on the Family.

Sylva, K. and Roy, C., 1980, *Child Watching at Play Group and Nursery School*, Grant McIntyre.

Tiger, L. and Fox, R., 1974, *The Imperial Animal*, Paladin.

Tizard, B., 1975, *Early childhood education*, NFER.

Tizard, J. and Tizard, B., 1975, 'The Institution as an Environment for Development', in Brown, and Stevens (eds.), *Social Behaviour and Experiences*, Hodder & Stoughton.

Tizard, B. and Reese, J., 1975, The Effects of Early Institutional Rearing on the Behavioural Problems of Affectional Relationships of Four Year Old Children', *Journal of Psychological Psychiatry* 16, 61–73.

Tizard, B. and Hughes, M., 1984, *Children Talking*, Fontana.

Tolson, A., 1977, *The Limits of Masculinity*, Tavistock.

Townsend, P., 1963, *The Family Life of Old People*, Penguin.

Townsend, P., 1975, *Sociology and Social Policy*, Penguin.

Townsend, P. and Davidson, N., 1982, *Inequalities in Health*, Penguin.

Toynbee, P., 1983, 'Guardian Women', *Guardian*, 26 September.

Toynbee, P., 1984, 'Bed and Breakfast', *Guardian*, 5 March.

TUC Working Party, 1977, *The Under Fives*, TUC.

Turnbull, C., 1981, 'Mbuti Womanhood', in Dahlberg (ed.) (*vide supra*).

Turner, D. H. and Smith, G. A. (eds.), 1979, *Challenging Anthropology*, McGraw-Hill, Canada.

Union Place Collective, 1976, *As Things Are*, Bonfire Press.

Van der Eyken, W., 1982, *The Education of 3 to 8 year olds in Europe*, Longman.

Vaughn, B., Egeland, B., Sroufe, L. A. and Waters, E., 1979, 'Individual

Differences in Infant Attachment at 12 and 18 months', *Child Development* 50, 971–5.

Wallerstein, J. S. and Kelly, J. B., 1980, *Surviving the Break-Up*, Grant McIntyre.

Waters, E., Matas, L. and Sroufe, L. A., 1975, 'Infant Reactions to an Approaching Stranger', *Child Development* 46, 348–56.

Weir, A. and McIntosh, M., 1982, 'Towards a Wages Strategy for Women', *Feminist Review* 10.

Weitzman, L., 1981, *The Marriage Contract*, Macmillan.

Welburn, V., 1980, *Post-natal Depression*, Fontana.

Whitfield, R., 1980, *Education for Family Life: Some New Policies for Child Care*, Hodder & Stoughton.

Winnicott, D., 1964, *The Child, the Family and the Outside World*, Penguin.

Winnicott, D., 1965, *The Family and Individual Development*, Tavistock.

Wood, D., McMahon, L., and Cranstoun Y., 1980, *Working With Under Fives*, Grant McIntyre.

Zetkin, C., 1968, 'From My Memorandum Book', in Bezveselny and Grinberg (eds.) (*vide supra*).

Zimmerman, I., Steiner, V. and Pond, R., 1969, *Pre-school Language Scale*, Charles E. Merrill.

AUTHOR INDEX

SUBJECT INDEX

abortion 46, 50
adolescents 344 (*see also* children)
adoption 87, 139
adults 23, 24, 30, 31, 82, 88, 89, 114, 118, 122, 137, 141–8, 157, 243–5, 268–9, 278, 283–4, 291, 302, 305
adventure playgrounds 125
after-school facilities (*see also* school-age facilities) 24, 117, 125–8
age 33, 98
    hierarchy of 263–4, 335, 344, 347
    as principle of social organization 33
Agta 28
ambivalence 181–2, 301
America (*see also* Canada, South America, USA) 34, 115, 121
anthropologists 27, 28, 34, 36, 167–8, 174–7
anti-feminism 44, 81
Asians 87, 321
at risk register 74
attachment 114, 157–77
    hierarchy of 165–6, 169
    theory of 165–9, 192–3, 252
au pair 101, 107
Australia 110, 147, 168, 346
    aboriginal women 30, 36

babies
    care of 24, 27–8, 30, 35, 39, 71, 92, 123, 136, 139–41, 157–77, 179–83, 186–7, 192, 325, 342, 348
    in nurseries 114, 263
    social capacities 163–5, 247–51, 295
    stranger anxiety 250–51
backgrounds (*see also* class) 59–61, 189, 288–90, 312
befriending schemes 74–6
Belgium 105–7
biology
    connection between men and children 205
    parenthood independent of 339
birth (*see* childbirth)
black economy 100
black families 61, 80
bonding 172–4, 226–7
boys 27, 34, 35, 36, 82, 119, 122, 123, 127, 139–41, 147, 170, 219–24, 302, 317, 320–21
breast-feeding 30, 31, 35, 39, 83, 162, 173–4, 176–7, 179
Britain
    child care in 88, 99, 102, 104, 105, 107, 110, 120, 124–5, 253, 263
    demography of 85, 99, 101

A CHOICE OF
PELICANS AND PEREGRINES

☐ **The Knight, the Lady and the Priest**
  Georges Duby   £5.95

The acclaimed study of the making of modern marriage in medieval France. 'He has traced this story – sometimes amusing, often horrifying, always startling – in a series of brilliant vignettes' – *Observer*

☐ **The Limits of Soviet Power** **Jonathan Steele**   £3.50

The Kremlin's foreign policy – Brezhnev to Chernenko, is discussed in this informed, informative 'wholly invaluable and extraordinarily timely study' – *Guardian*

☐ **Understanding Organizations** **Charles B. Handy**   £4.95

Third Edition. Designed as a practical source-book for managers, this Pelican looks at the concepts, key issues and current fashions in tackling organizational problems.

☐ **The Pelican Freud Library: Volume 12**   £4.95

Containing the major essays: *Civilization, Society and Religion, Group Psychology* and *Civilization and Its Discontents*, plus other works.

☐ **Windows on the Mind** **Erich Harth**   £4.95

Is there a physical explanation for the various phenomena that we call 'mind'? Professor Harth takes in age-old philosophers as well as the latest neuroscientific theories in his masterly study of memory, perception, free will, selfhood, sensation and other richly controversial fields.

☐ **The Pelican History of the World**
  J. M. Roberts   £5.95

'A stupendous achievement . . . This is the unrivalled World History for our day' – A. J. P. Taylor

A CHOICE OF
PELICANS AND PEREGRINES

A CHOICE OF
PELICANS AND PEREGRINES

☐ *Crowds and Power* **Elias Canetti**   £4.95

'Marvellous . . . an immensely interesting, often profound reflection about the nature of society, in particular the nature of violence' – Susan Sontag in *The New York Review of Books*

☐ *The Death and Life of Great American Cities*
   Jane Jacobs   £4.95

One of the most exciting and wittily written attacks on contemporary city planning to have appeared in recent years – thought-provoking reading and, as one critic noted, 'extremely apposite to conditions in the UK'.

☐ *Computer Power and Human Reason*
   Joseph Weizenbaum   £3.95

Internationally acclaimed by scientists and humanists alike: 'This is the best book I have read on the impact of computers on society, and on technology and on man's image of himself' – *Psychology Today*

These books should be available at all good bookshops or news-agents, but if you live in the UK or the Republic of Ireland and have difficulty in getting to a bookshop, they can be ordered by post. Please indicate the titles required and fill in the form below.

NAME _____ BLOCK CAPITALS

ADDRESS _____

_____

_____

Enclose a cheque or postal order payable to The Penguin Bookshop to cover the total price of books ordered, plus 50p for postage. Readers in the Republic of Ireland should send £IR equivalent to the sterling prices, plus 67p for postage. Send to: The Penguin Bookshop, 54/56 Bridlesmith Gate, Nottingham, NG1 2GP.

You can also order by phoning (0602) 599295, and quoting your Barclaycard or Access number.

Every effort is made to ensure the accuracy of the price and availability of books at the time of going to press, but it is sometimes necessary to increase prices and in these circumstances retail prices may be shown on the covers of books which may differ from the prices shown in this list or elsewhere. This list is not an offer to supply any book.

This order service is only available to residents in the UK and the Republic of Ireland.